The Poli

The Politics of Appearances

REPRESENTATIONS OF DRESS IN REVOLUTIONARY FRANCE

Richard Wrigley

Oxford • New York

First published in 2002 by
Berg
Editorial offices:
150 Cowley Road, Oxford, OX4 1JJ, UK
838 Broadway, Third Floor, New York, NY 10003-4812, USA

Berg is an imprint of Oxford International Publishers Ltd.

Library of Congress Cataloging-in-Publication Data
A catalogue record for this book is available from the Library of Congress.

British Library Cataloguing-in-Publication Data
Wrigley, Richard.
    The Politics of Appearances : representations of dress in revolutionary
France / Richard Wrigley.
        p. cm.
Includes bibliographical references and index.
    ISBN 1-85973-504-5 – ISBN 1-85973-509-6 (pbk.)
    1. Costume–Political aspects–France–History. 2. Costume–France–
History–18th century. 3. France–History–1789–1793. I. Title.
    GT867 .W75 2002
    391'.00944–dc21
                                                                2002011075

ISBN 1 85973 504 5 (Cloth)
      1 85973 509 6 (Paper)

Typeset by JS Typesetting Ltd, Wellingborough, Northants
Printed in the United Kingdom by MPG Books, Cornwall

Contents

Abbreviations

Sources

Actes Comm	*Actes de la Commune de Paris pendant la Révolution*, ed. Sigismond Lacroix, Paris, 1894–1914, 16 vols
AHRF	*Annales historiques de la Révolution française*
AN	Archives Nationales, Paris.
Arch Parl	*Archives parlementaires de 1787 à 1860*, 1st series 1787–1799, 100 vols, 1914–2000
BHVP	Bibliothèque Historique de la Ville de Paris
BL	British Library, London
BNF	Bibliothèque Nationale de France, Paris.
BSHAF	*Bulletin de la société de l'histoire de l'art français.*
Caron	Pierre Caron (ed.), *Paris pendant la Terreur. Rapports des agents secrets du Ministre de l'Intérieur*, 6 vols, Marcel Didier: Paris, 1910–1964.
RACSP	*Recueil des actes du comité du salut public*, ed. F.A. Aulard, 28 vols, Imprimerie nationale: Paris, 1939–1951.
RAM	*Réimpression de l'Ancien Moniteur*, 32 vols, Paris, 1863–70.
Schmidt	Wilhelm Adolf Schmidt, *Tableaux de la Révolution française, publiés sur les papiers inédits du département de la police secrète de Paris*, 3 vols, Leipzig, 1867–71.
Tourneux	Maurice Tourneux, *Bibliographie de l'histoire de Paris pendant la Révolution française*, 5 vols, Paris, 1890–1913.
Tuetey	Alexandre Tuetey, *Répertoire général des sources manuscrites de l'histoire de Paris pendant la Révolution française*, 11 vols, Paris, 1890–1914.

Revolutionary Calendar

vend.	vendémiaire
brum.	brumaire
frim.	frimaire
niv.	nivôse
vent.	ventôse
germ.	germinal
flor.	floréal
prair.	prairial
mess.	messidor
therm.	thermidor
fruct.	fructidor

Acknowledgements

In bringing this book to completion, it is both gratifying and chastening to realise how much I have depended on the support, advice, practical assistance and forebearance of friends and colleagues. Although research, writing, and thinking can at times seem to require a solitary bent, it is thankfully true that none of these things are possible without the sustaining presence of a community of friendship and collaboration. Wherever possible, I have thanked individuals in the notes for providing me with specific references and aperçus. As the roots of this book run deep into the past, I should also thank those to whom I owe a debt of gratitude accumulated along the way who I have inadvertently overlooked. On reflection, I realise that the book's distant origins lie in a visit to the Artemis Gallery in London, and an encounter with Pierre-François Delauney's *Offrande à la Liberté*. My research into this painting, which led me to explore the relation between Liberty's cap, and that adopted by French revolutionaries, and thereby to start thinking about the politics of dress in the French Revolution, was generously encouraged by the late David Carritt; Neil Macgregor gave me the chance to present the initial results of this research in a paper to the Association of Art Historians.

Thanks to Philippe Bordes, Ting Chang, Penelope Curtis, Colin Jones, Sophie Matthiesson, and Beth Wright for being willing to read and comment on drafts of parts of the text in various forms. I am particularly grateful to Tony Halliday for generously sharing his deep knowledge of the period. I have also had the benefit of discussing aspects of the material with Marie-Claude Chaudonneret, Dario Gamboni, Etienne Jollet, and Dominique Poulot. Tom Howrie kindly came to my aid by checking a reference and expediting a photographic order in Paris at a late stage. Along the way, audiences at various seminar presentations of parts of this material have provided valuable feedback. Thanks to the editors of *French History* and Oxford University Press for permission to republish in revised form an article on the libety cap, which here forms chapter four.

The research and writing would not have been possible without the help of staff at the following institutions: in England, the British Library, London; the Brotherton Library, University of Leeds; in France, the Bibliothèque Historique de la Ville de Paris, Bibliothèque Nationale (latterly de France), Archives Nationales, Archives des Musées Nationaux, Musée Carnavalet, and the Musée de la Mode et du Costume. Alain Chevalier and his staff at the Musée de la Révolution Française, Vizille, deserve special thanks, not only for the exceptional conditions from which I, as many other, researchers on the Revolution, have benefited, but also for allowing me the privilege of being able to stay *sur place*. More specifically, I am indebted to Alain Chevalier for permission to reproduce an image of the museum's collection of cockades on the cover. As ever I am immensely grateful to Mme Auffray and her staff at the Institut Francophone, Paris for providing timely and congenial accommodation, as have Etienne Jollet and Agnès Bouvier, and Laure and Olivier Meslay, in less institutional but equally *sympathique* surroundings. The pleasures of working in Paris have regularly been enhanced by the company of Ting Chang and Brian Grosskurth, honorary Parisians and indefatigable *habitués* of the BN.

I gratefully acknowledge having been awarded a grant from the Research Leave Scheme, jointly funded by the Art and Humanities Research Board and the School of Humanities at Brookes, and also smaller grants from the AHRB towards research costs. My colleagues in the Department of History of Art, Oxford Brookes University, have always been supportive, and helped to keep the commitment to research and writing alive, despite the intrusive bureaucracy with which Higher Education has become so increasingly damagingly burdened.

I would also particularly like to acknowledge the role of John Perkins, Head of the School of Arts and Humanities, who has worked extremely hard to foster and protect research culture with the School. I must thank Carol Tulloch, whose inspired idea it was to approach Berg as a publisher. At Berg, Sara Everett patiently and efficiently steered me and the book towards seemingly unattainable deadlines. George Pitcher's expertise as a copy-editor saved me from numerous faux pas.

Finally, and most importantly, I owe an incalculable debt of gratitude to Penelope Curtis, who came to realise to her cost how overwhelmingly the politics of dress in revolutionary France was, and is, capable of transforming the fabric of daily life.

Shepherd's Bush, Headingley

Introduction

In no other period [than the Revolution] was dress more dominated by political events, or did it react to them more; this was so to such a degree that their double history is as if confused, such that the description of one is almost always the description of the other . . . Dress imposed itself despotically, both for those whose opinions it articulated, and for those who had neither the courage nor the power to combat it. The crime of *lèse-costume*, if one can so describe it, was a crime expiated on the scaffold'[1] (Horace de Viel-Castel, 1834).

VIEL-CASTEL's judgement on the inescapable politicization of dress during the Revolution has the ring of retrospective exaggeration, indulging in an association of choice of dress and the cut of people's clothes with the repressive justice meted by the guillotine. Nonetheless, for all that he repudiates the brutal imposition of a form of vestimentary conformism, he recognised that there were varieties of intention at work beneath what he represents as the obligatory adoption of a homogenized régime of appearances. In this respect, Viel-Castel's conclusion is salutary, for, if it has been a commonplace to acknowledge the degree to which revolutionary dress was implicated in political life, what too often gets left out of account is the diversity and complexity of how dress functioned across institutional and personal levels of experience. Whereas, for censorious commentators such as Viel-Castel, the realm of dress as a form of personal identity was taken over by a fearsomely authoritarian mix of prescription and proscription, it could be argued that the crucial question facing historians of this aspect of revolutionary politics is precisely how, and how far, aspects of individual dress were adapted to express more general forms of identity. Thus, the prime aim of this study will be to explore how in practice dress served such ends, and to trace how such practices were represented across diverse genres of commentary and interpretation, both textual and visual. It is primarily conceived as an analysis of a specific episode in cultural history, seeking to define the multifarious roles and shifting meanings of dress in the dramatic and turbulent conditions of the French Revolution.

Such is the evolving and diverse nature of the history of dress,[2] and of the Revolution, that a statement about aims and methods seems appropriate, and some remarks on these matters are duly provided in this introduction. These questions are addressed more directly in the detailed studies that make up the book's chapters, each of which explores the evolving significance of particular forms of dress in relation to the specific semantic, representational, and political contexts within which it came to prominence. I use the term dress rather than fashion, since the former is much more inclusive, without fashion's connotations of a relatively circumscribed manipulation of style. Indeed, it could be argued that the elaborate and widespread currency of dress-as-fashion for which Paris was renowned in the late eighteenth century was rendered redundant during much of the Revolution, partly through the collapse of the luxury trades and élite markets on which it depended, and because of the primarily political significance with which dress came to be endowed.

In recent times, revolutionary dress has received a considerable degree of attention, both from specialised dress historians and from researchers engaged in defining revolutionary political culture. Various historical studies have contributed to the establishment of the history of dress as a culturally complex phenomenon. In terms of types of historical analysis beyond the specialised confines of dress history, Lynn Hunt, in her extremely influential *Politics, Culture and Class in the French Revolution* (1984), expanded our understanding of the ways in which the historical study of revolutionary dress should be located within the 'symbolic forms of political practice' and the politicization of everyday objects. The great virtue of her approach was to keep in play, and seek to integrate, the first three terms of her title. When dress is discussed, it is treated as a highly significant site for the articulation of beliefs and ideas, and a key ingredient in the consolidation of a new political culture. As she concluded in a subsequent article: 'questions of dress more broadly conceived [than fashion] went to the heart of the Revolution in both its democratic and totalitarian aspects'.[3] James A. Epstein's 1994 study of the political culture of popular protest in Britain from the time of the Revolution to the mid-nineteenth century showed how crucial an understanding of the complex meanings of emblems was to the lived experience of such politics.[4] Although addressing a later period and a different national context, Epstein's study is highly suggestive of how one might approach similar issues in the French Revolution. His approach is exemplary in its recognition of the multiple layers of contested meaning surrounding the polemical and ritual utilisation of objects such as liberty caps; and his closely contextualized account is richly dependent on primary sources, which he reveals as containing a hitherto unrecognized intensity of concern about such symbolic forms of political expression. In terms of showing how intimately dress could be embedded in and expressive of changing ideologies during the revolutionary period, Philip Mansel's brilliant article 'Monarchy, Uniform, and the Rise of the *Frac* 1760–1830', represents an extremely revealing case study of one particular form of dress, the *frac*, following its evolving polyvalent status as an item of court and official costume.[5] Mansel's article is a model of what can be learnt from close analysis of how individual types of dress undergo radical transformations of meaning, in different contexts embracing often conflicting emblematic significance

A more general but nonetheless innovative study in the development of a critically historicised analysis of dress was Philippe Perrot's *Les Dessus et les dessous de la bourgeoisie. Une histoire du vêtement au XIXe siècle* (Fayard: Paris, 1981). Perrot's main concern was the nature of the symbolic and material economy of Parisian dress and fashion in the mid- and later nineteenth century, yet he provides some highly pertinent remarks on the transformations worked by the Revolution on the inherited 'vestimentary system' of the Ancien Régime. His work represents a new generation of cultural historians, whose conception of culture and its dynamics was informed by semiotics – both the streetwise anti-bourgeois Barthes of *Mythologies* and the fastidious system-builder of *Système de mode*[6] – but was also grounded in empirical reconstruction of its conditions of production and consumption, and was alive to the symbolic complexities of dress in general and fashion in particular as a form of social represent-ation of status and identity.

Among the deluge of publications that coincided with the bicentenary in 1989, two major books and two substantial exhibition catalogues appeared, which together considerably added to our picture of the dynamic and multifarious interrelation of dress and Revolution. Aileen Ribeiro's *Fashion and the French Revolution* (Batsford: London, 1988) and Nicole Pellegrin's *Les Vêtements de la Liberté. Abécédaire des pratiques vestimentaires françaises de 1780 à 1800* (Alinea: Paris, 1989) offered contrasting kinds of synthesis of a wide range of historical and visual material. While Ribeiro's study was specifically located within the history of dress, and was presented in the form of a broadly narrative and profusely illustrated survey, Pellegrin arranged her material in the form of a critical and analytical dictionary, creating a remarkably richly detailed conspectus ranging across items of dress, style, and terminology, drawing on a wealth of unfamiliar primary sources. The exhibitions, *Modes et Révolutions 1780–1804* (Musée de la mode et du costume, Paris), and *The Age of Napoleon. Costume from Revolution to Empire: 1789–1815* (The Metropolitan Museum of Art, New York), were accompanied by substantial catalogues containing essays on key aspects of the dress of the period. *Modes et Révolutions* had more to say about the Revolution, including important essays on aspects of the subject, notably by Daniel Roche and Jean-Marc Devocelle.[7] In both these exhibition catalogues, attention was, however, weighted towards the Ancien Régime, Directory, Consulate, and especially Empire. Among the exhibits, revolutionary dress was in fact strikingly little in evidence – though this was more a consequence of its remarkably poor rate of survival than a deliberate evasion. The conservation problems associated with the display of dress meant that the objects gathered together for these exhibitions were normally invisible. In addition to these large-scale and high-profile exhibitions in major metropolitan institutions, we should also take account of the numerous exhibitions dedicated to the impact of the Revolution on particular localities, in which items of dress emerged so to speak obliquely from little-known public and private collections.[8]

The most important study on the history of dress in France during the seventeenth and eighteenth centuries to have appeared in modern times has without question been Daniel Roche's *La Culture des apparences: une histoire du vêtement (XVIIe–XVIIIe siècles)* (Fayard: Paris, 1989). Roche had earlier addressed clothing in *Le Peuple de Paris* (Aubier Montaigne: Paris, 1981),[9] as an aspect of consumption and lifestyle, but his 1989 study embraced society, and the uses it had for dress, in all its aspects. Even though Roche only touches on the Revolution, his study is fundamental for any attempt to comprehend the nature of the changes that occurred after 1789. Roche constructed a series of interlocking historical perspectives on the fabrication, maintenance, consumption and circulation of dress new and old, combined with extensive investigation of the way the representation of dress carried with it elaborate and evolving symbolic functions, as manifest in literature, medical and moral discourses. He placed the particular dynamics of fashion within a much larger vestimentary system. And he positioned his own study within a wide-reaching historiographical tradition, embracing anthropology, and historical perspectives at once social, cultural, and economic. Crucially, Roche's history of dress positions it within a complex of discourses on appearances and their meanings.[10]

The principal conclusion I draw from his study is that, in engaging with dress as a historical phenomenon, one needs to balance reflections on long-term processes of evolution with detailed analyses of individual and collective usage and the way this is represented across diverse textual and visual sources. General remarks on the changing forms and meanings of dress need to be seen as inseparable from the elaborate forms of decoding evident in the way contemporaries write about the régime of appearances which informed attitudes to dress.

In addition to the specific usefulness of Hunt's and Roche's expansion of the horizons within which a history of dress can be conceived, I would also acknowledge a more general debt to Richard Cobb's commitment to micro-histories of revolutionary society based above all on primary sources. However, in approaching dress in the light of such a mode of analysis, I come to contrary conclusions. That is, whereas Cobb was always sceptical of the impact of the ideologies of revolutionary politics on everyday life, which he celebrated as carrying on in spite of the zealotry of official and institutional interference, I would rather want to define revolutionary political culture as something which was as much manifest in its quotidian experience as in matters of rhetoric and legislation. As this book hopes to demonstrate, attitudes and responses to dress are a touchstone for matters of collective and self-representation, and the negotiation of questions of identity apprehended through the culturally complex business of the legibility of appearances.

I have addressed the politics of revolutionary dress through a series of case studies, each of which traces the creation and currency of specific forms of dress, taking account of the respective interventions made by legislation, debate, and observation of use and misuse. These case studies are framed by an opening chapter which explores the material history of revolutionary dress, and its historiographical fate, and a concluding chapter which suggests that the discourse of appearances, as it was registered through attention to dress, was a crucial element in the lived experience of the various institutions and practices which made up the Revolution's new political culture. The wide variety of sources used substantiate the proposition that the politics of dress was a multifarious, ubiquitously assimilated phenomenon that informs revolutionary culture at both individual and collective levels, and indeed at the interfaces of these artificially opposed terms.

It will immediately be apparent that the material covered in this book does not attempt to be comprehensive. The selection of material followed the degree of importance attached to some of the key items in the revolutionary vestimentary lexicon – notably the cockade, the liberty cap and the *sans-culotte*. Taken together, the topics addressed do provide a loosely chronological account of the Revolution. But close focus on each specific topic has been preferred to an integrated, precisely linear account in order to take full acount of the complexities attendant on the introduction and currency of each type of dress. Consistent with Hunt's survey of the politicisation of the everyday, fashion as such has not been isolated from a more inclusive conception of dress. Whenever possible, visual resources have been integrated into the account – that is, on an equal basis – within analysis of textual sources. Indeed, this study originally arose out of the need to date a figure of Liberty in a painting, leading to an investigation of the revolutionary history of liberty caps as emblems and as dress, and their interrelation.[11] It has remained a premise from which I have worked, that visual culture should be treated as continuous, across different media – including art and dress; the intersection of these different forms of representation, and their differing visual codes, should be understood as being rooted in the same historical circumstances, each being subject to revisions of form and meaning as topical exigencies required. In saying this, I would strongly resist the implication that paintings, drawings and prints provide us with a convenient or necessarily reliable documentary record of changing forms of dress. To this extent, the complex politics of dress which pertained in revolutionary France is merely an extreme instance of the need to see both dress and its representation as being subject to comparable contextual constraints and expectations. Nevertheless, I have tried not to lose sight of the materiality of dress, and have drawn attention to matters of fabrication and practicalities of diffusion whenever feasible. Indeed, it was a direct result of trying to get to grips with revolutionary dress as a material object that the first chapter came to seem essential, in the sense of having to confront the disappearance of the objects which are the focus of the study.

The choice of subjects for case studies follows the most prominent items of dress which we find recurrently enmeshed in the new political culture of the Revolution. It is part of the contention of this book that an understanding of the complex roles played by dress as a form of representation is essential to taking stock of how that new political culture worked in practice – in clubs, in the National Assembly, in festivals and ceremonies, and in the diverse, less manageable public spaces in which revolutionary politics was lived out in argument, confrontation, surveillance, and the display of forms of self-identification with different collectivities and constituencies. There was not, therefore, a single politics of dress, but rather a spectrum of competing, dissonant interpretative ideas and beliefs. Attitudes to dress are as fragmented, contested, and unstable as the political landscape in which they were mobilised. That is to say, the revolutionary politics of dress are more complex, less neatly circumscribed than is often assumed to be the case.

The ambition to forge a new political culture led in practice to a protean process of legislation, around which debates and partisan interventions proliferated. This inherent instability is vividly manifest in the intensive scrutiny of people's vestimentary identity, alert to the crystallisation of new groups, parties, clubs, factions, and allegiances both overt and covert. It is significant that almost all the legislation which directly addressed matters of dress was driven by a desire to impose much-needed control on conflicts arising out of inflammatory disputes and disturbances in streets, theatres, and other public spaces. Items of dress, such as the cockade, liberty cap, or *sans-culotte* costume were a form of public assertion of varieties of adherence to revolutionary beliefs and patriotic ideals. Rather than being self-contained emblematic entities buoyed up by currents of new ideas, they were in fact unstable markers of the changing ebb and flow of consensus, continually sucked down into the turbulent waters of political conflict. It follows from this that none of the types of dress considered here have a simple, straightforwardly reconstitutable unitary identity. Reconstructing the history of these forms of dress must also pay close attention to their reception.

The most obvious way in which dress was directly involved in revolutionary politics was in the propensity to propose new forms of costume, badge and insignia to identify members of incipient national and local institutions. In considering the generic phenomenon of official dress, we will see how, although such costumes and insignia were invested with the responsibility of making visible new institutions, their implementation was beset by both practical and theoretical obstacles. Practical, in that fabrication and distribution were frequently difficult to organize and coordinate, and once introduced, new costumes and insignia were as much a catalyst for dissent as they were an encouragement to and assertion of consensus. Theoretical, in that giving emblematic form to institutionalised manifestations of authority was necessarily premised on differing

conceptions of who had the right to exercise that authority. This produced
a fundamental scepticism about the employment of any form of
distinction which would single out certain individuals from society in
general. Such resistance to the potential misuse of new costumes and
insignia was resolved, at least in principle, by a recurrent insistence,
inherited from the Ancien Régime, that occupancy of a given official post
or role only corresponded to a temporary conferment of authority on
behalf of the people at large. Indeed, many of these new badges and
costumes were specifically instituted in order to identify officials as they
carried out their duties among their fellow citizens. In the case of the
National Guard and army, they were a concrete means to proclaim the
inception, and guarantee the survival, of a new political order. Taken
together, these practical problems and theoretical doubts meant that the
currency of new types of costume and insignia was subject to different
forms of resistance and revision. For all the extended legislative reflection
and disputation devoted to defining such official forms of identity, they
nonetheless had to make their way in the uncertain public space beyond
the Assembly, the revolutionary tribunal, the garrison, and the often
choreographed ceremonial of festivals.

The cockade was a remarkably consistent element in the repertoire of
revolutionary symbolism. But it is precisely its breadth of diffusion which
engendered a strikingly nuanced diversity of form and meaning. Legislation struggled to define a protocol for its use which could survive the
shifting practices of its employment. Beneath the illusion of a ubiquitous
national symbol was a counter-discourse of repudiation, misappropriation, and deformation. To this extent, the cockade was a primordial
catalyst for the assertion and challenging of patriotic credentials. Tracing
the currency of the cockade shows how the high-minded celebratory
rhetoric of national – that is, revolutionary – identity was continually
accompanied by the often violent negotiation of its adoption. The
adoption of the cockade also exemplifies the way that any understanding
of the politics of dress must situate its currency within the repertoire of
gestures and behaviour by means of which adherence to or distancing
from revolutionary beliefs was signalled. In this sense, the cockade's meanings, and those of other forms of badge and insignia, are inseparable from
the specific contexts within which they were displayed and scrutinised.

The liberty cap brought with it a considerable historical and symbolic
baggage, which sustained its central presence in revolutionary emblematics. This was primarily classical in origin, but also including an

eclectic variety of historical precedents and parallels. Once caps started to be worn, they took on a very different political dimension, in so far as who wore them, and why they chose to do so, had to be taken into account. The nature of emblems has to be redefined when they are items of dress, rather than rhetorical or visual figures – this tension was fully recognised by contemporary commentators, whether as a source of celebration or as one of disquiet. The social origins of the cap as that of the common man presented the opportunity to propose a novel political role for the popular. What is at stake here is not a simplistic identification of the inter-related presence of popular and classical culture, but rather the question of what happens when an emblem such as the liberty cap becomes translated into an item of politicised dress, in the context of a revol-utionary situation. The liberty cap became a site for the negotiation of variant meanings, in which past and present are simultaneously elided and in collision. Such meanings are always contingent rather than inherent. As with the cockade, a fundamental element here is to track the interplay of the liberty cap's changing usage, both recommended and censured, as revealed in the prodigiously abundant range of comments on it across journalism, pamphlets, discourses, speeches and tracts, and also within different forms of imagery. As throughout, we are primarily reliant on items in the press, as well as brief mentions in the proceedings of the National Assembly, Convention, Paris Commune, the Jacobin club, the Committee of Public Safety, and the reports of police agents, for accounts of particular incidents. This mosaic of sightings, protests, recommendations, and, of course, denunciations, constitutes an essential dimension to tracing the liberty cap's revolutionary career.

In exploring the vestimentary stereotype of the *sans-culotte*, we are dealing with a particularly elaborate and explicit politics of dress. The coming into existence of the *sans-culotte* in its new revolutionary meaning is, of course, dependent on a more widespread politicisation of dress. The *sans-culottes'* pungent presence was, however, relatively short-lived. Their demise spawned a vestimentary idiom of subversion and parody. The stereotype had depended on a paradoxical assertion of the transparency of appearances: true patriotic virtue could be expressed by the adoption of a costume. Yet the manipulation of items of dress was manifestly open to abuse. Thus we find that the currency of the *sans-culotte* was accomp-anied by apprehensive reflections and proscriptive recommendations on the need sceptically to survey people's dress and appearance. Indeed, it was the recognition that dress was being manipulated that constituted the most incontrovertible evidence of counter-revolutionary scheming. The case of the *sans-culotte* also opens onto the question of what was at stake in the transformation of the representation of the popular, and how far Ancien Régime prototypes in fact laid the foundations for a phenomenon designed to epitomize allegiance to a particularly militant form of the new political culture. The semantic complexity of the stereotype emerges all the more fully when the visual representation of this new player on the revolutionary stage is considered.

The final chapter reviews the extent to which the emblematic and expressive functions of all forms of revolutionary dress were continually undermined by what was recognised to be the essentially unreliable nature of vestimentary appearances, a dimension of social life inherited from the Ancien Régime 'culture of appearances', but which was given an urgent and perplexing redefinition in conditions of social and political revolution. In so far as dress was considered as a universal expression of particular forms of identity, it became subject to intensive scrutiny, and promised to reveal evidence of counter-revolutionary deviance, if not calculated attempts to foster conspiracy. The discourse of denunciation which emerged from the earliest days of the Revolution at times relied on dress as evidence of the legibility of appearances, more specifically when they had been subversively contrived. Thus the central theme to this chapter is disguise, a phenomenon which depended on dress as an indicator of identity, but was simultaneously undermined by recognition of its inherent susceptibility to being used as an instrument of dissimulation.

A coda suggests that the legacy of the revolutionary politics of dress was fundamentally ambiguous. On the one hand, there was a comprehensive repudiation of the adoption of explicitly political badges and dress codes, which were seen as part of the redundant baggage of the repressive politics of *sans-culotterie* and Jacobin republicanism, cathartically superseded in the aftermath of Thermidor. On the other hand, as an expression of social identity, dress was instrumental in defining the evolving contours of post-Thermidorian society, not only in the confrontational form of *incroyables*, who paraded their hatred for former Jacobins and *sans-culottes*, but perhaps more revealingly in relation to the status and appearance of *parvenus*. The resentful derision aimed at these illegitimate and ostentatiously visible *nouveaux riches* exposed a deep-seated sense of comprehensive social displacement. This also spawned attempts to re-map the social landscape in terms of a newly ordered, harmonised status quo, yet at the same time inevitably undermined the concrete plausibility of such schemes. As society became progressively militarized under the Empire, the recognition of and desire for a reinstituted hierarchical structure was to a large extent displaced onto the proliferating presence of uniforms.[12] Although civilian dress eschewed explicitly political identifications as redundant and divisive, this vestimentary denial was recognized as being informed by the memory – if not the trauma – of the Revolution. The ultimate inheritor of the playing out of the politics of revolutionary dress was the type of the blackclad bourgeois, whose formation and inherent complexity have been overshadowed by the opulence of imperial Napoleonic culture.[13] Although in due course this costume was to be widely perceived as a norm to be subverted, when seen against the backdrop of the Revolution and its aftermath the proliferation of 'men in black' stands as a conscious antithesis to the republican politics of dress most pungently enshrined in the *sans-culotte*, with which the Revolution was censoriously, if reductively, identified.

Notes

1. 'Jamais, à aucune autre époque, le costume ne fut plus dominé par les événemens politiques et ne réagit davantage sur eux; c'est à tel point que leur double histoire se trouve comme confondue, et que la description de l'un est toujours le récit des autres . . . Le costume s'impose despotiquement, et à ceux dont il indique l'opinion, et à ceux qui n'ont ni le courage ni le pouvoir de la combattre. Le crime de lèse-costume, si l'on peut s'exprimer ainsi, devient un crime qu'on expie sur l'échafaud' (*Collection de costumes, armes et meubles, pour servir à l'histoire de la Révolution française et de l'Empire* (Paris, 1834), pp. 9–10).

2. For a critical review of the discipline's current state of methodological diversity, see Lou Taylor, 'Doing the Laundry?: an assessment of object-based dress history', *Fashion Theory*, December 1998, vol. 2, no. 4, pp. 339–44.

3. 'Freedom of Dress in Revolutionary France', in Sara E. Melzer and Kathryn Norberg (eds), *From the Royal to the Republican Body. Incorporating the political in seventeenth- and eighteenth-century France* (University of California Press: Berkeley, Los Angeles, London, 1998), p. 249.

4. James A. Epstein, 'Understanding the Cap of Liberty: Symbolic Practice and Social Conflict in Early 19th-century England', *Past and Present*, February 1989, no. 122, pp. 74–118, and *Radical Expression. Political Language, Ritual, and Symbol in England 1790– 1850* (Oxford University Press: New York and Oxford, 1994).

5. *Past and Present*, no. 96, August 1982, pp. 103–32.

6. Barthes' articles on dress and fashion have recently been gathered together, *Le bleu est à la mode cette année et autres articles* (Éditions de l'Institut Français de la Mode: Paris, 2001).

7. Daniel Roche, 'Apparences révolutionnaires ou révolution des apparences' (pp. 105–27); Jean-Marc Devocelle, 'D'un costume politique à une politique du costume' (pp. 83–103), based on his important thesis, 'Costume politique et politique du costume: approches théoriques et idéologiques du costume pendant la Révolution française', Université de Paris I, mémoire de maîtrise, 2 vols, 1988.

8. Epitomized by an exhibition dedicated to one such object, *Le Soulier de Marie-Antoinette. Essai muséologique* (Musée des beaux-arts, Caen, 1989). See also, for example, Monique Ray and Jacques Payen, *Souvenirs iconographiques de la Révolution française à Lyon* (Éditions lyonnaises d'art et d'histoire: Lyon, 1989), and *Dix ans de médailles, insignes et récompenses révolutionnaires. Souvenirs historiques, 1789–1799* (Musée de Charleville-Mézières, 1989).

9. *The People of Paris. An essay in popular culture in the 18th century*, trans. Marie Evans with Gwynne Lewis (Berg: Leamington Spa, 1987).

10. Although important studies by Dorinda Outram (*The Body and the French Revolution. Sex, Class, and Political Culture* (Yale University Press: New Haven and London, 1989)), and Antoine de Baecque (*Le Corps de l'histoire: Métaphores et politique (1770–1800)* (Calmann-Lévy: Paris, 1993)) do not deal with dress directly, they have nonetheless enriched our sense of the context in which it must be understood by analysing the representation of the body in the Revolution.

11. 'Pierre-François Delauney, Liberty and St Nicholas', *Burlington Magazine*, December 1981, pp. 745–7.

12. See *Cérémonial de l'Empire français contenant; 1. les honneurs civils et militaires à rendre aux autorités militaires, civils et écclesiatiques de l'Empire; 2. les grands et petits costumes et uniformes des autorités civiles et militaires de l'Empire; 3. les fonctions et attributions des ces mêmes autorités; ce qui a rapport aux cérémonies publiques*, par L.I. Pxxxxx, Paris, 1805.

13. See John Harvey, *Men in Black* (Reaktion: London, 1995); Richard Wrigley, 'The Class of '89?: cultural aspects of bourgeois identity in France in the aftermath of the French Revolution', in Andrew Hemingway and William Vaughan (eds), *Art in Bourgeois Society 1790–1830* (Cambridge University Press: Cambridge, 1998), pp. 130–53.

1

Revolutionary Relics

IN THE political culture of revolutionary France, dress played many complex and powerfully symbolic roles, but the costumes, clothes, and badges themselves have all but disappeared.[1] This absence is not, however, simply the result of a gradual and inevitable process of material disintegration and accidental disposal. There is a history to be reconstructed which embraces the transformation of dress from being an active ingredient in political culture, and a means of representing that culture, to conservable and collectable object. In practice, this encompasses a transition which moves from the domain of the personal possession, being passed down either through networks of family, friendship, and shared allegiance, or through a commercial market, supplying private collections, which were in turn often donated to public museums.[2] Under what conditions, and by virtue of what attitudes and values did dress survive or disappear? The answer to this question is not, of course, merely a matter of reconstructing the 'life cycle' of clothes, in terms of calibrating their variable material durability, and consequent rarity. It is, rather, a matter of locating the history of such survival, and of attitudes to dress and costume as an expression of the past, within a larger framework of diverse and dissonant attitudes to the Revolution.

In terms of established attitudes to the treatment of domestic objects, the Revolution was at a crossroads between, on the one hand, what Annick Pardailhé-Galabrun describes as 'a world where nothing was thrown away out of respect for the objects',[3] and, on the other, the world of modern consumerism, in which objects were destined to have a shorter life. The nineteenth century was also, of course, the age of museums, during which evolving protocols of collecting and conservation came to be applied to a wide variety of cultural material, from the high culture of art and antiquities to more banal and quotidian artefacts. As we will see, the history of the survival and collecting of revolutionary dress intersects with these transitions, while at the same time being subject to the ebb and flow of contested political ideologies.

Far from being an inert residue of times past, items of revolutionary dress were indelibly marked by powerful associations, whether dangerous or inspiring, and their survival was therefore a highly charged and uncertain matter. In the context of the successive transformations which marked French history from the 1780s through the nineteenth century, political forms of dress were correspondingly prone to obsolescence. Revolutionary objects were the subject of conflicting desires; once their practical usefulness as active badges and means of identification had been superseded, they acquired the status of highly affective, and often inherently partisan, *aide-mémoires*.[4] Indeed, it was precisely the efficacy of such objects in evoking what many regarded as a painful or compromising past that ensured their disposal, if not destruction.[5] Recollections of the liberating relinquishment of items of political dress are as much a way of devaluing the Revolution – reducing such manifestations of its emblematic vocabulary to the status of repugnant, dispensable ephemera – as they may, in fact, be accurate descriptions of the fate of such items. As we will see in relation to the *bonnet rouge* and *sans-culotte* costume, discontinuing the practice of wearing such items was itself a highly symbolic assertion of the recognition of a transition to a new political situation, albeit that such renunciation was far from expressing a homogeneous set of attitudes.[6]

The active preservation of souvenirs and memorabilia was a more low-key practice, a style of conservation considerably encouraged by a prevailing climate of anti-revolutionary proscription through the early nineteenth century. Moments when the republican version of the Revolution could be celebrated in the form of public display – the aftermath of the 1830 Revolution, and the early days of the Second Republic – were exceptional. Otherwise it was a question of varieties of private or clandestine subculture or cult. It was not until the Third Republic that institutionalized commemorations of the Revolution were viable. At the time of the Centenary in 1889, the mounting of a large exhibition to survey the Revolution's history, containing imagery, texts, and multimedia souvenirs, was presented as only having become possible in the new republican climate. The exhibits were confined to the period up to 1804, because the inception of the Napoleonic Empire was deemed to have closed a chapter of French history: 'at this moment, the forms and fashions of the Revolution, like its images, disappeared, while its spirit led the clandestine life of conscience'.[7] The nation – or those within it who held to political principles rooted in the Revolution – had had to wait almost to the end of the century to be able to enjoy the freedom to celebrate this founding epoch in a way that had direct contemporary political relevance. Reviewing the historical exhibition dedicated to the Revolution, Maurice Tourneux reflected on the cumulative effect of such attitudes:

> What was spared by political and religious influences, which contributed so much to the destruction of the greater part of these objects, either remained buried in closets or was exposed to damaging conditions. Many families destroyed with their own hands unwanted or hateful heirlooms; even more denied any connection with this past, and did not care to have it revived; but eventually, such scruples diminished, points of view changed, indifference gave way to respect, even vanity came into play, and today people exhume what would have been hidden thirty years ago.[8]

Broadly speaking, in the course of the nineteenth century, partisan motivations for the destruction or cult of such souvenirs-cum-political relics tended to be resolved or neutralized by claims to historical object-ivity (in a manner analogous to the competing claims to museological rectitude made from the 1790s onward). In terms of the evolution of attitudes to the history of dress, the revolutionary episode was subsumed within a larger history of styles. Within this framework, the ideological identity of dress was translated into a generalized but reductive set of assumptions about the status of material culture as a form of transparent historical evidence, in such a way as to isolate it from the complexities of social and political life.

CONTEMPORARY USE: CEREMONIES AND FESTIVALS

In narrating the Revolution, dress figures repeatedly as tangible evidence by means of which to articulate the present's relation to the past, whether for reasons of celebration and commemoration, or for those of condemn-ation and denunciation. The preservation of special items of dress as highly charged and cherished souvenirs is a phenomenon that is evident from the earliest days of the Revolution.

New protocols for interpretation and display of the banal and quotidian evolved in order to politicize the present, transforming the ephemeral into the monumental and memorable. That is, not simply adopting items of dress as a form of badge (whether of national significance, as in the case of the tricolore cockade, or more localized factional signs and symbols), but treating it, so to speak, at one remove, in a sense isolating items of dress as a way of highlighting their expressive function. The artisans of the new political culture were fully alive to the rich symbolic charge of dress, and promoted its potential for expressing key revolutionary ideas and concepts, articulated in relation to topical exigencies. Equally, the highlighting of new forms of revolutionary dress in such public occasions also engendered diverse comments registering doubts, scepticism, and explicit challenging of their coherence and legitimacy. Festivals also encouraged independent or individualized forms of costume, exemplifying the eclectic nature of the creation of new vestimentary vocabularies.

Perhaps the most important context for the display of dress and other material elements of revolutionary history is that of festivals, funerary ceremonies, Pantheonizations, and other forms of ceremonial. The model for this kind of synthetic narration of the Revolution's ongoing progress is Palloy's patriotic entrepreneurial overhaul of the Bastille. As well as models of the prison distributed to all the communes of France, the reconstituted Bastille found its way into the costumes of the Assembly's ushers in the form of badges made from its chains.[9] These tokens were reminders of the dramatically foundational moment of the taking of the Bastille. [10]

The fundamental importance of the Bastille is evident in the presence of 'Vainqueurs de la Bastille' in festival processions from the Festival of the Federation in 1790 onwards. The *Vainqueurs* were a select and carefully vetted group of patriotic pioneers, rewarded and thenceforward identified, by a medal.[11] This is an early example of the creation of a new generation of revolutionary badges, which replaced forms of official medal and badge current during the Ancien Régime. *Vainqueurs*, and those who claimed to be *Vainqueurs*, continued to display their 'historic' dress as a badge of patriotic courage. In 1791, when Philippe Chapelle was arrested for having shouted 'Down with the National Guard!', he explained that, although he was no longer a member of the guard, he was wearing its uniform, having been given it by the 'Nation' in recognition of his exploits as a *Vainqueur*.[12]

Other participants in the founding day of 14 July 1789 held on to the clothing worn on that day as signs of an honourable revolutionary pedigree.[13] Initially, this would have been a matter of individual action, before the institutionalization of the *Vainqueurs*. In the spring and early summer of 1792, we find citizens from the faubourg St-Antoine and former French guards claiming the right to wear the clothes and carry the arms that they had used in July 1789. In April 1792, the procession for the Châteauvieux festival included as its second group 'A large number of male and female citizens carrying different arms and objects which were used in the conquest of liberty, on the day of 14 July 1789. They surrounded the model of the Bastille and the standard of this fortress, carried by the citizens of the faubourg St-Antoine, and former French guards, wearing their old uniform'.[14] Similarly, in June of the same year, a deputation from faubourgs St-Antoine and St-Marcel wished to plant a liberty tree on the terrace of the Feuillants, on the occasion of the anniversary of the 'Oath of the Tennis Court', and to present petitions 'relative to the present times' to the National Assembly and the king; they asked the *Conseil général* of the Commune for authorization 'to dress in the clothes they had worn in 1789, and to carry their arms'.[15]

In 1793 it was decided that the women who had participated in the march to and from Versailles on 5 and 6 October 1789 were to be allocated a place in civic ceremonies as 'citoyennes patriotes'; they were to carry a banner on one side of which was an 'inscription offensive to Louis XVI'; on the other 'Femmes des 5 et 6 octobre'; and would be accompanied by their husbands and children. An element of updating is, however, evident in that it was stipulated 'that they would knit' – a reference to the infamous 'type' of the *tricoteuses*, women who formed a popular, vociferous group of spectators in the public galleries of the Assembly.[16]

The display of dress as an *aide-mémoire* for recalling the Revolution's early days was at one and the same time impressively authentic, but was also inevitably subject to mythologizing. The soldiers of the Châteauvieux regiment who had been sent to the galleys for their part in a mutiny, sparked by an episode of insubordination symptomatic of the spread of revolutionary ideas, in Nancy in August 1790, were reclaimed as martyrs to Liberty in the spring of 1792 thanks to revised attitudes to the notion of public order and popular political action. In the Festival of Liberty arranged to celebrate the soldiers' liberation, the passage of historical time, and the freedom that a changed political climate had made possible, was performed by the soldiers themselves who replaced their galley convicts' costume with their old uniform. The chains of the ex-convicts, which had been carried by women in the procession, were attached to the vault of the Jacobin club as a reminder of former despotism, and also of the pointedly partisan nature of the organization of this event.[17] In May 1792, as part of the Festival of Law dedicated to Jacques-Guillaume

Simonneau, the mayor of Étampes who had died trying to quell a food riot, his mayoral sash, a token of his official role as the guardian of public order, was suspended from the vault of the Panthéon.[18]

MARTYRS

Some of the most striking uses of items of dress occur in the elaborate obsequies dedicated to revolutionary martyrs. Bloody clothes were displayed as martyrs' attributes – signs of their mortal sacrifice, and the violence of the Revolution's enemies.[19] It is difficult not to be reminded, not only of the religious cult of relics and the sacramental connotations of blood – especially where the body of the martyr is absent – but also, as we will see, of the compulsive attraction to royal blood witnessed at the scenes of the executions of Louis XVI and Marie-Antoinette.

The *conventionnel* Lepeletier de Saint-Fargeau was murdered for having voted for the death of the king on the day of the execution. In his address to the Convention on 22 January 1793, Marie-Joseph Chénier outlined his proposal for a ceremony to honour his colleague:

> This is no common death; the funeral should be given an equally exceptional character. Let superstition abase itself before the religion of liberty; let truly holy, truly solemn images speak to moved hearts; let the body of our virtuous colleague, exposed to all eyes, display the fatal wound which he received in the cause of the people; let there be an inscription describing with an energetic simplicity, the glorious reason for his death; let the parricidal blade, sanctified by a patriot's blood, glitter before our eyes, as testimony to the fury of tyranny and its vile worshippers; let his bloodied clothes strike the sight of citizens, and pronounce the impending judgement of death on the motherland's murderer.[20]

Jean-François Delacroix proposed that Lepeletier's last words – 'I am satisfied to shed my blood for the motherland; I hope that it will serve to consolidate liberty and equality, and to expose its enemies' (Je suis satisfait de verser mon sang pour la patrie; j'espère qu'il servira à consolider la liberté et l'égalité, et à faire reconnaître ses ennemis) (an obvious echo of those attributed to Louis XVI on the scaffold) – be inscribed on his tomb.[21] Mercier recalled that: 'This ceremony had an exceedingly remarkable character'; the body was accompanied by the members of the Convention and the Jacobin club (Figures 1 and 2):

Figure 1 Anonymous French School: Funeral procession of Lepeletier de St-Fargeau (24 January 1793), 1793, drawing. Musée Carnavalet, Paris, Inv. D 03534. Photograph: Photothèque des Musées de la Ville de Paris (Habouzit).

Figure 2 Detail.

They had their own banner, and next to it one saw another they had created: for pennant it had the shirt, jacket, and above all the breeches of Lepeletier, still disgustingly covered in blood. Everyone could see the dead man who, judge of Louis XVI, had preceded him into the tomb. It was a spectacle designed to make a deep impression, as it did. The hideousness of the ceremony disappeared before the awful images that it offered.[22]

In Marat's obsequies on 16 July 1793, held at the Cordeliers club, four women carried his bath, and, hoist on a pike, 'the bloody shirt of Marat'.[23] The shirt and bath were then displayed in front of the draped body. Both were later reused by some of the Parisian sections.[24] In the ceremony commemorating the assassination of French plenipotentiaries at Rastadt, the bloodstained coat of Jean de Bry (who, in fact, survived) was central

to the occasion. On a platform carried by two veterans, stood a figure of
the Justice of Nations, holding in one hand a raised sword, and pointing
with the other at the clothes that had been worn by de Bry when he was
attacked, which were decorated with olive branches. The draperies
hanging from the platform had inscribed on them the words with which
de Bry bequeathed – so he thought – his bloodstained clothes to his
children: 'Bless Providence, and Curse Austria' (Bénissez la Providence,
et maudissez l'Autriche).[25] In the Convention, funereal crêpe and 'bright
robes' were laid in the places occupied by the two other victims, the
plenipotentiaries Bonnier and Roberjot.[26] Bloody clothes and posed
official costumes stood in for their absent, violated bodies. Antoine de
Baecque has noted how the Convention was treated to the parading of
wounded and mutilated patriots for the inspiring edification of the
assembled representatives, turning such damaged bodies into animate
emblems of patriotic valour and sacrifice.[27]

   In these lugubrious spectacles, we see the presence of what might be
called a kind of documentary realism, intertwined with a theatricalized
didacticism. A further leitmotif of revolutionary justice was to reuse the
effects of the proscribed or executed in a way that was at once retributive
and purgative. Thus, in planning Bailly's elaborately stage-managed
execution, Chaumette argued that, rather than burning the red flag
denoting Bailly's declaration of martial law prior to the massacre at the
Champs de Mars, it would be better to employ it for the benefit of the
peuple; the material should be sold, and the proceeds given to the
commission de bienfaisance for distribution among the poor.[28]

ROYAL DEBRIS

The decline of royal authority is expressed in a prolific trail of discarded
and bestowed items of dress, ending with those retrieved from Louis XVI's
and Marie-Antoinette's respective final moments. Clothes had long
flowed down the social hierarchy, whether inherited, resold, or stolen, but
without the affective significance which accrued from their owners'
incarceration.[29] Royal items of clothing were, it would seem, given with
a clear sense of the intense value attached to them, and that they might
provide a tangible stimulus to enduring fidelity to the crown, even, or
especially, when it was all but effaced. We should remember, however,
that royal objects had been treated with exceptional reverence before the

Revolution. Hanet, valet to the king's sister (and brother of Cléry the king's valet), describes the intense emotions elicited by contact with a damaged pair of Marie-Antoinette's gloves in his possession, enabling commoners a rare opportunity to experience a vicarious but nonetheless exhilarating sense of direct contact with the royal body.[30]

Our awareness of the role played by 'relics' in the revolutionary dismantling of royal power owes much to the cult of the royal family as martyrs to the sanguinary violence of Revolution[31] – a cult that has been faithfully, not to say obsessively, upheld ever since. The collecting, conservation, and display of royal mementoes provides a key element in our understanding of the parallel or complementary cult of the Revolution. The decline of royal authority is not a separate episode, but an integral part of revolutionary history.

The invasion of the Tuileries palace on 10 August 1792 facilitated the widespread, collective dissemination of royal detritus. In a simple, practical sense, the disorder consequent on the invasion allowed unprecedented access to the contents of the royal apartments.[32] Looting-cum-souvenir hunting was, however, short-lived; on 11 August, the Legislative Assembly placed seals on the palace,[33] and then moved quickly not only to outlaw looting, but also to counteract such pilfering as had already occurred, and co-ordinated the gathering in of objects which had been taken from the Tuileries. In the first instance, this was a matter of collecting objects which had, almost by default, become national property. A decree of 13 August instructed that all the objects found in the palace, which had initially been gathered in the safekeeping of the Maison Commune, were to be deposited in the Archives Nationales.[34] Such legislation was also an expression of the desire to re-establish the Assembly's authority in the aftermath of the momentous and traumatic events of 10 August. In this context, it is perhaps surprising to find that items from the king's cabinet were later sold.[35]

Pieces of the palace's furniture and decoration may have been taken for their material value more than for their souvenir status, but certain things specifically identified as having been acquired on the day of the invasion also include banal items of royal dress.[36] Such objects acquired a special poignancy in so far as they corresponded to the moment when the royal household was physically and politically shattered. We should remember that, for all the uncertainties of the king's political position, he and his family and retinue had continued to lead a residual 'vie de château' while installed in the Tuileries.

THE TEMPLE AND CONCIERGERIE

A subsequent generation of souvenirs flowed from the king's trial,[37] and more numerously, the captivity of the royal family in the Temple, and Marie-Antoinette's incarceration in the Conciergerie. The royal family had existed in public all their lives, but at no period were they so intrusively scrutinized as during their imprisonment. At the time of the trial and execution of the king and queen, the surveillance which they were subject to intensified because of fears of escape plots. This episode is heavily documented – that is to say variously mythologized – both in offical records of the treatment of the royal prisoners, and in memoirs of their retainers, guards, and other witnesses.[38] Small items were smuggled out of the prison, in the process being transformed into precious, illicit relics.[39] The more constrained the royal family's sphere of action, the more intense the aura invested in their bestowed effects, further heightened by a sense of imminent, fatal closure. Recalling a dress given to her by Madame Elisabeth, the duchesse de Tourzel endowed it with an intense emotive charge: 'It is for me the token of an eternal memory; I keep it with a sacred respect, and I will preserve it for the rest of my life'.[40]

During the king's incarceration, he gave numerous items to his attendants. Some items were requested by his guards and the staff in the Temple. Recalling the king's gift of a pair of gloves to one of the staff in the temple, Cléry judged that: 'Even in the eyes of several of his guards, his remains were already sacred.'[41] On another occasion, the prison's staff were intermediaries in the supply of such royal tokens. Fragments of a damaged border to one of Marie-Antoinette's dresses, which had been replaced by the daughter of Bault, a *commissaire* at the Conciergerie, were distributed 'to several people who insistently asked me for them'.[42] Moëlle, another of the *commissaires*, wishing to have something which belonged to one of the princesses, took possession of one of the king's sister's leather gloves (which he describes precisely as 'couleur merde-oie') during their daily promenade on the terrace of the tower.[43] For royalist chroniclers, the fact that the royal family's gaolers willingly participated in the diffusion of relics was evidence of a conflict between their official role and their more humane sympathies. Royal relics also had an immediate currency for the royal family's fellow prisoners. On one extraordinary occasion, the officer guarding Marie-Antoinette gave one of her shoes to inmates, whose undimmed attachment to the crown was evident in the way they reverently passed it around and fervently kissed it.[44]

To judge from the relatively large quantity of such objects that found their way into collections of royal relics during the nineteenth and twentieth centuries, it is clear that, once acquired, they were carefully preserved. Objects whose provenance could be traced back to the royal family's last moments had a special place in exhibitions and museum collections. Indeed, the exhibition *Marie-Antoinette et son temps*, held at the Galerie Sedelmeyer in Paris in 1894, was organized around the authenticating provenance of the objects. The section dedicated to 'Souvenirs personnels' includes items traceable back to the duchesse de Tourzel,[45] the governess of the royal children, which had been inherited by two of her grandsons, the marquis de Villefranche, and the duc de Cars; objects which originally belonged to Cléry, the king's *valet de chambre* in the Temple;[46] and a series of objects belonging to the chevalier Hüe, grandson of another of Louis's *valets de chambre*, who had been imprisoned with him in the Temple. As with other exhibitions, news of the event brought to light new or lost objects. In this case, the remains of garters and other fragments of clothing which had been collected when, in 1815, Marie-Antoinette's remains were disinterred and given to Louis XVIII, were offered to the exhibition by the duc de Cars on behalf of their current owner, the duc de Blacas, whose forebear had supervised the exhumation.[47]

Numerous items now in the Musée Carnavalet which were included in the 1993 exhibition, *La Famille royale*, were donated in 1911 by descendants of Etienne Lasne, commissaire at the Temple between 11 germinal an III/31 March 1795 and 6 brumaire an VI/27 October 1796. A larger group derive from from the king's last *valet de chambre*, Cléry – together they provide enough to equip a reconstructed room in the current display dedicated to the royal family's incarceration in the Temple.[48]

Olivier Blanc's study of the 'last letters' of the condemned demonstrates that the behaviour of the royal family and their dependents in preparing themselves for death was entirely typical. As the king had paid especial attention to keeping locks of his family's hair, so others not only consigned such intimate souvenirs to their friends and family, but religiously cut their own hair prior to execution to this end, in order to avoid having it sullied by the executioner's hands.[49]

Mortal remains

The respective executions of the royal couple constitute the most intensely symbolic moments for the acquisition of mementoes and souvenirs. Daniel Arasse has noted the echoes of Christ's passion in descriptions of the cutting up of Louis XVI's jacket, and distribution of this and his hair, cut for execution, as well as the dipping of handkerchiefs, walking and smearing of hands in the king's blood, within accounts of the execution. He observes that republican texts stress the keenness to dip items in the blood as a kind of antidote so as to demystify this royal death. Pro-royal accounts omit such gory details (even though it is clear that royalists sought such relics).[50]

Surveillance reports of the execution's aftermath interweave these ambiguities. Antoine François Maingot was arrested for having walked in the kings' blood and wiped his shoes with his handkerchief. He claimed in his defence that, like many others, he had only walked on it with the intention of effacing it.[51] Another unnamed individual was arrested by Commandant Hanriot whose intervention saved him from nearly being killed by a mob after soaking his hands in Marie-Antoinette's blood while 'making uncivil remarks'.[52] Jacques Roux's laconic report of the king's execution, published in the *Courrier français* – 'His head has fallen. Citizens dipped their pikes and soaked their handkerchiefs in his blood' (Sa tête a tombé. Les citoyens ont trempé leurs piques et leurs mouchoirs dans son sang) – bespeaks a spirit of ritualistic negation.[53] The sense of uncertainty as to the feelings of the crowd, and indeed, of the soldiers who provided the guard, emerges all the more clearly in nineteenth-century texts concerning the collection of relics from the scene. A sample of Louis XVI's hair offered to the Musée des Souverains in 1868, was claimed to have been collected by a soldier standing at the foot of the scaffold, who discreetly put his foot on the fallen locks, until he could pocket them unnoticed.[54]

Particular care was taken to ensure that the king's body was irretrievable, being buried in a deep grave under a double layer of quicklime. A report confirmed that head and body, still wearing the clothes from the execution, were inside the simple coffin. Even his punitively rudimentary obsequies were given a didactic point. Santerre reported that the cadaver was placed between the remains of those members of the crowds who had been accidentally killed on the occasion of festivities celebrating Louis's wedding, and the victims of 10 August 1792.[55] Seals were placed on the room Louis had occupied prior to his execution, and the bed he had slept in, the clothes he had worn, and all other contents were burned on the place de Grève, as scrupulously witnessed by *commissaires*.[56] In like spirit, according to Louis Larivière, one of the gaolers at the Conciergerie, the executioner Sanson put Marie-Antoinette's hair in his pocket, and after her execution, this was burnt in the Temple.[57] The availability of the possessions of the royal family was further increased by the posthumous sale of Marie-Antoinette's effects.[58] However, to my knowledge, none of the existing relics relating to Marie-Antoinette has been traced to this sale. The single item which has received the greatest attention is a shoe owned by the Musée des Beaux-Arts in Caen, which reputedly was worn at her execution (Figure 3).[59] The traffic in illicit royal relics was noted as early as September 1793, as reported by the police agent Rousseville:

It seems certain that the fancy-goods merchant on rue Saint-Honoré, at the corner of rue de l'Echelle, at the sign of the Green Monkey, is selling little boxes in which there are locks of Capet's hair, and that several jewellers make large silver rings, which have secret openings, containing in their upper part, made convex for this purpose, a small piece of the coat of Monsieur Veto, who has become a saint for having murdered his people.[60]

Containers for this material sometimes took the traditional form of mourning jewellery, or more elaborate reliquaries, such as that created to house the items which had been given to the duchesse de Tourzel and her daughter by Madame Royale (Figure 4).[61]

The fabrication of modern relics of the recently dead should be compared with the treatment of the royal tombs at St Denis in October 1793. As recounted by the central protagonist, Alexandre Lenoir, once the bodies had been disposed of, the coffins were recycled for their lead. Interestingly, where items of clothing and jewellery were found to have survived, they were similarly treated so as to denature and obliterate their royal identity.[62] Lenoir's account gives no indication that it was possible to recognize or imagine the historical significance of the survival from medieval times of such items of dress, despite the fact that the Musée des Monuments Français's 'programme' specifically identified the representation of historic costume in sculpture as one of the resources it made newly available to artists and historians.[63]

Revolutionaires' Relics

By comparison with the reverent cult of the royal family's effects, the history of the conservation and collecting of revolutionary material is

Figure 3 'Marie-Antoinette's shoe'. Inscribed on the insole: 'Soulier que portait la Reine Marie-Antoinette le jour néfaste ou elle monta à l'échafaud. Ce soulier fut ramassé par un individu au moment où la Reine le portait et acheté immédiatement par Monsieur le comte de Guernon-Ranville' (Shoe which Queen Marie-Antoinette wore on the ill-fated day she mounted the scaffold. This shoe was picked up by an individual at the moment the Queen wore it and immediately bought by the comte de Guernon-Ranville). Musée des Beaux-Arts, Caen. Photograph: Musée des Beaux-Arts, Caen: Martine Seyve Photographe.

more elusive. It is significant that a satirical text on the varieties of political types published in an VI (1797–98) refers to 'exclusifs' who continued to wear republican dress, and 'who have faith only in their relics'.[64] Such assertions of the obsolescence of examples of earlier politicized dress are paralleled by the editing out from political language of revolutionary neologisms, or, as in the case of the *carmagnole*, confining its meaning to the Ancien Régime.[65] Republicans' accoutrements were deemed – by

Figure 4 Reliquary of Royal Mementoes created for the duchesse de Tourzel. Musée Carnavalet, Paris. Photograph: Photothèque des Musées de la Ville de Paris (Joffre).

their antagonists at least – to be vestiges of a lost, irretrievable past. Their subsequent dispersal is hard to trace. During the first half of the nineteenth century, the traffic in such mementoes remained private, and largely clandestine. By the third quarter of the century, a market had developed. The collections formed at this time in turn contributed to the institutional presentation of displays of revolutionary objects, including dress, notably in the newly created Musée Carnavalet (discussed below). That the centenary of the Revolution occurred under the Third Republic ensured that, as part of the celebrations which did as much to legitimize the new régime as to commemorate its antecedent, the opportunity was taken to bring together material from a wide range of sources – testimony to the survival of republican values, which had in turn ensured the preservation of mementoes and souvenirs.

The fate of the effects of famous, and infamous, revolutionary figures is much more fragmentarily ascertainable than that of those which derive from the royal family. In the case of those who were guillotined, this can be explained by the treatment of victims' clothes and belongings. By tradition, executioners had taken possession of the clothes victims had with them in prison and at time of their execution.[66] However, under new revolutionary law, the belongings of those condemned to death became the property of the Republic, and this seems to have extended to the clothes they were wearing at the time they were executed.[67] This was a source of considerable complaint from Sanson, who explained that the increased responsibilities required of him, as of other executioners, entailed much greater expense from the wear and tear of equipment and clothing, and that he risked being out of pocket.[68] The clothes were sent to the Hôtel-Dieu, renamed the Hospice de l'Humanité.[69] Thus, in a manner that repeats a common theme of revolutionary justice, the immediate effects of those proscribed by the Tribunal révolutionnaire were transformed into objects of charity. Victims' other effects and property were sold. In the case of St-Just, this occurred over a year after his execution: he was guillotined on 10 thermidor an II/28 July 1794, the sale of his belongings took place on 12 fructidor an III/29 August 1795.[70] Beyond administrative process, this time lag, whether deliberately intended or not, would also have had the effect of defusing the political relevance and increasing the curiosity value of such effects.

Considerable attention has been paid to the survival of Robespierre's effects, but with very little result – perhaps an example of collectability being in inverse proportion to availability.[71] Very few of Robespierre's

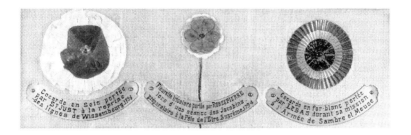

Figure 5 Left to Right: 'Cocarde en soie portée par St JUST à la reprise des lignes de Wissembourg 1793' (Silk Cockade worn by St-Just at the retaking of the line at Wissemburg, 1793); 'Fleurette tricolore portée par ROBESPIERRE lors d'une séance des Jacobins préparatoire à la Fête de l'Être Suprême 1794' (Tricolore flower worn by Robespierre at a meeting of the Jacobins prior to the Festival of the Supreme Being 1794); 'Cocarde en fer blanc porté par LEBAS durant sa mission à l'Armée de Sambre et Meuse' (Iron cockade worn by Lebas during his mission to the Army of Sambre and Meuse). Musée Carnavalet, Paris, Inv. OM 0536. Photograph: Photothèque des Musées de la Ville de Paris (Degraces).

belongings are known to have survived. A waistcoat – 'decorated with revolutionary figures and inscriptions, which had belonged to Robespierre, and been given by him to one of his friends from Arras' – was in Lavedan's collection.[72] Madame Tussaud claimed to have dressed her model of Robespierre in a coat and breeches which had been acquired directly from him (the implication being that a model was planned before his death).[73] Carnavalet possesses a cockade that allegedly belonged to Robespierre displayed with other cockades belonging to Saint-Just and Lebas (Figure 5), as well as a lock of his hair (Figure 6), and his shaving bowl.[74] In the case of figures who died 'honourably', as in the case of Marat, the ultimate destination of their effects is in fact equally hard to trace. We know from a letter in the *Journal de Paris* of 5 ventôse an III/23 February–March 1797, that even a 'relic' as precious (or odious) as Marat's heart could go missing.[75] The only surviving item of clothing attached to Marat is a waistcoat from the pre-revolutionary period.[76]

Some items of revolutionary dress were preserved initially through their identity as family mementoes, often testimony to the achievements of a forebear, or a revered revolutionary figure. In addition, objects with plausible provenances would also have been found more desirable by more scrupulous and exigent collectors, and in due course correspondingly

Figure 6 Medallion containing a lock of Robespierre's hair. Musée Carnavalet, Paris. Photograph: Photothèque des Musées de la Ville de Paris (Degraces).

more acquirable by modern museums.[77] But these are exceptions to the more general disappearance of clothing. Thus the scarlet cloak now in the Musée Carnavalet, worn by an unidentified member of the Conseil des Anciens or Conseil des Cinq-Cents, is the only intact example from at least 750 produced to survive.[78] The *bonnet rouge* in the Musée de la Révolution française at Vizille belonged to 'C.V.M.L.', discoverer of a method of steering aerostats, inherited by Auguste Hesse from his father, tailor to the Convention.[79] In the case of material from Lyon, these have predominantly been preserved as an homage to victims of the republican army.[80] While there are relatively numerous examples of special dress, or dress made in some sense special through its biographical connection, surviving (Figure 7),[81] the fate of anonymous items, especially more banal, quotidian types of dress, was far more obscure and precarious.[82] Writing of popular dress from the Revolution, Albert Soboul lamented this historical lacuna:

Figure 7 *Bonnet rouge*, cockade, pike head, laurel, and document. Musée Carnavalet, Paris. Photograph: Photothèque des Musées de la Ville de Paris (Joffre).

As for the items of dress themselves, they no longer exist. Worn until completely threadbare, the clothing of the petite bourgeoisie and the people has completely disappeared: none were shown at the exhibition devoted to French eighteenth-century costume at the Musée Carnavalet, in November 1954.[83]

Indeed, interest in revolutionary dress has habitually been overshadowed by, on the one hand, a fascination for the decorative pleasures of late eighteenth-century fashion, and on the other, the lavish military and official uniforms inaugurated under the Directory and massively multiplied under Napoleon. There has also been a tendency for royal items to receive more attention than revolutionary objects – encouraging the assumption that the former were more cherished, more scrupulously conserved than the latter, however much this inverts the probable quantitative reality qua survival.[84]

IMPERIAL DESTINY

The disposal and acquisition of the royal family's effects was by turns opportunistic, haphazard, and illicit; the fate of clothing belonging to revolutionary victims and martyrs is obscure and elusive. The case of Napoleon suggests a more coherent and stage-managed desire on the Emperor's part to control the fate of his belongings from beyond the grave. While we might take this as evidence of a new, or consolidated, sensibility regarding the conservation of personal relics as historical evidence, we should also remember that under the Restoration, images of, and objects pertaining to, Napoleon were proscribed.[85] Napoleon's will sought not only to resist the break-up of his official *patrimoine* and financial estate, but also, in a manner that was entirely conventional, to ensure that his personal effects were conveyed exclusively to those whom he designated. His prime concern was to make sure that his son, the Roi de Rome, took possession of specific effects, and that his family and faithful servants would acquire the rest. After the Roi de Rome's premature death, Napoleon's mother inherited the clothes which were to have been given to his son. On her death in 1836, they were was dispersed to Napoleon's brothers and sisters. The remaining clothes were bequeathed to Bertrand, Marchand, and Monthalon, the Emperor's faithfuls who had shared his exile in St Helena.[86] One of their obligations was to send cuttings of his hair to his family. When Napoleon's head was shaved prior to the taking of a death mask, Marchand took formal possession of the hair with this end in view.[87] Interestingly, the will specifically forbade the sale of items;[88] Napoleon was determined to ensure that his memory, and indeed his residual dynastic rights and property, be safeguarded, but on his own extremely controlling terms. In the event, his wishes were to a very large extent carried out, such that the greater part of the corpus of personal Napoleonic memorabilia remained within the Bonaparte family.[89] His executors, Bertrand, Marchand, and Montholon, strove to prevent the British from appropriating any Napoleonic effects, but the sale of the furniture from his residence on St Helena created a set of privately owned items outside Napoleon's wished-for direct line of descent. That some of these were in due course offered by their British owners to the Musée des Souverains (discussed below) is evidence of the way the burgeoning Napoleonic cult transcended national and political boundaries. In 1840, on his return from the expedition to recover Napoleon's ashes from St Helena, Bertrand gave part of his collection of Napoleonic material to the museum of his home town, Châteauroux, which in turn received his own uniforms and arms from his daughter.[90]

That the cult of Napoleon depended on the elision of reverence for royalty and patriotic veneration of French cultural heroes is illustrated by Vivant Denon's remarkable adaptation of a fifteenth-century reliquary, creating a personalized pantheon-in-miniature. Denon inserted two complementary sets of relics. On one side, Denon placed romantic souvenirs: fragments of the bones of El Cid and Chimène (heroine of Corneille's *Le Cid*), and locks of the hair of the Romantic heroine Inès de Castro and Agnès Sorel (mistress of Charles VII). On the other, historic French material: a fragment of Henri IV's moustache, and from the shroud of Turenne, fragments of bone from Molière and La Fontaine, one of Voltaire's teeth, and a lock of Desaix's hair. The assemblage was completed by Napoleonic items: his signature, a fragment from a bloodied shirt from Napoleon's last days, a lock of his hair, and a leaf from the willow adjacent to his grave on St Helena.[91] On another level, of course, this composite object was also a testament to Denon's own history as a roving collector, which had given him exceptional access to both living and dead heroes.

These examples form part of a larger movement towards the synthetic reconstruction of the past, finding its expression in new museums which accorded documentary status to relatively humble objects as well as more established media.[92] Complementing this is the growth of publications in the early nineteenth century which sought to classify historic costume, almost exclusively drawing their illustrations from sculpture, manuscripts and other representations.[93] Both Empire and Restoration publications of this type shared the aim of establishing – or, after 1814, re-establishing – links between the present and past traditions of national and royal identity. They also demonstrate a rather sombre recognition of the way the Revolution had indelibly assimilated politics to the business of dress.[94] However, as in the case of the series of volumes published by comte Horace de Viel-Castel, narrating this history in terms of the changing forms of dress was also a means to defuse this still pungently remembered episode, by placing it within an essentially typological and stylistic history of dress, anticipating what Roche calls 'l'effet Quicherat'.[95]

THE MUSÉE DES SOUVERAINS

The first major transformation in the official culture of collecting historical memorabilia comes with the creation by Napoleon III of the Musée des Souverains in 1852. The museum occupied five rooms in the east wing of the Louvre: the first two contained arms from François Ier to Louis XIV, the third was dedicated to the Ordre du Saint-Esprit, the fourth covered the period from Dagobert to Henri IV, and the fifth contained the Napoleonic material, which constituted over half the exhibits.[96] The Revolution appears only in so far as this marked the temporary end of the Bourbon dynasty, by means of 'royal relics'. The museum was instituted as a means of establishing Napoleon III's historical legitimacy, and can be understood as a more modest sequel to the Musée historique created by Louis-Philippe at Versailles; indeed, it is referred to in official correspondence as the 'new Musée historique'.[97] The idea for its creation was attributed to Louis-Napoléon himself. When visiting the historic interiors of the Henri II, Henri IV, and Louis XVIII rooms in the Louvre, he conceived the project to gather together 'curious relics' as a 'reminder of our emperors and kings, having escaped the vandalism of revolutions and the destruction of time'. In the Corps législatif, Dalloz commented that it was desirable to gather such precious relics together, 'to revisit with their help, the pages of our history, often brilliant, sometimes painful, always instructive'.[98] Other than the royal identity of the assembled objects, the key criterion, which was strictly applied, was that every object had to have belonged to or have been used by a French monarch, or a member of his family.[99] The museum was envisaged as drawing on objects from state and private collections. It was assumed that new material would come to light in response to the museum's existence. Marchand lent items that he had inherited, and a small number of personal mementoes acquired during his lifetime; in these cases, it is not clear whether they were gifts from Napoleon, or treasured as precious souvenirs.[100] Other Napoleonic memorabilia were lent by British owners.[101] Indeed, it is significant that it was assumed that there was a reservoir of personal souvenirs which could be drawn upon. To this extent, the museum put into practice a double-sided kind of democratization, both in terms of the sources of the collection, and also in its quasi-domestic assemblage of diverse objects – from coronation crowns to prayer books. By the same token, the very heterogeneity of its contents left open to visitors how they might reflect or respond to them. Mac'Vernoll, writing in *Le Monde illustré*, enthused over the 'striking contrasts' created by the juxtaposition of diverse historical material: 'What noble relics! The imperial crown of Charlemagne and the prestigious little hat of the founder of the new empire of the West.'[102] This ideological acquiescence, linking the Second Empire to the annals of history, was, however, only one form of response.

Collecting the Revolution

The linkage of royal and revolutionary collecting is evident in a remark by a pioneer in the latter activity, Champfleury. Writing in 1866 (the same year as the publication of the first catalogue of the Musée des Souverains), he asked: 'Has not the moment arrived, after so much accumulation of battle pictures, to collect the objects made by and for the people, which would form a natural and logical sequel to the Musée de Souverains?'.[103] It is interesting that he put forward this initiative as something 'natural' and 'logical', rather than as a politically polemical proposition. Although his initial involvement with collecting and documenting popular arts had shared the polemical thrust of his contributions to the critical debate around Courbet and Realism, such views had been superseded by a more conservative, fatalistic vision of popular culture.[104] In the 1860s, he assembled an unrivalled collection of popular imagery, patriotic ceramics, and revolutionary prints, and published historical monographs on the same topics. Such items of dress as he collected seem to have been acquired because of their explicit illustration of revolutionary imagery.[105] His pursuit of revolutionary ceramics and prints helped to stimulate a new generation of collectors of revolutionary souvenirs. The crystallization of such a market was partly evident in the production of fakes – which merely sharpened collectors' desire to track down authentic objects.

One of Champfleury's companions in his collecting trips across France deserves particular mention here because of his key role in the constitution of the revolutionary collections of the Musée Carnavalet. This is comte Alfred de Liesville (1836–1885), who assembled a huge multi-media collection of revolutionary objects, which he bequeathed to Carnavalet, where he was *conservateur-adjoint*, in 1880 prior to his early death.[106] De Liesville came from an aristocratic Normand family. Marius Vachon described him as a passionate republican.[107] However, his experience of 1848 and 1870–1 engendered an antipathy to revolutions, 'those moments of fever to which France is unfortunately too subject'. He nonetheless claimed that his collecting was 'free of any political concern'.[108] His importance as a collector was acknowledged in an obituary, which compared him to Edmond du Sommerand, the son of the founder of the Musée de Cluny.[109]

De Liesville's collection could be said to be a hybrid. On the one hand, it conforms to the old model of the collection of curiosities – apparently trivial objects valued for their links to history, and their extraordinary, charismatic provenance; and its display, which had taken over his house in Batignolles, seems to have lacked any systematic aesthetic or scientific rationale – it was the sheer density and profusion of diverse objects which struck visitors.[110] On the other hand, his making of the collection, dedicated to a phase of French history which was at once neglected and contested, and also its donation to the City of Paris, exemplifies a more modern kind of public-spirited ideology. The idea of cultural collecting, and the public display of the results of that collecting, as a constructive form of citizenship, had been established during the Revolution,[111] and was revived in officially sanctioned form under the Third Republic. As Edmond Bonnaffé asserted in his study of the history of French collecting: 'We should all – each in their own way – respect, look after, rescue the works of the past; we should encourage interest in collecting, popularise it, link everybody's efforts to the great national undertaking of conservation. To make a collection is the act of a good citizen.'[112] Marius Vachon claimed that it was the donation of his collection to the Musée Carnavalet which had transformed the display, hitherto merely a 'bazaar of diverse objects'.[113]

However, the application of this mode of collecting and display to forms of cultural history that were popular, material, and also explicitly political, was new.[114] Disparaging comments in the press on the revolutionary galleries at Carnavalet, known as the de Liesville donation, indicate that it was not just the inherently political associations of the material which were found unpalatable by different elements of the political spectrum, but also the anti-hierarchical approach to its display, which was dismissed as a motley assemblage of bric-a-brac. We find this kind of point recurring in responses to exhibitions and displays of revolutionary material from the later nineteenth to the early twentieth centuries; what was construed as merely an assemblage of trivia by the right,[115] was criticized for lacking a coherent historical, social, and political narrative by left-wing historians.[116]

To collect the Revolution was not in and of itself to express sympathy for it – indeed many leading collectors through the nineteenth and twentieth centuries were royalist or right-wing.[117] Such collections were a form of challenging its sanguinary republican associations, whether through providing a framework of notional comprehensiveness or even-handed objectivity, or explicitly denouncing its values, as in the case of those collections exclusively dedicated to royal objects.[118] It is a striking paradox that the most important collection of revolutionary materials asssembled in the later nineteenth century was that of de Liesville, a Normand aristocrat. When Jules Cousin paid homage to his late colleague at Carnavalet, he endorsed the collection as a resource for the proper, that is, high-minded and abstracted, study of History. The Revolution had been:

> a period to which he had devoted his life's work and a significant part of his fortune, and generously gave [his collection] to his adopted city . . . [It was] a period which he had treated as a veritable cult . . . and even those whose personal convictions made them exceedingly antipathetic to revolutionary ideas, understood the high philosophical significance of this impartial evocation, of this rigorous display of one of the most extraordinary phases of Humanity.[119]

In France, the collecting of historic dress, and more especially the development of a literature on the history of dress, was faced with an unavoidable political choice when it came to acknowledging the undeniable role played by the Revolution in radically transforming or, at the

least, interrupting, any kind of progressive stylistic evolution. In the case
of the historical exhibition organized in 1874 by the Union Centrale des
Beaux-Arts Appliqués à l'Industrie – innovative if for nothing more than
the sheer quantity of material assembled (approximately 6000 exhibits)
– the broad sweep of time and place covered, beginning with Byzantine
objects, and including Africa, the Far and Near East, effectively meant
that the few objects from the Revolution on show among the section
entitled 'Fin du XVIIIe siècle', which itself followed two whole sections
on the eighteenth century, were detached from any precise sense of social
and political historical specificity. Indeed, the adjacent, and final, section
was devoted to 'Costumes de théâtre'.[120] The rationale for the exhibition
was to inform and stimulate contemporary designers, hence a preference
for ample use of prints, paintings and drawings, to show dress as something living (if at one remove), in preference to the 'cold, limp, dead
display' that would have resulted from rooms full of dressed-up mannequins.[121] The absence of any commentary in the catalogue followed from
the fact that it was drawn up once the objects had been displayed, and
hurriedly produced so as to be available for visitors. To this extent, the
general assumptions underlying the status given to historic dress were left
at the level of a simple assertion of the relevance of this material as a
potential resource for modern designers and artists, and, of course, for the
education of collectors.

The more elaborate catalogue of the 'Musée rétrospectif' of 'costume
et ses accessoires' that formed part of the Paris Exposition Universelle
Internationale in 1900 is more forthcoming regarding attitudes to dress
as a form of historical evidence. First, it is striking that just over half of
the collectors who loaned material were women (though in several cases
their husbands are also named separately as lenders).[122] But there is no
simple gender divide corresponding to the collecting of women's clothes
as a feminine pursuit; while Georges Cain applauded Mme Henri Lavedan's
encyclopedic collection of 'feminine knick-knacks', the best collection of
female clothes from the era of Louis XV and Louis XVI belonged to the
artist Maurice Leloir. Clearly, as already evident in 1874, the collecting
of historic dress was a widely diffused activity. In the preface, Cain
observed that some exhibits were family heirlooms; Mme Lavedan's
collection contained umbrellas which were 'relics of youth', having
remained in mint condition since being wrapped in tissue paper years
before; other items had been trouvailles in unexpected locations – 'du
Barry's skirt, rediscovered in 1868, at Marly-le-Roy, on the waist of a salad

seller'.[123] The organization of the catalogue made a simple distinction between 'costumes et souvenirs historiques', where provenance and association were the key criteria, and 'costumes de style', that is to say, fashion, consisting of examples of evolving garment design. Significantly, exhibits from the third and final general category, 'costumes locaux', were predominantly drawn from museum collections, notably the Musée Ethnographique at Trocadéro and the museum at Clermont-Ferrand, indicating that the desire to collect, preserve, and study clothing as evidence of a disappearing regional culture was shifting onto urban forms of culture.[124] In the introduction to the 'costumes de style' section, Maurice Leloir observed that the key transformation in French dress had occurred during the Revolution (he cited the adoption of trousers and tall hats for men as the central development). Yet, in what is admittedly a short text, he fails to acknowledge the underlying political and social causes and significance of this phenomenon. Rather, his account is couched in a recherché technical language, which luxuriates in enumerating esoteric matters of tailoring and fabric.

Leloir (1853–1940)[125] was also the moving spirit behind the creation of a key institution in the transformation of the collecting and study of historic dress – or dress as history – from being the preserve of private collectors to being a matter of collective *patrimoine*, by the foundation of the Société de l'Histoire du Costume in 1907.[126] Other founding members worthy of note include the painters Edouard Detaille, Luc-Olivier Merson, Ernest Meissonier, Georges Gustave Toudouze, Henri Lavedan (who collected revolutionary materials),[127] and Georges Lenôtre, the indefatigable popular and erudite historian of the Revolution. The initial collection predominantly excluded military items, given the existence of the Musée de l'Armée. This was, however, in part the result of a historical accident, in that, on his death in 1915, Edouard Detaille had left his collection of uniforms and arms to the society, together with his Parisian hôtel, which was intended to provide a suitably spacious museum. But a legal aberration meant that his legacy passed to the state, which transferred it to the Musée de l'Armée.[128] It was the extensive collection assembled by the society's members which formed the nucleus of the Musée Carnavalet's costume collection, following a donation in 1920. However, Carnavalet's refusal to display foreign and regional material, as well as 'reconstructions' and 'mannequins réalistes', was an obstacle to co-ordinated use of the collection. It was not to open in a separate annexe as the Musée du Costume until November 1956.[129]

Shortly after this, the museum's holdings were further enhanced by the gift by Mme Edmond de Galéa's family of her collection of French costumes.[130] The Musée de la Mode et du Costume entered its current home in the Palais Galliera in 1974.

The broad ethos of the Société de l'Histoire du Costume was designed to situate the history of dress within the domain of the decorative arts, and to assert the prodigious and long-established creativity of French fashion, underpinning its contemporary authority by celebrating past glories.[131] Within this framework, dress and fashion are thus mapped across a model of stylistic evolution, essentially defined by an already given pattern based on the succession of monarchs and régimes, and as such glides over less neatly periodized problems of historical change and conflict. Indeed, as Daniel Roche has argued, such a narrow conception of the history of dress excludes the social in any meaningful sense.[132]

Other evidence of the growing interest in collecting historic dress around the turn of the century is the founding of several journals, including the short-lived journal, *Le Bonnet phrygien, publication mensuelle, illustrée des curiosités historiques et révolutionnaires* in 1907, *Costumes et uniformes. Revue historique documentaire* (from 1912), published with the support of the Société, and the *Bulletin de la société de l'histoire du costume*. These brought together at least three potentially overlapping constituencies: specialist collectors of revolutionary material; collectors of military uniforms and paraphernalia (who had had the *Sabretache. Revue militaire rétrospective* since 1893); and artists, who relied on authentic costume to give an aura of empirical authority to their historical genre scenes.

There had long been a pragmatic tradition, or convention, of artists borrowing clothes from their sitters for portrait-painting, but during the nineteenth century, this takes on a historical dimension, in two senses. First, sitters' clothing was sometimes kept by the artist, and thereby became a souvenir both of the person and of their associated historical situation.[133] Secondly, the vogue for historical scenes, from the *genre troubadour* onward,[134] encouraged interest in, and pursuit of, costumes from the past, and was therefore a major contributory factor in the creation of a buoyant market for historic dress.[135] Meissonier, one of the founder members of the Société de l'Histoire du Costume, specialized in producing Napoleonic images; after his death, a large collection of uniforms and military paraphernalia was given to the Musée de l'Armée in the Invalides by his family.[136]

The collections of the Musée de l'Armée in the Invalides were the main repository of material from the Napoleonic era beyond the collection of the Bonaparte family. This was augmented by the acquisition of the remarkable collection created by Jean Brunon and installed in what became the Musée de l'Empéri at Salon-en-Provence.[137] The Musée de l'Armée is the most extensive, and most atmospheric, display of dress from this period.[138] It is also the most affective – outfits are displayed with a minimum of artifice, essentially chronologically, and by regiment. For all their less than immaculate inertness, they gain an increased resonance from their obvious sense of having been used. These are objects which still bear the rude imprint of history and its at times fatal violence – unlike their owners, they survived. Indeed, in a way that is reminiscent of aspects of revolutionary ceremonies and festivals discussed above, the most powerfully poignant effects are produced by encounters with clothing cut, slashed, and in some cases with holes blasted through it.[139] This is in contrast to the usual museum protocols which emphasize an illusion of pristine conservation, encouraging a perception of dress – from haute couture to street style – which at one and the same time assimilates it to a still current régime of fashionable appearances, and presents it as an archaeological sign of times past.

This was nowhere more evident than in exhibitions devoted to the Revolution at the time of the bicentenary, where political dress was, in fact, all but absent beyond a handful of *bonnets* and cockades. Some recognition of the symbolic power with which dress had been imbued during the Revolution was, in a sense, displaced onto the bicentennial ceremonies and latter-day festivals, where, in a blend of civic ceremony and commercial opportunism, tricolore outfits and *bonnets phrygiens rouges* were visible in festive, if ultimately awkwardly theatrical, abundance.[140] Yet, given the breadth and extent of these celebrations, it would be mistaken to assume that such garments held no political resonance for their wearers. Just as in 1939, at the time of the 150th anniversary of the Revolution under the final moments of the Front populaire, the recreation of what Pascal Ory calls a pastiche of revolutionary art and emblems was linked to a discordant spectrum of political ideologies.[141]

In reviewing the historiography of revolutionary dress, it could be suggested that attitudes to it oscillate between two conflicting views. On the one hand, its fragility is construed as a metaphor for the mutable ephemerality of the values and principles of revolutionary politics. In

Jules Vallès's novel *L'Insurgé* (1886), the decay to which clothes were inevitably subject is used as a metaphor for the obsolescence of the values and principles of revolutionary politics. The author's alter ego, Jean Vingtras, repudiates the revolutionary legacy of the 'Jacobin' militants of 1869–71: 'All that rubbish of the legend of '93', reminded him 'of a pile of frayed and faded clothes taken to père Gros, the rag man, in his draughty shop on the rue Mouffetard'.[142] Vallès's metaphor replays cognate judgements on the Revolution for having failed to produce lasting monuments of marble and bronze, instead only fabricating temporary structures of plaster and papier mâché.[143]

On the other hand, forms of politicized dress are placed in the foreground of retrospective images of the Revolution – an emblematic extension of the widespread adoption of new ideas. Thus, when revolutionary crowd scenes are represented, whether in nineteenth-century historical genre painting or films like Abel Gance's *Napoléon*, *bonnets rouges* and hirsute *sans-culottes* are ubiquitous ingredients.[144] As will be argued later, this is misleading. Revolutionary costume in its multifarious guises was less widely diffused and more restricted in its use than is commonly assumed. Such items were predominantly confined to relatively special occasions, such as political club meetings, where they would normally only be worn by presidents, secretaries, and those who spoke from the tribune; or else at festivals, and as part of ceremonial processions. Indeed, as often as not they weren't worn, but placed on *autels à la patrie* or on liberty trees; they were, that is, primarily ritual objects. Similarly, the wearing of *sans-culotte* costume was a minority practice. The piece-meal survival of such items appears correspondingly less surprising. The cockade is an exception, explicable insofar as it was not an item of practical dress, and was the only truly national, and therefore durable, example of political dress to survive the revolutionary decade. Moreover, each form or type of dress to be studied, however limited or extensive its degree of circulation, was always accompanied by challenges regarding its meaning and legitimacy. Indeed, the very question of how universal or restricted the adoption of revolutionary emblems should be was at the heart of such interpretative commentaries – from sceptical journalistic observations to the more high-flown rhetoric in which legislative proposals were debated.

Notes

1. Daniel Roche, *La Culture des apparences: une histoire du vêtement (XVIIe–XVIIIe siècles)* (Fayard: Paris, 1989), p. 147.

2. Exceptionally, items of dress survived as pieces of police evidence, as in the case of a royalist white cockade; AN, AE v347.

3. Annick Pardailhé-Galabrun, *La Naissance de l'intime. 3000 foyers parisiens, XVIIe–XVIIIe siècles* (PUF: Paris, 1988), p. 177. See also Daniel Roche, *The People of Paris: an essay in popular culture in the eighteenth century* (Berg: Leamington Spa, 1987), p. 193, as well as more extensive treatment in *La Culture des apparences*, pp. 478 et seq., and *Histoire des choses banales. Naissance de la consommation XVIIe–XIXe siècles* (Fayard: Paris, 1997), pp. 209–37.

4. Louise Weiss recalled her mother approvingly showing her buttons supposedly from Robespierre's waistcoat (*Souvenir d'une enfance républicaine* (Denoël: Paris, 1937), pp. 7–8.

5. As Georges Duval recalled of someone who had been among the first to adopt the *bonnet rouge*: 'ce qu'il y a de certain, c'est qu'aujourd'hui il a mis son vieux bonnet rouge dans sa commode' (*Souvenirs de la Terreur de 1788 à 1793*, 4 vols (Paris, 1841), vol. 2, p. 42).

6. A.E. Gibelin, *De l'Origine et de la forme du bonnet de la liberté* (Paris, an IV), p. 6. On the disavowal of the *bonnet rouge* see Chapter 4.

7. *Catalogue des objets formant l'exposition historique de la Révolution française* (Société de l'Histoire de la Révolution Française: Paris, 1889), p. ix.

8. Maurice Tourneux, 'L'Exposition historique de la Révolution française', *Gazette des beaux-arts*, 1889, vol. 30, pp. 405–6. In the period leading up to the Centenary, Etienne Charavay noted correspondance debating whether enough material still survived to make an exhibition possible (*Le Centenaire de 1789 et le musée de la Révolution* (Paris, 1886), pp. 8–11). See also Barbara Nelms, *The Third Republic and the Centennial of 1789* (Garland: London, New York, 1987), pp. 127–33.

9. Louis Combes, *Épisodes et curiosités révolutionnaires* (Paris, n.d.), p. 8.

10. Palloy's donations continued until November 1793; see *Discours prononcé à la société de Sceaux-L'Unité, le 10 frimaire, jour de la Fête de la Raison, en présence de toutes les autorités constituées* (Palloy papers, BHVP, 10412, no. 16).

11. A decree of 19 June 1790 accorded to the *vainqueurs* 'un armement complet, un brevet d'honneur, le droit de porter une couronne murale appliquée sur le bras gauche ou sur la poitrine à côté du revers gauche de l'habit, une place distinguée à la prochaine fédération du 14 juillet etc' (Michel Hennin, *Histoire numismatique*, 2 vols (Paris, 1826) vol. 1, p. 55); see Chapter 2 for further discussion of the *vainqueurs*.

12. David Andress, *Massacre at the Champ de Mars. Popular Dissent and Political Culture in the French Revolution* (Royal Historical Society/Boydell: Woodbridge, 2000), pp. 8–9.

13. François-Louis Marin, a gunner who had been one of the first to enter the Bastille, kept his bloodstained trousers, which he displayed whenever an appropriate occasion arose (Hans-Jürgen Lüsebrink and Rolf Reichardt, *The Bastille. A History of a Symbol of Despotism and Freedom* (Duke University Press: Durham, NC, and London, 1997) p. 92).

14. *Patriote françois*, 7 April 1792, no. 791, pp. 393–4, cit. Maurice Genty, 'Le Mouvement démocratique dans les sections parisiennes du printemps 1790 au printemps 1792', thèse de doctorat d'état, Université de Paris I, 1981–82, 4 vols; vol. 4, p. 825.

15. Ibid. This was not, in the event, discussed.

16. *Arrêté* of 26 December 1793/6 nivôse an II, *Moniteur*, 31 December 1793, cit. Hennin, *Histoire numismatique*, vol. 1, p. 55.

17. E. Seligman, *La Justice en France pendant la Révolution (1791–1793)*, 2 vols (Plon-Nourrit: Paris, 1901–1913), vol. 2, p. 79.

18. See decree of 12 May 1792, cit. Tuetey, vol. 4, no. 542, p. 69. For the programme, see *Archives Parliamentaires*, vol. 44, p. 359. Simonneau's sash was ejected when Marat's remains entered (Jean-Claude Bonnet, 'La Mort de Simonneau', in *Mouvements populaires et conscience sociale XVe–XIXe siècles* (Maloire: Paris, 1985), p. 676).

19. See Antoine de Baecque, 'L'Offrande des martyrs: le corps meurtri de la Révolution', in *Le Corps de l'histoire: métaphores et politique (1770–1800)* (Calmann-Lévy: Paris, 1993), pp. 343–74.

20. *Arch Parl*, vol. 57, pp. 541–2, cit. Jeannine Baticle, 'La Seconde Mort de Lepeletier de Saint-Fargeau. Recherches sur le sort du tableau de David', *Bulletin de la société de l'histoire de l'art français*, 1988, p. 141.

21. Baticle, 'La Seconde Mort de Lepeletier de Saint-Fargeau', p. 141.

22. Louis Sébastien Mercier, *Le Nouveau Paris*, Jean-Claude Bonnet (ed.) (Mercure de France: Paris, 1994), p. 138. Ozouf points out that ceremonies held in the provinces employed an effigy of Lepeletier with bloodied clothes ('Le Simulacre et la fête', in Jean Ehrard and Paul Viallaneix (eds), *Les Fêtes de la Révolution, Colloque Clermont-Ferrand, juin 1974*, (Société des Études robespierristes: Paris, 1977), p. 329).

23. Jacques Guilhaumou, 'La Mort de Marat (13 juillet–16 juillet 1793)', in Jean-Claude Bonnet (ed.), *La Mort de Marat* (Flammarion: Paris, 1986), p. 71. Marat's shirt was later ironically compared to a holy shroud by the author of *La Vie criminelle et politique de J.P. Marat*, cit. François Gendron, *The Gilded Youth of Thermidor* (McGill and Queen's University Press: Montreal, Kingston, London, Buffalo, 1993), p. 63.

24. As on 8 August 1793, three weeks after the murder, in the church of St Eustache; see *Arch Parl*, vol. 73, p. 301, cit. de Baecque, *Corps*, p. 360, and *loc. cit.* for further discussion of the bringing of such simulacra to the Convention.

25. *Cérémonie funèbre en mémoire des ministres français assassinés près de Rastadt par les troupes autrichiens. Programme, 3 prairial an VII*, p. 5. See Mona Ozouf, *Fête révolutionnaire*, p. 134. This had a bizarre, not to say macabre, sequel in England where a type of jacket was named after de Bry; see Gillray's print (18 November 1799), 'French-Taylor, fitting John Bull with a "Jean de Bry"', ill. Draper Hill, *The Satirical Prints of James Gillray* (Dover: New York, 1976), plate 68. In the *Bulletin décadaire* (19 floréal an VII), Babbet proposed that Roberjot and Bonnier's bodies be displayed, and their bloody clothes used as a flag over the Convention, later to be exhibited across France 'afin qu'elle[s] serve[nt] à nos conscrits d'étendards militaires', cit. P. Montalot, L. Pingaud (eds), *Le Congrès de Rastatt (11 juin 1798–28 avril 1799). Correspondance et documents*, 3 vols (Picard: Paris, 1913), vol. 1, p. 277.

26. *Corps législatif. Conseil des Anciens. Motion d'ordre de Moreau (de l'Yonne), séance du 21 prairial an VII*, pp. 3–4; *RAM*, vol. 29, no. 278, 26 June 1799, p. 719 (séance 4 messidor an VII).

27. De Baecque, *Corps de l'histoire*, pp. 343–74. Yet, outrage was provoked when the bloodied clothes of Basseville, murdered in an anti-revolutionary riot in Rome, were sent to his widow via the Minister of France in Naples; see *Gazette de France nationale*, 3 May, cit. *Chronique de Paris*, 5 May, cit. Christoph Cave, Denis Reynaud, Danièle Willemart and Henri Duranton, *1793 L'Esprit des journaux* (Presses Universitaires de Saint-Etienne, Saint-Etienne, 1993), p. 135.

28. *RAM*, vol. 18, p. 413, 14 Nov. 1793; p. 441, 18 Nov. 1793/28 brumaire an II. On Bailly and his death, see George Armstrong Kelly, *Victims, Authority, and Terror. The parallel deaths of d'Orléans, Custine, Bailly, and Malesherbes* (University of North Carolina Press: Chapel Hill, 1982), pp. 149–210, and Andress, *Massacre at the Champ de Mars*. Chaumette also proposed that 'aristocrates' should be invited to give their shirts to 'les défenseurs de la patrie' (Tuetey, vol. 18, p. 385). See also Nicole Pellegrin, 'Les Chemises patriotiques. Essai sur les dons civiques en Haut-Poitou pendant la Révolution', in *Le Centre-Ouest dans la Révolution* (Poitiers, 1988), pp. 77–85.

29. See Roche, *The People of Paris*, pp. 183–4, and *Culture des apparences*, pp. 313–45.

30. Jean-Pierre-Louis Hanet, dit Cléry, *Mémoires de P.L. Hanet Cléry, ancien valet de chambre de Madame Royale, aujourd'hui Dauphine, et frère de Cléry, dernier valet de chambre de Louis XVI (1776–1823)*, 2 vols (Eymery: Paris, 1825), vol. 1, pp. 77–81. See Jeffrey W. Merrick, *The Desacralisation of the French Monarchy in the Eighteenth Century* (Baton Rouge: Louisiana State University Press, 1998), and George Armstrong Kelly, *Mortal Politics in Eighteenth-century France* (University of Waterloo Press: Waterloo, Ontario, 1986), pp. 208–34. William Doyle presented a critique of this overused concept in a paper, 'Desacralizing Desacralization', delivered at the Annual Conference of the Society for the Study of French History, University of Sheffield, 2000. Timothy Tackett makes the point that although desacralization of the monarchy had a long pre-revolutionary history, in the sense of disbelief in the king's divine right, there remained a deep-seated emotive attachment to the monarch ('Conspiracy Obsession in a Time of Revolution: French Elites and the Origins of the Terror 1789–1792', *American Historical Review*, June 2000, p. 710.

31. Louis XVI was declared a 'royal martyr' by Pope Pius VI on 17 June 1793. See David P. Jordan, *The King's Trial. The French Revolution vs. Louis XVI* (University of California Press: Berkeley, Los Angeles, London, 1979), p. 224.

32. On the spectacle of debris and corpses, see Mercier in *Le Nouveau Paris*, pp. 160–2.

33. Seals were placed on the Tuileries on 11 August 1792, prior to the taking of an inventory, which process continued until January 1793 (*La Famille royale à Paris. De l'histoire à la légende* (Musée Carnavalet, Paris, 1993), p. 50). See also Ferdinand Boyer, 'Deux documents sur les Tuileries· l'état des appartements en septembre 1792 et l'inventaire des peintures en décembre 1793', *BSHAF*, 1964, pp. 193–9.

34. See Tuetey, vol. 4, no. 2574, p. 327; and *ibid.* nos 2534–2611, pp. 322–33, for documentation of the handing in of objects taken, and the apprehension of looters. For examples of items that seem to have come from the Tuileries but not been handed in, see also Caron, vol. 2, p. 180 (15 niv. an II/4 Jan. 1794: an unnamed *valet de chambre* of the king, who possessed a necklace, jacket, sword of the Ordre [du Saint Esprit?], and other jewels); vol. 4, p. 50 (23 pluv. an II/11 Feb. 1794: Dardevillier, who had been noted as present at the king's execution, owned an *écritoire* of the king's, and an *épingle à brillants* which belonged to Madame Elizabeth).

35. 'Boîte travaillé au tour par le roi Louis XVI', gift of Elie Petit, February 1852, who describes its acquisition at a sale after 10 August by sieur Maëlrondt 'marchand de curiosités fameux sous l'Empire', whose widow gave it to Petit's father; see Henry Barbet de Jouy, *Notice des antiquités, objets du Moyen Âge, de la Renaissance, et des temps modernes composant le Musée des Souverains* (Paris, 1866), p. 182, no. 137.

35. 'Boîte travaillé au tour par le roi Louis XVI', gift of Elie Petit, February 1852, who describes its acquisition at a sale after 10 August by sieur Maëlrondt 'marchand de curiosités fameux sous l'Empire', whose widow gave it to Petit's father; see Henry Barbet de Jouy, *Notice des antiquités, objets du Moyen Âge, de la Renaissance, et des temps modernes composant le Musée des Souverains* (Paris, 1866), p. 182, no. 137.

36. Of the shoes claimed as Marie-Antoinette's, two have a provenance which stretches back to 10 August 1792. One is in the Musée Carnavalet, Paris: 'Soulier de Marie-Antoinette arraché le 10 août 1792 des mains de l'un des envahisseurs par M. d'Ennecey de Champuis qui défendit le château des Tuileries comme grenadier des Filles Saint-Thomas. Don de Henry C. Moreau, arrière-petit-neveu de M. d'Ennecey de Champuis' (*La Famille royale à Paris* (Musée Carnavalet: Paris, 1993), no. 310, p. 181, fig. 45, p. 42). Another was on loan to the Musée des Souverains in the Louvre: 'Soulier de Marie-Antoinette', 23 cm. Long; gift of M. Salvador dit Chéri, in 1853. According to his letter which accompanied the shoe's loan, it had been acquired by capitaine Dorville on 10 August 1792 from one of the queen's rooms; he offered it to Salvador's mother: 'depuis cet époque, il a été religieusement conservé dans ma famille' (Barbet de Jouy, *Notice . . . Musée des Souverains*, no. 143, p. 186; current location unknown; this would have been returned to the family on the disestablishment of the museum). On other shoes, especially that owned by the Musée des beaux-arts at Caen, which François Macé de Lépinay argues has the best chance of having been worn by her on the scaffold, see *Le Soulier de Marie-Antoinette. Essai muséographique* (Musée des beaux-arts: Caen, 1989), p. 42.

37. See the 'cravate de Louis XVI', used to mop the king's brow at his trial and given to his defence lawyer R. de Sèze, from whom it was inherited by the comte de Sèze (*Famille royale*, no. 267 p. 179); a cockade reputedly worn by Louis XVI at his trial is in the Thatcher collection, Library of Congress, Washington (Ribeiro, *Fashion in the French Revolution* (Batsford: London, 1988), p. 65, Fig. 35). Incriminating evidence in the dossier on Tronson de Coudray, who had defended Marie-Antoinette, included two gold rings and a lock of her hair (Tuetey, vol. 10, no. 184).

38. Jean-Baptiste Cléry, *Journal de ce qui s'est passé à la tour du Temple pendant la captivité du roi Louis XVI roi de France* (London, 1798) (an 1800 London edition of the *Mémoires de Cléry . . . ou journal de ce qui s'est passé dans la tour du Temple, pendant la détention de Louis XVI, avec détails sur sa mort, qui ont été ignorés jusqu'à ce jour*, sometimes attributed to François Daujon, is described by the British Library as a 'falsification' of Cléry's text); *Récit exact des derniers momens de captivité de la Reine, depuis le 11 septembre 1793, jusqu'au 16 octobre suivante, par la dame Bault, veuve de son dernier concierge* (Paris, 1817); Claude Antoine Moëlle, *Six journées passées au Temple et autres détails sur la famille royale qui y a été détenue* (Dentu: Paris, 1820); duchesse de Tourzel, *Mémoires de Madame la duchesse de Tourzel, gouvernante des enfants de France, pendant les années 1789 à 1795* (Paris, ed. 1969); Charles Goret, *Mon témoignage sur la détention de Louis XVI et de sa famille dans la tour du Temple* (Paris, 1825); Lafont d'Aussonne, *Mémoires secrets et universels des malheurs et de la mort de la Reine de France* (Paris, 1825). The most scholarly

and thorough collection of such texts is that by the marquis de Beaucourt, *Captivité et derniers moments de Louis XVI, récits originaux et documents officiels, recueillis et publiés pour la société d'histoire contemporaine*, 2 vols (Paris, 1892).

39. For further details of the traffic in these relics, see Pierre de Vaissière, *La Mort du Roi (21 janvier 1793)* (Perrin: Paris, 1910), p. 189.

40. Duchesse de Tourzel, *Mémoires*, p. 405.

41. Cléry, ibid., cit. *Famille royale*, p. 85. On another occasion in January 1793, Vincent, *commissaire* at the Temple, asked the king for something which belonged to him: 'Sa Majesté détacha sa cravate et lui en fit présent' (ibid.).

42. *Récit exact . . . par la dame Bault*, p. 7.

43. Moëlle, *Six journées*, p. 52, cit. *Famille royale*, pp. 85–6.

44. 'Déclaration de Rosalie Lamorlière, native de Breteuil, en Picardie', in Lafont d'Aussonne, *Mémoires secrets et universels des malheurs et de la mort de la Reine de France*, p. 337.

45. Duchesse de Tourzel, *Mémoires*.

46. See P. Le Verdier, 'Les reliques de la famille royale et les descendants de Cléry', *Revue des questions historiques*, 1896, vol. 60, pp. 264–80.

47. Germain Bapst, preface, *Marie-Antoinette et son temps* (Galerie Sedelmeyer: Paris, 1894), p. 20. See also Louis Barbier, *Notice sur l'exhumation du corps du roi Louis XVI* (Paris, 1815). Other royal-related items have found their way into public collections. For example, the 'Habit à la française, veste et culotte, vers 1775', worn by Barthélemy, archiviste du Temple, in whose apartment the royal family were housed from 13 August 1793 while they waited for the apartment of the Grande Tour to be prepared for them, is now in the Musée de la mode et du costume, Inv 60.58.64, *Modes et Révolutions*, no. 2, p. 138, detail ill. p. 108.

48. The Temple's demolition in 1809–11 prevented its treatment to the kind of cult that focused on the Conciergerie; see François Macé de Lépinay and Jacques Charles, *Marie-Antoinette du Temple à la Conciergerie* (Caisse Nationale des Monuments Historiques and Taillandier: Paris, 1989), p. 26.

49. As the princesse de Monaco wrote: 'C'est le seul legs que je puisse laisser à mes enfants; au moins faut-il qu'il soit pur' (Olivier Blanc, *La Dernière Lettre. Prisons et condamnés de la Révolution 1793–1794* (Robert Laffont: Paris, 1984), pp. 91–3; see also pp.143–4, 163, 236. Ronald Schechter notes a similar remark in the duchesse d'Abrantès's memoirs ('Gothic Thermidor: the *bals des victimes*, the fantastic, and the production of historical knowledge in post-Terror France', *Representations*, no. 61, winter 1998, p. 91). Many thanks to Sophie Matthiesson for drawing these sources to my attention. Locks of Louis XVI's hair were found on the person of Marie-Antoinette (Tuetey, vol. 10, no. 69). On the tradition of preserving locks of the deceased's hair as part of *le travail du deuil*, see Marcia Pointon, 'Materialising Mourning: Hair, Jewellery, and the Body', in Marius Kwint, Christopher Breward and Jeremy Ainsley (eds), *Material Memories: Design and Evocation* (Berg: Oxford, 1999), pp. 39–57.

50. Daniel Arasse, *La Guillotine et l'imaginaire de la Terreur* (Flammarion: Paris, 1987), pp. 80–4. See also Antoine de Baecque, 'Louis XVI, ou les restes sacrés', in *La Gloire et l'effroi. Sept morts sous la Terreur* (Grasset: Paris, 1997), pp. 109–48; and P. and P. Girault de Coursac, *Louis XVI, un visage retrouvé* (Éditions de l'OEil: Paris, 1990).

51. Tuetey vol. 10, no. 187, p. 29; also cit. in E. Campardon, *Marie-Antoinette à la Conciergerie* (Paris, 1863), pp. 161, 165.

52. Caron, vol. 1, p. 248 (20 vend. an II/17 Oct. 1793), also cited Tuetey, vol. 10, no. 190, p. 30. One example of a relic that presumably was believed to have come from the scene of the king's execution is owned by the Musée Carnavalet: 'Sang de Louis XVI, Fragment de tissu taché du sang du roi. Donné à Cléry par la marquise de Chastellux; Mme Giovanelli, son arrière-petite-fille; duc de la Salle de Rochemaure; Mme de Forceville. Don, 1930. Musée Carnavalet, E. 12462 (*La Famille royale*, no. 304, p. 181). This provenance also indicates that Cléry added to his own set of such objects. A towel used by Louis XVI on the morning of his execution was given to Cléry's descendants by Lepite; this appeared in the sale in Rouen of Cléry's effects in 1896; see Georges Lenôtre, *Notes et souvenirs* (Calmann-Lévy: Paris, 1940), p. 105. A drawing of 'Agnus Dei', made around a blood stain, purportedly that of Louis XVI according to an inscription, is owned by the Louvre, Rothschild collection, N. 3799 DR, ill. D. Arasse, *La Guillotine dans la Révolution française* (Musée de la Révolution française, Vizille, 1987), no. 95, p. 86.

53. 'Rapport de Jacques Roux', *Courrier français*, 23 January 1793, cit. Beaucourt, vol. 2, p. 309, doc. CCXXX.

54. See Archives des Musées Nationaux, Musée des Souverains, dossier 57, letter 12 February. 1868, where this royal relic is offered to the museum. The soldier in question, Peron, a drummer in the bataillon de la Haute-Garonne, gave it to his mother in Toulouse before leaving to fight. She then distributed samples among sympathetic friends, one of whose descendants, M. Chose, offered it to the museum. It was not accepted because its provenance was considered too fragile. Grace Dalrymple Elliott recalled encountering one of the 'king's workmen' from Meudon, who had attended the execution in case any attempt was made to save the king, but had only been able to dip his handkerchief in the royal blood; he gave her a fragment (*Journal of my Life during the French Revolution* (Bentley: London, 1859), pp. 122–3).

55. Letter dated 21 January 1793, Tuetey, vol. 10, no. 1158, p. 165. Louis's head was the object of a proposal which would have turned it into a grisly warning for future generations. See 'Lettre du sieur Merland, chirurgien aide-major à l'hôpital militaire ambulant de Sainte-Marie, au camp de Meaux, à la Convention nationale, la priant de lui donner la tête de Capet, qui doit tomber pour le bonheur de l'humanité, afin de la faire sécher et de graver dessus les inscriptions les plus propres à témoigner aux peuples toute l'horreur qu'ils doivent avoir pour ces monstruosités' (11 December 1792, Tuetey, vol. 8, p. 158, no. 1115). It is perhaps not surprising that this document didn't find its way into Beaucourt's collection.

56. Conseil général de la Commune, séance du 24 septembre 1793, cit. Beaucourt, vol. 2, p. 324, doc. CCXLIV. A letter from the Comité de sûreté générale to the president of the section du Mail expresses concern at the apparent disappearance of a hat belonging to the king which had last been noted as being in the section's possession (22 January 1793, Tuetey vol. 10, n. 1163, p. 166).

57. 'Relation de Louis Larivière, porte-clé à la Conciergerie', in Lafont d'Aussonne, *Mémoires secrets*, p. 356.

58. *La Famille royale*, p. 80; Emile Campardon, *Marie-Antoinette à la Conciergerie*, p. 135; *Le Tribunal révolutionnaire de Paris*, vol. 1, p. 151; cit. Tuetey, vol. 10, no. 177, p. 27.

59. *Le Soulier de Marie-Antoinette: essai muséographique* (Musée des Beaux-Arts: Caen, 1989). See above note 36.

60. Caron, vol. 1, p. 198, 25 September 1793/4 vend. an II. Louis did not wear a coat at his execution, so this must relate to another garment – assuming these were not fakes.

61. Musée Carnavalet, Paris, E.21929. This contains hair from the king, Madame Royale, the dauphin, a piece of the stocking worn by Marie-Antoinette the day of her execution, and a straw from her mattress. See also the croix de Saint-Louis of the Vendéen leader, Charette, enclosed in a kind of triptych with profiles of Louis XVI and Marie-Antoinette (Nantes, Musées départementaux de Loire-Atlantique. Musée Dobrée, ill. Pellegrin, *Vêtements*, p. 54). An example of the numerous royalist reliquaries is that sold at the Hôtel Drouot on 31 March 1989 (*Drouot 1989. Art and Auction in France* (Paris, 1989), p. 313). On the wider cult of royal relics considered in its discursive historiographical dimension, see Beth S. Wright, *Painting and History during the French Restoration. Abandoned by the Past* (Cambridge University Press: Cambridge, 1997), 'Precious Relics from the Shipwreck of Generations: the morality of local colour', pp. 31–76.

62. Similarly, when Saint Louis's shirt was brought before the Convention as part of an iconoclastic parading of religious paraphernalia, it was found to be a woman's shirt, and ordered to be burnt (*RAM*, vol. 18, no. 58, 28 brum. an II/18 Nov. 1793, p. 441).

63. Alexandre Lenoir, *Description historique et chronologique des monumens de sculpture, réunis au Musée des monumens français*, 6th edn (Paris, an X, 1801), pp. 338–56 ('Notes historiques sur les exhumations faites en 1793 dans l'abbaye de Saint-Denis'). See also Suzanne Glover Lindsay, 'Mummies and Tombs: Turenne, Napoléon, and Death Ritual', *Art Bulletin*, September 2000, vol. 82, no. 3, pp. 478–502.

64. Beauvert, *Caricatures politiques* (an VI), pp. 7–8, cit. Ribeiro, *Fashion in the French Revolution*, p. 87.

65. See Devocelle's discussion of the supplement to the 5th edition of the *Dictionnaire de l'Académie française* (an VII), where terms such as *cocarde nationale*, *écharpe municipale*, *tricolore* [flag], *costume des factionnaires*, and *carmagnole* are dealt with ('La Cocarde directorielle: dérives d'un symbole révolutionnaire', *AHRF*, 1992, vol. 69, no. 3, p. 356).

66. Georges Lenôtre, *La Guillotine et les exécuteurs des arrêts criminels pendant la Révolution* (Paris, 1893), p. 189.

67. 'Les biens de ceux qui seront condamnés à la peine de mort seront acquis à la République, et il sera pourvu à la subsistance des veuves et des enfants, s'ils n'ont pas de biens d'ailleurs', Titre II art. II, *Moniteur*, 12 mars 1793 (H. Wallon, *Histoire du Tribunal révolutionnaire de Paris* (Paris, 1880), vol. 5, p. 59). For examples of inventories drawn up by prison concierges of the effects of the executed, see Tuetey, vol. 9, nos 2562–4, pp. 680–3. In the case of Vergniaud, claims to have observed his coat becoming a relic are challenged by C. Vatel, who cites the letter from Sanson's assistants (complaining of the removal of their rights to victims' effects) as evidence that they would have taken possession of his coat, and the confiscation of the condemneds' belongings (C. Vatel, *Recherches historiques sur les Girondins: Vergniaud. Manuscrits, lettres et papiers, pièces pour la plupart inédites, classées et annotées*, 2 vols (Paris, 1873), vol. 2, pp. 380–2). The *accusateur public* from the department of the Doubs sent silver buckles that had belonged to François-Joseph Robert, an *émigré* priest, who had been guillotined, to the Convention (*Arch Parl*, vol. 85, p. 216 (30 pluv. an II/18 February 1794), 'Etat des dons').

68. See a letter from Sanson to Fouquier-Tinville asking to keep 'les dessous, mouchoirs, bottes et souliers, etc', even if he would no longer take possession of the clothes (Vatel, *Recherches historiques* (Paris, 1873), vol. 2, p. 382, cit. Pellegrin, *Vêtements*, pp. 35–6). On

executioners' rights and salary, see a circular setting these out published in Auguste Cochin and Charles Charpentier, *Les Actes du gouvernement révolutionnaire 23 août–27 juillet 1794*, 3 vols (Picard: Paris, 1920), vol. 1, pp. 175–6.

69. See Lenôtre, op. cit., pp. 189–90. This policy is echoed in the comments on the red flag of martial law used in Bailly's execution (see above). However, Lenôtre also publishes a document from 9 messidor an II/27 June 1794, which suggests that some clothes may have been sold. This requested the setting up of a table in the Picpus cemetery to facilitate the taking of an inventory of the deceased's effects: 'Toute la dépense . . . n'ira jamais à 50 livres, et une seule redingote oubliée peut être souvent une perte de plus de cent livres pour la nation . . .' (*La Guillotine*, pp. 194–5).

70. G. Lenôtre, *Vieilles Maisons, vieux papiers*, 3rd series (1906), pp. 78–9. See chapter 5 of the present volume for further discussion of St-Just's wardrobe.

71. For a summary of literature on this, including a discussion of the taking of Robespierre's death mask, and the fate of his house, see Gérard Walter, *Robespierre* (Paris, 1936), p. 454 note 2. See also Georges Michon, 'La Maison de Robespierre rue de Saintonge, à Paris', *AHRF*, vol. 1, 1924, pp. 64–6; and *ibid.*, vol. 3, 1926, pp. 217–24, on the battle over the location of a commemorative plaque. On the sale of his effects, see a document published by Vatel, *Recherches historiques*, vol. 2, p. 468.

72. Illustrated in Albéric Cahuet, 'Les souvenirs révolutionnaires de la collection Lavedan', *L'Illustration*, 15 April 1933, no. 4702, p. 452.

73. Daniel Arasse, *La Guillotine dans la Révolution française*, no. 197, p. 167.

74. 'Plat à barbe de Robespierre, donné par Mme Lebas (Mlle Duplay), veuve du constitutionnel Lebas à Didée, le séide de Robespierre (Colln. M. H. Didiée)', *Catalogue des objets formant l'exposition historique de la Révolution française* (1889), no. 1087, p. 122. Carnavalet also possesses a reliquary containing a 'poil de la veste de l'immortel Chalier' (OM 0368). For an extreme example of the collectability of minutiae, see the sale catalogue, *Collection d'un amateur. Révolution française. Dessins, estampes, médailles, livres, documents, hôtel Drouot, Paris, 12 Oct. 1973*, no. 199, p. 15: 'Morceau d'étoffe provenant du fauteuil de Robespierre, et aquarelle fin XIXe représentant ce fauteuil'.

75. René Farge, 'Le local du club des Cordeliers et le coeur de Marat', *AHRF*, no. 4, 1927, pp. 345–6. Marat's vital organs had been removed prior to the obsequies to offset the process of decomposition, accelerated by the exceptional heat, and were displayed with his body in the garden of the Cordeliers club. His heart was deemed to be the property of the club (See Jacques Guilhaumou, 'La Mort de Marat à Paris (13 juillet–16 juillet 1793)', in Jean-Claude Bonnet (ed.), *La Mort de Marat* (Flammarion: Paris, 1986), pp. 70–3).

76. A twentieth-century provenance exists for an embroidered silk waistcoat claimed to have been Marat's ('gilet, soie brodée d'argent', Lavedan sale, Drouot, Paris, 26–27 April 1933; see Cahuet, 'Les souvenirs, p. 452, where it is treated as a prerevolutionary item).

77. For a discussion of the problematic authenticity of several caps in museum collections, see Nicola J. Shilliam, '*Cocardes nationales* and *bonnets rouges*: symbolic headdresses of the French Revolution', *Journal of the Museum of Fine Arts, Boston*, 1993, vol. 5, pp. 105–31.

78. 'Manteau de représentant du peuple (Conseil des Anciens ou Conseil des Cinq-Cents)', 1798, as decreed 29 brum. an VI/19 Nov. 1797 (Carnavalet); *Modes et Révolutions*, no. 70, p. 148. See Madeleine Delpierre, 'A propos d'un manteau de représentant du peuple de 1798 récemment offert au musée du Costume', *Bulletin du Musée Carnavalet*, 1972,

no. 1, pp. 13–23. Carnavalet also possesses a fragment of the border of another cloak worn by François Aubert, deputy for the department of the Seine at the Conseil des Cinq-Cents (ibid., p. 13).

79. *Musée de la Révolution française, Vizille. Premières Collections* (Conseil Général de l'Isère: 1985), no. 120, p. 72. Philippe Bordes proposes General Meusnier La Place as the dedicatee; see Philippe Bordes and Alain Chevalier *Catalogue des Peintures, Sculptures, et Dessings*. Musée de la Révolution française, Vizille, 1996, p. 254.

80. See Monique Ray and Jacques Payen, *Souvenirs iconographiques de la Révolution française à Lyon* (Editions lyonnaises d'art et d'histoire: Lyon, 1989), pp. 75, 99.

81. See the mayoral sash that belonged to Leperdit (Musée de Bretagne), ill. Pellegrin, *Vêtements*, pp. 92/93. Leperdit was a moderate Breton, wounded when he opposed Carrier's intention to execute prisoners in Rennes. See the painting by Moreau de Tours, *Leperdit maire de Rennes* (1887 Salon; private collection, Paris), ill. *Bretons ou Chouans . . . Les paysans bretons dans la peinture d'histoire d'inspiration révolutionnaire au XIXe siècle* (Musée des Beaux-Arts, Quimper; Musée d'Histoire, St-Brieuc, 1989), p. 19).

82. By contrast, as a result in part of their greater durability, a number of metal *bonnets de la liberté* survive: two from French naval ships are in British collections, one in the family of Viscount Exmouth, another in the Royal Naval Museum, Portsmouth; a cap from atop a local church spire is in the Musée de Pithiviers.

83. Albert Soboul, *Sans-culottes parisiens en l'an II* (Clavreuil: Paris, 1958), p. 650.

84. This was strikingly the case with two bicentennial exhibitions dedicated to dress, *Modes et Révolutions, 1780–1804* (Musée de la mode et du costume, Paris), and *The Age of Napoleon: costume from Revolution to Empire: 1789–1815* (Metropolitan Museum of Art, New York).

85. On bonfires of effigies of Napoleon in Orléans and Puy in 1816, and the fact that shouting 'vive l'Empereur' or displaying the tricolore flag were punishable by deportation, see J. Lucas-Dubreton, *Le Culte de Napoléon 1815–1848* (Albin Michel: Paris, 1960), pp. 50–1.

86. Most of the effects inherited by imperial family are now in the Musée Napoléon at Fontainebleau. See Colombe Samoyault-Verlet, 'The Emperor's Wardrobe' (pp. 203–15), and Raoul Brunon, 'Uniforms of the Napoleonic Era' (p. 215), in *The Age of Napoleon: Costume from Revolution to Empire 1789–1815* (Metropolitan Museum of Art, New York, 1989).

87. *Mémoires de Marchand, premier valet de chambre et exécuteur testamentaire de l'Empereur*, Jean Bourguignon and Henry Lachouque (eds), 2 vols (Plon: Paris, 1955), vol. 2, p. 341.

88. See Jean Lemaire, *Le Testament de Napoléon. Un étonnant destin 1821–1857* (Plon: Paris, 1975), pp. 200–7.

89. On the complex sequence of inheritance within the Bonaparte family, see Colombe Samoyault-Verlet and Jean-Pierre Samoyault, *Château de Fontainebleau. Musée Napoléon Ier. Napoléon et la famille impériale* (Editions de la Réunion des Musées Nationaux: Paris, 1986), p. 4.

90. M. Naudin, 'Les Souvenirs Napoléoniens du Musée de Châteauroux', *Revue de la société des amis du Musée de l'Armée*, 1958, no. 61, p. 35. Bertrand was given an aviary by Darling, who had bought a lot from the sale of remaining effects after Napoleon's death. A further Napoleonic collection was that given by baron Barbet de Vaux to the Ecole d'application de la cavalerie et du train at Saumur, where it was displayed in the salle

d'honneur (see unidentified press cutting [May] 1936 in the dossier on Kellermann's sabre, Musée de la Révolution française, Vizille, 85.605).

91. *Dominique-Vivant Denon. L'oeil de Napoléon* (Editions de la Réunion des Musées Nationaux: Paris, 1999), pp. 420–1, where the reliquary is dated 1821–1840. The Molière sample was presumably acquired when his remains were transferred to the Musée des Monuments Français in 1799 (ibid., p. 383).

92. See Stephen Bann, *The Clothing of Clio: a study of the representation of history in nineteenth-century Britain and France* (Cambridge University Press: Cambridge, 1984), pp. 77–92. On the metaphor of dressing up in historical clothes as a means of facilitating 'living the past', and thereby confronting the problems of the contemporary world, see Stephen Bann's discussion of Macchiavelli, and Marx's assessment, in *The Eighteenth Brumaire of Louis Napoleon*, of the limitations of French revolutionaries' adoption of Roman costume and phrases (*Romanticism and the Rise of History* (Twayne: New York, 1995), pp. 132–4).

93. On the tradition of 'Les recueils de costume', see Roche, *Culture des apparences*, p. 19. Interestingly, L. Rathier and F. Beaunier justified closing their book with the period of Louis XIV because 'à dater de cette époque, les costumes sont connus, et dans les mains de tout le monde' (*Recueil des costumes français, ou Collection des plus belles statues et figures françaises, des armes, des armures, des instruments, des meubles, etc. dessinés d'après les monuments, peintures et vitraux, avec un texte explicatif suivi d'une notice historique et cronologique [sic]; devant servir à l'histoire de l'art du dessin en France, depuis Clovis jusqu'à Louis XIV inclusivement* (Paris, 1810), prospectus p. 1). A good survey of such publications is contained in *Catalogue d'une très belle collection de recueils de costumes XVIIIe et début du XIXe siècle, aquarelles originales, appartenant à M. le vicomte J. de Jonghe* (Giraud-Badin: Paris, 1930).

94. See Horace de Viel-Castel, *Collection de costumes, armes et meubles, pour servir à l'histoire de la Révolution française et de l'Empire* (Paris, 1834), pp. 9–10. Beth Wright notes Antoine Béraud's recognition of the historical significance of nuances of dress: 'Dans les temps de commotions populaires, la forme d'une coiffure est une pensée profonde, la coupe d'un habit un symbole adoré' (*Histoire pittoresque de la Révolution française* (Paris, 1833), introduction, cit. *Painting and History during the French Restoration*, pp. 168, 245).

95. Roche, *Culture des apparences*, pp. 29ff. As Ting Chang notes, Charles X was a prominent subscriber to his *Collection des costumes, armes, et meubles pour servir à l'histoire de France* (1827), the fifth and last volume of which appeared in 1832. From 1850, Viel-Castel was general secretary of the national museums; in May 1852 he became keeper of the Musée des souverains; and in the Second Empire, curator of the Louvre, until he was sacked by the comte de Nieuwerkere in May 1863 (*Mémoires du comte Horace de Viel-Castel sur le règne de Napoléon III 1851–1864*, ed. Pierre Josserand, 2 vols (Le Prat: Paris, 1979), vol. 1, pp. 11–12). He seems to have lacked any abiding political allegiance ('Alfred Bruyas: the Mythology and Practice of Art Collecting and Patronage in Nineteenth-century France', University of Sussex, D.Phil., 1996, pp. 42–3).

96. Items 168–408 (the last item) of the 1866 catalogue are Napoleonic. For further items, see *État des effets ayant appartenu à l'Empereur et dont il n'a pas disposé par ses divers testaments, les effets et d'autres objets délivrés par ordres des exécuteurs testamentaires aux légateurs ou à leurs agents, avaient été laissés en dépôt par l'Empereur à M. le Comte de Turenne lors de son départ de Fontainebleau et de l'Elysée, en 1814 et 1815*: 'tout ce qui est porté sur cet état a été remis le 4 février 1852 au Prince Napoléon, à l'Elysée, par le Cte de Turenne, accompagné de son fils aîné', attached to *Livre d'entrée faisant suite à l'inventaire du Musée*

des Souverains, p. 136, AMN, Musée du Louvre, Paris. Following its disassembly, many items from the Musée des Souverains were allocated to the Musée de l'Armée.

97. See letter of 16 March 1852 to Sauvageot, inviting him to join the commission (AMN, MS 1). In seeking to identify the Second Empire as part of the continuity of French history, this museological logic replicated the larger project, itself inherited from earlier centuries, to 'complete' the Louvre, set in train with the acceptance of Visconti's plans in March 1852 (Matthew Truesdell, *Spectacular Politics. Louis-Napoleon Bonaparte and the fête impériale 1849–1870* (Oxford University Press: Oxford, 1997), pp. 56–8).

98. Corps législatif, Session 1852. no. 124. Annexe du procès-verbal de la séance du 26 juin 1852. Rapport fit au nom de la commission chargé d'exécuter le projet de loi . . . par M. Edouard Dalloz, AMN, MS 1.

99. 'tout ce qui portait l'empreinte ou qui était comme une émanation de la personne, . . . tout ce qui la représentait contemporainement d'une manière flagrante' (27 March 1852, AMN, MS 1). See also 'Dons et legs non-acceptés (ou non suivis d'effet)', MS 57.

100. Nos. 381–402 were lent by the comte Marchand; Napoleon's handkerchief was a gift from Pierron, *ancien maître d'hôtel* of the Emperor on Elba and St Helena (no. 404, pp. 259–60); M. Duplan, son of Napoleon's hairdresser, offered a lock of Napoleon's hair from 1814 (no. 405, p. 260).

101. On the gaming table which had originally been acquired by the St Helena postmaster, see Barbet de Jouy, *Notice des Antiquités*, no. 367, pp. 248–9. On Napoleonic cults, see Robert Gildea, *The Past in French History* (Yale University Press: New Haven and London, 1994), pp. 89–111.

102. 22 May 1858, no. 58, p. 324.

103. Champfleury, *Histoire des faïences patriotiques sous la Révolution* (Paris, 1867), p. xii. In arguing against the museum's closure, in favour of its being expanded to include all men who had contributed to French greatness, Albert Babeau noted the irony that it was to be under a government headed by a historian, Thiers, that it was to close (*Le Louvre et son histoire* (Paris, 1985), p. 317).

104. See Amal Asfour, 'Champfleury and the Popular Arts', D.Phil., Oxford University, 1990.

105. He lent a white silk waistcoat with embroidered emblems of the Third Estate, and a pair of gloves with a revolutionary emblem of Justice on to an 1874 exhibition of historical costume (*Union centrale des beaux-arts appliqués à l'industrie. Quatrième exposition 1874. Musée historique du costume* (Paris, 1874), pp.112, 114).

106. *Bulletin de la société de l'histoire de Paris*, vol. 7, 1880, p. 163. See Madeleine Dubois, 'Les Origines du Musée Carnavalet. La Formation des collections et leur accroissement 1870–1897', 3 vols, 1947, École du Louvre. A copy exists in the Documentation of the Musée Carnavalet. I am extremely grateful to Philippe Bordes for drawing this to my attention.

107. *Le Temps*, 4 February 1881, MS 2118 fo 94.

108. A.R. de Liesville, *Histoire numismatique de la Révolution de 1848, ou Description raisonnée des médailles, monnaies, jetons, repoussés, etc. relatifs aux affaires de la France* (Paris, 1877), p. xi.

109. 'Deux antiquaires', *Le Gaulois*, 8 February 1881, MS 2118 fo 117–18.

110. Jules Cousin described it as: 'Entassés et comme enfouies dans cette petite maison des Batignolles dont ses amis connaissent seulement le chemin' (*Procès-verbal de la séance du 24 février 1885, Comité des inscriptions parisiennes*, de Liesville papers, BHVP, MS 2118,

fo 83). See also the unsigned article in *La Petite République française*, no. 1764, 9 February 1881, p. 2.

111. For a comprehensive overview, see Dominique Poulot, *Musée, nation, patrimoine 1789–1815* (Gallimard: Paris, 1997), and *'Surveiller et s'instruire': la Révolution française et l'intelligence de l'héritage historique* (Studies on Voltaire and the Eighteenth Century, vol. 344, 1996).

112. Edmond Bonnaffé, *Les Collectionneurs de l'ancienne France* (Paris, 1873), p. x. See the discussion of this remark, first published in *Paradoxes*, 1872, pp. 4–7, in Chang, 'Alfred Bruyas', p. 67.

113. *Le Temps*, 4 February 1881, MS 2118 fo 94–5.

114. See *Notice sommaire des monuments et objets divers relatifs à l'histoire de Paris et de la Révolution française exposés au Musée Carnavalet suivant l'ordre des salles parcourues par les visiteurs* (Paris, June 1881).

115. 'nous les Français, ne serions-nous pas capable de souhaiter et de demander que le secret de tant d'infamies cessât d'être enseveli dans nos archives? . . . la mode présente est de rechercher les curiosités de l'époque révolutionnaire. On en fait des musées. Ce genre de bric-à-brac a rencontré de nombreux adeptes' (article signed 'Y', in *La Liberté*, 13 December 1885, cit. Dubois, 'Les Origines du Musée Carnavalet', vol. 2, p. 365).

116. See Albert Mathiez on the 1928 exhibition held at the Bibliothèque Nationale, Paris, where he criticizes the suppression and exclusion of the popular, and the implicit pro-royal slant to the display, avoiding reference to violence or hardship: 'L'histoire, au fond, n'est là qu'un prétexte à exhiber des curiosités. On a copié Carnavalet et le Musée Grévin. On expose des clefs, des insignes, des reliques, toutes sortes de choses hétéroclites' ('L'Exposition de la Révolution française', *AHRF*, 1928, vol. 5, p. 169, also published in *L'OEuvre*, 1 February 1928). On the tradition of waxwork tableaux as manifest at the Musée Grévin and Madame Tussaud's, see David Bindman, *The Shadow of the Guillotine. Britain and the French Revolution* (British Museum: London, 1989), pp. 212–14, and Uta Kornmeier, 'Madame Tussaud's First Exhibition in England 1802–1803', *Object*, no. 1, October 1998, pp. 45–61.

117. On John Wilson Croker (1780–1857), M.P., extreme Tory, and First Secretary to the Admiralty, whose collection of revolutionary texts provided the core of the British Library's French Revolution 'tracts', see Audrey C. Brodhurst, 'The French Revolution Collections in the British Library', *British Library Journal*, vol. 2, no. 2, autumn 1976, pp. 138–58.

118. See *Fleurs de lys et bonnet phrygien. Raymond Jeanvrot et Jacques Calvet. Deux collectionneurs bordelais regardent la Révolution française*. Catalogue réalisé à partir de collections conservées au Musée des Arts décoratifs et aux Archives municipales de Bordeaux (1989–1990) (Association des Conservateurs des Musées d'Aquitaine: Périgueux, 1989). While Jeanvrot was an obsessive royalist, Calvet was a more eclectic collector of local history.

119. Extrait du Procès verbal de la séance du 24 février 1885, Comité des Inscriptions Parisiennes, fᵒ 83–4, Liesville papers, BHVP, vol. 1, MS 2118, pp. 1–2.

120. *Union centrale des beaux-arts appliqués à l'industrie. Quatrième exposition 1874. Musée historique du costume* (Paris, 1874). A pair of patriotic 'Mules de la Révolution' were to be found in the section made up of Jules Jacquemart's shoe collection (p. 9). These may be the same shoes now in the Musée de la Chaussure, Romans, ill. Pellegrin, *Vêtements*, pp. 124/5. On Champfleury's loans to this exhibition, see above, note 105.

121. Ibid., p. vi.

122. 90 women, 85 men (*Musée rétrospectif des classes 85 et 86. Le Costume et ses accessoires à l'Exposition universelle internationale de 1900 à Paris* (Paris, 1900), pp. 189–91).

123. Ibid., p. 8.

124. See *Hier pour demain. Arts, traditions et patrimoine* (Editions de la Réunion des Musées Nationaux: Paris, 1986), pp. 70–1.

125. On Leloir, see Georges Gustave Toudouze, 'Maurice Leloir, la Société de l'histoire du costume, et le Musée du costume à Paris', *Revue du vêtement*, no. 15, August 1943, and his preface to the *Dictionnaire du costume et de ses accessoires, des armes, et des étoffes, des origines à nos jours* (Günd: Paris, 1951).

126. See Jean Lequime, *La Société de l'histoire du costume et le Musée du costume* (Proba: Paris, 1946); Madeleine Delpierre, 'Le Musée de la mode et du costume de la Ville de Paris au Palais Galliera', in *I Duchi di Galliera* (Marietti: Genoa, 1991); and *Mémoires de mode* (Palais Galliera, Musée de la mode et du costume: Paris, 1994).

127. Henri Lavedan (Orléans 1859–1940). See Albéric Cahuet, 'Les souvenirs révolutionnaires de la collection Lavedan', *L'Illustration*, 15 April 1933, no. 4702, pp. 450–2, on the occasion of a sale at the hôtel Drouot, Paris on 26–27 April; see *Catalogue des objets d'art, de curiosité et d'ameublement ... appartenant à M. Henri Lavedan* (Hôtel Drouot, 26/27 April 1933). The remaining collection was dispersed when Lavedan's château de Loubressac changed hands sometime after 1980 (see correspondence in 'Collections' dossier, Musée de la Révolution française, Vizille). The Musée de la Révolution française at Vizille subsequently acquired two items which had been part of this collection: 'un petit portefeuille en tissu décoré de broderies à motif révolutionnaire' (Inv. MRF 1991–86); and a 'panneau de boiserie' (Inv. MRF 1992–13).

128. *De Neuville/Detaille: deux peintres témoins de l'histoire* (Editions I.O.P.: Musée du château de Vançay, 1981), cat. no. 55 (unpaginated).

129. Françoise Vittu, 'Maurice Leloir, peintre et historien du costume', in *Maurice Leloir: de Guy de Maupassant à Douglas Fairbanks* (Maison Fournaise, Chatou, 1995), pp. 2–7.

130. *Musée de la Ville de Paris/annexe du Musée Carnavalet. Collection de Madame Edmond de Galéa. Costumes français de 1750 à 1900. Don de Monsieur Christian de Galéa* (Paris, 1962).

131. One manifestation of this dovetailing of past and present is the increasingly widespread phenomenon of fashion designers collecting historic dress.

132. Roche, *Culture des apparences*, pp. 29–48.

133. On Isabey's collection of Napoleonic relics as described by Pierre-Nolasque Bergeret, *Lettres d'un artiste sur l'état des arts en France* (Paris, 1848), p. 164, cit. Aileen Ribeiro, *The Art of Dress. Fashion in England and France 1750–1820* (Yale University Press: New Haven and London, 1995), p. 5. Maurice Rheims illustrates a shoe (private collection) given to the artist Louis-Auguste Brun when he was painting Marie-Antoinette's portrait (*La Vie étrange des objets. Histoire de la curiosité* (Plon: Paris, 1959) p. 49).

134. See Wright, *Painting and History during the French Restoration*. On nineteenth-century painting of revolutionary subjects, see Marie-Claude Chaudonneret, 'Le mythe de la Révolution', in Philippe Bordes and Régis Michel (eds), *Aux Armes et aux arts! Les arts de la Révolution 1789–1799* (Adam Biro: Paris, 1988), pp. 313–40.

135. See the notice of a sale at the hôtel Drouot, *Le Bonnet phrygien,* 12 May 1907: 'des marchandises composant un fonds de costumier exploité à Paris, place Valois, par le sieur B ***, consistant en costumes anciens et reconstitués civils et militaires, du XIV au XVIII siècles à l'usage des artistes peintres et sculpteurs. Habits et robes de cour et de ville, livrées, costumes de magistrats et du clergé, bonnets, chapeaux, coiffures diverses, chaussures, lingerie, bonneterie, accessoires, uniformes militaires au majeure partie de Premier Empire . . .' Boudin *commissaire-priseur,* Courtois *expert,* and a similar sale at Drouot, salle no. 4, 3 May 1907 'vente après décès de M. X***, artiste-peintre', ibid., May 1907, no. 2, supplement. Such material remained on sale throughout the twentieth century; see, for example, the advertisement: 'Au Costumier Ch. Vachet, successeur du Costumier Fiatfilen, 17 rue Rodier, Paris 9e. Vous trouverez tous les costumes civils et militaires de toutes époques et tous styles en location pour vos défilés et reconstitutions historiques', in *Revue de la société des amis du Musée de l'Armée,* 1958, no. 61, [unpaginated, at back of the issue]. Leloir modernized this application in his capacity as a *costumier* to the cinema, following his trip to Hollywood to work with Douglas Fairbanks Jnr and Mary Pickford on *The Man in the Iron Mask*; see *Maurice Leloir: de Guy de Maupassant à Douglas Fairbanks.*

136. Meissonier lent to the 1889 'Exposition rétrospective militaire du Ministère de la Guerre', of which he was a member of the organizing committee (as was Edouard Detaille); see Thoumas, *Exposition rétrospective,* vol. 1, p. 131; vol. 2, pp. 249, 261, 266–7, 272–3.

137. See Colonel Bernard Douene, 'Hommage à Jean Brunon', *Revue de la société des amis du Musée de l'Armée,* 1984, no. 89, pp. 5–18.

138. On the allocation of Bonaparte family material to different museums, see above note 86. Numerous Napoleonic collections were created in the nineteenth century: Anatole Demidoff, who had married a descendant of Jérôme Bonaparte, in 1851 installed an 'opulent Napoleonic museum' in the Villa S. Martino on Elba (*Anatole Demidoff, Prince of San Donato (1812–70)* (Wallace Collection, London, 1994), pp. 19, 25). In England, Mme Tussaud is only the best-known of exhibitors of Napoleonic material; see Bindman, *Shadow of the Guillotine,* p. 212; Richard D. Altick, *The Shows of London* (Belknap: Cambridge MA, London, 1978), pp. 238–42.

139. For example: the breastplate of Carabinier Antoine Fauvreau of the 2nd regiment, 4th company, killed at Waterloo, 18 June 1815 (CC 206) (as a further gesture towards historical accuracy, the vitrine containing this spectacularly lugubrious object also houses canon balls and shot from the field of battle); and Captain Marbot's hat, damaged at Eylau on 8 February 1807, when attempting to save the 4th line regiment's eagle standard (25175). Examples of damaged clothing which either stand for miraculous survival, or rather as graphic evidence of injury and death, are not, of course, confined to the Revolution. An instance of the latter is the felt hat, pierced by a bullet, traditionally said to have been worn by Hendrick Casimir, Count of Nassau-Dietz (1612–1640) at Hulst in Flanders, where he was killed by a pistol shot to the head (*Chapeau, Chapeaux! 40 Hats from the Collection of the Rijksmuseum* (Rijksmuseum-Foundation: Amsterdam, 1997), p. 48). I am grateful to Louise Millar for providing me with a copy of this catalogue. Gustavus Adolphus III of Sweden gave the clothes in which he was wounded in 1627, in the war against Poland, to the armoury for preservation; similarly, the uniform worn by Charles XII when he fell at Frederikshald in Norway also remained part of the royal

wardrobe; see Torsten Lenk, 'La Garde-robe royale historique du cabinet royal des armes de Stockholm', in *Actes du Ier Congrès international d'histoire du costume*, Centro Internazionale delle Arti et del Costume, Palazzo Grassi, Venice, 31 August–7 September 1952 (Stampa Strada: Milan, 1955), pp. 187–96.

140. For some indicative photographic records, see *89 Le Livre du Bicentenaire*, Mission du Bicentenaire de la Révolution française et de la déclaration des droits de l'homme et du citoyen (Le Chêne-Hachette: Paris, 1990), *passim*.

141. Pascal Ory, 'Le Cent-cinquantenaire', in Jean-Claude Bonnet and Philippe Roger (eds), *La Légende de la Révolution au XXe siècle: de Gance à Renoir, de Romain Rolland à Claude Simon* (Flammarion: Paris, 1988), pp. 139–56.

142. Cited by Robert Gildea, *The Past in French History*, p. 43. On Vallès's changing attitude to the revolutionary heritage, see Roger Bellet, 'Mythe jacobin et mythe révolutionnaire chez Jules Vallès de 93 à la Commune de Paris', in Yves Charles (ed.), *Mythe et Révolutions* (Presses Universitaires de Grenoble: Grenoble, 1990), pp. 227–44.

143. Werner Oechslin, 'L'Architecture révolutionnaire: idéal et mythe', in *Les Architectes de la Liberté 1789–1799* (Ecole des Beaux-Arts: Paris, 1989), pp. 359–60. For a comprehensive critique of this simplistic devaluation of the Revolution's consequences for art, see Annie Jourdan, *Les Monuments de la Révolution 1770–1804. Une histoire de représentation* (Honoré Champion: Paris, 1997). On early 19th-century narratives of the Revolution, and the significance ascribed to dress as a manifestation of 'personal properties', see Ann Rigney, *The Rhetoric of Historical Representation. Three Narrative Histories of the French Revolution* (Cambridge University Press: Cambridge, 1990), pp. 153–61. See also Steven Laurence Kaplan, 'The Bicentennial Destiny of Robespierre', in *Farewell Revolution. Disputed Legacies, France 1789/1989* (Cornell University Press: Ithaca and London, 1995), pp. 441–69.

144. See Bonnet and Roger, *La Légende de la Révolution au XXe siècle*; Roger Icart, *La Révolution française à l'écran* (Editions Milan: Toulouse, 1988); Sylvie Dallet, *La Révolution française et le cinéma. De Lumière à la Télévision* (L'Herminier: Paris, 1988); Sylvie Dallet and François Gendron, *Filmographie mondiale de la Révolution française* (L'Herminier: Paris, 1989).

2

Representing Authority: New Forms of Official Identity

THE RECOGNITION of the coming into existence of a new era was expressed by a desire both to efface and abolish the symbolic apparatus and paraphernalia which belonged to that régime henceforward designated as 'ancien', and to replace these with a new generation of signs, badges and costumes. Yet, as became apparent from the earliest days of the Revolution, it was easier to renounce old signs than it was to expunge them from social space. Moreover, the definition and implementation of alternatives were to prove to be a protracted and tendentious business. As with iconoclastic revision and renewal in the realms of visual culture, such initiatives were accompanied by often prolonged, incomplete, uneven, and therefore semantically complex processes of substitution.[1] However forthright the enunciation of a principled rejection of old forms, or enthusiastic the desire for new ones, this left unresolved the practical matter of not only reaching agreement as to acceptable designs for revolutionary costumes or badges, but also seeing through their fabrication and dissemination. Furthermore, once instituted, such signs had to stand up to pressurized public scrutiny; in almost every case, problems of contestation, misuse and misunderstanding arose. In due course, changing political events necessitated revision, replacement, and sometimes abandonment.

Attitudes to old and new official costume and badges were based on a fundamental contrast between distinctions and decorations. The gamut of 'distinctions' inherited from the Ancien Régime came to be rejected because their prime function had been to fix people's identity within the royal state.[2] Moreover, they were conferred by, and in the name of, the crown, and therefore reinforced a position of subjection to higher authority. Such reservations about the problematic political import of external badges remained active throughout the revolutionary decade. In a report on the creation of official costumes produced in May 1799, Fénelon's opinion on the nature of costume – that 'signs' were considered as distinctions, reinforcing the hierarchy of the status quo – was deemed irrelevant to the changed circumstances prevailing at the end of the 1790s because it had only applied to a now defunct monarchical system. By contrast, in a republic, it was asserted that such signs should only be 'decorations', and as such not signifying a title 'but a job which ultimately is not given to the man but to the official'.[3] The idea that costumes and signs were nothing more than temporary indicators of a person's fulfilment of an official role was an attempt to avoid self-aggrandizement and the confusion of the person with the post and thereby to prevent such signs from being abused or misappropriated – something of which by 1799 there had been all too much evidence.[4] Furthermore, we will see that the introduction of new forms of decoration was recognized to be in tension with the principle of equality, and the belief that this should remain consistently expressed in physically visible form. The desire to separate the person of the office-holder from the job was to become intensified as examples of the misuse of such positions proliferated.

The demands and expectations of official costume were shaped by the changing role of officialdom in different contexts – local, legislative, ceremonial – centrally informed by the need to identify and assert authority, in the sense of giving publicly visible form to the new political status quo. The need for authority to be represented – and to be consolidated by such representation – was rendered urgent by resistance to, or competition with, 'the constituted authorities'. The urgency of the matter induced a pragmatic approach – yet the process of implementation was rarely expeditious, since the creation of new symbolic forms of dress was taken extremely seriously.

In the case of deputies, this applied in two quite different but complementary situations. First, when they were gathered in the National Assembly or Convention, engaged in the business of legislation and government. As the Assembly was an inherently public space, it produced a need, beyond any more symbolic purpose, to distinguish between the deputies and members of the public, between representatives and those whom they represented. Secondly, when they engaged in activities further afield, whether on occasions such as festivals, which were a ceremonial extension of their official duties, or else when caught up and needing to intervene in the context of public disorder. In episodes such as the *journées* of prairial an III (May 1795), when the authority of the Convention was dramatically challenged, these two conditions of visibility merged. Both types of situation produced a need for the deputies to be identifiable. Indeed, as we will see, the degree of disorder experienced in the *journées* was in part attributed to deputies' lack of a distinguishing costume, a circumstance which reinforced the argument that one should be created. In the latter case, there was also an anxiety that it was possible for people to pass themselves off as representatives of authority by appropriating or simulating its outward signs for destructive or disruptive ends. To this extent, the creation and currency of vestimentary forms of official identity enshrines questions to do with legitimacy and its legibility which will be explored more generally in relation to various forms of patriotic dress and emblem in succeeding chapters.

The unresolved nature of proposals for new official costume was complemented by a more piecemeal institution of what might be called badge culture – what Sophie Turckheim-Pey has characterized as 'insigno-manie'[5] – whereby identification and recognition of officials centred around the quasi-emblematic form of sashes, badges, medals and ribbons. For all their physical concision, these insignia nonetheless carried a considerable symbolic burden: they were a touchstone for the assertion and challenging of new forms of political authority and patriotic legit-imacy. For those who wore them, they were a means of identification with a larger political order, both through individuals' exercise of the respons-ibility conferred upon them, and in the sense that they functioned as tangible personifications of that new order. In the turbulent and contested public space in which revolutionary politics was enacted, they were also the focus for highly testing scrutiny, a form of representation continually under pressure. Such forms of official identity were also paralleled, and often challenged, by the currency of independent forms of political costume and badge corresponding to clubs, *sociétés populaires*, and other modes of localized collective identity.[6] To this extent, a review of new types of revolutionary official insignia and costume provides a necessary prelude to consideration of the wider politics of identity expressed through the dimension of vestimentary appearances.

The earliest episodes concerning official costume in the Revolution revolve around acts of renunciation and abolition. The point of departure for subsequent debate on the necessity and form of official costumes was the Estates General. Mirabeau drew attention to the political significance of the distinctions expressed by the costumes stipulated for the three estates. It was not, he argued, that the Third Estate was or should be humiliated by the simple dress that had been allotted to them, over-shadowed by the more elaborate outfits of the nobility and clergy; rather his objection was that the whole scheme involved submitting to a master of ceremonies whose authority he challenged. To give different costumes to the respective deputies was to reinforce unwanted distinctions between the orders, 'which one can regard as the original sin of our nation, and of which it is absolutely necessary that we be purified, if we hope to regenerate ourselves'. It was, he asserted, up to the Assembly to decide its own costume, if there was to be one. Uniformity of dress would be the symbol of equality of rights and power.[7] These remarks inherit a suspicion of signs of subordination that had been articulated in the later Ancien Régime, based on the belief that such notionally honorific indications of relative status accorded to the nobility and *gens en place* had been devalued by being awarded to undeserving dishonourable men.[8] The author of the *Lettre d'un provincial, député aux Etats-Généraux, sur le costume de cérémonie* (1789) shared Mirabeau's refusal to submit to an imposed costume, and further objected that outer distinctions were invidious, for they constituted esssentially false distinctions of identity. Deputies should remain serious and majestic, and not let themselves be coerced into participating in 'an indecent masquerade' – articulating what was to be a leitmotif of the discourse on official costume, namely that it was a superfluous distraction from more serious matters of political debate and legislation. He concluded in lapidary manner: 'I will keep my dress, my character, and my liberty'.[9] There was, indeed, some resistance to discussing this matter. In Le Doyen's opinion (25 May 1789), this would expose the Assembly to criticism that they were neglecting more important issues in favour of the relatively trivial matter of costume.[10]

It was not until 15 October 1789 that the Estates' different costumes, as all other distinctions of rank, and *places*, both in the Assembly's meetings and ceremonies, were suppressed. This internal reform anticipated the decree of 6 August 1790 which suppressed all decorations and exterior signs based on distinctions of birth.[11] The diversity of the assembled deputies' dress which resulted from this rejection of the adoption of any shared costume also caused practical problems for ushers in distinguishing members of the public; in response to this an identity card was instituted on 9 November 1789.[12] Discussion of the need for an official costume for deputies was not to resurface until late 1792, when the inception of a republican order brought with it a new conception of what officialdom represented.

Beyond the deputies' concerns for their own appearances within the Assembly, one of the chief objects of critical review of the inherited vestimentary order from the Ancien Régime was that of religious costume, corresponding to a type of quasi-official constituency which, once disestablished, nonetheless remained contentiously visible. All forms of religious community were abolished on 14 September 1790.[13] However, although religious costume was thereby disconnected from its former institutional focus, it continued to be worn, creating a subject of disquiet regarding the political implications of the spectacle of such an officially obsolete item. In arguing for the abandonment of such costumes in April 1792, the bishop of Paris, Pierre-Anastase Torné, comprehensively analysed the problems presented in a way which strikingly echoes later harder-edged debates on the politics of costume, informed by a desire to survey and, as it were, test people's political credentials by focusing critically on their forms of dress. Former members of religious communities, he argued, should distinguish themselves by their virtuous behaviour rather than seeking to retain signs of their separate identity and thus avoid becoming 'a holy caste separated from the profane'. Considered in this light, the abolition of ecclesiastical costume 'appears to the legislator as a measure justified by greater political considerations, whereas, in the eyes of the superficial man, it only seems like a frivolous question of *toilette*'.[14] In proclaiming that he had no desire to recommend the limiting of freedom of dress, he anticipated some of the arguments which were to result in the decree of 8 brumaire an II/29 October 1793 which forebade anyone from coercing others as to what and how they dressed. He pointed out, nonetheless, that the law in fact already had a considerable say on how people dressed, in the sense that reasons of decency and morals constituted well-established prohibitions:

> Tell me, I ask you, would one permit either sex to wear the habitual dress of the other whenever they wished? Would one tolerate that citizens made a habit of wearing a mask in society or in places of public assembly?[15]

In this view, dress lent itself to being a means of unnatural and inherently immoral dissimulation, inimical to a new régime of freedom and equality.

In August 1792, the Conseil général of the *commissaires* of a majority of the sections meeting in the Paris Commune called for the prohibition of religious costumes, since they were 'badly regarded' by the people, who viewed them as provocatively divisive. They could be deliberately exploited as, at best, a sign of a lack of patriotic engagement, at worst, a declaration of intransigent refusal to participate in the new political order.[16] Religious costume was subsequently prohibited on 15 August 1792, consistent with legislation accompanying the declaration of the 'patrie en danger' on 6/7 July 1792, which formalized a heightened régime of anxious surveillance engendered by the threat of invasion, and endemic internal division.[17] Significantly, religious costume was, with disguise ('travestissement'), one of the exceptions to the freedom of dress instituted on 8 brumaire an II (October 1793). Such outmoded dress was, however, mobilized in the context of festivals dedicated to dechristianization, where it was parodically paraded before being burnt.[18] An alternative fate for such outfits was to be recycled as theatrical costume for similar purposes of ridicule.[19] In due course, religious costume reappeared in the resuscitated carnival as a popular form of satirical 'travestissement'.[20]

THE NATIONAL GUARD

The earliest days of the Revolution had seen the creation of the National Guard, an institution whose adoption of a uniform corresponded to the expression of a newly forged patriotic unity. To some extent, this proved to be a relatively uncontentious phenomenon in so far as the creation of a uniform was consistent with the essentially military nature of the Guard. Uniforms were, however, strongly associated with hierarchy. In the case of the Guard, this related to the social status of its members and those who were excluded. As a result, uniforms were an ongoing site for discussion and debate over the Guard's constitution and authority. As had been the case with military uniform in the Ancien Régime, Guard uniforms were also a usefully easily appropriated form of unofficially assumed identity for a mixture of political and criminal motives.

The Guard's uniform was regularized in a decree of 23 July 1790, having been defined in readiness for the Festival of Federation on 14 July 1790, when guards were required to discontinue wearing any previously adopted forms.[21] Those who had joined between September and November 1789 were allowed to keep their old uniforms once new ones had been acquired; those who had joined after 1 January 1790 had to hand them in.[22] Following the decree of 21 June 1791 on the reorganization of the Guard, suppression of the 'uniformes de fantaisie', which had been adopted in an ad hoc manner in 1789, was reiterated.[23] Such retrospective enforcement was evidently a response to the existence of local variants and inconsistencies.[24] However, in addition to the inherent variety that resulted from the different sources of fabrication, when provision of uniforms became a matter of government responsibility, problems of ensuring supply rapidly became evident. In March 1792, even though 6 million francs had been provided by the war ministry, sufficient uniforms were not forthcoming; moreover, there were already requests for repairs to existing uniforms.[25]

The appearance of people in the Guard's uniform marked a break with established forms of identity. The uniform of the Guard replaced, or overlaid, the recognizable social differentiation that varieties of dress and fashion had hitherto ensured, in a way that could be understood as patriotically progressive, or disconcertingly levelling. Such defamiliarization could be seen as amusing or simply confusing.[26] Madame de Campan recalled how the king had been shocked to encounter his servants wearing Guard uniform, which he henceforward forebade in his presence; equally, if not more, offensively, Guard uniform was assumed by an Italian soprano who performed mass with the musicians of the royal chapel.[27] Resistance to the authority conferred on people who adopted the uniform was, indeed, most trenchantly expressed when women were concerned, as was the case with sightings of Théroigne de Méricourt wearing a National Guard jacket in the Assembly.[28] For Ferdinand Dutailly, the presence of 'des filles ou femmes poissardes' wearing military uniform beneath their white aprons, and carrying sabres in the procession for the Pantheonization of Voltaire's remains on 11 July 1791, epitomized the disreputable character of the event as a 'carnival madness (folie de carnaval)'.[29]

Uniform was the single most tangible sign of the Guard's identity, but the constitution of 1791 made emphatically clear, in a way that was to apply to all later forms of official dress, that this was only a means to signal a temporarily assumed role by people who, beneath their red, white and blue outfit, remained citizens, subject to the (new) law of the land: 'National guards do not form either a military body, nor an institution within the State; these are citizens themselves called to the service of the public militia' (titre IV, art. 3). Distinctions of rank, and the exercise and recognition of the authority that went with this, applied only during active service (art. 5). Citizens wearing their guard uniforms could not vote in political assemblies.[30]

Attention to the maintenance of consistency of appearance extended to the smallest details of the uniform, and was expressive of the desire to realize that political order which the Guard both enshrined and was mandated to protect. This is manifest in the extraordinary amount of attention given to the design of its buttons. Button design became a matter of long-running legislative clarification centring on their emblematic decoration. In July 1790, the *comité de constitution* decided that buttons would have the name of the district on. The *comité militaire* recommended that buttons should carry the words 'law' and 'king', and the name of district, but left the choice of material to individuals ('gilded wood, gilded bone, solid copper gilt or copper gilt plate').[31] A new model was necessitated when it was discovered that some of those already supplied had come from London. A report, drawn up by the assembled constitutional, military, agricultural and commercial committees recommended the buttons should be: 'yellow or gilded copper, and mounted on bone or wood, attached by a cord in gut or any other material; it will bear the central inscription 'The nation, the law, the king' surrounded by a civic crown; between the border and the crown will be inscribed 'District of . . .' In districts where there are several sections, they will be specified by a number placed after the name of the district.'[32] However, legislation struggled to synchronize adaption of changed forms of design. Introduction of the new form of button had to be postponed since it was noted that manufacturers had already made considerable advances toward their fabrication; a delay of 18 months in its introduction was agreed, with the changeover to take place on 14 July 1792.[33]

The Guard's members were responsible for paying for the acquisition of their uniform, a requirement which immediately highlighted social differences, and was to be an increasing cause of resentment and friction. A uniform cost 4 *louis*, which automatically excluded 'petits gens'. However, as it was agreed not to be possible to exclude those whose service dated from the very first moments of spontaneous revolutionary mobilization on 13 July 1789, exceptions were inevitable, a situation which was often resolved by the local district where the battalion was based covering the costs, or else, once the Guard was integrated into the military, 'patriotic subscriptions' to provide uniforms for poor volunteers.[34] Alternatively, prior to 14 July 1790, requests were made that the old uniforms of the French guards be employed for this purpose,[35] or that guards who were unable to afford to procure uniforms be allowed to perform their service without them.[36] Those who were excluded claimed that their patriotic credentials should be enough to justify their membership.[37] It was not until the immediate aftermath of the invasion of the Tuileries on 10 August 1792 that the distinction between 'active' and 'passive' citizens, which had determined membership of the Guard, was abolished.[38]

The symbolic value of uniform was a subject of considerable contestation. On the one hand, an anonymous pamphlet celebrated the role of the uniform as a sign of national identity: 'The Lacedemonians said: we are proud when we wear our national dress; Parisians can repeat the same words when they put on their uniform.'[39] On the other hand, it was precisely the excessive importance which guards were accused of attaching to their uniforms that provoked criticism from both within and outside the Guard. Indeed, by 1795, the type of the self-regarding national guard with his 'gleaming epaulettes' had become a stock figure for satire.[40] The volunteers of the Saint-Gervais district repudiated the need for officer's epaulettes: 'this mark of superiority [would be] as frivolous in philosophy as dangerous in politics, and . . . would be rather the sign of vanity than patriotism'.[41] Opinions varied as to how far Lafayette was responsible for fostering this reprehensible form of self-importance, which was but a token of the perversion of patriotism. An anonymous pamphlet denounced his dangerous example: 'See his ostentation, see his luxury, how it seems to insult the unfortunate citizen.' Since all citizens were soldiers, such showing off was indicative of a worrying state of affairs, wherein the Guard might assume the role of an arrogant pseudo-praetorian guard, creating an environment in which the king might be diverted from his own patriotic best interests.[42] Mercier recalled the Guard's uniform as a cause of the corruption of its unified patriotic purpose. Liberty had been threatened by the institution of 'these distinctions always dear to the mercenaries who hurry to serve under the command of an individual to fight against the *patrie*'. Nonetheless, he concluded that, whatever vain self-indulgence it elicited, the uniform had ultimately served as a means to bind together different classes.[43]

The Guard's uniform was attractive not only to its members, but also to those who, in a way that was hardly invented by the Revolution but was yet to be highly significant in its vestimentary culture, had various nefarious reasons for seeking to exploit the respect with which it was regarded. Misuse of military uniforms in the context of public disorder had been evident from the summer of 1789.[44] Following the Guard's role in the massacre at the Champ de Mars in July 1791, their patriotic credentials were called into question; in this context those concerned with public order were considerably exercised over the unauthorized use of its uniform.[45] At the time of the Châteauvieux festival in April 1792, the controversial nature of the event and associated 'fermentation' prompted alarm that former army officers from outside Paris were ready to assume Guard uniform on the day of the festival in order to cause trouble.[46] In

May 1792, Michel Gentil reported from the Department of the Loiret that uniforms were being misappropriated to prepare an uprising: 'The wolf is dressing in sheep's clothing (C'est le loup qui se revêt de l'habit du berger)'. But, as he pointed out, there was as yet regrettably no law to forbid this, as was the case with military uniform.[47] Other problems were the continued use of the uniform by individuals who had been expelled from the Guard's ranks, and the less transgressive but equally irregular employment of servants wearing their masters' uniforms when replacing them for periods of duty.[48] Penalties for misuse by members of the Guard were severe, in tune with military conventions. When Combe de Saint-Génie wrongly wore the uniform of a captain of the Guard to which he was not entitled, he was subjected to wearing the 'carcan' (iron collar) and 'écriteau' at the Palais Royal, and banished for three years.[49] As a means of limiting uniform's misuse, in 1791 the Commune de Paris proclaimed that no one outside the Guard could wear it, and forbade tailors and second-hand clothes sellers from hiring or selling it without the presentation of a certificate of enrolment.[50]

MILITARY UNIFORM

From 14 October 1791, the established uniform of the Guard was adopted for standard military use. However, as already noted with regard to the Guard's uniform, problems of fabrication and supply were a perpetual obstacle to the military being fully equipped and consistently dressed. Moreover, soldiers in the established army initially continued to wear their white uniforms after the new blue ones had been introduced; Xavier Vernière, for example, kept his new uniform in his backpack and only used it for reviews.[51] Symptomatic of the fears concerning the army's as yet unproven patriotic fidelity were stories about caches of old uniforms made of royal blue (*bleu de roi*) material embroidered with 'Victory or death (Vaincre ou mourir)', that had been made up in readiness for a royalist insurrection.[52] In May 1793, the Convention commanded infantry officers to lay aside their white uniforms and don the blue coats of the volunteers, the national uniform as it was called.[53] Some officers enacted their own form of retrograde protest by sewing fleur-de-lys buttons on to their new white coats.[54] Such buttons evidently remained in use for some time. Although they were disapproved of by both military and civil authorities, it was recognized that their continued circulation was not itself evidence of subversive intent; that such buttons were found to be openly on sale in the public space of the Palais Royal was interpreted as reassuring proof that they were not intended as a rallying sign (*signe de ralliement*).[55] By contrast, when in March 1793 a volunteer was found to be wearing a button with the arms of France on his hat, he was arrested.[56] The fact that uniform was at first volunteers' responsibility, before being taken on by local administrations and then the state, increased the possibility of both intentional and accidental variety.[57] The motley image of the revolutionary armies is a well-worn cliché, simultaneously serving the purposes of counter-revolutionary satire and yet also evidence of the dedicated patriotism of underequipped soldiers, but is nonetheless materially accurate.[58]

Equipping the army with uniforms necessitated drawing on diverse forms of collective and ad hoc resources. Popular donations were seen as a way of signalling support for valiant comrades.[59] In 1793 it was proposed that prostitutes be set to work knitting stockings for the army.[60] In the Gers in September 1793, obsolete Ancien Régime costumes – 'robes et chaperons consulaires' – were recycled to meet the shortage of red fabric, in a way which had a symbolic as well as practical logic:

> Thus, these hoods with signs of livery of the former lords of the robe which gave to the town municipalities an air of superiority over the municipalities of the country, these red robes which on judges were the emblem of the gold and blood of the litigants on which they gorged themselves, will end by serving as clothes for the valiant defenders who will deliver us from the oppression of kings and lords.[61]

One endemic problem of supply was trafficking. In the case of shoes – the most needed item of military equipment – in order to avoid the siphoning off of such supplies, it was proposed that a way of making them easier to trace was for the shoes produced for soldiers to be distinctively square-toed.[62] Concern over the lack of consistency in uniforms, or what passed for them, was offset by the recognition of the prime importance of mobilization and recruitment. As had been the case with the doubts expressed over the dispensable nature of discussion regarding the possible creation of a costume for the deputies in the National Assembly, basic matters of supply took precedence over niceties of regularization. None-theless, the diversity of the resulting military uniforms was to remain a contentious issue until the Empire.

Daniel Roche has argued that the political uniformity of which the new military uniform was hoped to be an exemplary expression was defeated not just by practicalities, but also by the 'prestige' of uniform, which constituted a space for the expression of individualism and fashion.[63] This view was shared by Colonel Bardin, who in 1812 drafted the report of a commission of generals on the reform of military uniforms. He concluded that earlier regulations had suited 'powerful and coquettish colonels, in leaving them to choose colours as they pleased, and which suited them best'. It was time, he proposed:

> That military dress be no longer subject to the caprices of frivolity and the metamorphoses of fashion; the inconstancy of military fashions is only equalled by female fashion . . . that of generals is decided by tailors and makers of trimmings (*passementiers*), and not by regulations and orders.[64]

DISTINCTIONS

Translating the new revolutionary order into the realm of external appearances was effected by the complementary processes of, on the one hand, the abolition of inherited orders, signs, and decorations, and, on the other hand, their replacement by new signs which expressed the social and political principles of equality and patriotic virtue. The latter process was to prove considerably more troublesome to implement. The discussions surrounding the creation of new honorific signs are extremely revealing of the aspirations and limits that were understood to subtend the material expression of new forms of social and political identity.

The case of the *Vainqueurs de la Bastille* illustrates the deep-seated ambivalence surrounding attitudes to the singling out of those who had distinguished themselves by patriotic deeds. It also illustrates the tension between the individual and collective desire to create new badges or signs of honour, and the reluctance of the Assembly and the commanders of the National Guard to countenance such spontaneous manifestations.[65] On the evening of 14 July, Henri Dubois, one of the heroes of the day, was singled out by being given a cross of St Louis, which had supposedly been taken from De Launay, the governor of the Bastille. He passed it on to Lafayette. In due course, it was given to Arné, another prominent figure in the storming. When he was led in triumph through the streets of Paris, he wore the cross as well as a laurel crown. On 17 July, the district of the Petits-Augustins minted a medal for the *vainqueurs*; this was not to be officially recognized until 6 March 1790. The *vainqueurs* themselves sought official recognition for their patriotic deeds. One group of *vainqueurs* were given military medals of honour by the marquis de la Sale, commander of the Guard, on his individual initiative. The *vainqueurs* as a whole were granted the right to wear the uniform of the National Guard. On 19 June 1790, they were also granted a badge ('insigne') – a miniature castellated crown suspended from a tricolore ribbon[66] – and also received a 'fusil de récompense' and 'sabre gravé'. In due course, on 20 August 1793, the badge was replaced by a medal commemorating 10 August 1792 (also distributed to *commissaires* of the *assemblées primaires* and members of the Convention). However, crucially, they were forbidden to wear it, or their medal of Federation, as a form of decoration, 'under pain of being treated as a traitor to the Republic'.[67] Indeed, the introduction of medals of honour had been disputed by Marat among others from the summer of 1790. The award of the *insigne* to the *vainqueurs* caused immediate resentment on the part of the Parisian National Guard and especially former *gardes françaises*, who felt that the distinction attaching to the medal that they had been awarded in August 1789 had been compromised.[68] The situation was to be resolved on 25 June 1790 by the *vainqueurs* renouncing their new decoration in the interests of 'public tranquillity'.[69] However, almost all the *vainqueurs* continued to demand, and were granted, further decorations, which took the form of sword belts and rifle slings with their names on, as well as certificates confirming their participation on 14 July.[70]

Two other cases where involvement in a significant episode of early revolutionary action was translated into badge form were those of the women who had marched to Versailles on 5/6 October 1789, who requested some form of emblematic reward, which was duly distributed on 18 November 1789,[71] and the 'Défenseurs du Trésor de la ville' (5 October 1789), who had to wait until 11th May 1790 (Figure 8).[72] Less specifically, women who donated their jewels to the 'patrie en danger' were granted shoe buckles as a reward ('boucles de récompense').[73] These examples indicate that, in addition to a desire to express visibly patriotic distinction, a dynamic of self-distinction also informs such badges' creation. Furthermore, there was a degree of fractious competition evident between the recipients of such national honours.

In formulating what new forms of distinction should look like, and the protocols for their award and display, the insistence on ensuring that

Figure 8 Medal and ribbon awarded to participant in defence of Trésor de la Ville, 5th October 1789 ('Trésor de la Ville sauvé et conservé le 5-8bre 1789'). Musée Carnavalet, Paris, Inv. ND 00951. Photograph: Photothèque des Musées de la Ville de Paris (Ladet).

these new distinctions were consistent with the principles of equality tended to result in recommendations which were impractically idealistic. At the same time, early discussions regarding the award of a new generation of national distinctions are particularly sensitive to their relation to the abolished badges that had been employed under the Ancien Régime.

All orders of chivalry, corporations, and all decorations and exterior signs corresponding to differences of birth, were abolished on 30 July 1791, though military decorations survived.[74] For Charles de Villette, 'a medallion, a ribbon, always has a certain aristocratic character which offends equality'. His remarks were prompted by having mistaken some *juges de paix* for chevaliers. This offensive and potentially confusing form of badge was especially disagreeable in private, fraternal assemblies.[75] In the aftermath of 10 August 1792, it was proposed that crosses of Saint Louis be handed in as a contribution towards funds to support the widows and children of victims of violence, and that these be substituted by the existing military medal signifying ten years service, to be awarded to those who made sacrifices for equality.[76] In October 1792, the Convention banned the wearing of the 'ordre des chevaliers de Saint Louis et ses agréments'; it was, however, not to be until July 1793 that the crosses themselves, and other suppressed royal orders, were ordered to be handed in to local municipalities, at a time when such vestiges became, as it were, increasingly anomalously visible in the context of an intensifying climate of republican proscription.[77]

The Convention's ban of October 1792 prompted a wide-ranging commentary in the *Révolutions de Paris* on the general phenomenon of national distinctions. It was noted that the question as to whether they should be replaced by a modern alternative was currently being studied by the *comité militaire* and *comité d'instruction*. Such decorations from the past, it was claimed, had long ceased to be recognized by public opinion. Moreover, the necessity or desirability of such decorations was called into question: 'Can it be doubted that any distinction challenges equality and violates its principles?' Nature did not differentiate people by their exteriors according to their respective merits. Such decorations were like toys 'with which tyrants dazzle the multitude and make themselves creatures to contain it'. Only 'enslaved' or 'bastardized nations' exploited vanity in order to subjugate their peoples. As a way of avoiding such undesirable features, the award of a 'civic crown' was proposed. This would only briefly be placed on the the head of the person to be honoured or congratulated by the president of the Convention, who would assure the grateful recipient that he would be further rewarded by being dispatched to defend the Republic wherever the danger was greatest. This was the most valid form of reward an individual could receive from the Republic: 'Isn't that worth more than a round or lozenge-shaped medal, a ribbon, or a sword embroidered on your coat?'[78] On the related subject of official costume, there was no need to be concerned about problems of identifying the Republic's representatives in crowds, for their position was assumed to be itself sufficiently imposing. Suspicion of the need to single out people was as much political as practical: 'under the reign of equality, let us avoid anything which tends to create separate gangs'. True patriots, it was confidently asserted, repudiated such paraphernalia.[79] Such arguments are consistent with the rhetoric of virtuous transparency and the repudiation of compromising external self-adornment at the heart of the new ideology accompanying the consolidation of the *sans-culottes'* political prominence. In practice, 'récompenses nationales' were not actually awarded until the spring of 1793, after the battle of Jemappes, employing a ceremony in which the first recipient, Bretèche, had an 'oak-leaf crown' placed on his head by the president, who also gave him a 'civic embrace' and a sabre inscribed 'La République Française à Bretèche'.[80] The award of these 'récompenses' was evidently somewhat *ad hoc*, and it was not until the Directory that attempts were made to systematize them.[81]

*

By countenancing the introduction of official costume, the institutionalization of a new political culture was to be made visible and publicly disseminated. This was the subject of extensive discussion, generated by the need to tailor legislative proposals to the exigencies of political principles. Key roles which were the subject of legislation defining their new costumes and identifying features were legal and municipal officials, and deputies.

THE LAW

The reorganization of the legal system in the summer of 1790 brought with it the creation of new costumes for its constituent functionaries. In June 1790, the 'municipal officers who deliver justice in the Police Tribunal' were invited to renounce their more elaborate Ancien Régime robes for the 'short cloak'.[82] A decree of 12 September 1790 prevented *avocats* from forming a corporation or 'order', and forbade them wearing any particular costume.[83] However, as had been the case with the deputies in the Assembly, it was equally argued that judges should not be subjected to an imposed costume, in a way that conflicted with their symbolically highly visible status as free men and instruments of the laws governing their peers, but should be permitted to wear whatever they wished. A petition to the *comité de constitution* recommended that they should have no other distinctive marks than 'their virtues, their talent and their integrity'.[84] In the event, judges were to wear a new ensemble consisting of 'black outfit', that is, breeches and coat, and a 'round hat turned up and with a plume of black feathers',[85] with the difference that the hats of *commissaires du roi* were to be 'turned up at the front with a golden button and braid'; clerks of court (*greffiers*) had the same costume, but without the plume; *huissiers* were to be dressed in black, with a gilt chain and black cane with an ivory knob.[86] Early in 1791, 'ushers, commercial guards, and other executors of judgements' were required to carry a white cane and a medal in their buttonhole with the inscription 'Action of the Law'.[87] *Juges de paix* and *prudhommes* had no new specific costume, but in March 1791 were granted an oval fabric medallion with a red border around a blue centre on which was inscribed 'Law and Peace'.[88] Officials in the *Tribunal de cassation* wore a black costume, and had a tricolore neck ribbon and a gilt medal inscribed with the words 'The Law', as well as a round hat with black feathers; *commissaires du roi* had the same costume, but with gold button and braid on their hats and 'The law and the king' on their medal.[89] These new identifying costumes and insignia were consistent with their dual role as both mobile purveyors of justice and its judgements, and administrators operating within their dedicated premises. Simple and effective as they were as identifying features, with the increased concern about public disorder in the summer of 1792, they nonetheless came to need the protection of legislation to outlaw their misappropriation.[90]

The best-known element in the creation of new costumes for representatives of the law is the subsequent substitution of the liberty cap for the hat with black feathers *à la* Henri IV worn by judges, which had been introduced on 2 September 1790.[91] Whether judges wore the earlier Henri IV feathered hat, or, as was popularly recommended in February 1794, they appeared 'in trousers and *bonnet rouge*', such costume was an integral part of the process of judgement: 'the costume of liberty must be the first object which strikes the eyes of the cowards who have betrayed it'.[92] However, as Jean-Marc Devocelle has noted, this in fact only occurred in a few instances and was a matter of local will, not national regulation. In the Vaucluse, the president of the *tribunal criminel* proposed an alternative to the *chapeau à la Henri IV*, not the *bonnet rouge*, but a so-called '*bonnet à la Jean-Jacques*, crowned with feathers in the three [national]

colours and national blue coat'. Only the Verdun tribunal put the replacement of 'monarchical' costume by the *bonnet de la liberté* into practice.[93]

In the case of officials whose duties required them to engage in public
activities, it was recognized that they needed a prominent form of identifying feature. Thus a 'hood in the three national colours' was proposed
for *commissaires de police* when on duty, which would mark them out in
times of trouble, for example among theatre audiences, allowing them to
be seen from all sides.[94] The issue of the public visibility of officials is
particularly relevant to municipal officers and their potential role when
intervening in moments of public disorder.

The sash (*écharpe*), instituted on 20 March 1790 as the 'distinguishing
mark' of municipal officers,[95] exemplifies the temporary nature of signs
of officialdom in the way that it could be quickly put on, thereby
transforming someone outwardly no more than an ordinary citizen into
an embodiment of law and, in theory at least, order. As David Garrioch
has noted, in the context of a local political culture in which office holders
were more likely to be unknown to the people whom they represented,
such forms of the external identification of representatives of authority
were correspondingly necessary.[96] Given the minimal material form of
the sash, it is not surprising that it did not escape the misappropriation
visited upon all forms of revolutionary costume and badge.[97]

In the aftermath of the invasion of the Tuileries on 20 June 1792,
officials' inconsistent willingness to assert the authority conferred on
them by their sashes on this occasion was a point of bitter recrimination
which came to light in the lengthy official report on the day's controversial
events. For example, the procurator of the Paris Commune, Mouchet,
was accused of failing to use his sash, and of remaining in the crowd as an
anonymous individual. Desmousseaux, who saw Mouchet in the crowd,
equipped with his sash, but without having put it on, had advised him
not to try to intervene since his probable chances of exerting any control
were slim and, indeed, 'hardly consistent with the dignity of which it is
the sign'.[98] Sergent, by contrast, stated that it was because of his sash that
he was able to get through the crowd and give the following orders:
'Citizens, this is the sign of the law; in its name we invite you to retire,
and to follow us'. His confidence was perhaps bolstered by being accompanied by two *officiers de la paix* with white batons.[99] Leroux took a more
positive line in claiming that 'le peuple' had indeed given proper respect
to the sash, a mark of authority which had been instituted on their
behalf.[100] It is ironical that Pétion, whose delayed intervention in the
events of 20 June 1792 earned him the opprobrium of the king and his

outraged supporters, was to use his sash as an instrument of crowd control a month later, when he quelled attempts to force a way into the precinct of the Tuileries (which had been closed off to the public after 20 June), which had been provoked by the inflammatory rumour that deputies were being murdered. Interestingly, a contemporary image of this episode shows him holding the sash before him, displaying it to the crowd, signalling his identification as an authority figure, and rendering it all the more an emblematic sign, rather than an item of dress as such.[101] A print endorsed Pétion's authority by showing him being given his sash by Liberty.[102]

DEPUTIES AND REPRESENTATIVES OF THE PEOPLE

Among the new official costumes and identifying features either projected or actually introduced, the one over which most ink was spilt was the proposal that members of the Convention should have their own costume. As the representatives of national government, the identification of their occupancy of this primordial role was intensely symbolic. By comparison, it is significant that the Commune de Paris never adopted any costume, or even a badge or medal for its members.[103]

The desire that, in addition to the *cartes d'identité* that had been in use by deputies in the Assembly since 9 November 1789,[104] some form of costume or badge be introduced was recognized as a matter of quotidian practicality, especially by the ushers of the Assembly, in order for them to be able to distinguish between mere spectators and deputies.[105] This recommendation took on a more urgent character in the summer of 1792, following the emergency legislation introduced under the aegis of 'la patrie en danger'. In the Assembly, Tardiveau spoke of the beneficial effect of such a form of decoration on constitutional equality, which was all the more desirable in the context of the need for deputies' authority to be visible and imposing.[106] What emerged from these discussions were badges for magistrates and departmental and district administrators, and *procureurs-généraux-syndics*, agreed on 11 July 1792.[107]

Recommendations of the adoption of official costume articulated an awareness of the egalitarian foundation on which progressive revolutionary institutions rested, namely, as enshrined in the 1791 constitution (13 September), that: 'Social distinctions can only be based on common utility' (art. 1); and that, equal before the law, all citizens were admissible to public roles 'with no other distinction than their virtues and their talents' (art. 7). The Constitution of 'an I', 1793 reiterated the essentially

COSTUME
*d'un Représentant du Peuple François près les Armées de la
République, institué par la Convention Nationale. L'An 1er de
la Répub^{que}1793. (V. S.) Dessiné d'après Nature sur les lieux.*

Figure 9 Pierre Duflos: 'Costume d'un Représentant du Peuple François près les Armées de la République, institué par la Convention Nationale, l'An Ier de la Répub[li]que. V[ieux] S[tyle]1793. Dessiné d'après Nature sur les lieux' (Costume of a representative of the people with the Armies of the Republic, instituted by the National Convention, Year One of the Republic. Old Style 1793. Drawn after nature on location), 1795, coloured etching, 12 x 8 cm. Musée de la Révolution Française, Vizille. Photograph: Musée de la Révolution Française, Vizille.

temporary nature of public functions: 'they cannot be considered as distinctions nor as rewards, but as duties' (art. 30).

As Jean-Marc Devocelle has pointed out, despite abundant but unresolved discussion of the need for a costume for deputies and other officials before the Directory, only one costume was actually put into practice: that of the 'représentant du peuple aux armés', consisting of a tricolore waist sash, and hat 'with three feathers, with striped braid in gold covering a part of the cockade' (Figure 9). This came into use on 30 April 1793, having been provisionally established by a decree of 4 April. Yet one year on, only 225 complete costumes had been issued. The participation of the Convention at the Festival of the Supreme Being, and the need for deputies to appear consistently apparelled, led to an accelerated distribution; that is to say, in lieu of the as yet unresolved costume which deputies should have worn.[108] As Devocelle has remarked: 'This costume of the representative of the people was in any case the great official uniform of the Revolution'.[109]

Wide-ranging proposals for the introduction of a national costume, including those for officials, took place in the Société populaire et républicaine des arts between March and June 1794. These discussions included a rare proposal to address the question of women's costume; however, this was agreed to already be much closer to a state of 'regeneration', and therefore less in need of the society's attention. A kind of chauvinistic primitivism was evident in the appeal to Gallic precedent, which was claimed to be more 'natural'. These discussions were, in fact, superseded by the series of costumes designed by Jacques-Louis David. Morever, prescribing a new outfit was recognized as being potentially at odds with the Convention's deliberations of freedom of dress.[110] In order to inform the society's discussions, a short pamphlet was published laying out the rationale for a new national costume, and soliciting proposals. The keynote here was regeneration. Under 'the empire of despots', dress had been subject to the 'vicissitudes of fashion', thereby departing from its original natural function. Dress ceased to be a practical matter; rather, it became 'an object of representation, directed by fantasy, appropriated by pride'; it was used to distinguish between rank and wealth. In the new circumstances of the republic, by contrast, dress should be used to identify people by age and their public function, without denaturing the 'sacred basis of equality'. Furthermore, such a new costume would be better suited to artistic representation.[111] The prototypes of new national costume were only essayed in public by a few artists, and more institutionally by the Elèves de l'Ecole de Mars.[112] In both cases their reception was no better than equivocal. The Elèves de l'Ecole de Mars were viewed as 'operatic' by inhabitants of Neuilly;[113] Lesueur's caption to his gouaches of this costume recalls that they were sceptically regarded 'like actors'.[114] Although, in practical terms, little was achieved in terms of any form of national dress, these initiatives express a deep-seated desire to institute a new régime of appearances, in which the uncertain meanings of individualized forms of dress would be replaced by transparently recognizable signs of exemplary identity. St Just's outline of a codified set of identifying features is well known.[115] Similarly, in C.F.X. Mercier's *Comment m'habillerai-je?* (1793), he recommended the explicit differentiation of people's identity, in a manner corresponding to their profession or job, by varieties of coloured clothing.[116] The resulting stability would, he asserted, only disadvantage malcontents, servants, and the public executioner.

After the *journées* of prairial (May 1795), it was decreed that the Convention should meet 'in costume' and armed, something, as it was pointed out, that would have saved time in their being 'delivered', as they would have been conveniently visibly differentiated from the insurgents.[117] These events prompted reconsideration of the whole question of the use of signs and other forms of official and quasi-official identity. On the one hand, the constitution of an III (5 fructidor/22 August 1795) suppressed all political societies – outlawing all public meetings, correspondence, any conditions of eligibility or exclusion, and the use of 'any exterior sign of their association' (art. 362); political rights were only exercisable in *assemblées primaires* or *assemblées communales* (art. 363). Furthermore, as an updated form of republican tabula rasa, all 'distinctive marks which recall the exercise of earlier functions or services rendered' were proscribed (art. 368). Complementing this was the institution of a new costume and sign of authority for members of the *Corps législatif* and all officials in the exercise of their duties, whose form was to be established (art. 369). The abbé Grégoire was charged to present a report on the costume to be adopted.[118]

Here we may draw out certain features of Grégoire's text, and that by Jean-François Barailon, which preceded it, regarding the vestimentary representation of governmental authority.[119] Barailon's motto, quoting himself – 'above all let us avoid the ridiculous!' – is indicative of the enduring concern over the tendency for costume, whether official or merely fashionable, to express incongruous superfluity.[120] At the same time, still uncomfortably aware of the experience of the prairial *journées*, he understood the usefulness of a visually striking means of asserting political authority. Such disorder might have been avoided if the representatives had been equipped with a costume 'which announces the power and grandeur of the French people, [and] which consequently commands and imposes respect for its representation'.[121] In reviewing the effects of official costume from former ages, he clearly preferred a minimal, emblematic form to elaborate outfits: 'is not a single ear of corn in the hand equal to the robe of Heliogabalus? If it doesn't have the same effect, is it any the less a distinctive mark? Vanity loses nothing.'[122]

Grégoire argued that it was incumbent on those responsible for government to be aware of the power of 'the language of signs': 'distinctive costumes are part of this idiom; they awaken ideas and feelings analogous to their object, above all when they seize the imagination by their impressiveness'.[123] The drawbacks of costume – its potential for satisfying vanity and ambition – were counterbalanced by the way that physically personifying the law could impose respect for it.[124] Understanding this was necessary in order the better to accomplish social duties. In this sense, Grégoire applauded the Estates General costume, and regretted its lack of a sequel. The tyrants of the Terror and the adherents of *sans-culotterie* had manifested their scorn for the Convention through elevating not only proper dress but 'almost cleanliness and decency to the rank of counter-revolutionary crimes'. The respect which should be accorded men of the law was nothing more than the respect required for the nation, and therefore of the individual citizen as part of the nation. Thus, although adoption and use of costumes was strictly conditional, in that they were to be confined to the role of identifying men engaged in their official duties, they were also expressive of a larger political and social order.[125] The legitimate desire for individualistic freedom of dress that had been manifested in the National Assembly was superseded by a recognition that the members of the Convention required some form of collective identification, making of the congregated deputies a striking spectacle. In recommending the creation of an official costume, he recalled how a foreigner, encountering the spectacle of the Convention in session, had asked 'Where are the deputies?' He divided the bodies in need of costumes into four categories: *corps législatif, pouvoir exécutif, corps administratif,* and *pouvoir judiciaire*. His conception of what kind of costume was suited to each type of function was at once symbolic and practical, based on whether they were essentially sedentary, such as the *corps législatif,* and therefore capable of wearing long robes, inducing a decorous sense of calm; or active, such as the *corps administratif,* who required something more suited to their mobility.[126] The Directoire executif would have both normal dress, and a ceremonial costume for occasions such as festivals.[127] Grégoire's proposals drew on a well-established critique of modern dress as both unhealthy and unsuitable for artistic represent-ation.[128] To this extent, he imagined that a new official costume might engender a corresponding reform in ordinary dress, indicative of an ideological homogenization. Grégoire's sensitivity to the public image of the Convention, including the desirability that its members be suitable subjects for artistic representation, clearly expresses the degree to which its socially visible effects were founded on a symbolic language in a way which took priority over more practical considerations of implement-ation.

A new commission to modify the form of deputies' costume was set up on 1 January 1797.[129] Following slow progress, and also problems of fabrication, the Conseil des Cinq-Cents resolved on 19 November 1797 to adopt the following new costume: 'French outfit, national blue colour, double-breasted and below the knee; waist sash of tricolore silk, with a golden fringe; scarlet Greek-style cloak, decorated with embroideries, in wool; velvet cap, with a tricolore plume'. This was introduced for the ceremonial transfer of the legislative body to its new location in the Palais Bourbon on 21 January 1798 (although the scarlet cloaks were not ready until 19 February).[130] For the *Moniteur*, the costume recalled that of high priests seen in the theatre; this was, however, taken as a compliment: 'this costume has something beautiful about it, something imposing and truly senatorial'.[131]

Following the coup of 18 brumaire an VIII, a commission of the Conseil des Cinq-Cents returned to the question of the costume of members of the *Corps législatif* as part of putting the new constitution into practice. Dissenting voices, such as Riouffe, questioned whether legislators needed a costume, as was by contrast the case for the executive, military and magistrature. Costume was not needed outside the chamber; inside, where representatives were at work, costume was superfluous, since they were only a spectacle to each other. Such costume also appealed to the vanity of men who wished to stand out by means of 'frivolous and extravagant marks, . . . as if equality were for them an unbearable burden which they continually sought to evade'. Although modified in 1800 and 1803, the costume of the *Corps législatif* was retained under the Empire.[132]

Beyond the premises of the Assembly or Convention, the only other situation when deputies publicly performed their role as representatives of the people was in festivals and related ceremonies. On these occasions, officials occupied an intermediate position, in that they were not engaged in their duties as such, nor were they simply at large in public space.

Festivals were an occasion for the performative restatement of authority, hence the need to formalize representatives' public image, and thereby maximize its proselytizing potential. In the planning of and comment-aries on festivals, official costume was to prove a touchstone for attitudes to the relation of these authority figures to the people.

Preparations for the Festival of Federation in July 1790 raised questions as to how participants beyond the National Guard should dress. For example, members of the *conseil* of the Paris Commune were advised by the mayor that no costume as such was required; they were simply to wear black, but without their cloaks, swords and 'en bourse' (a 'petit sac de taffetas noir' for hair, in the form of a pig-tail).[133] This form of low-key outfit was a sign of semi-official participation, reconciling the desire to present some form of collective presence while yet remaining essentially private individuals, in tune with the consensual nature of the occasion. This forgoing of any ceremonial formality – a collective dressing down offset by the spectacle of the assembled National Guard – was recognized as undermining in symbolic form the singular distinctiveness of the king's authority: he was reduced to the level of an accessory. Indeed, his appearance 'without sceptre, without crown, without royal cloak' was polemically read as a sign of his desire that he wanted nothing to do with this 'superficial spectacle'.[134]

By contrast, critiques of the Festival of Law dedicated to the murdered mayor of Étampes, Simonneau, censured the degree to which it resembled a hybrid of religious procession and military review in a way that was denounced as a means of marginalizing the people.[135] The presidents of the sections were compared to churchwardens. Indeed, for the *Révolutions de Paris*, this unpalatable spectacle suggested that there was a need for a decree regarding the costume of presidents, secretaries and *commissaires* of the sections, as had been done for legal costume, with the implication that such costumes should be used in festivals.[136]

Republican festivals were to take up this theme in so far as they were structured so as to enact a discourse of equality. In the case of the descript-ion of the procession in the programme of the Festival of Republican Unity on 10 August 1793, this was expressed through a calculated refusal to segregate groups of officials. Thus, 'all individuals useful to society will be indistinctly mingled together, although identified by their distinctive marks'; the president of the provisional executive council would walk side by side with blacksmiths; mayors, wearing their sashes, would be side by side with butchers and masons.[137]

When the Convention appeared en masse they were surrounded by an emblematic frame in the form of a tricolore ribbon, carried by the personifications of the four ages. That is, they were only identified as a generic collective entity, at once embodying solidarity, and suppressing any identification of individuals.[138] The projected, but unrealized, festival celebrating the martyrs Bara and Viala was to be the occasion when members of the Convention would appear in their new official costume. As this was not yet ready, they were instructed to adopt the costume of 'representatives of the people to the armies and in the departements'.[139]

This vestimentary subordination of the individual within a collective public image of authority did not escape criticism. Rejecting plans for representatives to adopt a costume to attend the festival celebrating the anniversay of the king's execution on 21 January 1795, Lecomte objected to the way this would detach him from the crowd:

> As for costume, I am honoured to dress myself in the national colours; but this should be a festival of the people; I want to be able to mix with my brothers, to shout 'Long live the Republic!' among them, without standing out. For this, I intend to go as I am at this moment, wrapped in my cloak.[140]

One of the incriminating statements in the dossier on Vincent, who was arrested as part of the liquidation of Hébertistes in March 1794, was his reported dismissal of the costume of the member of the Convention, which he considered as an 'aristocratic decoration' designed to satisfy a sense of self-importance. He imagined using a mannequin dressed in the costume as a means to attract a crowd in the Tuileries gardens, which he would then address on the need to distrust a government which relied on such contrived self-aggrandizement.[141]

After 1795, official costume was used in festivals in a more restricted manner; the *corps legislatif* was excluded from ceremonies by the Constitution – only members of the Directory were permitted to participate. In tune with the limiting of representative political power, its public display was strictly confined within the premises of the Convention. Their exclusion from festivals was a conscious backlash against the autocratic pretensions of Robespierre et al. At the same time, the bureaucratic apparatus of the state proliferated, and acquired distinguishing uniforms. However, in the reorganized administrative order of the Directory, these were clearly separated from political responsibility.[142]

Beyond the progressive, if intermittent, formulation and implement-ation of a new generation of signs, costumes and badges, corresponding to the evolving apparatus of officialdom, there lies the crucial matter of their currency in public spaces, and the way that this elicited critical commentary, in so far as the symbolic manifestation of authority was frequently found to be compromised by unwanted political effects and implications. Spectators at festivals were extremely sensitive to any evidence of individuals seeking to single themselves out in a way that was not sanctioned by law. When members of the local *société populaire* appeared at a festival in the section de Beaurepaire in January 1794, the fact that they wore their medals, which should have been restricted to their meetings, was condemned: 'this is to wish to revive distinctions; equality would then be but a vain word'.[143] More generally, members of *sociétés populaires* who continued to wear their *bonnets rouges* and medals in the street were frowned on. This was 'contrary to the principles of equality', for it singled them out from their fellow citizens. Such behaviour fuelled calls for the comprehensive proscription of all 'distinctive marks'.[144] Moreover, it was observed that men who were excluded from sections might retain and misuse their medals and ribbons; the existence of this 'class of men apart' was certain to lead to disturbances, 'beyond thousand upon thousand woes which can still result from these distinctions' – that is, distinctions were inherently anti-republican.[145] These censorious comments are directed at the use of badges without any official sanction. People in general, and police agents in particular, would have become used to the growing prominence of badges, sashes and medals employed by people in positions of official authority and responsibility, and were therefore sensitized to recognize instances where such forms of display served to express misplaced individual pretensions, which were unhesitat-ingly considered political in their significance, and also to the more serious matter of intentional misuse.

A dimension to suspicion over signs and badges which elicited part-icular anxiety was their potential for echoing proscribed signs from the past. Thus, soldiers who continued to wear plaques signifying long service on their chests were subject to reproach, and were expected to sacrifice this honorific distinction. For the police agent who recorded this anom-alous practice, such signs were too similar to vestiges of the monarchy, notably the croix de Saint-Louis. It was argued that the sight of soldiers wearing these plaques was equivalent to judges attending the theatre with their official costume of medal and black cloak: 'There should not exist any distinction between citizens outside of the carrying out of the responsibilities with which they may be entrusted . . . We should survey carefully all those who seek to distinguish themselves from others; these are not true republicans'.[146] Moreover, the currency of such signs was vigorously denounced in so far as it was perceived as seriously under-mining the foundations of republican equality. Indeed, suspicion of 'distinctive marks' in general was such that even legitimate bearers of bona fide medals found themselves challenged. A member of a departmental *comité de sûreté générale* equipped with his official medal was refused free entry to the Théâtre de la Gaité, being told by the usher: 'I don't recognize the medal you wear: no ticket, no entry.'[147] When faced by a hostile crowd, a *commissaire de section* 'with a large medal' who tried to arrest a baker only succeeded with difficulty, even though he had shown his medal and declared: 'I arrest you in the name of the law, and you are going to follow me.'[148]

∗ ∗ ∗

Official costume constitutes only one element, and far from the most important in quantitative terms, in the creation of a new régime of revolutionary appearances. In reviewing the proposals for and institution of military, legal, and governmental costume and other more concise distinguishing features, we find a consistent slowness in their realization, characteristically accompanied by an underlying scepticism about the necessity for such potentially divisive attire. From the early days of the National Assembly to the Directory, proposals for official costume encountered considerable resistance in so far as it was commonly viewed as being in conflict with the fundamental values of equality, especially when transformed into republican form. As we have seen, in practice, such signs of authority most commonly took the form of badges, medals and ribbons.[149] Although these were more easily produced and distrib-uted, deriving an extra level of differentiation from their diverse artisanal sources, their small scale, and numerous variations of form and emble-matic content, brought with them a profusion that could be as troubling as it was reassuring, creating problems of inconsistent legibility and the uncertain recognition of legitimacy. It is this dimension, far more than the extremely limited usage of full formal costume, in which the new identity of revolutionary political culture predominantly existed.

The next three chapters will show how the vestimentary and emble-matic dimension of the Revolution's incipient political culture was subject to intense and multifarious expectations. The form and content of such material signs was unstable and fluctuating, and correspondingly prone to elicit conflicting degrees of recognition and repudiation. To this extent, exploring matters of the visual or material form and currency of dress in its diverse manifestations cannot be separated from densely tangled layers of commentary, interpretation, and contestation. Legislation which sought to stabilize such matters was almost always introduced as a retrospective attempt to prevent further disturbances, social discord, and the scope for subversion. At the same time, precisely because of this complex contest of meaning, vestimentary appearances emerge as a crucial site for the articulation of new forms of socio-political identity at both the collective and the individual level. In tracing the history of the national cockade in the next chapter, I shall demonstrate the complexities underlying the representation and recognition of emblematic forms of political dress in more detail.

Notes

1. On the inception and meanings of the term Ancien Régime, see Diego Venturino, 'La naissance de l' "Ancien Régime"', in *The French Revolution and the Creation of Modern Political Culture*, vol. 2, Colin Lucas (ed.), *The Political Culture of the French Revolution* (Pergamon: Oxford, 1988), pp. 11–40. On iconoclasm, see Richard Wrigley, 'Breaking the Code: interpreting French revolutionary iconoclasm', in Alison Yarrington and Kelvin Everest (eds), *Reflections of Revolution, Images of Romanticism* (Routledge: London, 1993), pp. 182–95; *Révolution française et 'Vandalisme'*. Actes du colloque international de Clermont-Ferrand 15–17 décembre 1988, Simone Bernard-Griffiths, Marie-Claude Chemin, Jean Ehrard (eds) (Universitas: Paris, 1992); Richard Clay, 'Signs of Power: Iconoclasm in Paris 1789–1795', Ph.D. University College London, 1999, and 'Saint-Sulpice de Paris: art, politics, and sacred space in revolutionary Paris 1789–1795', *Object*, no. 1, October 1998, pp. 5–22.

2. In the *cahier de doléance* produced by the nobility of Bazes, distinctions were supported 'so that moderation in ideas may be maintained and subordination in the behaviour and conduct of all men may be preserved' (as John Markoff notes, this idea derives from Montesquieu's *L'Esprit des lois*, book 5 chapter 9). In like manner the *nivernais* nobles asked: 'Help us put on the mask of authority . . . and our faces will grow to fit that mask' (*The Abolition of Feudalism. Peasants, Lords, and Legislation in the French Revolution* (Pennsylvania State University Press: Philadelphia, 1996), pp. 530–1).

3. AN F[17] 1232 pièce 5 f° 30–40, 15 floréal an VII [4 May 1799]. See Fénelon, *Les Aventures de Télémaque, fils d'Ulysse (1699); Telemachus, son of Ulysses*, ed. and trans. Patrick Riley (Cambridge University Press: Cambridge, 1994).

4. The distinction between an individual's public, official identity and his or her identity as a private person was certainly understood clearly in the Ancien Régime. Megan Vaughan has written of the case of Benoît Giraud, who was hanged for attacking the Intendant-elect of Martinique in August 1777; Giraud explained that, as Foucault was 'en bourgeois' at the time of the assault, this was, in effect a matter between two free men. In the Revolution, what was at stake, in radically redefined ways, was the relation between public and private roles ('I am my foundation', *London Review of Books*, 18 October 2000, p. 15). I am grateful to Penelope Curtis for drawing this reference to my attention.

5. Sophie Turckheim-Pey, 'Les Insignes révolutionnaires de la collection Côte', in *Autour des mentalités et des pratiques politiques sous la Révolution française*, 112e Congrès national des sociétés savantes, Lyon, Histoire moderne et contemporaine (Comité des travaux historiques et scientifiques: Paris, 1987), vol. 3, p. 139. The problem with this term is its implication that this kind of practice was aberrant, not to say pathological. Rather, I would argue that it was indicative of a pragmatic way of coming to terms with the need to reinvent forms of official identity.

6. On the chronology and incidence of *sociétés populaires* and other forms of local political groupings, see Jean Boutier and Philippe Boutry, *Les Sociétés politiques* (Éditions de l'École des Hautes Études en Sciences Sociales: Paris, 1992), part 6 of *Atlas de la Révolution française*, eds Serge Bonin and Claude Langlois; Isabelle Bourdin, *Les Sociétés populaires à Paris pendant la Révolution française* (Sirey: Paris, 1937); and Michael L. Kennedy's three-volume study of the Jacobin club (see Bibliography).

7. *Lettre à ses commettans* (10 May 1789), cit. Edmond Launay, revised André Souyris-Rolland, *Costumes, insignes, cartes, médailles des députés 1789–1898* ([1899] 1981), p. 11.

8. See Antoine de Baecque, 'Le discours anti-noble (1787–1792): aux origines d'un slogan '"Le Peuple contre les gros"', *Revue d'histoire moderne et contemporaine*, 1989, vol. 36, p. 13.

9. *Lettre d'un provincial*, pp. 5, 7. Others argued that by retaining the black costume, the vanity of the rich would be banished.

10. Launay, *Costumes, insignes, cartes, médailles des députés*, p. 12.

11. Jacques Boedels, 'Le Costume des gens de justice pendant la Révolution de 1789 à 1793', in Robert Badinter (ed.), *Une Autre Justice, 1789–1799. Contributions à l'histoire de la justice sous la Révolution française* (Fayard: Paris, 1989), p. 337.

12. Launay, *Costumes, insignes, cartes, médailles des députés*, p. 13. Deputies were also for the most part mutually unknown to each other (Timothy Tackett, *Becoming a Revolutionary. The Deputies of the French National Assembly and the Emergence of a Revolutionary Culture (1789–1790)* (Princeton University Press: Princeton and London, 1996), p. 122). Tackett also notes La Revellière-Lépeaux's adoption of brightly coloured clothes.

13. See Louis Trichet, *Le Costume du clergé, ses origines et son évolution en France d'après les règlements de l'église* (Cerf: Paris, 1986), and Chanoine Jourand, 'De la suppression (1790) au rétablissement (1805) du costume ecclésiatique', *La Semaine religieuse du diocèse de Lyon*, 1963, no. 70, pp. 230–7.

14. Torné, *Discours de Pierre-Anastase Torné, évêque de la métropole du centre, sur la suppression des congrégations séculières et du costume ecclésiastique, 6 avril 1792*, pp. 15–16.

15. Ibid., p. 18. Torné's reasoning was paralleled at precisely the same moment by a debate in the Jacobin club regarding the pressure to discontinue the wearing of the *bonnet*

rouge: 'La robe monacale, la soutane, la culotte, plus pernicieuses encore que les bonnets rouges, étaient autant de signes entretenant un esprit de parti' (18 April 1792), cit. Jean-Marc Devocelle, 'Costume politique et politique du costume: approches théoriques et idéologiques du costume pendant la Révolution française', mémoire de maîtrise, Université de Paris I', 1988, 2 vols, vol. 1, p. 27.

16. *Municipalité de Paris. Commissaires des 48 sections réunis à la Maison commune. Extrait des déliberations du conseil général des commissaires de la majorité des sections, du dimanche 12 août 1792, l'an 4me de la Liberté* (affiche).

17. J.M. Devocelle, 'Costume et citoyenneté', *Révolution française, Actes des 113e et 114e Congrès nationaux des sociétés savantes (Strasbourg, 1988–Paris, 1989), Section d'histoire moderne et contemporaine* (Editions du Comité des Travaux Historiques et Scientifiques: Paris, 1991), p. 314. However, religious costume could continue to be employed when priests were engaged in their duties (*Arch Parl*, vol. 48, 18 August 1792, p. 351).

18. Pellegrin cites a festival in Poitiers on 20 frim. an II/10 December 1793, where costumes representing popes, cardinals and bishops were visible, as well as the costumes associated with the defunct *corps de métier* (*Les Vêtements de la Liberté. Abécédaire des pratiques vestimentaires françaises de 1780 à 1800* (Alinéa: Paris, 1989), pp. 125–6).

19. Paul d'Estrée, *Le Théâtre sous la Terreur 1793–1794* (Émile-Paul: Paris, 1913), pp. 324–5.

20. A. Aulard, *Paris sous le Consulat. Recueil de documents pour l'histoire de l'esprit public à Paris*, 4 vols (Cerf: Paris, 1903–1909), vol. 1, pp. 178–9 (25/26 Feb. 1800).

21. 'Habit bleu du roi, doublure blanche, passepoil, parement et revers écarlates, collet blanc, vestes et culottes blanches, épaulettes jaunes et or' (*Moniteur*, pp. 200–1, cit. Georges Carrot, 'La Garde nationale 1789–1871', 3e cycle doctoral thesis, Université de Nice, 1979, p. 66). *Procès-verbal de la Confédération à Paris, le quatorze juillet mil sept-cent-quatre-vingt-dix* (Paris, 1790), pp. 24–5

22. This provided scope for treating such discarded uniforms as a kind of relic; *Actes Comm*, 2nd series, vol. 3, p. 605, Viguier de Curny report (16 April 1791).

23. Georges Saint Mleux, *Souvenirs d'un fédéraliste Malouin* (Saint-Servan, 1911), p. 25, cit. Roger Dupuy, *La Garde nationale et les débuts de la Révolution en Ille-et-Vilaine (1789–mars 1793)* (Klincksieck: Paris, 1972), p. 156.

24. *RAM*, 16 August 1791, p. 28.

25. *Arch Parl*, vol. 39, p. 698, 14 March 1792.

26. The same applied to military uniform. The sight of emigré financiers and parlementaires adopting counter-revolutionary uniforms caused considerable merriment to noble onlookers (Philip Mansel, 'Monarchy, Uniform, and the Rise of the *frac* 1760–1830', *Past and Present*, no. 96, August 1982, p. 129). This was a phenomenon still relevant to modern times. When, on leave from his French military posting in October 1944, Richard Cobb revisited a Parisian family whom he had not seen since 1939, he was greeted with the exclamation: 'Mais, Richard, te voilà déguisé!' (*Paris and its Provinces 1792–1802* (Oxford University Press: Oxford, 1975), p. 7).

27. Cit. J. Quicherat, *Histoire du costume en France depuis les temps les plus reculés jusqu'à la fin du XVIIIe siècle* (Hachette: Paris, 1875), p. 623, and Pellegrin, *Vêtements*, p. 93.

28. As observed by John Moore on 17 August 1792 (*A Journal during a Residence in France, from the Beginning of August to the Middle of December, 1792*, 2 vols (London,

1794), vol. 1, pp. 116–17); see also the gouache by Lesueur, *Mlle Méricourt* (Musée Carnavalet, Paris, D.9061).

29. Letter to Claude Ferdinand Faivre 12 July 1791, cit. Pierre de Vaissière, *Lettres d' "Aristocrates". La Révolution racontée par des correspondances privées 1789–1794* (Paris, 1907), p. 297.

30. *Arch Parl*, vol. 21, 5 December 1790, p. 238.

31. *Actes Comm*, 2nd series, vol. 1, pp. 621–2.

32. *Arch Parl*, vol. 18, p. 589 (5 September 1790); see also *ibid.*, vol. 21, p. 64 (23 December 1790).

33. *Arch Parl*, vol. 22, p. 274, 15 January 1791.

34. Maurice Genty, *L'Apprentissage de la citoyenneté: Paris 1789–1795* (Messidor/Éditions sociales: Paris, 1987), p. 28; C.L. Chassin and L. Hennet, *Les Volontaires nationaux pendant la Révolution*, 3 vols (Paris, 1899–1906), vol. 1, pp. 138, 144–5.

35. *Actes Comm*, Ist series, vol. 4, p. 252, 1 March 1790.

36. *Arch Parl*, vol. 44, p. 454, 1 May 1792; and ibid., p. 551 (4 June 1792, Berthelot, *orateur* for section de l'Observatoire).

37. See *Adresse présentée par les clercs de notaires de Paris* (n.d. [1789?]). *Représentations de la livrée de Paris à Monseigneur le Maire de ladite ville* (n.d.[1789]), argued that their service shouldn't exclude them from the Guard.

38. Genty, *Apprentissage*, p. 183.

39. *A Messieurs de la garde nationale parisienne, sur le prix qu'ils doivent attacher à leur uniforme* (n.d.), p. 8.

40. See Amaury Duval's sarcastic remarks on portraits in his review of the 1795 Salon: 'But you see the deputy with his tricolour plume, the National Guard with his gleaming epaulettes etc., etc., O vanity!' (*Décade philosophique*, 30 vend. an IV/21 October 95, no. 7, p. 145, cit. Tony Halliday, *Facing the Public. Portraiture in the aftermath of the French Revolution* (Manchester University Press: Manchester, 2000), p. 49).

41. 24 August 1789, cit. Maurice Genty, 'Controverses autour de la garde nationale parisienne', *AHRF*, January–March 1993, p. 74.

42. *Le Lutteur clairvoyant* (n.d.), pp. 11–13.

43. Louis-Sébastien Mercier, *Le Nouveau Paris*, ed. Jean-Claude Bonnet (ed.) (Mercure de France: Paris, 1994), pp. 123–4.

44. *Actes Comm*, vol. 1, p. 245, 16 August 1790.

45. David Andress, *Massacre at the Champs de Mars. Popular Ddissent and Political Culture in the French Revolution* (Royal Historical Society and Boydell Press: Woodbridge, 2000), p. 61. See *Le Babillard du Palais Royal*, no. 67, 19 August 1791, pp. 213–14 on the recruitment of 'brigands' disguised as guards.

46. *Le Réviseur universel et impartial et bulletin de Madame de Beaumont*, no. 44, 11 April 1792, p. 1.

47. *Arch Parl*, vol. 44, p. 454, 1 May 1792.

48. *Comité militaire de l'hôtel de ville de Paris, séant au palais Cardinal. Règlement concernant les abus introduits dans l'usage des habits d'uniforme, et dans la faculté de se faire remplacer* (14 April 1790), p. 1.

49. See *Actes Comm*, vol. 1, pp. 461, 468 (he received a royal pardon on 8 January 1790); see also *Arch Parl*, 1st series, vol. 1, pp. 538, 543.

50. *Actes Comm*, 2nd series, vol. 2, p. 723, 24 February 1791; anyone who contravened this was to be arrested, consistent with article 2, titre 7 of the 'règlement militaire' of

12 September 1789. See also *Commune de Paris. 14 mars 1793*, on a similar proscription on the resale of uniforms and equipment, partly in response to a denunciation from the Section de la Bonne Nouvelle of volunteers (Tourneux, vol. 2, no. 6309).

51. *Cahiers d'un volontaire de 1791* (n.d.), cit. Pellegrin, *Vêtements*, pp. 181–2.

52. *Le Babillard du Palais Royal*, no. 70, 22 August 1791, p. 237.

53. John A. Lynn, *The Bayonets of the Republic. Motivation and Tactics in the Army of Revolutionary France, 1791–1794* (University of Illinois Press: Urbana and Chicago, 1984), p. 83.

54. *Ibid.*, p. 158. On the reform of 'boutons d'uniforme fleurdelisés', Tuetey, vol. 9, no. 1430.

55. See Tuetey, vol. 7, no. 1187, p. 201, 15 August 1792.

56. Tuetey, vol. 8, p. 343, no. 2251.

57. Albert Soboul, *Les Soldats de l'an II* (Club français du livre: Paris, 1959), p. 153. That the provision of clothing for the army became a collective responsibility was consistent with the assertion of the 1793 constitution that: 'La force générale de la République est composée du peuple entier' (art. 107).

58. Jean-Paul Bertrand, *La Révolution armée. Les soldats-citoyens et la Révolution française* (Laffont: Paris, 1979), pp. 239, 243. The rudimentary elements which often passed for a uniform, and the administrative disorder of the autumn of 1793, meant that groups of bogus soldiers had a field day; see Richard Cobb, *The People's Armies. The armées révolutionnaires, instrument of the Terror in the departments April 1793 to Floréal Year II* (Yale University Press: New Haven and London, 1987), pp. 202–5.

59. *Adresse de la section du Marais à la Convention nationale* (n.d.), p. 2 (extract from the *registre* of the *assemblée générale* of the Marais section, 15 February 1792). On *dons patriotiques* toward the war effort between January and March 1793, see Tuetey, vol. 8, nos 1414–62, pp. 203–10.

60. Caron, vol. 1, p. 149, 20 September 1793.

61. Archives du Gers, Xw34, September 1793, cit. Bertrand, *La Révolution armée*, p. 239.

62. See Howard G. Brown, *War, Revolution, and the Bureaucratic State. Politics and Army Administration in France 1791–1795* (Clarendon: Oxford, 1995), pp. 157–8; and pp. 105–7, 122. Carla Hesse notes that during the Terror bad shoe manufacture could be deemed treasonous ('The Law of the Terror', *MLN*, vol. 14, no. 4, September 1999, p. 717).

63. Daniel Roche, *La Culture des apparences* (Fayard: Paris, 1989), pp. 242–4.

64. Marcel Baldet, *La Vie quotidienne dans les armées de Napoléon* (Hachette: Paris, 1964), p. 40. On the contemporary English culture of uniform, see Scott Hughes Myerly, *British Military Spectacle: From the Napoleonic Wars Through the Crimea* (Harvard University Press: Cambridge MA, London, 1996).

65. The following account is largely based on Hans-Jürgen Lüsebrink and Rolf Reichardt, *The Bastille. A History of a Symbol of Despotism and Freedom* (Duke University Press: Durham and London, 1997), pp. 86–95.

66. Jacques Godechot, *14 juillet 1789. La Prise de la Bastille* (Gallimard: Paris, 1965), pp. 323–4. The *insigne* is illustrated in *La Révolution française et l'Europe 1789–1799*, 3 vols (Council of Europe: Grand Palais, Paris, 1989), vol. 2, p. 400.

67. *Décret de la Convention nationale 20 Août 1793, an II* (BHVP 10530). Under the Empire, they tried to get the *légion d'honneur* (24 July 1804). André Souyris-Rolland, 'Les vainqueurs de la Bastille et leurs décorations', *Revue de la société des amis du Musée de*

l'Armée, vol. 88, 1983, pp. 68, 73 (59–80). See also Joseph Durieux, *Les Vainqueurs de la Bastille* (Paris, 1911).

68. See *Actes Comm*, 1st series, vol. 1, pp. 100, 121–2, 287–8, 5, 7 and 20 August 1789. This distinction was actively policed. Mary, who had been given a 'ruban particulier' by the mayor of Paris, was told to remove it by the commander of National Guard; it was decided that it would be acceptable as long as it did not use the same colours and design as the badge of the French guards (*Actes Comm*, vol. 1, p. 545, 11 September 1789).

69. *Actes Comm*, vol. 6, pp. 232–3.

70. Lüsebrink and Reichardt, *Bastille*, p. 95.

71. *Actes Comm*, 1st series, vol. 2, pp. 227, 258–9, 657, 661. This medal is illustrated in Michel Hennin, *Histoire numismatique de la Révolution française*, 2 vols (Paris, 1826), vol. 1, no. 64, pp. 52–5. Compare the comment in *Dictionnaire national et anecdotique* (1790): 'le civisme parmi les français ne connoît point de sexe' (p. 125).

72. *Actes Comm*, vol. 6, pp. 429–30, 7 July 1790; p. 683, 9 August 1790; p. 705, 14 August 1790; As Michel Hennin noted, only the ribbon was actually awarded; the medal seems to have been added to it by its recipients (*Histoire numismatique*, no. 60, plate 8, pp. 46–8).

73. *Dix ans de médailles, insignes et récompenses révolutionnaires. Souvenirs historiques, 1789–1799* (Musée de Charleville-Mézières, 1989), p. 42.

74. *Procès-verbaux de l'Assemblée Nationale*, vol. 24, pp. 10–12. On attacks on signs of feudal authority, see Markoff, *Abolition of Feudalism*.

75. 'Sur les décorations', *Chronique de Paris*, 25 October 1791, no. 298, pp. 1199–200.

76. *Arch Parl*, vol. 48, p. 625, 22 August 1792.

77. Jean-Marc Devocelle, 'Costume politique et politique du costume', p. 19. On the handing in of 'décorations royalistes', see Tuetey, vol. 10, nos. 284, 287–8, 314, and *RAM*, vol. 18, 15 frim. an II/5 December 1793, no. 75, p. 578. The autumn of 1793 was to see objections in the Paris Commune to the still visible coats of arms and other signs of livery on horses' harnesses (*RAM*, 27 September 1793, no. 270, p. 754). See also *Affiche de la Commune de Paris*, 28 June 1794, no. 13, in *Affiches de la Commune de Paris 1793–94* (Éditions d'Histoire Sociale: Paris, 1975).

78. *Révolutions de Paris*, 20–27 October 1792, pp. 214–18.

79. Ibid., pp. 214–18. The example of the victorious Anselme at Nice was cited; he responded to someone's call that he should be awarded a 'bâton de maréchal de France' by saying that he had no need for the 'hochets de l'ancien régime'.

80. Awarded to Bretèche on 5 May 1793 (Robert-Jean Charles, 'Armes de récompense et armes d'honneur', *Revue de la société des amis du Musée de l'Armée*, no. 60, 1957–1958, pp. 16–18).

81. See law of 1 vent., adopted 4 vend. an VIII (*RAM*, vol. 29, no. 13, pp. 832–3, 13 vend. an VIII/5 October 1799). Names were to be publicly pronounced and inscribed on departmental marble columns; there was no personalized decoration. They were replaced by the *légion d'honneur* from 26 mess. an XII, the anniversary of 14 July. A total of 2,104 sabres were awarded (Charles, 'Armes de récompense', pp. 16–18). See A. Souyris-Rolland, *Histoire des distinctions et des récompenses nationales*, 2 vols (PREAL: Paris, 1986–87). It is interesting to note that, although the *légion d'honneur* was created in May 1802, it was not until July 1804 that their badges were instituted (Colombe Samoyault-Verlet and Jean-Pierre Samoyault, *Château de Fontainebleau. Musée Napoléon Ier. Napoléon et la famille*

impériale 1804–1815 (Editions de la Rénion des Musées Nationaux: Paris, 1986), pp. 12–13).

82. *Actes Comm*, 1st series, vol. 6, pp. 23–4, 11 June 1790.

83. Boedels, 'Costume des gens de justice pendant la Révolution', p. 341.

84. See the submission to the comité de constitution, dated 5 August 1790 (mistakenly printed as 1789), cit. Jacques Boedels, 'Costume des gens de justice', p. 335, and *Les Habits du pouvoir. La Justice* (Antébi: Paris, 1992), p. 123.

85. See J.F. Fournel, *Histoire du Barreau de Paris dans le cours de la Révolution* (1816), pp. 173–5, cit. Pellegrin, *Vêtements*, pp. 155–6.

86. Art. II of tit. 13 of general decree on organization of 'l'ordre judiciaire', sanctioned 11 September 1790; see Boedels, 'Costume des gens de justice', p. 338.

87. Ibid.

88. 6–27 March 1791, Boedels, 'Costume des gens de justice', pp. 338–9.

89. Ibid., p. 339. These reforms lasted until Empire (*ibid.*, p. 344).

90. *RAM*, vol. 13, p. 712, 17 September 1792. See also the *Code pénal*, 2 vols (Paris, 1810), vol. 1, p. 63.

91. 'On a vu avec plaisir les juges du 2e arrondissement déposer leur costume monarchique et substituer le bonnet de la liberté, au chapeau de Henri IV' (Caron, vol. 6, p. 34, 2 germ. II/22 March 1794). On revolutionary legal costume, see Boedels, 'Costume des gens de justice', pp. 325–44.

92. Caron, vol. 4, pp. 64–5, 24 pluv. an II/12 February 1794; and p. 129, 27 pluv. an II/15 February 1794.

93. Devocelle, 'Costume politique et politique du costume', pp. 53–4. On the reorganization of the *appareil judiciaire* see the decree of 12 niv. an VIII/2 January 1800.

94. *Arch Parl*, 20 June 1791, vol. 27, p. 344.

95. Interestingly, they were deemed not to be part of 'charges publiques' or 'dépenses communes' (*Arch Parl*, 1st series, vol. 15, p. 509, 14 May 1790).

96. David Garrioch, *The Formation of the Parisian Bourgeoisie, 1690–1830* (Harvard University Press: Cambridge MA and London, 1996), p. 177. On the fast turn over of political personnel, see Lynn Hunt, *Politics, Culture, and Class in the French Revolution* (University of California Press: Berkeley, Los Angeles, London, 1984), p. 170.

97. On 14 September 1792, it was used as a 'disguise' to facilitate theft; on this occasion the perpetrator was the victim of summary, fatal, justice; see *Révolutions de Paris*, 8–15 September, no. 166, p. 496.

98. *Proclamation du Roi, et Recueil de pièces relatives à l'arrêté du conseil de département, du 6 Juin 1792, concernant le Maire de département et le Procureur de la Commune de Paris* (Paris, 1792), pp. 5, 53.

99. *Procès-verbal dressé sur les événemens du 20 Juin 1792, par M. Sergent, Administrateur du département de la police* (1792), pp. 8–9.

100. *Déclaration de M. J.J. Leroux, sur les événemens du 20 juin 1792*, p. 5.

101. Pierrette Jean-Richard and Gilbert Mondin, *Un Collectionneur pendant la Révolution: Jean-Louis Soulavie (1752–1813)* (Éditions de la Réunion des Musées Nationaux: Musée du Louvre, Paris, 1989), p. 51, no. 47, drawing for *Révolutions de Paris*, no. 159, 21–28 July 1792.

102. 'La liberté donnant l'écharpe municipale à Pétion', anon. Bibl. Nat., ill. Michel Vovelle, *La Révolution française. Images et récits*, 5 vols (Livre Club Diderot Messidor: Paris, 1986), vol. 3, p. 30.

103. On 21 September 1789 a costume was proposed but this was never followed up (*Actes Comm*, vol. 2, p. 21).

104. Launay, *Costumes, insignes, cartes, médailles des députés*, p. 14.

105. The Assemblée des électeurs used 745 medals offered by Palloy made from chains from Bastille chains for *huissiers*; the medal was suspended from a 'ruban à la nation', in place of the chains they had (Louis Combes, 'La Bastille et la patriote Palloy', in *Épisodes et Curiosités révolutionnaires* (Paris, n.d.), p. 8). Olivier Blanc notes two royalist agents (Louis-François Poiré and Rose du Rempart) who got jobs as *huissiers*, presumably to be close to the pulse of revolutionary politics (*La Dernière Lettre. Prisons et condamnés de la Révolution 1793–94* (Robert Laffont: Paris, 1984), pp. 214–15.

106. Launay, *Costumes, insignes, cartes, médailles des députés*, p. 23.

107. *RAM*, vol. 13, no. 196, pp. 124–5, 14 July 1792 (*séance* 11 July).

108. Devocelle, 'Costume politique', p. 74.

109. Ibid., p. 76.

110. See H. Lapauze (ed.), *Procès-verbaux de la Commune générale des arts* (Paris, 1903), pp. 270, 308.

111. *Considérations sur les avantages de changer le costume français par la société populaire et républicaine des arts* (n.d.), pp. 1–3.

112. Devocelle, 'Costume et citoyenneté', p. 317.

113. Ibid., p. 320.

114. Madeleine Delpierre, 'A propos d'un manteau . . .', *Bulletin du Musée Carnavalet*, no. 1, 1972, p. 21.

115. On the precedent of Fénelon's account of the expression of a hierarchy of status in Greek dress, see *Les Aventures de Télémaque, fils d'Ulysse (1699); Telemachus, son of Ulysses*, ed. and trans. Patrick Riley (Cambridge University Press: Press, 1994).

116. *Comment m'habillerai-je?*, pp. 6–8.

117. *RAM*, vol. 24, no. 246, 6 prairial an III/25 May 1795, p. 515 (séance 1 prairial). Use of *cartes d'identité* outside the Convention was approved on 2 December 1794; the *carte d'identité* was needed to leave Paris (1 May 1795; Launay, p. 28). On the fact that some deputies adopted the use of hats with mottoes on as worn by the insurgents, see Chapter 6.

118. L'Abbé Grégoire, *Rapport et projet de décret présentés au nom du comité d'instruction publique sur les costumes des législateurs et des autres fonctionnaires publics, séance du vingt-huit fructidor, l'an trois* [14 September 1795], in Bernard Deloche and Jean-Michel Leniaud (eds), *La Culture des sans-culottes. Le premier dossier du patrimoine 1789–1798* (Editions de Paris, Presses du Languedoc: Paris and Montpellier, 1989), pp. 295–303; see J.M. Devocelle, 'Costume et citoyenneté', pp. 313–32. See also A. Anninger, 'Costumes of the Convention: art as an agent of social change in revolutionary France', *Harvard Library Bulletin*, vol. 30, 1952, pp. 179–203.

119. Jean-François Barailon, *Projet sur le costume particulier à donner à chacun des deux conseils législatifs, et à tous les fonctionnaires publics de la République française, présenté à la Convention nationale, 13 fructidor an III* [30 August 1795].

120. Ibid., p. 6.

121. Ibid., pp. 5–6.

122. Ibid., p. 4.

123. Grégoire, *Rapport et projet de décret,* p. 296.

124. Ibid., p. 295.

125. Ibid., p. 297.

126. Ibid., p. 298.

127. Ibid., p. 299.

128. M.J. Chénier approved of Grégoire's proposals because of their suitability for artistic representation; he criticized prevailing forms of contemporary dress as 'inartistes' (séance 3 brum. an IV/25 October 1795, *Moniteur*, 3 November 1795, p. 165, cit. Launay, *Costumes, insignes, cartes, médailles*, pp. 33–5). See Roche, *Culture des apparences*, pp. 440–6.

129. Launay, op. cit., p. 37.

130. See Delpierre, 'A propos d'un manteau', p. 23, who notes that although 750 people wore them, surviving examples are extremely rare. 131. *RAM*, 21 February 1798/ 3 vent. an VI, p. 614, cit. Launay, p. 77. A largely satirical pamphlet, signed 'Sandalo-Philos', on representatives' costume argued that it should be pseudo-priestly rather than 'mondain' (*Le Costume des représentants conforme à la religion de nos pères* (n.d.), pp. 2–3. 132. Launay, pp. 105–13, 129.

133. *Actes Comm*, 1st series, vol. 6, pp. 482–3, 12 July 1790.

134. *Révolutions de Paris*, no. 53, 10–17 July 1790, cit. Christian-Marc Bosseno, 'Acteurs et spectateurs des fêtes officielles parisennes', in Valérie Noëlle Jouffre (ed.), *Fêtes et Révolution* (Délégation à l'action artistique de la ville de Paris: Paris, 1989), p. 116.

135. See Mona Ozouf's classic comparison of this festival with that of Châteauvieux, *La Fête révolutionnaire 1789–1799* (Gallimard: Paris, 1976), pp. 102–35.

136. *Révolutions de Paris*, cit. Ozouf, *Fête révolutionnaire*, p. 116.

137. *Rapport et décret sur la fête de la réunion républicaine du 10 août* [1793], p. 1. This festival also figured the centrality of work in having tools on the *autel de la patrie*.

138. Marie-Louise Biver, *Le Panthéon à l'époque révolutionnaire* (PUF: Paris, 1982), pp. 81–2.

139. Law of 7 prairial an II/26 May 1794, *Bulletin des lois*, an II, no. 2, p. 4.

140. *Procès-verbaux du Comité d'Instruction publique*, M. Guillaume (ed.), 7 vols (Paris, 1891–1957), vol. 5, pp. 422–3, séance 25 niv. an III/14 January 1795.

141. Tuetey, vol. 10, pp. 533–4, no. 2329, declaration of Louis Legendre (26 vent. an II/16 March 1794).

142. A parallel to this transition was the increased emphasis put on sporting events in festivals. Moreover, these generated a new form of apolitical badge. See the medal awarded for the 'prix de course de barres' at the Festival of the Sovereignty of the People, 30 ventôse an VI (20 March 1798), Musée de la Révolution française, Vizille, MRF 87.33, ill. in Jouffre, *Fêtes et Révolutions*, cat. no. 76, p. 133.

143. Caron, vol. 2, p. 279, 21 niv. an II/10 January 1794.

144. Caron, vol. 3, pp. 393, 400, 20 pluv. an II/8 February 1794.

145. Caron, vol. 4, p. 13, 22 pluv. an II/9 February 1794.

146. Caron, vol. 6, p. 104, 5 germ. an II/25 March 1794. The 'plumets', 'écharpe' and 'ceinture de couleur blanche' that had been the sign of veterans was reduced to 'un plumet aux trois couleurs' (*RAM*, vol. 18, p. 441, 28 brum. an II/18 November 1793). See also *RAM*, vol. 18, no. 75, 5 December 1793, p. 583 (séance 14 frim. an II).

147. Caron, vol. 2, p. 390, 27 niv. an II/16 January 1794.

148. Caron, vol. 3, pp. 147–8, 6 pluv. an II/25 January 1794.

149. See Turckheim-Pey, 'Les insignes révolutionnaires de la collection Côte', p. 139. She lists collectors of such badges, from Michel Hennin's *Histoire numismatique de la Révolution française* (Paris, 1826) onward.

3

Cockades: Badge Culture and its Discontents

FROM THE moment of its invention as a patriotic badge in the summer of 1789, the cockade was to remain a continual presence throughout the revolutionary decade and beyond. Tracing its history is therefore tantamount to traversing in microcosm the larger history of the Revolution. In particular, it is intimately involved in two of the defining moments in the dramatic unfolding of the revolutionary narrative: the events leading up to the taking of the Bastille, and the march to Versailles on 5 October, leading to the relocation of the royal family to Paris. The cockade's dissemination elides its original military role with forms of civilian action, identity, and authority, while at the same time continuing to function as a form of symbolic decoration, albeit adapted to express meanings that went deeper than mere varieties of fashionableness.

Throughout the cockade's history, we will see how crucial were matters of the minutiae of dress and their searching scrutiny. Such signs were extraordinarily potent – not merely as cues to the expression of antipathy or enthusiastic identification, but frequently also to violence at once personal and collective. At the heart of these reactions is the question of legibility – its complexities, uncertainties, and urgent necessity. We will see that reactions to the cockade are inseparable from perceptions of how it was worn, that is, particularly in terms of degrees of prominence or concealment, but also more subtly in the way its style of display could be treated as a manifestation of diverse beliefs and allegiances. To this extent, attitudes to the cockade are informed by the assumption that it was possible to treat people's dress, and its nuanced variety, as a deliberate index, not only of their social identity, but also of their political orientation. The close attention paid to the cockade exemplifies the kinds of scrutiny and interpretation applied to vestimentary appearances in general.

Strictly speaking, the cockade is an accessory, a decorative embellishment to hats, lapels, jackets and scarves. Although small in size, its profound political purpose ensured that it would command particular attention. It deserves separate treatment here because of its remarkable status as an enduring item of emblematic dress. Moreover, as the patriotic symbol par excellence, it was the object of a series of legislative attempts to define its identity and currency. The discussions of the need for, and effectiveness of, such legislation allow us to explore the complex of attitudes surrounding the politics of emblematic dress. By virtue of this longevity and widespread proliferation, its history illustrates certain central aspects of the contested negotiation of revolutionary emblems as they were assimilated into dress. This contestation is central to any understanding of the kinds of status and role ascribed to dress during the Revolution.

The story of the cockade begins with a clearly defined moment of invention. This centres on Camille Desmoulins' act of inspired, spontaneous exhortation in the Palais Royal, as he addressed in the Palais Royal a crowd exercised by the king's dismissal of Necker, and fearful of military intervention in reaction to incipient popular protest. Desmoulins' own account links the choice of a green cockade to the duc d'Orléans, but also to its emblematic association with hope.[1] In its account of the people looking for arms on 13 July, the *Révolutions de Paris* described the adoption of green cockades as a sign of solidarity and popular mobilization: 'in putting a cockade on his hat, each individual declared themselves a soldier for the *patrie*'.[2] However, not all early accounts cite Desmoulins; the *Révolutions de Paris* mentions neither Desmoulins nor the spontaneous invention of the cockade in the Palais Royal.[3] Desmoulins later made the episode a key element in the proclamation of his patriotic credentials, asserting in December 1793 that he had been the first to adopt the cockade, 'which you can't put on your hat without remembering me'.[4]

In contemporary texts, rather than Desoulins' auto-mythologizing, a recurrent theme is the way this episode is premised on the authority of popular choice. The dynamic instability of the situation is manifest in the decision to change from green to blue and red, as it became a codified part of the bourgeois militia's uniform. This choice was expressed in what was to be a fundamental style of triumphant repudiation – trampling underfoot, in this case, of the offending superseded green cockade,[5] in a way which dovetails an iconographical tradition familiar above all from monuments.[6] A further dimension to the cockade's enduring properties was the way it served as a catalyst for extremes of emotion. After hearing him out in silence, Desmoulin's audience was duly 'electrified by his courage', and suddenly let out 'violent cries'.[7]

The cockade moved from sign of popular mobilization to prescriptively national symbol when, on 17 July 1789, Louis XVI came from Versailles to Paris, and appeared at the Hôtel de Ville with the tricolore cockade that had been presented to him by Bailly, mayor of Paris.[8] Some accounts make the point that Louis did not wear the cockade, but held it with his hat – by holding it at a distance, he both facilitated the visibility of this action for the crowd, and also treated it as a self-contained emblematic entity.[9] He thus visibly proclaimed – one might say performed – the fact of royal approval to the events of the previous five days. Bailly recalled the sense of trepidation when he prepared to present the cockade to Louis: 'I did not know how the king would react, and if there was something out of place in making this proposition'.[10] According to Mercier's recollection, Bailly's equivocation was acerbically echoed by Marie-Antoinette, who subsequently remarked on finding the king wearing a cockade: 'I did not think that I had married a commoner.'[11] Further evidence of the tensions engendered in the court by the royal adoption of the cockade is the provocative wearing by the duc de Chartres (later d'Orleans) at Versailles of a 'magnifique' *cocarde tricolore*, indulging in what was to become his hallmark patriotic one-upmanship.[12]

Central to the narrating of the cockade's inception is the choice of its colours, and an emblematic gloss on their significance, with a degree of elaboration which predictably increases as it becomes more retrospective. In a letter of 16 July 1789 giving an account of the events of 12–14 July to his father, Desmoulins quotes himself: 'Let us all take up green cockades, the colour of hope'.[13] In the same letter, he goes on to describe the cockades worn by '800,000' people greeting the deputies from the Assembly as they arrived in Paris, which had replaced green with red – 'to show that we were ready to shed our blood', and blue – 'for a heavenly constitution'.[14] When, in 1793, Desmoulins reviewed his revolutionary career, he elaborated further on the 12 July episode. After asking the crowd what colours were to be adopted for the cockades he proposed, he was asked to choose himself. In addition to green, he now has himself ask the crowd if they prefer 'the blue of Cincinnatus, colour of American liberty and democracy?'[15]

But deciding on the meaning of colours opens out on to choices that are at once cultural and political. Louis's adoption of the cockade prompted Ferat to spell out an elaborate litany of its alleged meanings.[16] His explication shifts the cockade's meaning away from the highly charged arena of street politics into the domain of learned commentary. Nonetheless, he attributes to the cockade a dominating power: 'the sole aspect of this Royal Cockade intimidates or makes tremble the most intrepid of our enemies'. By contrast, Chantreau explained the cockade's changing colours as a direct response to political conflict. He claimed green had been abandoned because of its unwanted echo of the uniforms of the prince de Lambesc's troops (who had led a charge on civilians in the Tuileries gardens). Subsequently, 'saffron' (*aurore*), deriving from the colours of the city of Paris, had been temporarily replaced by red. But saffron had been reinstated once red ('colour of fire') had been compromised by its association with the red flag which signalled the declaration of martial law (after July 1791).[17]

Beyond this symbolic commentary, the cockade entered public life on two fronts: as part of the uniform of the National Guard, expressing the prime official manifestation of patriotic empowerment, and through popular dissemination, at times in ritualized form. The cockade played a prominent role as a sign of solidarity with revolutionary sentiments. As in the powerfully symbolic episode of the 17 October 1789, it was habitually employed as a special form of proselytizing patriotic gift. For example, the Paris Commune sent cockades to the mayor and procurator syndic of Rennes, who duly wore some themselves, giving others to be attached to standards of the garrison and distributed to the *milice nationale*.[18] Syonnet celebrated this form of patriotic gift as an exemplary antithesis to old forms of royal, hierarchical decoration: 'I saw a Frenchwoman, palpitating with joy, herself attach the ribbons of liberty to the hat of her lover. He was prouder of his cockade than the most vain aristocrat could be of all the ribbons of kings.' Syonnet invoked the precedent of Henri IV, who had exhorted his troops to follow his 'white plume', in order to celebrate the cockade as a means to express national unification, but such rhetoric was less a witness to a *fait accompli* than a response to its partisan status, as signalled by his identification of the cockade with the Third Estate.[19] This was momentously borne out by the events of 5–6 October 1789, when different types of cockade were catalysts for both disputation and reconciliation.[20]

The march to Versailles was provoked by rumours of the abuse of the *cocarde nationale* by the royal *gardes-du-corps*, and the subsequent adoption of both black and white anti-patriotic cockades by intransigent royalists.

Such calculated alternatives to the *cocarde nationale* had, however, been in evidence in Paris prior to this momentous incident. As the *Moniteur* reported, this was part of a variety of aristocratic provocations, including the allegedly orchestrated prevailing food shortages:

> Not content to work secretly to maintain general desolation, the aristocratic cabal seems still to triumph openly about it. Men of all ranks, all ages, wear the black cockade, and, out of the most insolent bravado, dare to present themselves, with this sign of an enemy faction, at a review of a division of the National Guard, on Sunday 4 October, on the Champs-Elysées.[21]

This led to disputes in which some of these cockades were torn off.[22]

In the events of 5–6 October, the *cocarde nationale* as gift could be not only a catalyst for conflict, signalling the solidarity of opposed viewpoints, but also a token of reconciliation. In his statement to the Assembly, Mettereau, *aide-de-camp* of M. d'Estaing, commander of the National Guard at Versailles, cited a captain of the royal bodyguard as stating that the 'enormous' white cockade he was wearing had been given to him by women in the court.[23] Maillard, the *vainqueur de la Bastille* who spoke for the women at the head of the deputation, received a *cocarde nationale* from the soldiers of the royal bodyguard as a token of their peaceful intentions, eliciting cries of 'Long live the king! Long live the royal bodyguards!'.[24] On 6 October 1789, the Queen and Mme Adélaïde each ordered 150 tricolore cockades from dressmaker Mme Eloffe to give to market women.[25] Later nine women from the market (who had not been on the march) were admitted to a meeting of the Paris Commune, where, having spoken with disapproval of public disorder, they were approvingly given ribbons and cockades.[26]

An article in the *Moniteur* regarding the events of 5–6 October 1789 warned of the harmful effects of a war of badges: 'Cockades of a single colour will be the signal for a civil war if they are allowed to multiply', and recalled the recent case of Holland, where 'the patriot party was lost . . . by a women and a cockade. Therefore, let us put down this insurrection by a terrible example.'[27] Bertier, president of the *comité militaire*, argued that the oath decreed by the Assembly as part of the procedure for joining the National Guard, which included the adoption of the 'cocarde nationale', would be a pretext for such civil war to erupt.[28]

The invention of the patriotic cockade was accompanied by attempts to define it, in terms of both its physical form and its symbolic meanings.

This was more urgently necessary after the traumatic events of 5–6 October, which crystallized the cockade as a matter of highly charged choice.[29] During 1790, as the cockade became more widely diffused, so conflicts over its meaning and authority proliferated, symptomatic of destabilizing divisions beneath the surface of patriotic unity. A royalist commentator reacted angrily to the imposition of cockades on the army; the cockade was nothing more than a 'standard of revolt in the name of liberty'; this 'sign of unity with the rabble has contributed to the defection of several regiments. They were [only] too happy that they might always have a sign which distinguished them from the national troops.'[30] By contrast, adherents of the new cockade argued that it deserved to replace established forms of military badge, such as the *cocarde rouge*, a sign of twenty years' service, for the latter might merely have been acquired through time-serving, whereas the new cockade was acknowledged as 'the distinctive sign of courage, the emblem of the hero'.[31] Gouvion, the major general of the National Guard, recommended to Bailly, mayor of Paris, that an *ordonnance* be published to require the wearing by civilians of either a ribbon in the buttonhole, or a tricolore cockade, in the form decided by the Assemblée des Electeurs on 14/15 July the previous year. Bailly replied that such an *ordonnance* 'would not be without problems', no doubt conscious of the scope this would provide for disputes.[32]

What had been promoted as the indispensable sign of unity was showing worrying signs of turning into a catalyst for dissent. At the end of May 1790, the uncertainties and friction consequent upon the wearing of different types of cockade prompted Louis XVI to issue a proclamation aimed at regularizing the situation.[33] Cockades other than the royally sanctioned patriotic one were forbidden, with the hope that this would remove a pretext for the excitement of conflict, the fomenting of division, and the disturbances that would follow.[34] The 'reform' of the cockade, whereby all other forms of cockade and uniform were in effect outlawed, was reiterated in a royal proclamation of the Assembly's decree (18 June 1790) regarding the inscription of active citizens on the National Guard's register.[35]

In so far as the threat of a royalist backlash remained a constant in the imaginations of patriots, the *cocarde blanche* persisted as a highly threatening symbol; to be accused of wearing such a cockade was one of the most unequivocal forms of denunciation.[36] In March 1790, a particularly notorious instance was the alleged fidelity to *cocardes blanches* at the Société des Amis de la Constitution Monarchique. Those arriving allegedly wore them; a crowd gathered at this provocative news, so as to challenge this 'sign of disorder'.[37] This incident had repercussions in the form of further ripples of conflict. Thus, on 3 April 1791, a man was arrested in the Palais Royal for tearing off suspect cockades with the comment: 'here's another who has a white cockade from the Club monarchique'.[38] However, the white cockade was also noted in popular contexts such as the *ateliers de charité*.[39]

The special attention visited upon the *cocarde blanche* as a sign of provocative unwillingness to embrace change, let alone compromise, should be seen in the context of endemic manifestations of deviant behaviour expressed through alternatives to the *cocarde nationale*. As a national guard argued in April 1791: 'The least things are important in revolutions, and I am astonished that no one remarks upon the *variations* in the colours of the national cockade, a sacred rallying-sign to which patriots should never permit any disfigurement'. The writer – 'S.G. National Guard' – went on to report the subtle variations in colour and design of the cockade he had seen 'with indignation', and concluded that their wearers 'appear suspect to me; and who assures that these modific-ations are not the means of recognition amongst enemies of the public good?'[40] In due course, people were indeed to remark vigilantly on the variations of the cockade.

Reports of people arrested for suspicious or provocative behaviour habitually include detailed notes on variant forms of cockade. A man arrested after a confrontation with workers at the Bastille was recorded as wearing a red cockade on the right side of his hat.[41] Two men who had 'stirred up a rumour' when entering Curtius's wax gallery were noted as wearing cockades of blue and white material, decorated in the middle with a red fleur de lys.[42] Absence of a cockade was accusingly noted when individuals were arrested for unpatriotic behaviour.[43] Similarly, women who wore their cockades beneath their kerchiefs, or partly concealed by the ribbons on their bonnets or hats, were subject to reproach.[44] In so far as there was no normative model, all variety could be construed as potentially subversive. To judge from recorded incidents, if any doubts arose, arrest was more than likely, or at the least a dispute.

The status of the cockade shifted markedly in July 1792, when conditions of war and heightened internal security led to the introduction of the *patrie en danger* legislation. This meant that the military function of the cockade, hitherto identified with the National Guard, was opened to all citizens. It became compulsory for men living or travelling in

France, with the sole exception of ambassadors and 'accredited agents' of foreign powers. All cockades other than those comprising the national colours were deemed 'signs of rebellion'; citizens were ordered to denounce or arrest those who were seen wearing such signs, failing which they would be considered accomplices. The punishment for wearing deviant cockades was death.[45] However, as pointed out by De Lacroix, problems might arise if each municipality made its own arrangements about how to implement this law. The law only stipulated the presence of the national colours. It was therefore clarified that different materials and forms of cockade were acceptable as long as they reproduced these colours.[46] As is the case with all legislation on the cockade until 1798, this was an attempt to stabilize and control a situation which was continually threatening to produce disorder and conflict. It is striking that here as elsewhere in legislation regarding the cockade, no norm for the combination of the *couleurs nationales* was stipulated.

In practice, the two components of these laws were found to be in conflict. The variety of cockades continued to provide grounds for suspicion. Thus, on 30 July an artillery officer arrested someone for wearing 'a very voluminous silk cockade whose colours seemed to be faded'.[47] In the summer of 1792, Stephen Weston observed Marseillais forcing all they met to remove their silk cockades, and commented that such incidents were likely to persist because different forms of cockade had been made up following the Assembly's formal consent to possible variety.[48] More programmatic evidence of deliberately factional cockades was found in the aftermath of the invasion of the Tuileries Palace on 10 August 1792. Citizens of the section Mauconseil claimed to have found a 'rallying sign' in the form of a tricolore cockade embellished with an L and a fleur de lys on the corpse of a Swiss soldier.[49]

Demands for further legislation to cope with the employment of different forms of cockade continued during the spring of the following year. In March, the Paris Commune declared that those found without cockades should be brought before the municipality.[50] In April, authorization was given to arrest soldiers, returned from Dumouriez's disgraced army, who were reported as having torn off cockades. In the preceding discussion, Sergent observed that, more generally, many people dispensed with the cockade, and that, although the sentinel on the Pont-Neuf forced them to buy them, this was hardly a sufficient solution.[51]

In the same month a deputation from the Section de l'Arsenal put a series of proposals to the Convention (8 April 1793) in order to regularize how to wear the cockade, and by extension to clarify recognition of deviance. Furthermore, they recommended the introduction of a penalty for contravention of such a law:

> 1. That the tricolore cockade be uniform for all without distinction, in size, the proportion of the colours, and the material; 2. That all other signs be prohibited; 3. That the position on hats be specified, and there be a penalty awarded against all who contravene these regulations.[52]

The call for official legislation by activists such as those from the Arsenal was prompted by continued uncertainty over how to deal with people who deliberately adopted subversive styles of wearing the cockade, as when it was partly covered by hat bands – termed 'cocardes à l'éclipse'.[53] The corollary to this was that it was also possible to signal identification with the equally provocative positive stereotype of the *sans-culotte* by choosing what form of cockade to wear. Thus, a moderate was defined as someone who eschewed the distinctive features of *sans-culotte* identity (French fabric, the label itself, and *coiffure* of *sans-culottes*), and who 'out of ill-will does not wear a cockade of three inches in circumference'.[54]

September of 1793 witnessed an intensive period of confusing crisis in attitudes to who should wear the cockade, and also how it should be worn, manifest in the fact that similar motives produced contradictory actions. The focus was whether women should be wearing it.[55] Women of the *halles* refused to wear it, fearing that such a policy was a ruse of counter-revolutionaries. They reportedly backed up this refusal by the laudable wish to receive official guidance from the Convention. This uncertainty was further expressed in terms of disputes over where the cockade should be worn. Squabbles were reported provoked by the belief that certain positions were a form of subversive code, or simply offensive to true patriots – as when cockades were worn on the bosom, or, as one journalist sarcastically suggested, on the bottom, which would be to confuse 'liberté' with 'libertinage', and true patriotism with parody.[56] When this was coupled with reports of *agents provocateurs* fomenting trouble, the result was confusion and conflict. An instance in which the wearing of cockades in different places sparked a disturbance was noted on 19 September:

> Men, probably paid to incite trouble in Paris, walking yesterday in the rue St-Denis and surrounding streets, spanked several women, some because they had no cockade, others because they wore it over their breast; they claimed that this was a rallying sign.[57]

Police agents concluded that: 'The cockade is the veil beneath which troublemakers today conceal their perfidious projects.'[58] The cockade was in little an instance of the fears of dissembling beneath a 'mask' of patriotism. In September 1793, cockades partly concealed by black crepe were enough to cause suspicion.[59]

As Soboul noted, we should see the resulting legislation (13 and 21 September) as corresponding to the Convention's response to a combination of popular pressure and public disturbance.[60] This legislation specified that, first, women must wear it when in public places. Failure to do so carried a sentence of eight days' imprisonment. Secondly, those who insulted or profaned it, or tried to remove it from others, would be imprisoned for six years (21 September).[61] As a way of encouraging observance of the new legislation, bodies such as the Versailles municipality publicly handed out cockades to women in *sociétés fraternelles*, accompanying this act with an explanation of the emblem's inspiring powers. Consistent with this is the 'religious respect' with which the women are described as accepting these gifts.[62]

Discussions around the proper policy regarding the wearing of the cockade had centred on whether women should wear them, an issue complicated by doubt and confusion over the true motives of those who encouraged such a policy, and also of the women who supported it. The same issues were at the heart of the decree protecting freedom of dress (8 brumaire an II, 29 October 1793), although this was, in fact, prompted by similar conflicts over the wearing of the *bonnet rouge*.[63] This legislation was again prompted by a call from outside the Convention. A deputation of women called for freedom of dress as a solution to the trouble that had been caused by women who had adopted the *bonnet* trying to force them to wear it.

Fabre d'Eglantine's speech in favour of the proposal linked a patronizing construction of female character with its potential exploitation by subversives. Women, he claimed, were vulnerable because of a weakness for 'their adornment'; by this pretext they would eventually be given arms, which situation would be exploited by 'bad subjects' who would know all too well how to make good use of them. Female revolutionaries would, he warned, be formed of:

> types of adventurers, female knight errants, emancipated prostitutes, female grenadiers (applause). I ask for two things as a matter of the greatest urgency, because women in *bonnets rouges* are in the street:

Article I.   No-one, of either sex, can force any citizen (citoyen ou citoyenne) to dress in a particular manner, all being free to wear whatever dress or adornment they see fit, under pain of being considered and treated as suspect, and pursued as a disturber of public peace.

Article II. The National Convention does not intend to derogate preceding decrees regarding the national cockade, on priests' costume, and on disguise, nor any other decrees relating to these same subjects.[64]

Thus, the decree sought to undercut subversive manipulation of dress by making this, in theory at least, a legitimate matter of personal choice.[65]

In tandem with these national decrees, local legislation sometimes sought to resolve ongoing uncertainties over proper conduct regarding the cockade by imposing specific restrictions. Thus, on 3 brumaire an II (24 October 1793) representatives of the people in Brest sought to eradicate inconsistencies in the form of cockades, whether innocent or calculated, and their potential for generating trouble, by forbidding cockades of silk or ribbon, or in material whose colours were likely to fade quickly, presenting at a distance 'the scandalous appearance of the white cockade'; cockades which were, or had become, 'disfigured' could be a 'sign of recognition which, in moments of trouble, would serve to rally ill-willed people'.[66] Yet white cockades in unadulterated form evidently went on being worn in 1793, presumably in some concealed manner (Figure 10).[67] In Paris, the wearing of cockades with an expanded white component led to arrests.[68]

After the wearing of cockades had been made compulsory, concerns continued to arise as to the potentially subversive meaning of different styles of doing so. In December 1793, a police agent reported that women were to be seen wearing cockades with plumes on their bonnets, making of it 'an object of coquettery'. He observed a 'brave sans-culotte' removing them with his pike, remonstrating with their wearers that the cockade was a symbol of liberty and equality, and not 'a luxury item'.[69] Other women who received similar criticism challenged this equation of embellishment with 'aristocratic' disrespect, pointing out to their assailant that decoration could be faultlessly republican, as when crowns had been placed on Marat's head.[70]

The September legislation was criticized for failing to stipulate where the cockade should be worn. While there was official encouragement for women to conform to the new law, this had failed to include

Figure 10 White Cockade, 1793. Archives Nationales, Paris, AE V 347. Photograph: Centre Historique des Archives Nationales, Atelier de Photographie.

any specific advice on how and where to wear them.[71] Police agents reported that: 'People want to place it on the right, on the left, on the front, behind, and this frivolous question, which is not yet decided on, has already caused violent brawls'.[72] That some wore it beneath kerchiefs, or tucked beneath ribbons of bonnets and hats, led to disputes: 'Would it not be best for the municipality to oblige people to wear them on their heads by means of a decree?'.[73] Underlying worries over the scope for coded communication between counter-revolutionaries was the objection that this manipulation of the cockade was inherently disrespectful to the national colours; not surprisingly, the National Guard called for them to be worn in a clearly visible manner 'in the place where people could most easily see each other's [cockades]'.[74] A mirror image of the cult of the cockade as universal microcosm of the revered national colours are the remarks recorded in 1792 by a police agent of a man whom he noted as wearing a suspiciously particular form of cockade. His culpability was confirmed in overheard remarks which mocked the naive patriotic cult of this invitingly manipulable emblem: 'Those buggers won't know what to make of it, for them it's just red white and blue'.[75]

These uncertainties remained in play, even after the introduction of more draconian legislation in the spring of 1794. As Jean-Marc Devocelle points out, following the decree of 27 germinal an II (16 April 1794) produced in the wake of Saint-Just's report on the policing of factional crime, which required all suspected of conspiracy to be brought before the Tribunal révolutionnaire, a further decree (14 floréal an II, 3 May 1794) specified that anyone found without a cockade would be treated as a counter-revolutionary, and judged according to the terms of the earlier decree.[76]

COST AND FABRICATION

Ubiquitous use, however contested, highlighted practical problems related to the fabrication and provision of cockades. In the context of discussions of *patrie en danger* legislation, Broussonnet noted that in the countryside many couldn't afford to buy a cockade; one consequence of this was that people made their own. This resulted in variations which were as disturbing as they were irregular, such that, in September 1793, 'revolutionary cavalry' decided it was advisable to ban them.[77] In order to avoid such trouble caused by the variety resulting from do-it-yourself types of cockade, it was urged that money be provided to subsidize this necessary form of patriotic expression.[78] During 1793, we find complaints about the cost of cockades.[79] In Amiens, the price of cockades was included in the *maximum*.[80] An extra allowance for cockades was given to *remplaçants militaires* under the Republic.[81] Following an incident when some national guards had broken ranks and torn off silk cockades from bystanders, Vivier called for all French people, including foreigners residing in France, to have to wear the popular woollen type of cockade.[82]

There was no control over the fabrication of cockades. Cockades could be made by dressmakers (as we saw with Madame Eloffe at the time of 5/6 October 1789), but of course did not require the elaborate resources at the disposal of an upmarket *couturière*. Those who sold cockades were in a position to denounce plans to distribute 'suspect cockades', as in the case of a second-hand clothes seller and distributor of cockades (made by Maret), who reported that she had been asked to supply four thousand of them by a man wearing ecclesiastical dress.[83] In recognition of this potential outlet for subversive badges, on 17 September 1792 the Legislative Assembly decreed the death penalty for any supplier or *fournisseur* who sold any form of cockade other than the national one.[84] Such legislation could not cope with the problem of the surviving stockpile of white cockades in military magazines which had been made in earlier times for troops of the line.[85] Individual form inevitably varied according to the maker, to the extent of having mottoes such as 'Freedom to nations enchained by kings, eternal war on crowned despots (Liberté aux nations par les rois enchaînés, guerre éternelle aux despotes couronnés)' worked into their design.[86]

ABUSE

The cockade could be a focus for counter-revolutionary nonconformity more explicit and violent than mere nuances of form and colour. Of those incidents which have been recorded, it seems to have been common to insult the cockade by associating it with animals' bottoms. In Amiens in 1790, an officer of the dragon-Dauphin put a cockade on the rump of a donkey. He was punished in a way which mirrored his offence: 'the long-eared animal, dressed in his degraded master's uniform carried him by all the town's crossroads on a market day'.[87] Similarly, a man who tied a cockade to his dog's tail was condemned by the National Gurard to kiss the dog's bottom three times (Figure 11). This custom remained active in 1800, when a cockade was attached to the tail of a pig, designated as 'citoyen', and driven through streets of a 'counter-revolutionary' town.[88] In the aftermath of the royal family's flight to Varennes in June 1791, a man was arrested for making the gesture of wiping his bottom with a cockade, saying 'he shit on the cockade.'[89] As well as these forms of humiliation, the cockade could itself be subject to violence. During the aftermath of the invasion of the Tuileries on 20 June 1792, the queen and others were alleged to have slapped cockades as a form of anti-patriotic catharsis.[90] Abuse of the cockade was an habitual form of symbolic repudiation of the Revolution.[91] Conversely, in some cases, deviant cockades were burnt.[92]

Exécution de la Sentence Nationale rendue par la Garde Bourgeoise de Sivrai en réparation de l'injure faite à toute la France et au Roi, par le C.... de ... qui avoit attaché la Cocarde Nationale à la queue de son chien dont il fut condamné de baiser trois fois le derriere.

Figure 11 Anonymous: 'Exécution de la Sentence Nationale rendue par la Garde Bourgeoise de Sivrai en réparation de l'injure faite à toute la France et au Roi, par le C . . . de . . . qui avoit attaché la Cocarde Nationale à la queue de son chien dont il fut condamné de baiser trois fois la derrière' (Execution of the National Sentence carried out by the Bourgeois Guard of Sivrai in reparation of the injury to all France and the King, by C . . . de . . , who had attached the National Cockade to his dog's tail whose bottom he was condemned to kiss three times) 1791?, etching. Département des Arts Graphiques, Bibliothèque Nationale de France, Paris. Photograph: Bibliothèque Nationale de France.

THRESHOLDS

Scrutiny of the wearing of the cockade occurred most consistently at the entrances to public spaces and institutions. The Tuileries gardens were a recurrent site for this. Its location immediately adjacent to the residence of the royal family, after October 1789, and the National Assembly meant that this space was especially sensitized to matters of patriotic decorum. While the royal family inhabited the palace, maintaining correct patriotic appearances was a form of confrontational challenge to the residual courtly life within. In November 1789, visitors to the Tuileries gardens were only admitted if wearing a cockade.[93] On 24 May 1790, a man, described as an 'aristocrat', and his wife narrowly escaped being lynched after they had been challenged by a sentinel, and had thrown down the cockade he made them take, protesting: 'I don't give a fuck about the cockade and those who wear it'.[94] During 1791, sentinels at the Tuileries gardens habitually arrested those who responded to their enquiries about irregular or missing cockades with insults.[95] In May 1793, the national guards posted at the entrances to the Tuileries were instructed to refuse entry to those without cockades.[96] In November 1796, this was also reiterated and augmented in relation to *nattes retroussées* (folded plaits), as part of attempts to counter the seditious activities of the *jeunesse dorée*.[97] In 1798, Faulcon saw this as a peculiarly feminine problem: the fact that women were perpetually changing their hats was bound to result in inadvertent omission of the cockade. For proof of this phenomenon, he referred to the entrance to the Tuileries.[98] Instructions on this require-ment, as it applied to both the precinct of the Tuileries and the tribunes of the two Conseils, needed to be reiterated frequently.[99]

Entry to clubs, cafés,[100] and theatres[101] was frequently refused to those without cockades. In 1791, the Club central in Lyon only allowed women in if they wore a 'patriotic ribbon'.[102] Similarly, in September 1793, the Section du Luxembourg decided not to admit women to tribunes with-out a cockade. Some Jacobin clubs required cockades to be worn.[103] On 16 September 1793, prior to the introduction of legislation by the Convention, the Conseil of the Paris Commune ordered that no one would be allowed into 'buildings, gardens, and public monuments' without a cockade.[104]

The cockade's status as a national emblem was intensified, but also rendered provocative, by the antagonistic reactions of France's neighbours to the Revolution. In January 1790, it was possible for *pensionnaires* of the Académie de France in Rome openly to wear large cockades in their hats, thereby deliberately snubbing the duchesse de Polignac.[105] Yet in September of the same year, an aristocratic satire challenged the cockade's value as a sign of patriotism, by emphasizing the confusions that occurred when crossing the French frontier: not wearing a cockade inside France caused the same problems as wearing one abroad.[106] The problems associated with revolutionary paraphernalia were derided as being symptomatic of the trivializing pretensions of the new politics. Such incidents were, however, potentially serious. When the sculptor Chinard was arrested in Rome because of his pre-revolutionary views, his hat, with a cockade on, was seized as evidence of his compromising culpability (even though he only wore this when at home).[107]

As part of the *patrie en danger* legislation, foreigners visiting or residing in France had to wear the cockade, the only exceptions, as noted above, being ambassadors and 'accredited agents' of foreign powers.[108] In October 1796, the Earl of Malmesbury, in Paris for confidential peace talks, described the difficulties that Parisian attitudes to the wearing of cockades created for foreigners:

> The wearing of the national cockade is so universal in the streets, and so unpleasantly enforced by the populace, that it is impossible to appear in them without it; the Government by no means insists upon it, and certainly it never shall be worn by any persons belonging to me, when I am acting in an *official* capacity; but it would inevitably make me liable to the most disagreeable species of insult, were they not to put it on when they walk out in a morning.[109]

Similar restrictions obtained at French embassies abroad. A courier to the French ambassador in Soleure, wearing a cockade on entering the town, encountered attempts to remove it – and narrowly escaped arrest.[110] In Vienna, Bernadotte ordered that his staff could only wear cockades in the embassy. However, he was overruled by the Directoire, and the publicly visible cockades cause a riot.[111]

The range of incidents described above bespeak the unstable, pressurized nature of revolutionary politics, and the multiplicity of undermining, deviant and subversive variants on the patriotically inspiring emblem of the cockade, an emblem which enshrined an ideal unity which was so elusive in practice. Complementary to this emblematic realpolitik was a more elevated discourse which envisaged the cockade as enshrining certain essential qualities.[112] The cockade's unchallenged status as the central revolutionary emblem was possible because of the generic nature of its emblematic ingredients.[113]

Siviniant's pamphlet, *Motion pour engager les Français et les Françaises à ne jamais cesser de porter la Cocarde nationale* (Brest, 1791),[114] reflected on the consequences of Louis XVI's proclamation that only the national cockade be used. Siviniant felt that this might yet provoke indifference or even play into the hands of those who could choose to reject it as a sign of their antipathy to the Revolution. Referring to the parading of *cocardes blanches* at the time of the flight to Varennes, he argued that although such 'apprehensions and . . . speculations might seem perhaps fanciful or pedantic', the deviousness of the Revolution's enemies was not to be underestimated. As a counter-measure, he therefore proposed that the cockade – the 'palladium' [safeguard] of freedom – be worn by all, all of the time, everywhere. The cockade was a 'sacred shield of liberty'. To the objection that it could just as well be worn by bad citizens, he reminded his readers of the 'terror' he had seen the emblem cause among the Revolution's adversaries. They would therefore certainly reveal themselves when confronted with the cockade. Moreover, an oath would put their true sentiments to the test. He called on women to encourage its universal adoption by wearing it in their hats and bonnets.[115] The wishful thinking underpinning this prescriptive policy is thrown into relief by the sceptical reflections of the pamphlet *Diogène à Paris* (1790). On being challenged as to why he wore no cockade, Diogenes retorted: 'But how can that allow one to distinguish between a good and a bad citizen, unless [the cockade] is a marvellous talisman which gives to others the facility of divining inner thoughts?'[116] The belief that the cockade rendered just such a type of searching political assay possible was to remain active throughout the Revolution.

For committed patriots, the cockade was indeed a powerful, charismatic talisman. In October 1789, the adoption of the cockade in Saint Domingo was apostrophized as 'the sacred sign of the redemption of peoples'.[117] It was claimed as a means to speak to the senses in a way which challenged the Ancien Régime's legacy of ridiculous absurdities. Liberty could and should face down fanaticism through the language of emblems. The new politics could not be a purely intellectual phenomenon as this would ensure its popular inefficacy.[118] In the wake of the flight to Varennes, the citizens of Beauvais were told to wear the national cockade 'as the capital sign to prevent all dissent and to make good patriots recognizable'.[119] It was, however, possible to propose variations on the national cockade in special circumstances. At the time of Marie-Antoinette's illness in April 1792, a woman at the Société patriotique at Marseille suggested that women should wear pink cockades on their arms 'as a sign of joy'; if the queen were to die, then this would be celebrated by wearing two cockades.[120]

The irreducible nature of the cockade was further asserted by contrasting it with the problems associated with the wearing of the liberty cap or *bonnet rouge*. Having witnessed the frictions generated by the vogue for *bonnets rouges* in March 1792, Robespierre urged that such divisive insignia be put aside in favour of the cockade, which was, he asserted, the only mark of authentic patriotism. It operated on a level which transcended mere display: 'by putting the *bonnet rouge* aside', he advised:

> citizens who have adopted it out of praiseworthy patriotism will lose nothing: with this sign of liberty [i.e. the cockade] in their hearts, all friends of liberty will easily recognize each other by the same language and signs of reason which restore virtue, whereas all other signs can be adopted by the aristocracy and the treacherous.[121]

In December 1793, the *bonnet rouge* was again criticized because it could be appropriated by aristocrats, thus devaluing its use by patriots. Similarly, it was recommended that tricolore bouquets and other elaborations of and variations on the cockade be forbidden.[122]

Although tricolore ribbons were here spoken against, they reappear as an extremely powerful form of symbol, constituting a kind of extension of the cockade beyond its role as personal badge. In the procession for the pantheonization of Rousseau's ashes (18–19 vendémiaire an III/9–10 October 1794), the members of the Convention were surrounded by a tricolore ribbon carried by the four ages, and preceded by the 'beacon of the legislators'.[123] In the offices of the Comité de Salut Public, the public were separated from the desks and personnel by a tricolore ribbon.[124] A similar ribbon divided the Tuileries gardens from the terrace des Feuillants, adjoining the Manège – where the National Assembly was located – which had been opened to the public at the end of July 1792.[125] More dramatically, a *commissaire* at the Temple, François Daujon, tied a tricolore belt across the entrance to the tower where royal family were being held, to create a barrier to prevent the entry of a violent mob brandishing the princesse de Lamballe's head. His act was a double vindication, both of the power of the tricolore ribbon and of the people's respect for it:

> At the sight of this revered sign, these hearts intoxicated with blood and wine seemed to put aside homicidal fury in place of national respect. Each of them used all their energy to prevent the violation of the sacred banner; to touch it seemed to them a crime.[126]

In stories of the deaths of revolutionary martyrs, the cockade served as an extremely economical shorthand for the values for which they had sacrificed themselves. As reported to the Convention, Chalier's last words at his execution by rebels in Lyon were poignantly inspiring: 'Insensible to his suffering and thinking only of *la patrie*, Chalier moved his dying head and cried to the rebels' executioner: "Put a cockade on me, I die for liberty".'[127] In presenting his plans for the ceremony to pantheonize Bara and Viala, David described Bara's last moments: 'At that moment, pierced by blows, he fell, pressing to his heart the tricolore cockade: he died, to live forever in the glorious annals of history'.[128] None of the other contemporary sources cited include this detail – one to be crucial for the compositional narrative of David's painting, in which the cockade enshrines those values of patriotism and republican unity for which Bara gave his life.[129] The role of the cockade as his martyr's attribute accords with the reading of his nudity as elevating the scene above mere documentary to a kind of apotheosis. The idea of the cockade as a self-sufficient emblem was elsewhere associated with the patriotic zeal of new recruits. In March 1793, a deputation from the Section des Quinze-Vingts declared to the Convention that they would willingly enrol, and only required arms and food. They needed no uniform, and were ready 'dressed as they stood, with no other distinctive sign than the tricolore cockade, declaring that when the legislators had decreed uniformity of costume, they had decreed uniformity of hearts'.[130]

Beyond the rhetoric surrounding revolutionary martyrs, we find a variety of special qualities being attributed to the cockade. In reports of the taking of Valenciennes by émigré forces, it was claimed that it was fitting that the enemies of the Republic did not wear the cockade, for it would have weighed too heavily on their servile heads.[131] In 1790, peasants in the Périgord had their *curé* put a cockade in with the Host;[132] as part of patriotic baptisms, a cockade was placed on the breast of the new-born baby.[133] Conversely, the white cockade could function in the same symbolically condensed manner, as when one of these cockades, hanging on the end of a ribbon, was used in a festival to represent the enemy crowd.[134]

AFTER THERMIDOR

Through the Thermidorian Reaction and the Directoire, further legislation sought to deal with increased licence in the ways of wearing the cockade, or neglecting to do so. Concern over this problem was in part a legacy of the intense scrutiny of such crucial minutiae in appearances that had been current in 1793–94. As the anti-Jacobin *Courier républicain* reflected in March 1795: 'If it is with political signs, rallying points, rosettes, ribbons and caps, that one disperses tyrants, it is also with these same signs that one re-establishes them'.[135] The *journées* of prairial prompted two new laws tightening up on observance of the wearing of the cockade. The first (2 prairial an III/21 May 1795) forbade any 'rallying sign' other than the 'cocarde nationale' (significantly implying that the *cocarde nationale* was one rallying sign competing with many others). It was, furthermore, specified that 'any other sign or device whether written or otherwise, on hats, banners . . . is expressly forbidden'. Anyone found wearing or bearing such sign or texts would be treated as 'rebel before the law'. The second (7 prairial an III/25 May 1795) made tearing or trying to tear a cockade by 'all individuals of either sex' an offence which rendered the perpetrator an 'enemy of liberty' and required that he or she be instantly brought before the military commission set up to judge those accused of the prairial conspiracy.[136]

There ensued a kind of excess of apprehensive observation driven, on the one hand, by worries over the apparent desuetude of republican ideals, and on the other, by the continued need to be alert to the different strands of oppositional political subculture, ranging from the seriously conspiratorial – as exemplified by the violence of prairial – to the flaunted complacency of the increasingly high-profile wealthy. In 1797, the prolific variety of types of cockade prompted the newspaper *Le Menteur* to conclude that every possible colour had been compromised by some royalist or anti-revolutionary association, and all that remained was 'the impossible colour'.[137] In 1796, Merlin de Douai, Minister of Police, reported that the cockade was almost totally abandoned in Orléans, having been replaced by 'white braids'.[138] In the department of the Sarthe, the administration responded to priests, even *constitutionnels*, refusing entry to churches to those with cockades, by instructing all citizens to wear it 'in the buttonhole of hats, or in the most visible place of head-gear'.[139] Wealthy women were reported in October 1794 as wearing cockades so small as to be easily hidden by 'ribbon rosettes'; others didn't wear it all.[140] At the 1798 Salon it was remarked that in the many portraits on show, hardly any cockades were visible on the hats as they should have been; heads were sometimes turned so as to give the appearance of concealment of the national emblem.[141] Whether by accident or by design, David's portraits of Monsieur and Madame Sériziat (Musée du Louvre), shown at the 1795 Salon, display precisely this kind of semi-concealment of their cockades.[142]

The cockade seems to have survived through 1795 and the *jeunesse dorée*'s campaign against revolutionary symbols associated with the Jacobins and *sans-culottes*, notably the *bonnet rouge*. We have seen how, in 1796, the Earl of Malmesbury found wearing of the cockade still being enforced. It is significant that one strategy for salvaging *bonnets* was to make them tricolore (discussed further in the next chapter). That the cockade had survived as a national symbol explains its immunity from reactionary proscription: it never became identified with a particular faction, and therefore remained adaptable to the nation's evolving constitutional forms. In so far as it was subverted, this was through cockades of other colours, and manipulation of its form.

The most extensive consideration of the nature of the cockade occurred in late 1798, when a commission was set up to draft new legislation to rationalize the accumulated laws produced to date.[143] This was primarily driven by concern about apparent neglect, and what this signalled about the unstable patriotic consensus. As Devocelle notes, these discussions took place in a difficult situation: the assassination of French plenipotentiaries at Rastadt, military reverses, and resistance to conscription.[144] Duplantier insisted that the new legislation had to be workable in time of war, which required a quite different approach from that of peacetime.[145] As further evidence of the need to regularize the situation, he cited the disrespect with which it was being treated: 'See how people who call themselves well-bred strive to render the cockade invisible. Although they have gone as far as making it almost lentil-like, they still are careful to hide three-quarters of it, and to give a wholly unsuitable place.'[146] (However, for others, such as Andrieux, who saw far less need to replace existing legislation, the wearing of the cockade was 'a general custom' and not a source of trouble.)[147] Legislation had to deal with the current tribulations; France was not yet in a condition when, liberty being universal, removing someone's right to wear the cockade would in itself be tantamount to a form of capital punishment.[148] There is also a sense in which the cockade had been so ubiquitously present in the Revolution's emblematic repertoire that it had only been necessary to resort to legislation to deal with circumstantial problems. Indeed, it was precisely this argument which justified the need to rationalize and unify existing legislation.

Roëmers' *projet de résolution* focused on three essential proposals: first, that wearing the cockade in a prominent manner be made compulsory for all; second, that foreigners be excluded from this; third, that there be a scale of penalties for failing to wear it, wearing it in a concealed manner, or abusing it.[149] The central issue raised in discussions of this text were whether it was proper for an emblem which enshrined France's new 'revolutionized' national identity to have any restrictions as to who could not wear it. The prime candidates for this exclusion were women, children, foreigners, and criminals.

Certain texts reiterated Rousseau's recommendation that woman's place was in the home, and not in public life. Women also denatured the cockade by reducing it to an item of adornment.[150] But this form of exclusion was challenged by Duplantier, who argued that the revolutionary cockade was not an exclusively masculine military sign; moreover, women had a key role to play in free states.[151] Children's exclusion was based on the argument that the values embedded in the cockade were ones which they would only appreciate when they had reached adulthood. The exclusion of criminals was justified by the sense that they would dishonour the emblem.

Foreigners should be excluded, for otherwise this would be to denature the notion of the cockade's status as the national sign (their identity was defined in articles 12 and 14 of the constitution of an III); an exception should be made for those who had participated in the fight for freedom. If foreigners were to be allowed to wear it, the sign would lose its meaning, and would in the eyes of the people become nothing more than 'a uniformity of dress which says nothing to their spirit', and which would encourage disrespect. They should wear their own national distinctive signs.[152] However, as Andrieux pointed out, this would create a field day for malevolent fabricators of subversive 'rallying signs', as it would be extremely difficult to keep track of the profusion of national badges in circulation: 'And what would you say to someone who adopted an invented cockade, and pretended that it was that of I know not which country, of China or the Congo?'[153]

J.F. Eude queried some of these conclusions, for they seemed to him at odds with the principles of good legislation. He rejected the idea that the cockade corresponded to the possession of 'civic rights', for this was in effect nothing other than 'the prerogatives dependent on the quality of being a French citizen', which amounted to the right to elect and be elected. Such political acts required no external sign, and in this respect were consistent with the constitution of an III, which stated that, outside of the exercise of their public functions, no 'distinctive sign' should differentiate citizens and officials.

Underlying these arguments as to how best the legislation should respect the cockade's symbolism, was unanimous recognition of its historical

importance in the heroic early days of the Revolution. For Faulcon, the
cockade was identified with the 'fine memory of the first days of the
Revolution', and 'recalls this wonderful epoch when the French, trans-
ported by a burning enthusiasm, full of emotions at once electric and
pure, unanimously adopted the cockade, as an indicator and token of
their nascent liberty'.[154] This heritage intensified the cockade's revered
symbolic function, but the emblem's sacred nature might be said to have
made attempts to reconcile this with practicalities of legislation all the
more difficult.

Broadly, there were two opposed currents running through these
discussions: on the one hand, an egalitarian spirit, which rejected any
imposed code of practice which might exacerbate divisive distinctions;
and on the other hand, a more repressive logic, anxious to counter
subversive misuse or exploitation of loopholes in the legislation. Eschasseriaux emphasized the egalitarian force of the cockade. It was:

> one of the republican institutions whose maintenance is essentially connected
> to our political existence . . . By means of memories equally dear and glorious,
> it ceaselessly awakens in the people's spirit, the sense of their rights, their power,
> and their dignity; it is the shield against which the impotent efforts of the
> enemies of its independence must henceforward be broken.[155]

Consistent with this critique, he spoke against the idea that servants
should not be allowed to wear the cockade, for this would be to accent-
uate a hierarchy based on wealth. If necessary some form of updated
sumptuary law might be needed to ensure that excessive displays of wealth
were avoided. Indeed, the universal wearing of the cockade would be a
means to bridge such differences. 'In a republican state, only a single body,
a single spirit is needed'; tolerance was therefore better than restriction.
The 'majesty' of the sign could cope with a few 'blemishes'.[156] Furthermore, if too many exclusions were imposed, this would expose those who
were legitimately allowed to wear it as potential targets for their counter-
revolutionary adversaries, especially in locations where dissension was
rife. If the cockade was not made compulsory, this would leave patriots
vulnerable to attack and facilitate repudiation.[157]

There was considerable reluctance to make of the cockade a pretext for
extensive surveillance, so as to avoid any unwanted echo of the Terror's
intrusively proscriptive régime. Gastin argued that the cockade's symbolic
power would deter most of its antagonists more effectively than any legal

measure: 'As the hydrophobe has a horror of water, the royalist fears, dreads the sign of our political regeneration, he has a horror of it.'[158]

Given that no new legislation emerged from the commission's proposals, it is appropriate to leave the last word on these discussions to Andrieux, one of the most sceptical contributors to the debate. He wondered whether the commission had not confused a sign with 'the thing itself', appearance with reality, and effect with cause. He urged that 'the public spirit' should first be encouraged in order to promote the wearing of the cockade rather than vice versa.[159] Legislation could only do so much, but there were numerous fundamental issues that were in urgent need of attention before deliberating on the cockade – republican institutions, public instruction, finances: 'Let us heal, as much as is in our power, the wounds of the Revolution; let us put aside the interests of parties . . . above all let us restore order and the economy.'[160] Indeed, he had difficulty in envisaging the cockade as an 'institution'; it lacked the physical substance to become 'an enduring institution. This sign is small, not very noticeable; it is something we have in common with other peoples, most of whom give it a very different meaning from ours'. He found much more plausible the idea of 'a form of dress, *a costume* [in original], a colour, exclusively dedicated to French citizens, when they are acting as citizens'.[161] Interestingly, his criticism of the efficacy of cockades cited what we have seen to be one of the habitual modes of proselytizing employment, and was based on essentially aesthetic criteria: 'A distribution of cockades preceded by a speech would be a ceremony without action, without movement, without life'. He wanted 'moving', 'electrifying', 'enflaming', 'tear-provoking' institutions of the types which had been so effectively evolved by priests and the Ancients, and which were so lacking in contemporary France: 'Do you think that our valiant soldiers, mortally wounded on the field of battle, are able to call to mind or to regret reading the *Bulletin décadaire*?'.[162]

Cockades continued to be worn during the Consulate. Occasions when they were a subject of concern were relatively few. For example, on the anniversary of the execution of Louis XVI on 21 January, agents reported that certain people who were not wearing cockades were also heard to make sarcastic remarks about republican institutions. Orders were sent out to monitor that cockades were indeed being worn.[163] But this was an exception. Cockades continued to be subject to variety of form; for example, the revival of cockades made of ribbon, which reminded observers of those worn in 1790, and cockades obscured by black ribbons, but this was judged to be a fashion concentrated among 'societies formed by luxury and pleasure', rather than corresponding to a seditious 'rallying sign': 'The mass of the inhabitants of Paris', it was reassuringly noted, 'continue to wear the cockades stipulated by the law and consecrated use'.[164] The fact that cockades were openly on sale in public was reckoned by to support lack of concern over what would have been a cause of anxiety in the mid-1790s.[165] Police reports express complete confidence that their surveillance would be enough to ensure that apparent negligence in the wearing of cockades would not be confused with any more seriously subversive initiative.[166] Nonetheless, in February 1801, police in Beauvais resorted to the banning of all cockades as a way of dealing with the display of *cocardes blanches* and other rallying signs.[167]

Like his soldiers, Napoleon wore the tricolore cockade. When he was exiled to Elba, a special cockade – with three red and white bees – was instituted. The cockade that he wore when bidding farewell to the Imperial guard at Fontainebleau, and also that which he wore on Elba, became precious Napoleonic memorabilia;[168] it may well have been from this period that collecting cockades became a way to encapsulate the fragmented diversity of France's recent political evolution.[169] With Napoleon's defeat, people had white cockades made up to signal their enthusiasm for the restored Bourbon régime. Louis Dessaux-Lebrethon published a pamphlet to establish his claim to have been the first (in St-Omer at least) to wear the *cocarde blanche*, 'this rallying sign so dear to the French, so revered by our good ancestors', and also to recount the temporary imprisonment he endured until the tide of opinion shifted to willing acceptance of the return of Louis XVIII.[170]

The history of the cockade, the most widely adopted of revolutionary emblems, exemplifies the dynamic interrelation between its dissemination and currency, retrospective legislation, and the difficulties in putting this into practice. The very ubiquitousness of the cockade generated a prolific diversity of reported adaptions and (mis)uses. Even within apparent patriotic consensus, the debate on whether women should wear the cockade highlights the way that restriction of the adoption of emblems exposed the limits of egalitarian rhetoric. Through its use in rituals and as a gift, the cockade was intimately bound up with forms of patriotic behaviour and comportment which gave active meaning to a new emblematic language. Despite, or because of, its material slightness, the cockade constituted an eloquent site for representation of, and identification with, the Revolution. Indeed, the survival of the cockade became a token of the enduring, if contested, viability of revolutionary idealism, managing to avoid being compromised by partisan misappropriation. For all its implication in moments of sceptical scrutiny, the cockade succeeded in transcending factional conflicts. It did so because it continued to symbolize an ideal of national unity, an ideal which was all the more precious for being recurrently in doubt.

Notes

1. '"Voulez-vous", dit-il, "le vert, couleur de l'espérance, ou le rouge [bleu?], couleur de l'ordre libre de Cincinnatus?" – "le vert! le vert!" répond la multitude. L'orateur descend de la table ou il était monté, attache une feuille d'arbre à son chapeau, tout le monde l'imite; les maronniers du palais sont presque dépouillés de leurs feuilles, et cette foule se rend en tumulte chez le sculpteur Curtius, pour y chercher les bustes de Necker et du duc d'Orléans, bustes qui sont portés en triomphe et voilés d'un crêpe, car le bruit de l'exil de ces hommes populaires s'était répandu' (Mignet, *Histoire de la Révolution française*, vol. I, pp. 65–6, cit. F. Pouy, *Histoire de la cocarde tricolore* (Paris, 1872), pp. 22–3. Mignet's account is based on Desmoulins' own version in his *Le Vieux Cordelier*, no. 5, 5 niv. an II/25 December 1793, produced to recall his services to the liberty (see the edition by Albert Mathiez and Henri Calvet (Colin: Paris, 1936)). See also *RAM*, vol. 1, no. 20, 17–20 July 1789, p. 170, note 2.

2. *Révolutions de Paris, dédiées à la Nation, et au district des Petits-Augustins*, 9th edn, no. 1, 12–17 July 1789, p. 7.

3. The accompanying print, 'Motions du Palais Royal le 12 J[uill]et 1789', shows an unidentified man addressing the crowd (*Révolutions de Paris*, pp. 2–3).

4. Desmoulins, *Le Vieux Cordelier*, no. 5, 5 niv. an II/25 December 1793, p. 137. The editors Mathiez and Calvet note (p. 139) René Farge's analysis of the occasion, and his conclusion that Desmoulins is in fact here quoting his own contribution to the text for this episode from the *Tableaux historiques de la Révolution française*, not written until 1790 ('Camille Desmoulins au jardin du Palais-Royal', *Annales révolutionnaires*, vol. 7, 1914, pp. 646–74).

5. 'Ce matin [14 July] une ordonnance des électeurs à la ville fixe l'état de la milice bourgeoise: hier on portoit la cocarde verte et blanche; aujourd'hui on la foule aux pieds, et l'on prend la cocarde bleu et rose; ce sont les couleurs conformes au blason de la ville' (*Révolutions de Paris*, no. 1, 12–17 July 1789, p. 10). Lynn Hunt notes the Duke of Dorset's observation that red and white were substituted for green because the former were the colours of the duc d'Orléans, the latter those of the comte d'Artois (*Politics, Culture, and Class in the French Revolution* (University of California Press: Berkeley, Los Angeles, London: 1984), p. 57).

6. See Etienne Jollet, 'Between Allegory and Topography: the Project for a Statue to Louis XVI in Brest (1785–86) and the Question of the Pedestal in Public Statuary in Eighteenth-century France', *Oxford Art Journal*, 2000, vol. 23, no. 2, pp. 49–78.

7. *RAM*, vol. 1, n. 20, 17–20 July 1789, p. 170.

8. When a deputation from the Assemblée Nationale at Versailles came to Paris on the 17th, they were given cockades along the way (Jacques Godechot, *14 Juillet 1789. La Prise de la Bastille* (Gallimard: Paris, 1965), p. 312).

9. *Journal encyclopédique*, vol. 6, part 1, August 1789, p. 159.

10. 'Je ne savais trop comment le roi prendroit la chose, et s'il y avait quelque inconvenance à cette proposition' (J.S. Bailly, *Mémoires* (1804), cit. Godechot, *14 Juillet 1789*, p. 418).

11. 'Je ne croyais pas avoir épousé un roturier' (L.S. Mercier, *Le Nouveau Paris*, ed. Jean-Claude Bonnet (Mercure de France: Paris, 1994), p. 282).

12. 25 August 1789, Evelyne Lever, *Philippe Égalité* (Arthème Fayard: Paris, 1996), p. 346. On the duc's alleged adoption of *sans-culotte* costume, see Chapter 4 of the present volume.

13. *Œuvres de Camille Desmoulins*, 2 vols (Paris, 1838), vol. 2, p. 22.

14. Ibid., p. 27.

15. *Le Vieux Cordelier*, no. 5, 5 niv. an II/25 December 1793, cit. ibid., vol 1, pp. 86–7.

16. 'Le RUBAN BLEU AZURE, nommé par quelques-uns couleur Saphirique, et céleste, signifie *justice, royauté, beauté* et *bonne réputation*. Le RUBAN ROUGE désigne *vaillance, hardiesse*, et *générosité*. Le RUBAN BLANC dénote l'Étendard et le Pavillon de la Monarchie Françoise qui de tous les tems a été sous la protection de *Marie*, mère du *Sauveur du monde*. Ce *Ruban* marque particulièrement *espérance, pureté, innocence*, et *charité*. La COURONNE de CERFEUIL au centre de laquelle se trouve placée la Cocarde, exprime par cette devise: Vertu partout' (P.S. Ferat, *Cocarde royale et de la liberté aux couleurs distinctives de l'Hôtel-de-Ville de Paris . . . A la gloire immortelle de la Nation françoise, régénérée le 17 Juillet 1789*. Explication des symboles emblématiques. Significations mystérieuses des trois Rubans de couleurs différentes, arboré pour cocarde par la Nation. 3rd edn); the text is reprinted from *Courrier de Versailles*, no. 13, p. 197.

17. *Dictionnaire national et anecdotique, pour servir à l'intelligence des mots dont notre langue s'est enrichie depuis la révolution, etc.* (1790), pp. 38–9.

18. *Actes Comm*, 1st series, vol. 1, p. 236, 16 August 1789.

19. In the spring of 1794, when 'rubans tricolores à la boutonnière' reappeared, it was contentiously recalled by a police agent that this early style of cockade had been encouraged by adherents of the Ancien Régime because 'des citoyens devenus libres se crussent de ressembler à des chevaliers de Saint-Esprit' (Caron, vol. 5, pp. 159–60, 18 vent. an II/8 March 1794).

20. 'On a mis la cocarde Henri IV! J'embrasserais volontiers le premier qui a eu cette heureuse idée. Il me semble encore entendre ce bon Prince s'écrier encore une fois: mes enfans, ne perdez pas de vue cette Cocarde; vous la verrez toujours dans le chemin de l'honneur' ([Jacques-Louis Gautier de Syonnet] Sionnet, *La Cocarde du Tiers Etat* ([1789]), p. 3). Raoul Girardet points out that references to the unifying function of this emblem overlook the fact that this remark occurred in the context of the wars of religion ('Les Trois Couleurs, ni blanc, ni rouge', in Pierre Nora (ed.), *Les Lieux de mémoire*, vol. 1, *La République* (Gallimard: Paris, 1984),p. 9).

21. *RAM*, vol. 2, no. 69, 9 October 1789, p. 20. See also Tuetey, vol. 2, item 594, on the arrest of a man for appearing in public with a black cockade.

22. *RAM*, vol. 2, no. 69, 9 October. 1789, p. 20.

23. *RAM*, vol. 2, no. 69, 9 October 1789, p. 19.

24. *RAM*, vol. 2, no. 68, 5–8 October 1789, p. 11.

25. Comte de Reiset (ed.), *Livre-journal de Madame Eloffe*, 2 vols (Paris, 1885), vol. 2, p. 431, cit. Nicole Pellegrin, *Les Vêtements de la liberté* (Alinéa: Paris, 1989), p. 118.

26. See Michel Hennin, *Histoire numismatique de la Révolution française*, 2 vols (Paris, 1826), vol. 1, p. 52, no. 64 pl. 9; and *Actes Comm*, 1st series, vol. 2, p. 215.

27. *RAM*, vol. 2, no. 69, 9 October 1789, p. 20. Dutch 'patriots' who identified with the French wore black and white cockades based on the lily in opposition to the orange of the Stadtholder; they mistakenly assumed the French would come to their help. A leading 'patriot', Princess Wilhelmina, was arrested. See Simon Schama, *Patriots and Liberators: Revolution in the Netherlands, 1780–1813* (Collins: London, 1977), p. 127.

28. *RAM*, vol. 2, no. 69, 9 October 1789, p. 19.

29. *Procédure criminelle, instruite au Châtelet de Paris, sur la dénonciation des faits arrrivés à Versailles dans la journée du 6 octobre 1789. Imprimée par ordre de l'Assemblée nationale* (1790). The pictorial version of the cockade, showing the Nation equipped with divers attributes, which was in effect a homage to its symbolic authority rather than a practical model, was reportedly accepted by Lafayette (17 October 1789); see *Révolutions de Paris*, no. 13, 3–10 October 1789, opposite p. 6; and the colour plate in the almanac, *La Cocarde citoyenne* (1790) (BHVP, Rés. 700 617).

30. *Nouveau Dictionnaire françois, à l'usage de toutes les Municipalités, les milices nationales et de tous les Patriotes, composé par un Aristocrate, dédié à l'Assemblée Nationale, pour servir à l'histoire de la Révolution de France, et c'est la vérité comme on dit toute nue* (Paris, 1790), pp. 10–11. Raoul Girardet notes a similar phase of diversity in the design of the newly ordained tricolore flag ('Les Trois couleurs, ni blanc ni rouge', p. 13).

31. *Dialogue entre le ruban rouge et le ruban aux trois couleurs. Fable* (Paris [1790?]), p. 2 (BL R.200(10)).

32. Cit. Tuetey, vol. 2, no. 3976 (28 March, 1 April 1790).

33. For example, the arrest of someone for the misuse of 'une grande cocarde aux trois couleurs' in clandestine recruiting 'contraires aux intérêts de la Nation' (15 October; 4 December 1789). The dossier, drawn up by the Comité de police de la Commune, included a cockade (Tuetey, vol. 1, no. 1176).

34. *Proclamation de Louis XVI lue à l'Assemblée nationale le 28 mai 1790, couleurs de la conciliation*; see *RAM*, 31 May 1790, no. 151, p. 497 on the Assembly's meeting of 29 May. This national action had, in fact, been anticipated locally; see 'Ordre à tous les citoyens de la porter rendu pour Montauban', *RAM*, vol. 4, 17 May 1790, p. 94.

35. *RAM*, vol. 4, p. 613 (séance 12 June 1790). Guards were, in theory at least, equipped with two cockades ('Etat des effets d'habillement, équipement et armement dont les gardes nationales devront être pourvus (5 August 1791)', cit. Ch.L. Chassin and L. Hennet, *Les Volontaires nationaux pendant la Révolution*, 3 vols (Paris, 1899–1906), vol. 1, p. 147).

36. See the *Adresse à l'Assemblée nationale, par les soldats du cent-deuxième régiment, accusés sans fondement d'avoir voulu arborer la cocarde blanche, ce signe de proscription qu'ils ont tous en horreur, présentée le 10 juin 1792, l'an quatrième de la liberté*, BL FR. 278 (8),

in which the regiment defended itself against the malevolent accusation that because they wore 'la livrée du ci-devant comte d'Artois', this 'marque extérieur étoit celle de nos sentiments', and also the more damaging one that the regiment was ready to adopt the *cocarde blanche* (p. 2).

37. *Actes Comm,* 2nd series, vol. 3, pp. 360–3, 368. The marquis de Ferrières claimed in his memoirs that scaremongering Jacobins produced *cocardes blanches* from their pockets (cit. Louis Blanc, *Histoire de la Révolution française*, 15 vols (Paris, 1878), vol. 6, pp. 117–19).

38. Cit. David Andress, *Massacre at the Champ de Mars. Popular Dissent and Political Culture in the French Revolution* (Royal Historical Society and Boydell Press: Woodbridge, 2000), p. 103. The man concerned, Louis Jean Gobrou, a 38-year-old servant, explained that he had been provoked by 'cockades on a white ground with a small addition in the centre, which announces in these cockades a difference with the national cockades'.

39. *Révolutions de Paris*, 2–9 July 1791, cit. *Actes Comm*, 2nd series, vol. 5, p. 263.

40. *Bouche de fer*, no. 37, 1 April 1791, cit. Andress, *Massacre at the Champ de Mars*, p. 103.

41. Tuetey, vol. 2, no. 2506, 21 September 1791.

42. Tuetey, vol. 2, no. 2748, 28 July 1791.

43. As in the case of M. d'Agoult, formerly a major in the gardes françaises, who was arrested on 19 August 1791 for scornful remarks on the Garde nationale (Tuetey, vol. 2, no. 1421).

44. Tuetey, vol. 9, no. 1451, 29 September 1791.

45. article 16: 'Tout homme résidant ou voyageant en France, est tenu de porter la cocarde nationale. Sont excepté de la présente disposition les ambassadeurs et agents accredités des puissances étrangères'; article 17: 'Toute personne revêtu d'un signe de rebellion sera poursuivie devant les tribunaux ordinaires; et en cas qu'elle soit convaincue de l'avoir pris à dessein, elle sera punie de mort. Il est ordonné à tout citoyen de l'arrêter ou de la dénoncer sur-le-champ, à peine d'être réputé complice; toute cocarde autre que celle aux trois couleurs nationales, est un signe de rébellion' (*Arch Parl*, vol. 46, p. 134, 5 July 1792).

46. *RAM*, vol. 13, no. 216, p. 311, 3 August 1792. A similar law was passed on 16 April 1796 (22 germ. an IV). See also, *Loi relative aux cocardes, 2 août 1792* (BHVP 125046), and *Arch Parl*, vol. 47, p. 792, 2 August 1792.

47. *Arch Parl*, vol. 47, p. 291.

48. Stephen Weston, *Letters from Paris, during the Summer of 1792, with Reflections* (London, 1793), p. 128. Hochon claimed that such incidents, which included fatal attacks on people on the Champs-Elysées, must have been perpetrated by 'de prétendus fédérés' (cit. Tuetey, vol. 4, no. 1394, 6 August 1792). The case of a lyonnais 'muscadin', whose hat bore a cockade with an image of Louis XVI, three fleurs de lys, and the motto 'La nation, le roi, la loi', might be understood as the resolute continued use of a cockade which had been tailored to an earlier stage of revolutionary politics (*RACSP*, vol. 7, p. 156, 30 September 1793).

49. Tuetey, vol. 4, no. 2302, p. 287.

50. When reviewing legislation dealing with the cockade in 1798, Roëmers pointed out that the order of 3 March 1793 'ordonne seulement d'arrêter et de conduire devant la municipalité les particuliers qui seroient trouvés sans cocarde' (Roëmers, *Corps législatif.*

Conseil des Cinq Cents. Projet de résolution présenté par Roëmers au nom d'une commission spéciale, sur le port de la cocarde nationale. Séance du 8 frimaire an VII [28 November 1798], p. 3).

51. *RAM*, vol. 16, 6 April 1793, p. 52, séance 6 April. See also *Commune de Paris, prescriptions touchant l'uniformité des cocardes* (Tourneux, vol. 2, no. 6318, 6 April 1793).

52. *Arch Parl*, vol. 61, p. 461, 8 April 1793. This was referred to the Comité de Salut public.

53. Tuetey, vol. 9, no. 577, p. 163, 9/10 May 1793, Bureau de surveillance de la police.

54. Walter Markov and Albert Soboul, *Die Sansculotten von Paris. Dokumente zur Geschichte des Volksbewegung, 1793–94* (Berlin, 1957), p. 4, cit. William H. Sewell Jnr, *Work and Revolution in France. The Language of Labour from the French Revolution to 1848* (Cambridge University Press: Cambridge, 1980), p. 104.

55. The most succinct and best documented account is Albert Soboul, 'Un épisode des luttes populaires en septembre 1793', *AHRF*, 1961, pp. 52–5. See also Dominique Godineau, *Citoyennes tricoteuses. Les femmes du peuple à Paris pendant la Révolution française* (Alinéa: Paris, 1988), pp. 163–6.

56. Caron, vol. 1, p. 192, 25 September 1793.

57. Caron, vol. 1, p. 137, 19 September 1793. In September 1793 in Beauvais, cockades worn on petticoats were deemed disrespectful (Maurice Dommanget, 'Le Symbolisme et le prosélytisme à Beauvais et dans l'Oise: la cocarde et l'autel de la Patrie', *AHRF*, 1925, vol. 2, pp. 134–5).

58. Caron, vol. 1, pp. 149–50, 20 September 1793.

59. Caron, vol. 1, p. 223, 28 September 1793.

60. Soboul, 'Episode', p. 55.

61. Pouy, *Histoire*, p. 44.

62. *RACSP*, vol. 7, p. 48, Versailles, 24 September 1793.

63. *RAM*, vol. 18, no. 39, 13 October 1793, p. 290. See also an *arrêté* of 7 January 1794 by the Paris Commune which reiterated this decree (Tourneux, vol. 2, no. 14301). See Annie Geffroy, '"A bas le bonnet rouge des femmes!": (octobre–novembre 1793)', in *Les Femmes et la Révolution française. Actes du colloque international 12–13–14 avril 1989, Université de Toulouse-Le Mirail*, ed. Marie-France Brive, 3 vols (Presse Universitaire du Mirail: Toulouse, 1989–90), vol. 33, pp. 345–52.

64. Ibid. Contrary to Fabre's alarmist view of women in *bonnets rouges*, they were on one occasion noted as standing guard armed with pikes to maintain order at the door of bakers (Caron, vol. 6, p. 270, 29 October 1793).

65. See Lynn Hunt, 'Freedom of Dress in Revolutionary France', in Sara E. Melzer and Kathryn Norberg (eds), *From the Royal to the Republican Body: Incorporating the Political in Seventeenth- and Eighteenth-century France* (University of California Press: Berkeley, Los Angeles, London, 1998), pp. 224–49.

66. Affiche, AN, AD XX C 73 (33). On 29 May 1792, a man was nearly killed after having mistakenly been accused of wearing a *cocarde blanche*, which turned out on closer inspection to be tricolore (Tuetey, vol. 5, no. 3240).

67. AN, AE v.347 (exhibited in *La Révolution française*, Bibliothèque Nationale, Paris, 1928, no. 887, p. 227).

68. Tuetey, vol. 9, p. 587, 13 May 1793; vol. 9, p. 489, 27–28 March 1793 on 'agents de l'aristocratie' who wore cockades 'où le blanc domine'.

69. Caron, vol. 1, p. 361, 3 niv. an II/23 December 1793. Another report called such women 'muscadines' (vol. 1, p. 339, 2 niv. an II/22 December 1793).

70. Caron, vol. 1, p. 322, 1 niv. an II/21 December 1793.

71. For example, the president of the *société populaire* of Rheims gave cockades to women present (Baron Marc de Villiers, *Histoire des clubs des femmes et des légions d'amazones 1793–1848–1871* (Plon: Paris, 1910), p. 200).

72. Caron, vol. 1, p. 192, 25 September 1793.

73. Caron, vol. 1, p. 226, 29 September 1793.

74. 12 floréal an II/1 May 1794, from 'L'ordre du jour de la force armée de Paris', Tuetey, vol. 11, no. 1902. This injunction was reiterated on 11 germ. an II/31 March 1794, Tuetey, vol. 11, no. 1013.

75. Tuetey, vol. 6, no. 277.

76. *RACSP*, vol. 13, p. 244, cit. Jean-Marc Devocelle, 'D'un costume politique à une politique du costume', in *Modes et révolution 1780–1804* (Éditions Paris-Musées; Musée de la mode et du costume, Paris, 1989), p. 102 note 46.

77. 14 September 1793; see Dommanget, 'Le Symbolisme et le prosélytisme: la cocarde . . .', vol. 2, p. 133.

78. *Arch Parl*, vol. 46, p. 132, 5 July 1792.

79. Pouy, *Histoire*, pp. 49–50.

80. Ibid., pp. 49–50 ('en taxant son prix en sus seulement de celui de 1790, Arrêté du Ier mois [vend.] de l'an II [September/October 1793]', Conseil général du district d'Amiens).

81. Ibid., p. 51.

82. *Arch Parl*, vol. 47, p. 290, 30 July 1792.

83. Tuetey, vol. 2, no. 727 (15 June 1790). See also the case of 'la dame Angelloz', who admitted that she had provided M. Boneton, rue Greneta, with four dozen 'rosettes noires à queue avec point blanc au centre' (Tuetey, vol. 5, no. 3932, 20 September 1793).

84. 17 September 1792, cit. Devocelle, 'Costume politique et politique du costume: approches théoriques et idéologiques du costume pendant la Révolution française', Université de Paris I, mémoire de maîtrise, 2 vols, 1988, vol. 1, p. 38.

85. *Arch Parl*, vol. 50, pp. 68–9, 17 September 1792.

86. Moreover, the maker's name was included on the reverse: 'Fabrique du Citoyen A . . . Fils, inventeur des cocardes devises républicains, n. 357 à Paris'. This cockade was included in a sale at Drouot Richelieu, Paris (commissaire-priseurs Pescheteau, Badin, Ferrieu, 2 December 1988, p. 28, no. 122). A cockade with the same maker's name was recorded in the deposition produced concerning an arrest on 13 May 1793 of two men wearing cockades with a suspiciously prominent proportion of white, with the difference that the maker's mark referred to him as 'inventeur des cocardes nationales' (Tuetey, vol. 9, no. 587).

87. *Anecdotes intéressantes et peu connues sur la Révolution* (Paris, 1790), pp. 47–8, noted *Annales révolutionnaires*, vol. 3, 1910, pp. 592–3. This also includes the Çivrai story.

88. Conseil des Cinq Cents, 29 flor. an VIII/19 May 1800, cit, Mona Ozouf, *La Fête révolutionnaire 1789–1799* (Gallimard: Paris, 1976) p. 114.

89. 21 June 1791; Andress suggests his motive was more likely disgust with the authorities and the National Guard rather than an attack on the Revolution (*Massacre at the Champ de Mars*, p. 149).

90. Letter from sieur Tripier aîné, rue Coquéron, cit. Tuetey, vol. 4, no. 825.

91. In an incident of rebellion against the French occupation, Augustin Spinola, at Arquata, had torn a cockade and raised the imperial standard (*Correspondance de Napoléon Ier*, 32 vols (Paris, 1858–1870), vol. 1, letter 627, 25 prairial an IV (13 June 1796), p. 397). See also the fate of Sauveur in the commune of Roche-Bernard in the département du Morbihan, which had been taken by 'brigands, émigrés ou prêtres'. They tore off his *cocarde tricolore*, and replaced it with a *cocarde blanche*, and forced him to make an *amende honorable* in a church to a profaned divinity, before brutally killing him (Léonard Bourdon, *Recueil des actions héroiques et civiques des républicains français*, no. II, premier ventôse, l'an 2 de la République une et indivisible (Paris, an II), pp. 11–12); and *ibid.*, no. III, pp. 15–16, for a similar story of a revolutionary's death for refusing to wear the *cocarde blanche* (29 frim. an II, commune of Sables). See also *Détail du combat qui a eu lieu à Metz, entre la Garde nationale, les troupes de la ligne, et des soldats de l'empereur, qui ont voulu forcer la garnison à prendre la cocarde blanche* (1790).

92. See Tuetey, vol. 2, no. 2555, on the arrest of Jean-François Gavarret, who had been apprehended in the Tuileries wearing a black cockade in his hat. The *croix de Malte* he was also wearing was broken at the same time that his cockade was burnt.

93. *Journal général de la cour et de la ville*, 9 November 1789, no. 52, p. 408.

94. They were taken by the National Guard to the prison of the Prévôté; *Punition terrible et exemplaire de trois brigands aristocrates, arrêtés et mis à la mort hier au soir par nos bons citoyens du fauxbourg Saint-Antoine. Cocarde nationale insultée aux Thuileries* [1790], pp. 7–8. The events are dated 24 May 1790 in an annotation on the copy in the British Library (R.659 (17)).

95. For example, a man wearing a red cockade (21 February 1791); a yellow and black cockade (19 April) (Andress, *Massacre at the Champ de Mars*, pp. 103–4).

96. In a regulation decided on 9 May 1793 by the *comité des inspecteurs de la salle* for the entries to the Tuileries (Tuetey, vol. 8, no. 2457).

97. *RAM*, vol. 28, no. 58, p. 490, 26 brum. an V/16 November 1796: see the letter to the *commandant de la place* from the *Bureau central*.

98. *Opinion de Felix Faulcon, Député de la Vienne, sur le projet de résolution relatif à la cocarde nationale. Prairial an VII*, p. 7.

99. See *Corps législatif. Conseil des Cinq-Cents et des Anciens. Les commissions des inspecteurs des conseils des Cinq-Cents et des Anciens, réunies. Extrait du procès-verbal du 6 vendémiaire, l'an sixième de la République française, une et indivisible*. Affiche, BL, FR 68 (9), regarding the desuetude, since '1 prairial dernier', of the *consigne patriotique* which required all to wear the *cocarde tricolore* 'ostensiblement'.

100. Those without cockades were made to leave the café de Chartres; at the café des Canonniers, a man without a cockade was made to stand on a table to be noted (Schmidt, vol. 2, p. 299, 13 March 1795/23 vend. an III).

101. At the Théâtre de la Montagne, three women were refused entry because they were not wearing cockades (and refused to put them on) (Schmidt, vol. 2, p. 259, 4 December 1794/15 niv. an III).

102. De Villiers, *Histoire des clubs des femmes*, p. 176.

103. Patrice Higonnet, *Goodness beyond Virtue. Jacobins during the French Revolution* (Harvard University Press: Cambridge MA, London, 1998), p. 227.

104. *RAM*, vol. 17, no. 259, p. 654, 16 September 1793. See the 'Ordonnance rendue par le tribunal criminal du département de Vaucluse séant à Bédouin l'infame, par Arrêté du représentant Maignet, qui condamne Rose Marcelin, Gabrielle Frutus, Rose Guelin et Rose Mazet, à rester huit jours dans la maison d'arrêt pour avoir paru au tribunal sans cocarde nationale. Du 23 floréal an 2 de la République/12 mai 1794.' Affiche.

105. *Chronique de Paris*, 11 January 1790, no. 11, p. 43; Jacques-Louis David read Topino-Lebrun's letter (dated 31 October) from Rome recounting this episode to the Convention (*RAM*, vol. 14, no. 327, 22 November 1792, p. 531).

106. *Les Différens Effets de la cocarde nationale, dédiée à la nation, ou lettre écrite par Dominique-Antonio-François-Jean-Népomucène-Pancrace Meresos y Poralipipos, à sa soeur, le 4 septembre 1789* ([Paris] 1790). According to Sainte-Beuve, the abbé Maury was arrested at Péronne 'sans rabat et sans cocarde' when trying to leave France after 14 July 1789 (*Causeries du lundi*, 15 vols (Paris, n.d.), vol. 4, p. 275, cit. Pouy, *Histoire* (p. 34), who places this in the *Nouvelles Causeries*). See the letter discussed in the Assembly regarding the difficulty of enforcing the wearing of the cockade in the canton of Soleure, where it was insulted (*Arch Parl*, vol. 30, p. 60, 30 August 1791).

107. J.J. Guiffrey and A. de Montaiglon, *Correspondance des directeurs de l'Académie de Rome avec les surintendants des bâtiments 1666–1797*, 18 vols (Schemit: Paris, 1887–1912), vol. 16, p. 124. An interesting comparison might be made here with a gouache miniature self-portrait by Girodet executed according to an inscription in Rome. This shows him wearing a *bonnet rouge*. Whether or not he owned such a cap, he could not have worn it in public. The image therefore probably constitutes a clandestine ideal self-image. The gouache was exhibited in *Nineteenth-century French Drawings and Some Sculpture* (15 June–14 July 2000), Hazlitt, Gooden and Fox, London, no. 3 [unpaginated] and is now in a private collection. Many thanks to Richard Thompson for alerting me to this fascinating work.

108. Article XVI. A 'Projet de décret' of 7 August 1793 proposed that foreigners granted a 'certificat d'hospitalité' should wear a tricolore armband on their left arms on which 'hospitalité' and the name of their nation be written (*Arch Parl*, vol. 70, pp. 452–3). After 1792, foreign soldiers who joined the French armies were exempt from the prohibition on foreigners wearing cockades. See also *RAM*, vol. 9, 27 August 1792, no. 239, p. 496.

109. *Diaries and Correspondence of the Earl of Malmesbury*, 3 vols (London, 1844), vol. 3, p. 269, 23 October 1796.

110. *Courier francais*, n. 192, 11 July 1791, p. 88.

111. Pouy, *Histoire*, p. 31. In 1798, when ambassador in Turin, Guinguéné insisted that all French residents should wear the cockade and swear allegiance to the Republic, otherwise they would be treated as émigrés and expelled (*RAM*, vol. 29, no. 224, p. 255, 14 floréal an VII/3 May 1798).

112. See Klaus Herding on *Le Nouvel Astre Français, ou la Cocarde tricolore suivant la cour du Zodiaque* (anon. aquatint, 1792, De Vinck Collection, 1751, vol. 10, p. 1223), in 'Visual Codes in the Graphic Art of the Revolution', in James Cuno (ed.), *French Caricature and the French Revolution 1789–1799* (Grunwald Center for the Graphic Arts: Los Angeles, 1988), pp. 83–100.

113. On its survival through to the early nineteenth century, and later episodes of republican government, see Girardet, 'Les Trois Couleurs, ni blanc, ni rouge', pp. 5–35.

114. Pouy gives 1789, but the text clearly refers to Louis XVI's May 1790 proclamation, and the flight to Varennes, which means it must be no earlier than the summer of 1791.

115. Siviniant, pp. 1–4.

116. *Diogène à Paris* (1790), BL R.200(13), pp. 13–14.

117. *Le Courier de Paris, ou le Publiciste françois*, 31 October 1789, no. 18, p. 148.

118. *RACSP*, vol. 7, p. 48, Versailles, 24 September 1793.

119. Dommanget, 'Le Symbolisme et le prosélytisme: la cocarde . . .', vol. 2, p. 133.

120. *Courrier des 83 départements*, 7 April 1792, cit. Villiers, *Histoire des clubs des femmes*, pp. 164–5.

121. F. A. Aulard, *La Société des Jacobins*, (6 vols, Paris, 1889–97), vol. 3, 19 March 1792, p. 444. However, in the Jacobin clubs of Marseilles and Avignon, frustration at the troublesome variety of cockades led to the alternative proposal that members should grow moustaches so that they would be able to 'recognize each other at first glance' (Michael L. Kennedy, *The Jacobin Clubs in the French Revolution 1793–1795* (Berghahn: New York and Oxford, 2000), p. 83).

122. Aulard, *Société des Jacobins*, vol. 5, 29 frim. an II/19 December 1793, p. 566.

123. *Journal de Paris*, cit. Marie-Louise Biver, *Le Panthéon à l'époque révolutionnaire* (PUF: Paris, 1982), p. 81.

124. See the print ill. in François Furet and Mona Ozouf (eds), *Dictionnaire critique de la Révolution française* (Flammarion: Paris, 1988)*,* p. 577.

125. Mercier, *Nouveau Paris*, pp. 287–8. An anonymous drawing for the print in the *Révolutions de Paris* (no. 160, 28 July–4 August 1792) is illustrated in Pierrette Jean-Richard and Gilbert Mondin, *Un collectionneur pendant la Révolution: Jean-Louis Soulavie (1752–1813)* (Éditions de la Réunion des Musées Nationaux: Musée du Louvre, Paris 1989), no. 51, p. 53, Fig. 51. Significantly, in the caption to the print, the responsibility for erecting this symbolic barrier is given to 'le Peuple': 'cette barrière fut respectée. Personne ne la franchit.' Restif de la Bretonne referred to the ribbon as a 'favour', but he also emphasized the fact that it was the people themselves who had put it up, symptomatic of their self-discipline and respect for public order, and noted that it was rapidly adorned with 'petits papiers, où étaient les sarcasmes les plus violentes contre les Rois, contre le *veto*, contre la Cour et ses Protégés' (*Les Nuits de Paris, ou le Spectateur nocturne*, 8 vols (Paris, 1788–1790), vol. 8, p. 347, 9/10 August 1792.

126. *Récit de ce qui s'est passé au Temple dans les journées du 2 et 3 septembre 1792, par un officier municipal de la Commune*, cit. *Journal de ce qui s'est passé à la tour du Temple pendant la captivité de Louis XVI roi de France par M. Cléry, valet de Chambre du Roi*, ed. Jacques Brosses (Mercure de France: Paris, 1987), pp. 197–8 note 41.

127. *Arch Parl*, vol. 79, p. 318, cit. Antoine de Baecque, *Le Corps de l'histoire: métaphore et politique (1770–1800)* (Calmann-Lévy: Paris, 1993), p. 354. These words appear in commemorative prints, for example, 'Joseph Chalier guillotiné le 15 juillet 1793', grav. Angelique Brisseau, *femme* Allais, 1793, de Vinck Collection 5396.

128. *Rapport sur la fête héroïque pour les honneurs du Panthéon à décerner aux jeunes Barra* [sic] *et Viala par David, séance 23 messidor an II*, cit. *La Mort de Bara. De l'événement au mythe. Autour du tableau de Jacques-Louis David* (Fondation du Musée Calvet: Avignon, 1989), p. 159. See Raymonde Monnier, 'Le Culte de Bara en l'an II', *AHRF*, 1980, pp. 321–37.

129. Similarly, the 'compagnie des amazones de Creil' and the 'compagnie de la capitaine Daru' wore a cockade over their heart, as did the *bordelaises* who gathered on the Champ de Mars on 20 June 1791 (Villiers, *Histoire des clubs des femmes*, pp. 92, 151, giving the *Chronique de Paris* as source). We might compare the imposition of the cockade on Charlotte Corday during her imprisonment as a kind of purgative retribution; see the terracotta portrait medallion by Pierre Chinard, dated 26 prairial an II (Petit Palais, Paris, Inv. PPM 71).

130. *Arch Parl*, vol. 59, p. 712, cit. Tuetey, vol. 8, item 1989 (8 March 1793).

131. In a discussion of the taking of Valenciennes by royalists (Caron, vol. 1, p. 3, 27 August 1793). See also the print 'Oh! quanto pesa questa libertà', 12th plate of *Varij ritratti ed altre stampe* (Naples, 1797–8), ill. *Premières Collections. Musée de la Révolution française, Vizille* (1985), p. 85, cat. no. 145.

132. An item in *Le Rôdeur*, noted slightly mockingly in a letter from Vergniaud to his brother-in-law, 16 January 1790 (*Annales révolutionnaires*, vol. 3, p. 1910, p. 592).

133. Jacques Godechot, *Les Institutions de la France sous la Révolution et l'Empire* (PUF: Paris, 1968), p. 269.

134. Mona Ozouf, 'Le Simulacre et la fête', in Jean Ehrard and Paul Viallaneix (eds), *Les Fêtes de la Révolution française*, Colloque Clermont-Ferrand (June 1974) (Société des Etudes robespierristes: Paris, 1977), p. 333.

135. *Courier républicain*, no. 491, 20 ventôse an III/10 March 1795, 'Nouvelles de Paris', pp. 77–8. The context for these remarks was the incident where representives of the people, Armonville and Guffroy, were baited by *jeunesse dorée* for wearing respectively a *bonnet rouge* and a badge in the form of one; see François Gendron, *La Jeunesse sous Thermidor* (PUF: Paris, 1983), pp. 120–7.

136. *RAM*, vol. 24, no. 251, 4 prairial an III/30 May 1795, p. 555, on the *séance* of 7 prairial an III/26 May 1795. Wicar's self-portrait, painted in Paris in 1795, shows him with a cockade pinned to his hat. This had been painted for his sister, whom he had wanted to see before departing for Italy, having been advised to do so by his friend the diplomat François Cacault following his imprisonment (3–25 June 1795) for having been involved in the prairial insurrection; see *Le Chevalier Wicar, peintre, dessinateur et collectionneur lillois* (Musée des Beaux-Arts, Lille, 1984), cat. no. 4, pp. 24–6.

137. *Le Menteur, ou le journal par excellence*, 'La Cocarde. Dialogue', pp. 95–8; undated beyond 'an V'.

138. Letter dated 17 ventôse an IV/6 March 1796 to administration municipale of Orléans, Bodin sale, summer 1983, no. 19, lot 130. On 27 germ. an IV/16 April 1796, a *signe de ralliement* in the form of a cockade with white braid worn high on the hat was noted (Schmidt, vol. 2, p. 157).

139. Administration du département de la Sarthe (printed Le Mans), Affiche, 21 germ. an IV/10 April 1796, Musée de la Révolution française, Vizille, 'cocarde' dossier, from unidentified sale catalogue.

140. Schmidt, vol. 2, p. 241, 22 vend. an III/13 October 1794.

141. *L'Indépendant*, 27 fruct. an VI/13 September 1798, no. 347, p. 4.

142. As Daniel Roche notes, Richard Cobb's failure to find any references to patriotic badges (in the morgue records which he analysed) follows not from their having been abandoned – in a way consistent with Cobb's scepticism about the penetration of revolutionary ideologies among ordinary people – but rather from the fact that cockades

would have been worn on hats and caps, which had in every case become separated from the body of the deceased (Richard Cobb, *Death in Paris 1795–1801. The Records of the Basse-Géôle de la Seine October 1795–September 1801 vendémiaire Year IV–Fructidor Year X* (Oxford University Press: Oxford, 1978), pp. 80–1; Daniel Roche, *The People of Paris* (Berg: Leamington Spa, 1987), p. 188).

143. Concerns about inconsistency in regulations continued to exercise legislators in 1798; punishment for those refusing to wear them were called for (see *Le Rédacteur*, 6 fruct. an VI [23 August 1798], no. 994). For an excellent discussion of the commission's report and associated pamphlets, see Jean-Marc Devocelle, 'La Cocarde directorielle: dérives d'un symbole révolutionnaire', *AHRF*, 1992, vol. 69, no. 3, pp. 355–66. To Devocelle's list of the published texts in connection to this legislation should be added René Eschasseriaux, *Corps législatif. Conseil des Cinq-Cents. Opinion de Eschasseriaux jeune sur le projet de résolution relatif à la cocarde nationale. 3 floréal an VII* (BL, FR 229 (18)).

144. Devocelle, 'La Cocarde directorielle', p. 360.

145. J.F. Duplantier, *Corps législatif. Conseil des Cinq-Cents. Opinion de J.P.F. Duplantier, député du département de la Gironde, sur le projet relatif à la cocarde nationale. Séance du 3 floréal an VII*, p. 2.

146. Ibid.

147. F.G.J.S. Andrieux, *Opinion d'Andrieux (de la Seine), sur le projet de loi relatif à la cocarde nationale. Séance du 14 floréal an VII*, pp. 18–19. It is certainly the case that cockades appear fairly regularly in visual imagery from this period. For example, in the work of Louis-Léopold Boilly, they are included in portraits (*Réunion d'artistes* [Isabey's studio], 1798, Louvre) on two of the hats worn and held; in a satirical genre scene, *La Marche incroyable* (1797, private collection, Paris), and in caricature (*Les Croyables* (1797), where a cockade is visible on the hat of a republican).

148. P.J. Pollart, *Opinion de Pollart (de la Seine), sur le port de la cocarde nationale. Séance du 13 floréal an VII*, p. 4.

149. Roëmers, *Projet de résolution . . . Séance du 8 frimaire an VII.* [28 November 1798].

150. *Opinion de Pollart*, pp. 3–4.

151. *Opinion de Duplantier*, p. 5.

152. *Opinion d'Eschasseriaux jeune*, pp. 9–10.

153. *Opinion d'Andrieux*, p. 7.

154. *Opinion de Felix Faulcon . . . Prairial an VII*, pp. 1–2.

155. *Opinion d'Eschasseriaux jeune*, p. 1.

156. Ibid., pp. 5–8.

157. Duplantier, p. 2, Pollart, pp. 4–5.

158. L.A. Gastin, *Opinion de Gastin, sur le projet de résolution relatif à la Cocarde nationale. Séance du 29 floréal an VII*, p. 4.

159. *Opinion d'Andrieux*, p. 3.

160. Ibid., p. 4.

161. Ibid., pp. 15–16.

162. Ibid., p. 17.

163. F.A. Aulard, *Paris sous le Consulat*, 4 vols (Cerf: Paris, 1903–1909), vol. 1, p. 113 (21 January 1800).

164. *Gazette de France*, 4 prairial an VIII, 24 May 1800, cit. Aulard, *Consulat*, vol. 1, pp. 357, 501 (10 July 1800); vol. 1, p. 604 (15 August 1800).

165. *Ibid.*, vol. 1, p. 299 (30 April 1800).

166. *Ibid.*, vol. 1, p. 604 (15 August 1800).

167. Dommanget, 'Symbolisme: la ccocarde . . .', p. 138 (16 pluv. an IX/5 February 1801).

168. See Henry Barbet de Jouy, *Notice des Antiquités, objets du Moyen Âge, de la Renaissance, et des temps modernes composant le Musée des Souverains* (Paris, 1866), no. 213, p. 212 ('Cocarde tricolore que l'empereur Napoléon Ier portait à son chapeau le jour où, à Fontainebleau, il fit ses adieux à sa garde.'), and nos 214 and 215, both of which are Elba-style cockades (p. 214).

169. See *Premières Collections*, pp. 27–9, no. 29, plate 6.

170. Louis Dessaux-Lebrethon, *Mes Angoisses de 30 heures, dans les journées des 5 et 6 Avril 1814, pour avoir, le premier, arboré le signe chéri des Français: la cocarde blanche* (Ghent, May 1815), pp. 1, 39. On 22 April, Jean Debry, prefect of Doubs, appeared at his window with white cockades and had servants distribute them to his officials (*Nouvelle Biographie Générale* (Firmin Didot: Paris, 1855), vol. 13, p. 290).

4

Liberty Caps: from Roman Emblem to Radical Headgear

UNLIKE the cockade, the liberty cap was never the object of specific legislation.[1] Its use and interpretation were, however, constrained by less precise but nonetheless influential beliefs about its symbolic import and social connotations. In reviewing its currency, we are of course dependent on contemporary comments, mostly speaking for – and against – the people who actually wore the caps. Although present in imagery and in emblematic form from 1789, it was not worn to any significant degree until the spring of 1792. At this point, it predominantly took the form of the *bonnet rouge*. From the autumn of this year, it acquired a quasi-official status, being a part of the ensemble of the *sans-culotte* (discussed more fully in the next chapter). Its career as an item of revolutionary dress ended with the Thermidorean Reaction, being reclaimed and relocated as a national emblem in the form of the *bonnet tricolore*.

I argue for a dynamic picture of the ways in which the liberty cap's meanings were selectively and polemically negotiated at different points in the Revolution, which takes account of both topical debate and retrospective interpretative rationalization. In whatever medium it was represented, whether mobilized as emblem or dress, the liberty cap was not simply understood as a stable, orthodox entity for which there was an agreed programmatic rationale; as is shown here in detail, the opinions that were projected onto, and clustered around, the generic idea of the cap were not only multifarious but inherently in mutual tension. Although the historical origins of the liberty cap are Roman, revolutionary commentaries provide a much more diverse – and frequently inconsistent – set of pedigrees for the emblem. The complexities of the liberty cap's currency during the Revolution are further investigated by considering its position within attitudes to the politicization of dress, and the inconsistencies and uncertainties that run through these attitudes. What emerges emphatically is that one cannot separate consideration of the cap as dress from the range of emblematic meanings it was given, as articulated across texts and imagery.

Origins

Historians writing about liberty caps in the Revolution use any one of three terms: *bonnet de la liberté*, *bonnet rouge*, and *bonnet phrygien*, the last two often being combined. Although they have commonly been employed as if they were interchangeable, it can be shown very easily that these three terms are by no means synonymous. Different usage corresponds to the particular circumstances that obtained at different moments of the revolutionary history of the liberty cap. Much of the confusion of terminology would seem to have arisen as a result of a failure to distinguish sufficiently clearly between liberty caps used as emblems and those that were actually worn at different stages of the Revolution.[2]

In France during the nineteenth century, and in consequence to a large extent elsewhere, the *bonnet phrygien rouge* came to be consolidated as the normative type of liberty cap.[3] This post-revolutionary process has obscured the absence of any contemporary explanation as to why it should have taken on a Phrygian form during the Revolution.[4] Although various authors have noted that Phrygian caps did not originally function as liberty caps, why they should have become so during the Revolution has not been satisfactorily addressed in relation to contemporary texts.[5] Benzachen, surely rightly, proposes that 'the origin of the cap's represent-ation is learned'.[6] Yet studies of the Revolution's debt to Antiquity by Parker, Boisneau and Mosse fail to provide any evidence for the classical origins of Phrygian liberty caps.[7] I have not yet found an eighteenth-century source which identifies the Phrygian cap as signifying liberty. Although we can find occasional representations of caps of Phrygian form from the beginning of the Revolution, they do not become common until 1793–94, and the term *bonnet phrygien* only appears with increasing regularity slightly later.

The earliest, and in some ways still the most pertinent, discussion of this matter is the pamphlet *De l'origine et de la forme du bonnet de la liberté* (an IV/September 1795–September 1796) by the history painter Alexandre-Esprit Gibelin. This is the only example of a revolutionary text which addresses the question as to why a liberty cap should be Phrygian, and Gibelin concludes that this is erroneous. His opening premise is that historical references, whether in political discourse or artistic imagery, should be archaeologically accurate, and he complains that contemporary artists and theatre designers have failed to study their sources carefully enough. The dissemination of the Phrygian liberty cap is a case in point for, as Gibelin explains in detail, there is no evidence to show that this is the historically correct form that liberty caps should be given. What Gibelin makes emphatically clear is the fact that the *pileus*, the cap given to enfranchised slaves by the Romans and the standard iconographical referent for the liberty cap as an attribute of Liberty, was not Phrygian. Both the *pileus* and the Phrygian cap evidently varied in shape, but they are, nonetheless, quite distinct: the former is usually round, occasionally slightly pointed, the latter has an unmistakable elaborate forward-falling peak, ear-flaps and trailing neck-piece (Figure 12).[8]

Gibelin was optimistic enough to hope that, once aware of this mistake, people would adopt a historically more justifiable type of liberty cap. His pamphlet is particularly interesting in that he was writing at the moment when, as we will see, liberty caps were undergoing a process of reformulation, which consisted in the substitution of *bonnets phrygiens* or *bonnets tricolores* for *bonnets rouges*. He failed to find a convincingly substantive source for the hybrid Phrygian form of liberty cap. However, in so far as it was assumed to depend on some classical source he suggests possible explanations that he thinks others might have had in mind when either proposing or accepting the *bonnet phrygien*. Castor and Pollux wore it, 'others think', as liberators of Greece, and also to signal their origins as Lacedemonians, who habitually fought wearing caps in order to show their hatred for kings and against tyrants.[9] However, although the word Phrygian has been claimed 'to mean free', Phrygia was, in fact, a source of slaves for Greece.[10]

The circumstances and reasoning behind the transformation of the *bonnet de la liberté* into the *bonnet phrygien* remain mysterious (putting aside for the moment the question of colour). A prosaic suggestion would be that, at some stage during the Revolution, it was thought that the floppy woollen caps which came to double as headgear and emblematic liberty cap resembled the Phrygian caps familiar from antique sculpture. As Phrygian caps were worn by Trojans, the popularity of subjects drawn from Homer's *Iliad* in late eighteenth-century French painting meant that such caps were a familiar item. The antique Phrygian cap and the contemporary common woollen cap would seem to have been conflated with the authentic example of the Roman *pileus*, to produce a confusing but nonetheless influential iconographical progeny.

Only a very approximate picture emerges if one seeks to trace the incidence of *bonnets phrygiens* in revolutionary imagery. One can find sporadic examples of what seem to be Phrygian caps of various colours

Figure 12 Attendant of Mithras (restored as Paris), marble, H 4' 6", 2nd century AD?. Roman sculpture. British Museum, London.

almost from 1789. An early example of the *bonnet phrygien* is the March 1790 project for a medal, where Moreau de St Méry and Delavigne are shown wearing caps with quite clear Phrygian peaks (though lacking the trailing side flaps) (Figure 13).[11] Augustin Dupré, one of the leading medallists of the revolution, was notably inconsistent in his treatment of the form of liberty caps.[12] The earliest dated example I have been able to

Figure 13 Project for medal to Moreau de St-Méry and Delavigne, presidents of Assemblée des Electeurs May-July 1789. Département des Arts Graphiques, Bibliothèque Nationale de France, Paris, D 98896. Photograph: Bibliothèque Nationale de France.

find of an unmistakably Phrygian cap is the 5 *centimes* piece introduced in August 1793.[13] Examples of dated Phygian caps in painting and sculpture are first consistently noticeable during 1793–94. In J.B. Regnault's *La liberté ou la mort* (dated an III, September 1793–September 1794),[14] for example, Liberty holds up a peaked cap with clearly visible side-pieces.

Textual references to the *bonnet phrygien* during the revolutionary decade are extremely rare: the earliest I have found, which refers to it in the context of a medal design, is from the summer of 1790;[15] Annie Geffroy notes two from March 1792.[16] The term does not seem to recur with any consistency until 1794. A poem datable to 27 germinal an III (16 April 1795) cites the Phrygian cap as the true liberty cap (but without pausing to explain why this is so), as distinct from the 'cap of the galley convicts (*bonnet des galériens*)' (i.e., the *bonnet rouge*) which had supposedly been promoted by Jacobins (on which see below): 'Whether error or foresight, / The Jacobins have adopted / the cap of evildoing, / not that of liberty; / For, remarkable by its form, / it is the cap of the Phrygians, / but they have taken as their uniform, / the cap of galley convicts.'[17]

In a discussion of a costume for the Conseils législatifs and public officials in August 1795, Jean-François Barailon somewhat ambivalently mentioned 'these Phrygian caps, whose outfit will soon, unquestionably, be admired by the whole universe, but which would be above all charming for a synod'.[18] In his study of the 'archaeology' of the *bonnet rouge*, Louis Combes states that he could not find the term in contemporary documents before an IV (September 1795–September 1796).[19] This is the same moment that Gibelin went into print to denounce the error of describing liberty caps as Phrygian.

One reason that the correspondance between liberty cap and Phrygian cap has not been scrutinized more thoroughly before is probably that it seems to fit with a well-established expectation that revolutionary discourse and imagery were saturated with classical ingredients. However, if we look at this point more closely, we find that the lack of an explicitly understood rationale for the Phrygian cap is, in fact, not inconsistent with the prevalence of generalized and approximate usage of classical references. Enthusiasm for the example of Antiquity did not necessarily guarantee precision in its citation. Moreover, with liberty caps as elsewhere, it is not uncommon to find interpretations which are manifestly supplementary to the episodes described. The *Patriote françois* gave the following gloss to the wearing of red woollen liberty caps in March 1792:

> This symbolic headgear, in addition to the fact that it recalls a truly dear idea, that of liberty, also pleases, because, hitherto abandoned to the least well-off part of the people, and later adopted by patriots of all estates and every degree of wealth, it seems to destroy the most demeaning of aristocracies, that of wealth.[20]

Paternalistic didacticism is also evident in comments in the *Révolutions de Paris* on the same phenomenon:

The sight of a *bonnet rouge* transports them [the people], something that should not be the occasion for mockery . . . They were told that this woollen cap was in Greece and Rome the emblem of the enfranchisement of all the enemies of despotism; this was enough for them; from this moment, every citizen wanted to have this cap.[21]

There is no shortage of citations of classical precedent for various aspects of political actions (whether to defer to such models, or to claim to have surpassed them).[22] But awareness of precise classical prototypes for the use of liberty caps is only very exceptionally made explicit. For example, in October 1792, Chaumet proposed that an Austrian deserter should be given a *bonnet de la liberté* as a sign of his adoption as a French citizen, citing the precedent of the enfranchisement of Roman slaves.[23] A medal struck to commemorate the death of Mirabeau (2 April 1791), copies a coin commemorating Brutus' assassination of Caesar, which bears a *pileus* between two daggers, and was illustrated in the *Révolutions de Paris*. But such erudite echoes would be lost on all but a tiny minority.[24]

The Thermidorian Reaction saw a rethinking of classical elements in political vocabulary, for they had become tainted by association with the Terror. According to *Le Propagateur*, an era of pseudo-classical politicking had gratuitously and erroneously invoked 'the opinions, the prejudices, the documents of history, and even the axioms of morality' in order to bolster an otherwise fragile legitimacy.[25] Classical names had lost their authority through having become too familiar as alibis for butchery and disorder. In June 1800, the *Propagateur* concurred with the *Moniteur*'s attempt to rehabilitate the two Brutuses from their association with the politics of the Terror, and its observation that such authentic historical figures had disappeared beneath the perfidious clichés of revolutionary rhetoric: 'one can make false applications; one can persuade an intoxicated populace which murders its magistrates, that any man who has a dagger in his hand and a *bonnet rouge* on his head, is a Brutus'.[26] A draft report on costumes for public officials stressed the same need to distinguish carefully between different eras from Antiquity; artists were too prone to confuse motifs originating from periods of oppression and freedom.[27]

Classical referents could nevertheless provide a reassuringly *savant* and bourgeois idiom in which to recreate a language of politics which superseded the violence of Jacobin and *sans-culotte* rhetoric. This does not, of course, get us any further toward locating an influential, recognized point of departure for resorting to Phrygian liberty caps. Nonetheless, however mysterious, the presumed classical pedigree of the Phrygian cap was strikingly different from that of the coarse *bonnet rouge de laine* associated with the *sans-culottes*. To this extent, the promotion of the Phrygian form of liberty cap is consistent with the cultural tenor of the Directory's bourgeois republicanism. One might see this in terms of a latent level of meaning coming to the fore as it became politically necessary to detach the emblem from its previously radical popular incarnation, the *bonnet rouge*.

The range of historical precursors and parallels for the liberty cap that occurs in revolutionary discourse extends beyond Antiquity. Such connections are, however, curiously selective. Thus, although Bianchi cites the precedent of the revolting Breton peasants in 1675 known as 'bonnets rouges', this does not seem to have been picked up on in revolutionary texts.[28] One might also have expected to have found some reference to the insurrectionary example of the seventeenth-century Neapolitan fisherman Masaniello, whose cap was sometimes construed by his contemporaries as being akin to the classical liberty cap, but I have not yet come across this idea in revolutionary texts.[29] By contrast, an obscure episode of Netherlandish history originating in 1350 was produced as a salutary precedent for the wearing of caps as political signs, specifically *bonnets rouges* by enemies of despotism.[30] Perhaps the most frequent alternative or supplement to classical prototypes for the liberty cap is that associated with the Swiss 'freedom fighter' William Tell. This form of headgear – in fact a brimmed and plumed hat – was that of the tyrant Gessler whom Tell had deposed,[31] and had occurred in pre-revolutionary prints and medals celebrating Tell's compatriot Necker.[32] Once again, we find that comprehension of the emblem's historical origins could be garbled in revolutionary commentaries. Thus, in the pamphlet *Les Bienfaits de la Révolution* (1791), the cap is described as belonging to Tell, not Gessler.[33] In the aftermath of the Terror, Gibelin compared the *bonnet rouge* to Gessler's hat, for it had likewise become a despised object of obligatory homage.[34] Gibelin suggests that liberty caps in the form of brimmed hats signify civic distinction, in contrast to the more truly democratic practice of wearing of *pileus*-like caps, in that the headgear normally worn by ordinary people has been elevated to the level of a political emblem.[35] This is perhaps what a journalist in the *Chronique de Paris* had in mind when claiming that 'the round shape of a cap [was] an emblem of equality'.[36] A contemporary commentator also correlated

different types of liberty cap with different types of freedom, in remarks
exposing Jacobins' ignorance of the Swiss historical precedent: 'we ask
Jacobin fashion merchants, if they know that this emblem of liberty
comes from the formation of the Swiss League? From the way in which
they treat this respectable nation, we would be tempted to believe that
they don't know this this. We draw to their attention, for the rest, that
the form of our *bonnets rouges* no more resembles that cap which was
the sign of liberty for the Swiss, than our liberty resembles theirs.'[37]
Alternatively, at the same period, the Tell version of the liberty cap could
stand in as a less inflammatory substitute for the discredited *bonnet
rouge*.[38] On another occasion, the story of Tell's exploits was recalled in
order to denounce the squalid and criminal origins of the *bonnet rouge de
laine*, identified as that of the galley convicts.[39] The claim that revolutionary symbols had been bogusly justified by a misguided reliance on
a hotch-potch of misunderstood precedents came to be a familiar form
of denunciation in the nineteenth century.[40]

THE BONNET ROUGE

If the instigation of the *bonnet phrygien* form of liberty cap depends upon
an elusive and almost certainly putative classical model, the *bonnet rouge*
might seem to have a less problematic origin and agreed meaning. But
this is far from the case. First, liberty caps were of no consistent colour
in the early Revolution;[41] secondly, the introduction of *bonnets rouges*
as liberty caps was a complex and contested episode. Perhaps no other
revolutionary item has been the object of such violently conflicting
interpretations.

Retrospective commentaries have been particularly influential. Jules
Michelet, for example, insisted that the colour of the *bonnet rouge* was
deliberately chosen in such a way as to reinforce his picture of a benign
People. He repudiated the claim that the red colour derived from blood,
and, moreover, denied the link with the cap of galley convicts supposedly
launched at the Châteauvieux festival: 'The colour red was preferred to
all others, being more gay, more striking, more pleasing to the crowd.'[42]
As Michelet's comments imply, the association that, from the period of
the Revolution onwards, weighs most heavily on the *bonnet rouge* is that
of bloodshed – it was red because it had literally been stained by the sanguinary excesses of the Terror.[43] Further negative connections were made

with the red shirt worn by those on their way to be executed,[44] or the red flag used to signal the declaration of martial law.[45] In 1791, for example, Charles Lameth's appearance at the Opéra dressed in red provoked an angry response: 'the people, for whom this colour recalled the red flag, forced him to withdraw, shouting: "Down with the red flag, down with matrial law!"'.[46]

As far as accounting for the origins of the red colour is concerned, three principal contexts have been cited – taken chronologically, these are: Girondins' espousal of bellicose populism, the festival organized to celebrate the release of the soldiers of Châteauvieux, and the rise of the Jacobins in the spring of 1792. It is important to recognize that the general interpretative context within which descriptions and commentaries on such new forms of dress were articulated during 1791–92 became progressively more fragmented and polarized. Liberty caps were increasingly remarked upon in so far as they were associated – both positively and negatively – with factions, groups, and clubs – that is, with the new institutional apparatus of the Revolution's evolving political culture.

The Girondins have been held to be responsible for encouraging the *bonnet rouge*, in tandem with the pike, as part of a political platform based on aggressive populism.[47] This attribution of an apparently simple cause both depends on and reinforces the idea that such emblems were essentially and exclusively badges belonging to neatly definable political clubs or societies. The association of *bonnet* and pike in the second half of 1791 was less the consequence of a concerted Girondin programme than a contingent reaction to popular items. An examination of Girondin texts shows that their explicit enthusiasm for *bonnets* is not evident until early 1792. In fact, secondary texts which make this claim rely almost exclusively on an article of 6 February 1792 in the *Patriote françois*, which deals with the speech by the Englishman Robert Pigott given in Dijon on 26 December at the Société des Amis de la Constitution – that is, a provincial Jacobin club, where the replacement of three-cornered hats by caps had been proposed.[48]

Pigott's speech is worth consideration as it indicates some of the associative repertoire ascribed to liberty caps at this point in the Revolution. He begins by decrying hats as having been introduced by priests and despots: 'as well as the servile and ridiculous ceremony of a salute which degrades a man, in making him bow his bare and submissive head before his equal'.[49] By contrast, he argued that caps:

make more gay, reveal the physiognomy, make it more open, more confident, cover the head without concealing it, elevate gracefully natural dignity and are susceptible of all kinds of embellishment in their varied form and colours.

Pigott casts his net wide in seeking a respectable pedigree for caps, including, without any particular emphasis, the Greeks, Romans and ancient Gauls, who wore them 'to distinguish themselves from barbarian peoples', and two revolutionary heroes – Rousseau, who is claimed as a partisan of the cap as symbol of liberty, and Voltaire, who 'wore it always'.[50] The cap shown at the head of the title page of his printed speech is fur-trimmed, and resembles that worn by Jean-Jacques Rousseau in his much reproduced portrait in Armenian costume by Allan Ramsay (1766).[51] As far as Pigott is concerned, his advocacy of the cap was, at this stage, decidedly not a populist policy: 'it is to the few, rather than the multitude that I address myself to effect the benign reforms by their example'. Great emphasis is put on the general example of Antiquity: 'it is the great examples of Antiquity which must be followed if you wish to carry through a reform'. He ends by celebrating the irresistible combination of cap – proud emblem of liberty, and pike – the means for its achievement beyond France's frontiers.[52]

One might expect that commentary on this text, in a journal partly written by Brissot and Manuel, two leading members of what later became known as the Girondin group, would provide some indicative amplification of their proselytizing attitude to the *bonnet rouge* as a politically provocative and cohesive symbol. Yet most of the article amounts to little more than direct quotation from Pigott's published discourse. Moreover, Pigott was speaking at the Jacobin club. The *Patriote françois* commentary makes nothing of the specificity of *bonnet rouge*, nor does it, in fact, insist on the coupling of cap and pike; an article the following week on the pike does not mention caps.[53]

Because of the later prominence of the *bonnet rouge* between late 1792 and 9 Thermidor, its rise has been seen as inevitable. However, we should consider the evolving currency of liberty caps in the context of the more general politicization of dress during the previous two years. The predominant impression from this period is that new forms of politicized dress were ad hoc, topical and individualistic. For example, in 1791 the proceedings of the National Assembly were interrupted by a curiously dressed man:

a character [arrived in the Assembly] in a costume which attracted everybody's attention. He was dressed from head to toe in white: a white hat *à la* Henri IV, with a tricolore plume; white coat, jacket, breeches, stockings and shoes; only his coat had blue piping, and his jacket red piping. A Spanish-style cloak hung over his back; this cloak was of silk and in the three colours; he held a laurel branch. His project was to present himself to the National Assembly, to deliver a very brief speech, and to present his Mercury's wand in hommage to the president . . . This strange character, of an advanced age, *and whose costume and actions provoked a thousand conjectures*, was an assessor for the *juge de paix* at Bar-sur-Seine, named Pial.[54] [my emphasis]

The dominant white colour and plume *à la* Henri IV seem to identify him with a broadly royalist outlook. As well as recalling the official costumes that were run up for the Estates General, this description of Pial's outfit also suggests a festive or theatrical flavour. His use of a bricolage of ceremonial attire is consistent with the predvailing do-it-yourself flavour of patriotic dress. Similarly, references to liberty caps at this stage of the Revolution indicate that they range from day-to-day fashion accessory to a device adopted for special occasions when a self-consciously emblematic purpose was required. For example, looking back to the summer of 1790, a liberty cap was noted as an emblem used by workers preparing the Champ de Mars for the Festival of Federation; one group had a flag with the motto 'the slaves of despotism have become the children of liberty'; another group carried a pole with a cap on top, 'symbol of liberty'.[55] The festivals of Federation were the first occasions when we find widespread ceremonial use of liberty caps as a prominent element.[56] In the spring of 1792, we also find the recommendation that the 'round hat', which stood for equality, rather than the *bonnet rouge*, replace the three-cornered hat, though this is clearly intended as an alternative to the common man's cap and its signification of populist politics.[57] More generally, liberty caps were to be found on buttons and worn as an ostentatious kind of fashion accesssory.[58] However, during the summer of 1791, *bonnet de la liberté* remains the standard form of terminology, *bonnets de laine* or *bonnet rouge* continuing to refer more specifically to a characteristic form of pre-revolutionary artisanal dress associated with the faubourg Saint-Antoine.[59] *Bonnets rouges* as the distinguishing feature of the faubourg Saint-Antoine were described as having been in evidence during the pantheonization of Voltaire's remains on 12 July 1791, well before any evidence of Girondin espousal of such items.[60]

It has been repeatedly claimed that the *bonnet rouge* form of liberty cap originated as a result of the festival given in Paris on 15 April 1792 to celebrate the release of the forty soldiers of the Châteauvieux regiment from the galleys after imprisonment as a reprisal for insubordination at Nancy during 1790. On this occasion, the soldiers and large numbers of onlookers were supposed to have worn *bonnets rouges*, the former as part of the clothing worn by *galériens*, the latter in sympathy and celebration, as liberty caps.[61] The idea that a cap denoting a modern form of slavery had been transformed into a liberty cap is obviously appealing, but was not, in fact, voiced at the time. It is true, of course, that the festival was also dedicated to Liberty. Indeed, in the Jacobin club, Collot d'Herbois claimed that: 'this festival was not that of the soldiers of Châteauvieux, but rather that of Liberty'.[62] This theme was primarily established by the inclusion of a large seated figure of Liberty in the festival's procession. However, the festival was not the site for the 'invention' of the *bonnet rouge*. The soldiers' reinstatement was to be demonstrated during the course of the festival by their changing *out of* the 'galley convict outfit' back into regimental uniform.[63] After returning from the National Assembly, forty men would carry 'the galley convicts' outfit and the chains of the forty patriot soldiers as a form of trophy'.[64] According to one source, in the festival's procession, the soldiers were accompanied by the *hats* given to them en route from Brest to Paris by the departments they passed through, which would have been a more appropriate sign of the restitution of respectability.[65] This festival – Châteauvieux/Liberty – is often set up in opposition with the Simonneau Festival of Law, but there too we find the 'bonnet rouge de la liberté' appearing in descriptions of the shields of the 48 sections of Paris.[66] Indeed, it is hard to find more than incidental references to *bonnets rouges* in connection with the Châteauvieux festival.[67] David Dowd records that the statue of Louis XV was blindfolded and give a *bonnet rouge*, but does not attempt to clarify to what extent caps were evident among the participants.[68] At first sight, blindfolding the royal statue might be assumed to be a form of ritual humiliation for a monumental spectator deemed to be unworthy of participation in the festival. But André Chénier uses blindfolding as a metaphor to signify the deliberate aversion of all true patriot's eyes – not just those of Louis XV (who literally stands in for Louis XVI) – from a degrading spectacle.[69]

Yet, it is certainly true that later antagonistic, counter-revolutionary texts play on the stigma attached to the *galériens'* cap as a means of

Figure 14 Anonymous: 'Au Roi dépouillé. Louis le dernier et sa famille conduits au Temple le 13 Aoust 1792' (To the Stripped king. Louis the Last and his Family taken to the Temple on the 13 August 1792), etching, 1792. Musée Carnavalet, Paris (Hist. GC 007 A). Photograph: Photothèque des Musées de la Ville de Paris (Andreani).

expressing distaste for the *bonnet rouge* of *sans-culottes* and Jacobins. An undated caricature attacking the Jacobins, entitled 'Le Jacobin royaliste', shows a galley slave branded with *fleurs de lys* wearing a cap, and has the caption: 'Having long governed the galleys, now he wants to govern affairs'.[70] Official recognition of the undesirable similarity between *galérien*'s cap and liberty cap did not come until 23 September 1793, when the former was abolished.[71] One reason why the link was not simple is that not all convicts wore *bonnets rouges*; some wore *bonnets verts*, or green caps with red borders.[72] The green version of the convict's cap was utilized to condemn Louis XVI in the aftermath of the invasion of the Tuileries on 10 August 1792 (Figure 14). However, the *bonnet vert* had another derogatory meaning, as it had been worn by bankrupts.[73] A print which was probably made soon after 20 June 1792 relies on this register to denounce Louis XVI (Figure 15). In 1797, Gibelin made it clear that an awareness of this ambiguity resurfaced at the time of the Thermidorean Reaction,

Figure 15 Anonymous: 'Aristocrates soyez tranquilles sur la santé du TRAITRE LOUIS XVI, il boit comme un Templier en attendant . . .(Aristocrats be calm regarding the health of the TRAITOR LOUIS XVI, he drinks like a Templar while waiting . . .)', etching, 1792. Département des Arts Graphiques, Bibliothèque Nationale de France, Paris. Photograph: Bibliothèque Nationale de France.

when the *bonnet rouge* had been drained of its intimidating power following the fall of the *sans-culottes* and Jacobins. He declared that those who had earlier adopted the *bonnet rouge* as a matter of political expediency were now free to discard it, having previously had to put prudence before a sense of disgust in wearing a cap which they considered had 'until this day only served us to cover the head of the convict'.[74] The final point against the Châteauvieux claim is that the *bonnet rouge* had already been made familiar in Paris because of the controversy surrounding its use at the Jacobin club in March.[75]

Jacobin Caps and Others

Between the spring and summer of 1792, the *bonnet rouge* was transformed from a factional badge loosely connected to *sans-culottes* and
Jacobins[76] to a national republican emblem, an evolution which corresponds to the elevation of Jacobins to a central role in government. Two
points need emphasizing in relation to this transformation. First, that
under the weight of nineteenth-century revolutionary and republican
traditions which sought to anchor their emblems in the Revolution, the
bonnet rouge was singled out for special status from among a highly diverse
range of forms of patriotic dress and adornment. Secondly, given the
unregulated nature of their manufacture, *bonnets rouges* inevitably
manifested considerable variations in form and material which gave
ample scope for being gratuitously or accurately interpreted as evidence
of different groupings' attempts to identify themselves and provoke
others.[77] If we trace the currency of the *bonnet rouge* between February
and April 1792, we find that its association with the Jacobins is decidedly
ambiguous, and was as much the result of derisive comments as of any
deliberate policy. By examining a range of 'readings' of liberty caps and
other items of dress, we get some insight into the unpredictable and
eclectic amalgam that is revolutionary imagery, perceived and interpreted
from intensely partisan perspectives.

   At the end of February 1792, *bonnets rouges* were described as having
been brandished on canes by members of the audience of the Théâtre
Italien in Paris to cries of 'Long live Liberty! Long live the Nation!'.[78]
Raising hats on canes and poles was a standard gesture of liberty.[79] In this
case people waving canes are identified as nothing more specific than
patriots out to provoke royalists. Furthermore, such behaviour was
probably only insured against official suppression by the traditional role
of theatres for demonstrations of political partisanship. In February 1792,
this risk was the greater as the municipality of Paris had earlier in the
month ordered, in connection with the control of the distribution of
pikes, that: 'No one can carry any rallying sign other than the cockade
or the national colours.'[80] It is probable that further comments on, and
manifestations of, the use of *bonnets rouges* could be found before the
second half of 1791, but it is in late February and March of 1792 that we
encounter a sudden profusion of references to *bonnets rouges* in the
Parisian press. The fact that the Jacobin club was centrally involved in the

publicity given to the wearing of *bonnets rouges* ensured that the episode was discussed in strongly polarized terms.

The wearing of the *bonnet rouge* by speakers at the tribune at the Jacobin club was first observed on 11 March 1792.[81] The practice was also reported at the meeting on 19 March, a session which was already newsworthy because of the presence of Dumouriez, then foreign minister, who wore the cap when he spoke. However, during the course of the meeting, a letter arrived from Pétion, the mayor of Paris, which was immediately read out. Pétion urged the Jacobins to relinquish the *bonnet rouge* as a potentially divisive symbol, which might be both harmful to their political prestige and, more importantly, detrimental to public order. He voiced his horror of conflict between antagonistic factions. The *bonnet rouge* might be a catalyst to internal dissention and disruptive of the consensual and peaceful implementation of the principles of 'liberté' and 'égalité'. The danger lay in the malicious use to which enemies of the constitution might put *bonnets rouges*:

> [They] would indeed like to present patriotic societies as a party, a faction, and would this not in some fashion be helping them by separating citizens by exterior signs who should rather be rallied to the same principles and the general interest? Whatever vogue these signs might have, they will never be adopted by all patriots, and a man passionate about the public good will be very indifferent for a *bonnet rouge*. In this form, liberty will appear neither more beautiful nor more majestic: such a form will add nothing to the natural love that the French have for the constitution . . . If the torrent of fashion is not halted, what will happen? Men who appear in public with *bonnets rouges* will be labelled Jacobins; the enemies of this Society will be the first to take up this costume to compromise them. They will provoke troubles, disorder, and this will be blamed on the Society . . . Soon you will seee green caps, white caps. When caps of different colours meet, then a bloody and ridiculous war will start, public order will be disturbed, internal peace disrupted, and perhaps liberty will be compromised.[82]

According to the minutes of the Jacobin club, this letter had an immediate effect: 'In the middle of reading this letter out, the President's cap had re-entered his pocket, and by the time he had finished not one was visible in the room.'[83] Robespierre then spoke at length in support of Pétion's recommendation, and a resolution was taken to cease wearing the *bonnet rouge*, both at their meetings and in public.[84]

Although the Jacobin club responded to this plea to abandon the *bonnet rouge* in its meetings,[85] its use continued to spread throughout Paris, occasioning contrasting responses. For the *Révolutions de Paris*, the cap was a patriotic sign, whose significance should not be compromised by petty disputes arising from indiscriminate use. Rather it should only be employed when 'the public interest was in danger': 'At the sight of the first *bonnet rouge* on the head of a good citizen well-known as such, let us rally around him, putting on [*bonnets rouges*] likewise.'[86] Such a recommendation steers the cap away from localized identification with a particular group, toward a usage akin to the adoption of the cockade inspired by Desmoulins in July 1789 as a rallying sign for popular mobilization.

The role of the Jacobins in the dissemination of the *bonnet rouge* was influential, but they clearly had no monopoly on its use.[87] That it was taken up outside the walls of the Jacobin club may well have been encouraged by the publicity given to their temporary adoption of it at their meetings. Jacobins' relinquishment of the headgear was contrasted to the more enthusiastic retention of it by others beyond the walls of the club. According to the *Patriote françois*:

> While cold reason thus proscribed the *bonnet rouge* at the Jacobin club, ardent enthusiasm made it triumph at the Théâtre de la Nation . . . They were performing *The Death of Caesar* . . . After this performance, the bust of Voltaire was carried on to the stage, and was crowned with the cap of Liberty.[88]

In the second half of March *bonnets rouges* were described as visible 'in all the walks, in cafés, in theatre auditoria, and above all in patriotic assemblies'.[89] The cap's appearance in theatres and in the official space of the National Assembly was attributed to Jacobins by the Abbé Fontenay on 15 March, and by the *Chronique de Paris* two days later.[90] Those who wore *bonnets rouges* after Pétion's letter to the Jacobins were labelled 'sedition-mongers'.[91] A number of violent incidents were reported as having been provoked by *bonnets rouges*.[92] The comte de Fersen expressed a beleaguered royalist view, claiming that the *bonnet rouge* would become 'a means of persecution as the national cockade used to be'.[93] The Marquis de Romé blamed *agents provocateurs* disguised as *sans-culottes*: their raggedness was contrived, their *bonnets rouges* were 'of the finest scarlet', and they were to be found in cabarets paying with newly minted coins – damning evidence that they were malevolent mercenaries, not authentic patriots.[94] The abbé de Fontenay described how Jacobins in theatre audiences 'brazenly paraded themselves';[95] six days later he sarcastically referred to the 'new Jacobin livery', made up of *bonnet rouge* and 'trousers and a single jacket'[96] (indicating that what was to become the outfit of the *sans-culottes* after 10 August 1792 and into 1793 was already perceived as a negative stereotype by the spring of 1792).[97] He goes on to denigrate the utility and value of this type of costume for both economic reasons – 'Commerce will not benefit' – and because of the confusion of established dress codes it implied: 'Liberty will lose much by the licence which authorizes the link that is made with the apparel of people on the wrong side of justice among others'. He concludes deprecatingly: 'this fury for *bonnets rouges* is our new craze' – like Pétion, relegating the phenomenon to the status of a modish aberration, but destablisingly dangerous nonetheless.[98]

On 16 March 1792, Condorcet observed the popularity and spread of the *bonnet rouge* and considered Pétion's attempt to reverse this trend. He was not optimistic about his probable success giving as reasons the impracticality of enforcement, for 'in a free country, everyone is master of their own choice of headgear'. Furthermore, with the abolition of the guild of *bonnetiers*, 'simple merchants have been able, without the consent of the jurors of their guilds, to stock up with as many as thirty thousand of these caps. In truth, having thought about this seriously, we can see no constituted authority which can deal with a disorder of this kind, and we are resigned to wait for it to disappear.'[99] An element of political modishness is also manifest in the appearance of 'red hoods' sported by women, as observed in the audience of the Théâtre de la rue de Richelieu (Comédie française) at a performance of *Caius Gracchus* on 18 March 1792.[100] According to the critical commentary of the *Feuille du jour*, the idealism enshrined in the liberty cap was undermined by a kind of fashion- and status-conscious élitism, fed by a sophisticated fashion industry in need of new clients: 'It is worth noting in passing, that this type of equality presents a certain aristocracy in the quality of material, since someone who disdained a woollen cap, had one made of cashmir, another of silk, etc., etc. What a subject of mockery for the rest of Europe! A great and brilliant nation all in *bonnets rouges*! For the rest, the price of caps has risen from 30 *sols* to 6 *livres*; at the Palais Royal they are worth no more than 20 *sols*'.[101] For *Le Spectateur et le modérateur*, the sudden spread of *bonnets rouges* could be explained as the result of 'the speculation of a Jacobin capmaker, who wanted to make one hundred thousand *écus*'.[102]

Writing from Paris on 25 March 1792, Jean Fourgeret claimed '[the *bonnets rouges*'] reign here is f :shed', ascribing this to the challenge of a 'coalition' of 'white caps, which had perhaps surprised [people] by their majority'.[103] Antoine Gorsas, a more sympathetic commentator attributed the cap's reduced visibility to patriots' realization that it would appear more 'respectable' if worn less.[104] Two months later, on 23 May, Fontenay reported with relief that: '*bonnets rouges* have finally disappeared from Paris, and one can hope that public tranquillity will no more be troubled by this ridiculous accoutrement. The Jacobins are looking for some other subject for a quarrel.'[105] Exactly the opposite of Condorcet's hope was to be realized. With the rise of what Soboul has called the 'mouvement populaire' during the spring and summer of 1792, the *bonnet rouge* was to figure in increasingly politically polarized confrontations. It was worn by *fédérés* converging on Paris in summer of 1792 and therefore associated with the violent incidents which they courted.[106]

20 JUNE 1792

A watershed in the evolution of the *bonnet rouge*'s symbolic status is the invasion of the Tuileries Palace on 20 June 1792. Reports of the events of this revolutionary *journée* manifest an extreme polarization between proponents of populist political action and defenders of royal authority. The part played by the *bonnet rouge* in commentaries on the invasion provides a central focus for the articulation of such views. In accounts of this occasion, we can also observe the pressurized evolution of a new emblematic language by means of which to articulate conflicting perceptions of the dissociation of a phase of constitutional monarchy.[107]

On 19 June, batallions from the faubourgs Saint-Marcel and Saint-Antoine had paraded before the National Assembly, planting an *arbre de la liberté*, and brandishing a *bonnet rouge*. Although this demonstration was accompanied by a speech that referred to the classical pedigree for the *arbre de la liberté*, it was viewed as a troubling manifestation of popular force, intended to challenge not only royal authority, but the authority of the Assembly itself. While the original aim of the popular march-past in the Assembly had been to commemorate the third anniversary of the oath of the Tennis Court on 20 June, the more urgent topical motive was to protest at the king's dismissal of the Girondin ministry, and his refusal to agree to a law banishing non-juring priests, or to the setting-up of a military camp on the edge of Paris. Pétion, the mayor of Paris, did nothing to quell this unrest, even when crowds – including groups from the faubourgs and National Guard – gathered in the grounds of the Tuileries on the morning of 20 June.[108]

Having entered the Tuileries more or less unchallenged, the crowds eventually reached the royal family and, like some subversive initiation, gave to the queen a cockade, and to the king and Dauphin *bonnets rouges* to wear. Chuquet writes that the king was 'constrained to put on the *bonnet rouge*'.[109] In his 1792 pamphlet on what he characterized as these 'sad events', de Rougeville, an ex-royal guard, recounts how a *bonnet rouge* was first put on the Queen's head by a courtier to whom it had been passed, and then on that of the Dauphin, who, pale and in tears, 'did not long have to bear this regicide vulgar cap'.[110] For de Rougeville, the imposed wearing of the cap is symbolic of an anarchic breakdown of the social order in the explicit form of a circumstantial threat to the king's life, as well as an implicit challenge to the legitimacy of his authority. Royalist accounts consistently insist on the king's calm bravery, but differ on whether he accepted the *bonnet rouge* from a grenadier and then drank the health of the nation, or was forced to submit to having it roughly pulled onto his head. Similarly, in one description of Marie-Antoinette's involvement in this episode, a courtier is described as playing the role of protective intermediary, passing the cap from crowd to queen.[111]

In the Legislative Assembly a shocked Dumas claimed that 'le peuple' had forced Louis XVI 'to debase himself in wearing the liberty cap'. Despite the use of the more neutral term 'liberty cap', which clearly corresponded to his refusal to name the *bonnet rouge*, he signalled his disgust at the convergence of popular headgear and both social and political infringement by damning the occasion as demeaning for the king and royal family.[112] By contrast, according to a report in the *Journal de Paris*, Isnard, an eye witness, asserted that: 'The King himself had willingly put on the liberty cap'.[113] Daubigny's version of events given in the Jacobin club was a direct riposte to Dumas's account. While he emphasized Louis XVI's compliance in accepting the *bonnet rouge*, he also stressed the essential incompatibility of king and the popular badge of liberty by pointing out that the king was only able to put the cap on with great difficulty: 'Well then, the king indeed put it on himself, for as it was too tight for his big head, he pulled with all his strength to have the peak facing forwards. All that was attached for him were two cockades on each side. They placed one of a prodigious size on the bosom of the queen.'[114] The significance of the episode as a moment of choice is also manifest in some accounts according to which the king was to be offered two cockades, one white and one 'national': 'if he takes the white one, we will call for his removal from the Assembly; if he chooses the red, we will force him to approve the decree against priests'.[115]

Prints of this episode are consistent with the main alternative versions of what occurred. On the one hand, as Annie Duprat has noted, contemporary prints seem predominantly to represent Louis as a rather passive protagonist, at best manifesting a regal bonhomie in agreeing to toast the Nation.[116] In contrast, images produced after the king's execution, such as that by Bouillon, emphasize his extraordinary courage (though not his approval of the invasion), demonstrated by his asking a grenadier to feel his heart, beating at its normal pace.[117] Although this incident may appear suspiciously melodramatic, it is also included in eyewitness accounts of the events of 20 June given by representatives from the Legislative Assembly sent to the Tuileries to confirm what was going on.[118]

Engravings after Boze's pre-revolutionary portrait of Louis XVI were updated in the wake of the invasion of the Tuileries by giving the king a liberty cap. The cap is crisply delineated, and sits stiffly above Louis's smiling features, with any hint of its popular source eliminated. In one version of the print, a lengthy caption censures the invasion and denounces the mixture of violence and compromise by means of which Louis was obliged to wear the *bonnet rouge*.[119] As was remarked at the time, Louis's temporary adoption of this new coiffure provided a concrete realization of the rhetorical apostrophization of the liberty cap as a new, democratized substitute for the royal crown. Versions of the cap-crown pairing could be categorized as confrontational[120] or parodic,[121] the cap serving as a democratized substitute for the crown: 'This headgear is the civic crown of the free man and the regenerated Frenchman'.[122]

Whichever way they were interpreted, the events of 20 June 1792 stand as a momentous, if ad hoc, elevation of the *bonnet rouge* to a quasi-official emblem of state. For royalists, this was a profoundly shocking flaunting of the king's authority. In terms of the detail of the narration, one way to try to defuse the impact of the popular challenge to royal authority was to shift the meaning of the *bonnet rouge*, not only by stating that he took it willingly, but further by playing up the claim that Louis had also accepted a cockade which he attached to the cap. This not only echoed his endorsement of the cockade on 17 July 1789, but overlaid the meaning of the cap as a provocative token of de facto insurrection with the less divisive import of the national colours.[123] Other commentators were more confrontational. De Gouy asked how people would have reacted if:

> These robbers, purposefully equipped with this deprobatory sign, which in the prison of our galleys distinguishes the criminal from the respectable man, had dared violently so to dress the President of the legislative body, [and] to exhibit him in this degraded state to the laughter of his accomplices.[124]

Other supporters of the king sought, somewhat desperately, and only in print, to wrest the *bonnet rouge* from the oppressive grip of the sections. Responding to Santerre's reported statement that the day had been 'a failed affair', Rosoi countered that it had in fact proved the grandeur of Louis XVI. Moreover, he asserted that the cap had emerged from the traumatic events as an object of royalist veneration:

> this very *bonnet rouge*, this sign which hitherto signified disgrace, ignominy, rebellion, this sign was placed on the head of the Hero of 20 June: from this moment, I adopted it, and I already know several hundred royalists, who, like me, will take up this sign that has become sacred since my King wore it. – Two mottoes will be embroidered on it. – On the front, *my King purified it*; on the back, the motto of the English Order and for the same reason, *Shame on him who sees a stain*. When the MAN GOD had expired on the cross, it became the sign before which all Nations bent their knee; *in hoc signo vinces*, said Heaven to Constantine. The rebels will abandon this purified sign after Louis XVI, and Marie-Antoinette and the royal child wore it. Sedition-mongers will blanch before it, there is nothing in Nature, which having been for them, will not be found to be against them.[125]

Louis reacted forcefully to the affair, seeking to reassert his authority. Annie Duprat has drawn our attention to the print in *Révolutions de Paris* showing the king's reproach to Pétion, mayor of Paris, the following day for failing to take any action to prevent the invasion until it was too late.[126] A lengthy investigation into how the palace had come to be invaded, with particular reference to the non-intervention of the municipal authorities, was set in motion.[127] As Philip Mansel has emphasized, Louis further manifested his intransigence through the medium of dress by subsequently refusing to appear in the uniform of the National Guard despite advice from the Guard's leaders that this would be a powerful way of commanding widespread – and much needed – support.[128] Yet, in the wake of 20 June 1792, the spread of the *bonnet rouge* corresponded to the consolidation of organized popular radicalism.

Usage and Status

In addition to the wearing of the *bonnet rouge* as polemical political headgear, associated with protest and provocation, it increasingly became a form of quasi-official dress in patriotic political clubs. However, we should not take this institutionalization to be either homogeneous or consistent. Decisions to adopt the *bonnet rouge* as a form of official dress were taken at local level, and without any central instruction. Despite certain moments of euphoric hyperbole, it is important to understand that the use of the *bonnet rouge* was increasingly confined to official or special occasions;[129] Dommanget notes that it is extremely rare to find references to the cap being worn in Beauvais in 1793–94.[130] Although police reports on public opinion in September 1793 note that there was a desire for all men to wear the *bonnet rouge*, it was also observed that this proposal was essentially a reaction to the legislation requiring women to wear the cockade.[131] We should, however, distinguish between usage and possession, in the sense that many people evidently owned caps but kept them in readiness in their pockets.[132]

The cap was in widespread use in provincial Jacobin clubs in March 1792, and became a common feature for its members during 1793.[133] While currency of the *bonnet rouge* was most often connected with Jacobins' influence during the spring and summer of 1792, we also find it used in other clubs such as the Cordeliers.[134] In January 1793, it was noted that, as there was no prohibition against wearing the *bonnet rouge*, so there was no need to institute a regulation to formalize the practice of speakers from the tribune at the Jacobin club wearing it.[135] Elsewhere, it was worn by the administration at the Lycée in 1794.[136] Presidents and secretaries of the sections' general assemblies adopted the *bonnet rouge* in the spring of 1793.[137] Daubenton was excluded from the assembly of the Section du Pont-Neuf for a year for having spoken from the tribune without wearing the cap.[138] Following a request from the *comité révolutionnaire* of the Section du Bonnet Rouge, who already wore it, it was adopted by the Commune de Paris on 16 brumaire an II (6 November 1793).[139] A proposal to limit the *bonnet rouge* to members of the Paris Commune's Conseil Général carrying out their duties was considered to be a response to the concern that wider dissemination might dilute the respect with which it was viewed, and also facilitate its potential use as disguise.[140] Employees of the government administration were advised only to wear it in their offices.[141] A police agent noted disapprovingly of members of *sociétés populaires* from the sections who, in February 1794, wore their medals and caps in the street, 'which is contrary to the principles of equality'.[142]

The vagaries of local implementation were a source of troublesome diversity. In January 1794 Joseph Le Bon reported from Arras to the Comité de Salut public that various types of cap were being introduced: 'some with frills and gilding, others in the three colours, and plain red was on the verge of being proscribed and scorned'. This had been the cause of disputes in theatres.[143] In Paris, a *marchande de chiffons* was attacked by women from les Halles for wearing one of the 'bonnets aux trois couleurs' which she was knitting for sale.[144]

Caps were used, in a fashion similar to the use of cockades, as part of secular baptism ceremonies, and worn by civic officials when conducting weddings (Figure 16).[145] In Nantes, Catherine Trinquand wore a cap decorated with *rubans tricolores* as part of her mourning dress at the funeral of her husband.[146] In Beaufort, a dying Jacobin asked to be buried in his.[147] *Bonnets rouges* were given to 'élèves de la patrie' to remind them that their fathers had died for the *patrie*, and that when old enough to carry arms they, too, would combat despots.[148] The cap could also be a focus for the synthesizing of sentiments of piety and patriotism, what Mona Ozouf has termed the 'transfer of sacrality', which was at the heart of many revolutionary practices.[149] In festivals, for example, the figure of Liberty was sometimes taken to be a saint. In February 1792, Varlet appeared at the Jacobin club with a pike on which was hoist a *bonnet rouge* to which was attached a shield with the inscription 'Apostle of liberty'.[150]

The sometimes elaborate nature of the authentic caps that survive reinforces the idea that they were treated as a form of dress associated with special occasions, or some official role. A cap in the Museum of Fine Arts Boston is made of wool, cotton, linen and silk, and has an embroidered roundel showing portraits of Lepeletier and Marat.[151] Whatever their materials and degree of elaborateness, caps served as objects of veneration, as expressed in their being offered, often collectively, as signs of solidarity to *sociétés populaires*. A 'liberty cap decorated with the national colours'

Figure 16 Jean-Baptiste Mallet: 'Republican marriage', 1794, drawing. Musée Carnavalet, Paris, Inv. D 09274. Photograph: Photothèque des Musées de la Ville de Paris (Ladet).

was presented to the Société des Amis de la Constitution at Belleville in return for twenty pikes presented to the Commune de Paris, and was tried on in turn by members of the *société*'s deputation during the meeting. The cap was to be hoisted on a pike and placed in the meeting room of the *société*.[152] According to the president of the district of Saint-Calais, responding to a donation of a number of caps by the *citoyennes* of the town in September 1792: 'The liberty cap, woven and offered by the hand of the Graces, will double, if that is possible, the civic ardour of the heads which this impressive sign must electrify.'[153]

In prints and paintings liberty caps primarily appear hoist on poles[154] and worn by central protagonists and isolated peripheral onlookers. In a drawing by François Gérard of the invasion of the Assembly on 10 August 1792 (produced in 1793), the presence of caps is confined to being either carried on a pole with a panel attached ('Plus de Roi') held aloft by a wounded insurgent, or worn by one of the central group of three figures (Figure 17). Similarly, as in Pierre Alexandre Wille's image of a village celebration of the festival of old age (Figure 18), the cap is very selectively

Figure 17 François Gérard: 'The 10th August 1792', 1793, drawing. Musée du Louvre, Paris. c Photo: Réunion des Musées Nationaux.

depicted as allegorical attribute and worn only by a small number of the participants. A metal cap on a wooden pole now in the Musée Carnavalet may well have been used for precisely this sort of ceremonial purpose.[155] Although the *bonnet rouge* became associated with the minimally equipped revolutionary armies, its role as a standard was every bit as ritualized as that found in *sociétés populaires*. Kellerman's 'ordre du jour' (15 July 1792) for the camp at Wissembourg was intended to proclaim 'the price which he attached to the liberty cap'. The cap was to be permanently maintained at the centre of the army, and always to be guarded 'as the symbol of French liberty'; and on the march, it was to be carried by the most senior *sous-officier*. It was forbidden for any soldier to wear a *bonnet de la liberté*, for this privilege would only be granted to individuals and groups as a 'reward for fine actions', thereby ensuring that it was recognized as 'the striking sign of civic and martial virtue'.[156] The extraordinary importance given to the cap by Kellerman was intensified by his liminal and embattled location. The cap's role as a signifier of French identity was consolidated by virtue of the publicity given to its proscription abroad. For example,

Figure 18 Pierre-Alexandre Wille: 'Festival of Old Age', engraved by J. Duplessi-Bertaux, 1794. Private Collection. Photograph: author.

in August 1793, the King of Prussia chose to enforce the suppression of the *bonnet rouge* as a way of eradicating Jacobin sympathizers symbolically as well as physically.[157] In February 1793, the wearing of a 'bonnet de la liberté' at the theatre in Madrid caused a major disturbance.[158] As reported in France, such incidents merely served to validate the need to remain faithful to republicanism's vestimentary proclamation.

From mid-1792 onwards, the career of the *bonnet rouge* was to be closely tied up with the political ascendancy and fall of the *sans-culottes*,[159] a phenomenon which will be discussed in the next chapter. The localized institutionalization of the *bonnet rouge* has been recorded in detail by Albert Soboul in his thesis on the Parisian *sans-culottes* of Year II (September 1793–September 1794).[160]

The prominence of the *bonnet rouge* during this phase of the Revolution encourages the belief that its widespread use corresponds to the existence of a unified and homogeneous ideology. Yet its actual currency was inherently fraught. That the *bonnet rouge* had achieved a temporary normative status was paradoxically demonstrated by its manipulation as a means to provoke citizens who had become used to treating it with respect. In December 1793, police reports note incidents where the misuse of the cap led to perplexity and resentment: 'The people still observe and ask that the conduct of the *bonnets rouges* is surveilled, who, far from using it as a sign of liberty and equality, instead treat it as a distinctive mark, and believe themselves free to create little despots.' In addition to such undermining of the cap as a sign of patriotic credentials, it was observed that the cap was becoming distanced from the *peuple* simply because of its cost.[161] These developments were echoed by the Jacobins' decision that the society's officers no longer be required to wear the cap, a decision which encouraged the recommendation that the 'autorités constituées' should also relinquish it.[162]

But, as with the case of the term *sans-culotte*, the *bonnet rouge* was a badge and a piece of political vocabulary subscribed to by a heterogeneous set of people for different reasons. As R.B. Rose has argued, the *sans-culottes* were socially diverse, thus making the unofficial adoption of a standardized outfit (trousers, *carmagnole*, *bonnet rouge*) all the more manifestly a matter of polemical or conformist façade.[163] By extension, it is important to emphasize that the increased currency of the *bonnet rouge* does not correspond to a simple upgrading of the ordinary clothing of the artisans and poor who made up the *sans-culottes* in the pre-revolutionary sense.[164] However, the politicization of the dress of common people was indirectly broached as a topic via references at this period to the cap worn by Janot, recalled from Dorvigny's 1779 vaudeville *Les Battus qui paient l'amende* (The Downtrodden who pay the Fine). In this play, Janot, a shop assistant, has his cap soiled by the contents of a chamber pot and spends the rest of the play vainly seeking retribution. He was used as a prototype by royalists, in order to ridicule the fashion for such vulgar caps, and by radicals, in order to highlight the new political importance of common people who were no longer destined to be passively on the receiving end of injustice and poverty.[165] Such references to Janot were symptomatic of the contested meanings given to the *bonnet rouge* at this period, reliant on contrasting reflections on an incident recalled from the Ancien Régime.

After Thermidor

The fall of Robespierre and the Jacobins led to an abrupt and comprehensive revaluation of the *bonnet rouge*. Not only were *bonnets rouges* removed from sight, and edited out of political vocabulary after germinal an II,[166] the iconography of the liberty cap underwent a significant reformulation. After 9 Thermidor, those who continued to display any form of *bonnet rouge* risked being attacked as despised survivors of a discredited régime. In nivôse an III (December 1794–January 1795), among other anti-Jacobin talk, there circulated 'the proposition to proscribe the *bonnet rouge* and to substitute one in the three colours'.[167] On 19 ventôse (9 March 1795), following the arrest of youths emanating from the café de Chartres as a result of their intimidation of the representative Armonville, who had provocatively persisted in wearing the *bonnet rouge*, the Comité de Sûreté générale agreed that, rather than sanctioning the defacement or removal of emblematic *bonnets rouges*, an acceptable compromise would be to substitute *bonnets tricolores* which, by carrying the national colours, thereby avoided being identified as the 'cap of the cut-throats'.[168] Indeed, such incidents prompted Fréron and other supporters of the iconoclastic *jeunesse dorée* to call into question the authority of political emblems, and their translation into dress:

> A jacket, a headdress, will these today be reasons for proscription? And will you declare war on powderless hair and trousers like the partisans of Robespierre did against tight-fitting breeches and powdered hair? Finally, is it on their conduct that you wish to model your own? Would you disturb public tranqillity for a *bonnet rouge*? Would you waste your efforts for ribbons? To repeat, it is not thus that one accomplishes a revolution.[169]

What was being rejected here was, indeed, the whole emblematic legacy of the Jacobin Republic. Fréron understood that promoting this kind of violent street politics could allow Jacobins to revive their languishing popular support.

The Comité seem to have been responding to the climate of opinion, for that evening, in theatres and many cafés, the *bonnet tricolore* was substituted for the *bonnet rouge* accompanied by 'the universal cries of Long live the Nation! Long live the Convention! Perish the cannibals and blooddrinkers!'[170] In due course, coloured versions of liberty caps were made 'tricolore'; a decree of prairial an III (June 1795) proposed placing *bonnets tricolores* on ships, vessels and public buildings.[171] As ever, the installation and revision of public emblems was accompanied by contestation symptomatic of latent conflicts of opinion. In the Falaise, some citizens appealed that *bonnets rouges* be removed from the bell towers of the region; the municipality agreed that they would be replaced by cockerels. However, 'Jacobins' persuaded administrators in Calvados to restore the *bonnets*. A conciliatory proposal was to have 'girouettes' (weathercocks) which was rejected by the administrators 'as an epigramme aimed against them', since 'girouette' also means turncoat, 'and the *bonnets* had the victory'.[172] It is notable that, apart from military caps, *bonnets tricolores* do not seem to have been adopted as headgear.[173]

By 1796, the liberty cap was redefined as a positive and consensual political symbol in ways which distanced it from the factional and obsolete *bonnet rouge*.[174] The *Gazette française* suggested that in festivals, cap and pike as Liberty's attributes be substituted by a volume on which was inscribed in large letters 'Constitution de 95'.[175] On 30 pluviôse an III (18 February 1795), the cockade was removed from the secretary's *bonnet rouge* at a meeting of the local *société populaire* in the Section des Lombards, thus separating national and factional emblems.[176] Alternatively, but with comparable effect, in an II, generic formulations such as *bonnet à la République* replace *bonnet rouge*.[177]

At around the same period we also find the group of Jacques-Louis David's pupils known as the 'Barbus' using sky-blue *bonnets phrygiens* as part of a pseudo-antique costume with no active political significance beyond that of demonstrating their withdrawal from earlier forms of revolutionary engagement.[178] Moreover, when David includes *bonnets phrygiens* in his *Sabines*, whose exhibition announced his return to public life after his imprisonment, he is careful to colour them grey (only one is a muted plum colour). As these caps are not present in the preparatory drawings for the picture, they must have been included nearer the date of the picture's exhibition in 1799 than that of its initial conception in 1795. In the pamphlet that accompanied the picture's exhibition, David includes an oblique mention of 'symbols of freedom', without specifying the presence of liberty caps. By depicting Phrygian caps in a classical subject and (with one exception) avoiding colouring them red, David minimized the possibility that any connection with *bonnets rouges* and his political career as a Jacobin deputy and regicide would be elicited. Rather, they would seem to be consistent with the overall 'antiquisant' tenor of the picture, even if, as Phrygian liberty caps in a Roman subject, they lack authenticity.[179] Evidence of contemporary awareness of the ambiguity of David's reputation – as leading history painter and disgraced Jacobin – surfaced in a comment that he was 'le Raphael des sans-culottes', alluding both to the picture's ostentatious show of nudity, and to David's concealment of his political past behind a façade of high-minded artistic dedication. By contrast, when Jean-Baptiste Regnault showed his *La Liberté ou la mort* (Liberty or Death), which had been painted in 1793, at the 1795 Salon, he was strongly reproached for including a liberty cap that, although Phrygian, was also red, because its colour recalled obsolete, but for many people still highly offensive, Jacobin associations.[180]

Another strategy, by means of which liberty caps could be simultaneously neutralized of any residual factional signification and nationalized, which came to the fore in the mid-1790s was to discuss the economic importance of instituting more elaborate official costumes. In this sense, the preceding equality of dress had amounted to no more than an imposed 'poverty of dress' on all, which had contributed to the devastation of French manufactures.[181] The *Citoyen français* also spoke up for the reviving fashion industry, which had continued to be the envy of Europe even when political matters had alienated foreigners.[182] According to Grasset de Saint-Sauveur, greater political stability fostered increased formality of official dress; this put before people's eyes in an impressive manner the workings of legitimate authority. He contrasted this new respect for dress with recent times of 'trouble and anarchy' when such things were either deemed superfluous, if not inherently 'aristocratic', or else treated as artificial and ephemeral by being derided as 'theatrical'. The designs he published were based on Greek and Roman clothes which guaranteed that they were 'modeled in nature', and hence ensured a timeless fitness for their symbolic purpose.[183] Emphasis on such august characteristics served to disengage the language of dress from topical polemic, and to promote an alternative discourse legitimized by the generic authority of Antiquity.

∗ ∗ ∗

By looking at the revolutionary currency and transformations of the liberty cap, it is clear that the emblematic language of which this formed part was in a continual process of differentiation, consolidation and fragmentation, produced under the pressure of unpredictable and unrelenting political conflict. Thus, attempts to fix or standardize versions of the liberty cap were bound to be the subject of energetic contestation. In the case of the particular forms and identity of either the *bonnet phrygien* and or the *bonnet rouge*, the multiplicity of interpretations generated has obscured the origins of such emblematic types. Subsequent historiography has tended to gloss over the discordant diversity of interpretation that is an integral part of the active life of such emblems, and instead to assume a direct correspondence between a given emblem and an apparently coherent revolutionary constituency such as the Girondins or Jacobins. By recognizing the inadequacy of such one-dimensional teleological readings of emblems, we open up a much richer, if perhaps less manageable, picture of the workings of revolutionary symbolism. Thus, as we have found with the *bonnet phrygien*, the assumption that the revolutionary inception of this specific emblematic form corresponds to the co-ordinated mobilization of an image or emblem with an understood conceptual referent turns out to be an oversimplification. The belief that one can isolate an emblem's originary moment, and that this will supply one with a definitive recognition of its essential meaning, can of course be found in revolutionary journalism as much as in history books. However, this is primarily the product of the desire to impose a rationalized, and inherently partisan, narrative on events. Such commentaries tend to leave out the unpredictability and contingency central to the formation and dissemination of meanings attached to emblems such as liberty caps, in whatever medium.

The history of the the liberty cap as an item of dress embraces a series of dramatic episodes. Initially, it remained within the realms of allegory, as an attribute of Liberty. In this form, it corresponded to the assimilation of a historical item of symbolic dress into the repertoire of political emblems. This origin was fully recognized, and cemented the dominant classical frame of reference for signalling the Revolution's attainment of an epoch-making transformation. Yet, on the one hand, the apparently erroneous linkage of the liberty cap with the Phrygian cap suggests that this classical provenance was at times creatively misunderstood; on the other hand, the claims of revolutionary rhetoric to universal relevance encouraged comparisons with other historical precedents, notably that of William Tell and the Swiss conquest of freedom. Although caps were used as concrete allegorical attributes in festivals and other rituals, they were slow to be adopted as dress. When they did so, in the spring of 1792, in the form of the *bonnet rouge*, the emblem was tainted by being identified with the polemical interventions of the Jacobins. During 1792, *bonnets rouges* appear as tokens of popular political engagement, in a way that had been anticipated in the summer of 1791 by the men of the faubourg Saint-Antoine, for whom it was a sign of their patriotic credentials. The remarkable episode of the invasion of the Tuileries Palace on 20 June 1792 did much to highlight the way in which a simple item of common dress had come to play an intensely complex role as a touchstone for partisan attitudes to the replacement of royal authority. With the consolidation of the collectivity of the *sans-culottes* in the aftermath of 10 August 1792 (discussed in the following chapter), the liberty cap took on a nationwide role as attribute of militant radical politics, such that its normative form was emphatically identified with the simple woollen *bonnet rouge*. In this guise, it was integrated into the institutions of local politics as a token of officialdom, and was correspondingly employed as a revered symbol in ceremonies. Thus, even during the time of its most widely diffused use as dress, it retained something of the aura of an allegorical attribute. After the demise of the *sans-culottes*, liberty caps as dress only persisted in the context of residual opposition. Nonetheless, the eclipse of *bonnets rouges* as an item of current political dress only served to intensify its status as a sign of a lost era. As we will see in the next chapter, even if a diluted form of *sans-culotte* costume survived as part of the vestimentary choices of republicans, this invariably omitted the *bonnet rouge*, too heavily marked by its association with the Terror and the oppressive conditions of the Jacobin republic.

Notes

1. This chapter is a revised and expanded version of Wrigley, 'Transformations of a Revolutionary Symbol: the Liberty Cap in the French Revolution', *French History*, 1997, vol. 11, no. 2, pp. 31–69.

2. According to A. Mathiez: 'le bonnet phrygien, plus communément appelé bonnet de la liberté, bonnet rouge, apparait déjà à la fête à la Fédération de Lyon en 1790, où il est porté au bout d'une lance tenue par une déesse de la liberté' (*Les Origines des cultes révolutionnaires* (Paris, 1904), p. 32). H.T. Parker's influential book, *The Cult of Antiquity and the French Revolutionaries* (University of Chicago Press: Chicago, 1937) follows this account. More recently, see for example Michel Vovelle's *La Chute de la royauté 1787-1792* (Seuil: Paris, 1972), p. 224: 'le bonnet phrygien rouge . . . connu comme symbole dès 1789 . . . devient coiffure usuelle des sans-culottes et de ceux qui se réclament d'eux à l'été de 1791'; and Gwyn A. Williams, *Artisans and Sans-culottes* (Edward Arnold: London, 1968), pp. 3, 33. In an otherwise carefully documented article, Jennifer Harris anachronistically refers to 'the red Phrygian cap, borrowed, like many of the symbols of revolution in France, from the period of classical antiquity' ('The Red Cap of Liberty: A Study of Dress worn by French Revolutionary Partisans', *Eighteenth-century Studies*, Spring 1981, vol. 14, no. 3, p. 283). Even the *Encyclopedia Britannica* makes this mistake: 'In Rome the Phrygian cap was worn by emancipated slaves as a symbol of their freedom' (15th edn, micropedia vol. 7, p. 408).

3. On ninetheenth-century republican imagery, see Maurice Agulhon, *Marianne au combat: l'imagerie et la symbolique républicaine de 1789 à 1880* (Flammarion: Paris, 1979) and *Marianne au pouvoir: l'imagerie et la symbolique républicaine de 1880 à 1914* (Flammarion: Paris, 1989); and Marie-Claude Chaudonneret, 'Le mythe de la Révolution', in P. Bordes and R. Michel (eds), *Aux Armes et aux arts! Les arts de la Révolution 1789-1799* (Adam Biro: Paris, 1988), pp. 313–40. Louis Combes's pioneering essay, 'L'Archéologie du bonnet rouge', attempted to counter official repudiation of the *bonnet phrygien rouge* as redolent of Communard anarchy and its forebears (*Épisodes et curiosités révolutionnaires* (Paris, n.d.), p. 117).

4. This point has been made at various times from the nineteenth century on, but not yet been assimilated into revolutionary studies. For example, Combes, 'L'Archéologie', p. 142; Pierquin de Gembloux notes sceptically that: 'Selon les Brutus et les Cassius de l'époque, cet hiéroglyphe de la liberté fut emprunté par eux aux Phrygiens', but gives no source (*Le Bonnet de la liberté et le coq Gaulois fruits de l'ignorance. Lettre à M. Viennet, Membre de l'Académie française, Pair de France, etc., etc.* (Bourges, n.d.), p. 9). Donna Hunter kindly drew my attention to this text. E.H. Gombrich, 'The Dream of Reason: Symbolism in the French Revolution', *Journal of the British Society for Eighteenth-century Studies*, Autumn 1979, vol. 2, no. 3, p. 196. I am very grateful to Professor Gombrich for allowing me to see his article when it was in typescript, and for discussing the problem. Bobbye Burke, 'The Liberty Cap in America and France 1765–1789', Masters thesis, University of Pennsylvania, 1971. Michael Vickers drew my attention to this unpublished study, and the author generously provided me with a copy. See also Alice Gérard, 'Bonnet phrygien et Marseillaise', *L'Histoire*, July–August 1988, no. 113, pp. 44–50. On mid-nineteenth-century attitudes to the iconography of the Republic, see Marie-Claude Chaudonneret, *La Figure de la République: le concours de 1848* (Éditions de la Réunion des Musées Nationaux: Paris, 1987). On the Phrygian cap of Classical times, see G. Seiterle, 'Die Urforme der Phrygischen Mütze', *Antike Welt*, 1985, vol. 3, pp. 2–13.

5. See Jean-Charles Benzaken, 'L'Allégorie de la Liberté et son bonnet dans l'iconologie des monnaies et médailles de la Révolution française', *Gazette des archives*, 1989, nos 146–7, pp. 338–77; Bernard Richard, 'Le Bonnet phrygien, couvre-chef de la République en France et ailleurs', *Marianne: image féminine de la République* (Centre Culturel Français de Turin, n.d.), pp. 339–48; Marina Warner, *Monuments and Maidens: The Allegory of the Female Form* (Weidenfeld & Nicolson: London, 1985), pp. 273–6. Nicola J. Shilliam notes how the *bonnet phrygien* and the *pileus* were 'apparently merged' ('*Cocardes nationales* and *Bonnets rouges*: Symbolic Headdresses of the French Revolution', *Journal of the Museum of Fine Arts, Boston*, 1993, vol. 5, p. 115). Yvonne Korshak claims that the red Phygian cap worn by Paris in J.L. David's *Paris and Helen* (1788–89) was an anticipation of the liberty cap, but neither in her article on this picture, nor in a further article on liberty caps in America and France, does she demonstrate that pre-revolutionary Phrygian caps (of whatever colour) were understood to function as liberty caps; see '*Paris and Helen* by Jacques-Louis David: Choice and Judgment on the Eve of the French Revolution', *Art Bulletin*, March 1987, vol. 69, no. 1, pp. 102–16, and the reply by Francis H. Downley, ibid., September 1988, vol. 70, no. 3, pp. 504–12, with Korshak's response, pp. 513–20; and 'The Liberty Cap as a Revolutionary Symbol in America and France', *Smithsonian Studies in American Art*, Fall 1987, pp. 53–69. Neil Herz discusses the transition from pileus to Phrygian cap in 'Medusa's Head: male hysteria under political pressure',

Representations, Fall 1983, no. 4, pp. 27–54. Herz draws on Eleonore Dörner's attempt to trace lines of connection between Phrygian cap, pileus, and *bonnet rouge* (*Études mithraïques* (Leiden, 1978), pp. 115–22).

6. 'L'Allégorie de la Liberté', p. 367.

7. Parker, *The Cult of Antiquity*; Jacques Bouineau, *Les Toges du pouvoir (1789–1799), ou la Révolution de droit antique* (Université de Toulouse le Mirail: Toulouse, 1986); Claude Mosse, *L'Antiquité dans la Révolution française* (Albin Michel: Paris, 1989).

8. A.L. Millin, *Dictionnaire des beaux-arts* (1806), cit. Jean-Charles Benzaken, 'L'Allégorie de la Liberté', p. 338. See L. and J. Heuzey, *Histoire du costume dans l'Antiquité. L'Orient* (Paris, 1935), plate XLV (2); C. Darenberg and E. Saglio, *Dictionnaire des antiquités grecques et romaines*, 5 vols (Paris, 1877–1919), vol. 4, pp. 479–81. Martin Henig kindly advised me on this point.

9. Gibelin, *De l'origine et de la forme du bonnet de la liberté* (Paris, an IV), pp. 10–11.

10. *Oxford Classical Dictionary*, N.G.C. Hammond and H.H. Scullard (eds) (Oxford, 1970), p. 892. For an account of the *pileus* see *Paulys Real-Encyklopädie der Classischen Altertumswissenschaft*, new edn, ed. G. Wissowa et al. (Stuttgart 1893; Munich, 1972), vol. 20, cols. 1328–1330, 'pileus'. In 1848, Théophile Gautier invoked the Mithraic Phrygian cap in seeking to explain the origin of the *pileus* in his review of the entries for the competition to choose a figure of the Republic: 'Le bonnet phrygien est le signe de l'initiation aux systèmes mithraïques, et c'est probablement par imitation de cette costume qu'on donnait le pileus aux esclaves affranchis, comme initiés à la liberté' (*La Presse*, 21 May 1848, cit. Marie-Claude Chaudonneret, *La Figure de la République*, p. 145).

11. Cabinet des Estampes, Bibliothèque Nationale de France, Paris, De Vinck Collection, M. 98896–7; see Benzaken, 'L'Allégorie de la Liberté', p. 356, Fig. 14.

12. See Rosine Trogan and Philippe Sorel, *Augustin Dupré (1748–1833), Graveur général des Monnaies de France. Collections du Musée Carnavalet* (Paris-Musées: Paris, 2000). One of the very few authentic surviving caps has a Phrygian peak but no side flaps and is dated by its inscription to 1793 (*Premières Collections. Musée de la Révolution française, Vizille* (Conseil Général de l'Isère: 1985), p. 72). As Shilliam observes, surviving caps are mostly of elongated conical form ('*Cocardes nationales* and *bonnets rouges*', p. 115).

13. V. Guilletaux, *Monnaies françaises. Colonies 1670–1942. Métropole 1714–1942* (Chaix: Versailles, 1937–42), no. 423. In descriptions of new 1, 2 and 5 *centimes* pieces the *Feuille de Paris* cites the decree introducing them (24 August 1793) but refers to a 'bonnet de la liberté' (25 August 1793, no. 371, p. 2). Benzaken illustrates a two *sous* piece which shows the same profile bust with a Phrygian cap (op. cit., p. 371, Figs 22 and 23).

14. On Regnault, see *French Painting 1774–1830: The Age of Revolution* (Detroit Institute of Arts, Cleveland; Metropolitan Museum of Art, New York: 1974), p. 137. Other examples are P.A. Hennequin's drawing *La République* (1793) (Musée des Beaux-Arts, Lyon); Joseph Chinard's sculptures, *La République* (12 April 1794) (Louvre, Paris); and *Liberté et Egalité* (Musée des Beaux-Arts, Lyon); Nanine Vallain's painting, *La Liberté* (an II) (Musée de la Révolution Française, Vizille, on loan from Louvre, Paris).

15. *Description fidèle de tout ce qui a précédé, accompagné et suivi la cérémonie de la confédération nationale du 14 juillet 1790*, p. 10, referring to a medal designed by Gatteau and given by him to participating deputies: behind a figure of France, 'un drapeau, dont la lance porte un bonnet phrygien'. This detail of the medal is described in similar terms in other contemporaneous pamphlets published by Garneray (*Cérémonial de la confédération*

française, fixé par la ville de Paris pour le 14 juillet 1790, p. 2, and *Description de la fête du pacte fédératif, du 14 juillet, fixé par la ville, avec règlement de la police. Grande Illumination* [1790] p. 1).

16. The following references are noted by Annie Geffroy in her 'Étude en rouge 1789–98', *Cahiers de Léxicologie*, 1987, no. 51, pp. 119–48. In a comparison to the *bonnet rouge de laine*, a preference was stated for `bonnets phrygiens pareils à celui que portoit Guillaume Tell', which were more elegant (*Père Duchêne de Lemaire*, 15 March 1792, 346th letter, pp. 1–2). The other text is almost of the same date and relates to a cap worn in a theatre audience: `Pendant l'entr'acte, nous avons vu des patriotes se coiffer d'un bonnet rouge dont la pointe se recourbe en avant *à la manière* du Corno Phrygien. Un de ceux qui en étaient coiffés a dit tout haut que ce bonnet rouge serait desormais, dans les endroits publics, le signal auquel se rallieront les patriotes' (*Journal des théâtres*, 10 March 1792) (*op. cit.*, p. 140). [my emphasis]

17. 'Soit erreur soit prévoyance, / Les jacobins ont adopté / Le bonnet de la malfaisance, / Non celui de la liberté; / Car remarquable par sa forme, / C'est le bonnet des *Phrigiens*, / Mais ils ont pris pour uniforme, / Le bonnet des galériens' ('Couplet sur le bonnet rouge, par le citoyen Hector Chaulsit', *Portefeuille politique et littéraire par le Citoyen L****, 27 germ. an III/16 April 1795, no. 25, p. 99).

18. 'ces *bonnets Phrygiens*, dont l'attirail feroit bientôt, sans contredire, l'admiration de l'univers, mais qui seroit surtout charmant pour un *synode*' (*Projet sur le Costume particulier à donner à chacun des deux conseils législatifs, et à tous les fonctionnaires publics de la République française, présenté à la Convention nationale* (13 fructidor an III/30 August 1795), p. 30 note).

19. Combes, 'L'Archéologie du bonnet rouge', p. 142.

20. *Patriote françois*, 21 March 1792, no. 954, p. 524, cit. Combes, 'L'Archéologie', p. 193.

21. *Révolutions de Paris*, 17-24 March 1792, no. 141, pp. 534–6.

22. See the article 'Les Enseignes, drapeaux, flammes, oriflammes, etc., etc., et du drapeau rouge', *Journal de la ville et des provinces*, 2 November 1789, no. 33, pp. 130–1.

23. F. Braesch, *La Commune du dix août 1792. Étude sur l'histoire de Paris du 20 juin au 2 décembre 1792* (Hachette: Paris, 1911), p. 1114 note 1 (21 October 1792).

24. *Révolutions de Paris*, 17–24 March 1792, no. 141, p. 534; on the Mirabeau medal, see M. Hennin, *Histoire numismatique de la Révolution française*, 2 vols (Paris, 1826), vol. 1, no. 207.

25. *Le Propagateur*, 20 niv. an VIII/10 June 1800, no. 738, p. 3.

26. Ibid., p. 3.

27. 'Rapport au chef de la cinquième division du ministre de l'Intérieur sur les costumes à donner aux autorités constituées et fonctionnaires publics', AN, F[17] 1232, dossier 3, 14 floréal an VII (3 May 1799), cit. Jean-Marc Devocelle, 'Costume politique et politique du costume: approches théoriques et idéologiques du costume dans la Révolution française', Université de Paris I, mémoire de maîtrise, 1988, 2 vols, vol. 2, pp. 27–8.

28. S. Bianchi, *La Révolution culturelle en l'an II. Élites et peuples 1789–1799* (Aubier: Paris, 1982). On the 1675 Breton revolt see E.S.B., A. de La Borderie and Boris Porchev, *Les Bonnets rouges* (Paris, 1975). Geffroy notes the anachronism of identifying these seventeenth-century caps as *bonnets de la liberté* ('Etude en rouge', pp. 132, 138). However,

Roger Dupuy and Jean Meyer have argued that the parishes which supported the *bonnets rouges* in 1675 in the Finistère were also those which supported the Republic in the 1790s, while the quiescent parishes supported the Chouans ('Bonnets rouges et blancs bonnets', *Annales de Bretagne et des pays de l'Ouest*, 1975, vol. 72, pp. 405–26, cit. Donald Sutherland, 'Chouannerie and Popular Royalism: the survival of the counter-revolutionary tradition in Upper Brittany', *Social History*, October 1984, vol. 9, no. 3, p. 351).

29. Peter Burke suggested the Masaniello connection and advised me on following it up. Although contemporary commentators such as M. Bisaccioni (*Historia delle guerre civili di questi ultimi tempi . . .* (Venice, 1653), p. 122, cit. *Storia d'Italia* (Turin, 1974), vol. 2, p. 420) and Giuseppe Donzelli write approvingly of Masaniello's simple fisherman's clothes, appropriate to the leader of a popular revolt, his cap was not interpreted symbolically (see *Partenope Liberata overo Racconto dell'Heroica risoluzione fatta dal Popolo di Napoli per sottarsi con tutto il Regno dall'Insopportabil Giogo delli Spagnuoli* (Naples, 1647), re-ed. Antonio Altamura (Naples, 1974)). Alessandro Giraffi's *Le rivoluzioni di Napoli* (Venice, 1648); trans. J. Howell, *An exact Historie of the late Revolution in Naples, and of their monstrous successes not to be paralleled by any Ancient or Modern History* (2 parts; London, 1650-52), contains a frontispiece showing Masaniello with a tassled cap: 'Effigie et vero Ritratto di Masianiello, comandante, in Napoli', and the further caption 'Liberator Patriae'. However, in the text his cap is described as a 'Mariner's flop' (part 2, pp. 16-17). Wendy Wassyng Roworth has noted the similarity between the French revolutionary liberty cap and Masaniello's cap ('The Evolution of History Painting: Masaniello's Revolt and Other Disasters in Seventeenth-century Naples', *Art Bulletin*, June 1993, vol. 75, no. 2, pp. 219–34). However, the example she illustrates (a medal showing Marat wearing a cap (Figure 12)) is certainly a nineteenth-century or modern object. I would like to thank Chloe Chard for drawing my attention to Dr Wassyng Roworth's article, and the author for kindly supplied me with an offprint. Rosario Villari has noted a French revolutionary reference to Masaniello, but this does not involve his cap; see 'Masaniello: Contemporary and Recent Interpretations', *Past and Present*, 1985, no. 108, pp. 117–32; and *The Revolt of Naples* (Polity/Blackwell: Oxford, 1993), pp. 153–70, where he also points out that the leaders of the Neapolitan republic of 1799 'repeatedly sought to use the myth of Masaniello' to appeal to the 'lower strata of society'.

30. F. Noël, 'Lettre au Rédacteur du Magazin encyclopédique, sur l'antiquité du BONNET ROUGE, considéré comme signe de la Liberté', *Magazin encylopédique*, 1793, no. 41, pp. 327–8. I owe this reference to Marie-Claude Chaudonneret.

31. See Jacques Proust, 'Sans-culotte malgré lui: contribution à la mythologie de Guillaume Tell', *Essays on Diderot and the Enlightenment in Honor of Otis Fellows*, ed. John Pappas (Geneva, 1974), pp. 268-81; Georges Andrey, 'Guillaume Tell, héros républicain ou les métamorphoses d'un mythe (XVIe–XVIIIe siècles)', in Michel Vovelle (ed.), *Révolution et République, l'exception française* (Kiné: Paris, 1994), pp. 67–81. On the iconography of Tell with particular reference to Switzerland, see *Emblèmes de la Liberté: L'image de la république dans l'art du XVIe au XXe siècle*, co-ordinated by Dario Gamboni and Georg Germann with François de Capitani (Berne, 1991), cat. nos 1–4, 50–2, 55–69. For similar hats in Netherlandish iconography in the revolutionary period, see A. Boppe and R. Bonnet, *Les Vignettes emblématiques sous la Révolution* (Berger-Levrault: Paris, 1911), p. 72, nos 114, 115.

32. Anon. 'Necker le vrai père du peuple', undated, Hennin Collection (no. 48), Cabinet des Estampes, Bibliothèque Nationale de France, Paris.

33. *Les Bienfaits de la Révolution* (1791), p. 5. An instance of a crossover in the reverse direction in Switzerland has been noted by Dario Gamboni. A *vaudois* patriot, arrested in 1791 for distributing French buttons, with the liberty cap on, defended himself by claiming that this was 'l'emblème de la liberté des Suisses . . . ce chapeau à jamais mémorable de Guillaume Tell ('"Instrument de la tyrannie, signe de la liberté": la fin de l'Ancien Régime en Suisse et la conservation des emblèmes politiques', in *L'Art et les révolutions. Actes du XXVIIe Congrès international d'histoire de l'art. Strasbourg 1–7 Sept. 1989. Section IV, Les Iconoclasmes* (Société Alsacienne pour le développement de l'histoire de l'art: Strasbourg, 1992), p. 220).

34. Gibelin, *De l'origine*, p. 8.

35. Ibid., pp. 25-7.

36. 16 March 1792, no. 76, p. 301.

37. *Le Spectateur et le modérateur*, 19 March 1792, no. 110, pp. 75–6.

38. *Programme de la fête de la victoire de 10 Prairial l'an IV* [29 May 1798], p. 2. See the print of the festival, engraved by Berthault after Girardet, in which Liberty holds a baton with Tell's cap on in one hand and the 'charte constitutionnelle' in the other (Jean Ehrard and P. Viallaneix (eds), *Les Fêtes de la Révolution. Colloque de Clermont-Ferrand*, juin 1974 (Paris, 1977), p. 323, note 55).

39. *Courrier républicain*, 20 vent. an III/10 May 1795, no. 491, pp. 77–8. A similar strategy was employed by Brissot who cited the precedent of British Roundheads, and quoted Shakespeare's *Julius Caesar* into the bargain, in support of short, powderless hair (*Sur les cheveux plats, coupés en rond, et sans poudre*, cit. *Chronique de Paris*, 2 November 1790, no. 306, pp. 1221–2).

40. See Pierquin de Gembloux, *Notices historiques, archéologiques et philologiques sur Bourges et le département de Cher* (Bourges, 1840), pp. 249–51, 'Histoire de la justice des bonnets verts.–Des bonnets blancs.–Des bonnets rouges.–Du Peuple.–Et du pot aux fleurs'. On some of the pre-revolutionary roots of liberty trees and liberty caps, see J. David Harden, 'Liberty Caps and Liberty Trees', *Past and Present*, February 1995, no. 146, pp. 66–102.

41. Elizabeth Liris notes that, of 23 caps used in the standards, their colour was follows: 5 red, 6 grey, 4 blue, 4 ochre, 1 beige, 1 white, 1 red and green ('De la liberté à l'union dans l'iconographie des drapeaux des districts parisiens', *AHRF*, 1992, vol. 64, no. 3, p. 346 note 11). Jean-Charles Benzaken discusses the diversity of shape and colour found in the liberty caps used in these standards ('L'Allégorie de la Liberté', p. 357).

42. J. Michelet, *Histoire de la Révolution française*, 2 vols (Bouquins: Paris, 1979), vol. 1, p. 675. This echoes a contemporary commentary on the patriotic associations of colours, which comments on red: 'Le rouge te retrace cette chaleur brûlante de l'âme, avec laquelle nous devons aimer et secourir nos frères; ce rouge nous retrace l'ardeur du patriotisme, qui nous porte à tout faire pour la félicité commune' (*Rougyff ou le Frank en vedette* [July 1793], no. 2, pp. 1–2). See A. Geffroy, 'Etude en rouge 1789–1798', for the most thorough and carefully analysed treatment of this issue.

43. For example, 'La couleur rouge figure le sang' (Condorcet, *Chronique de Paris*, 16 March 1792, no. 76, p. 301); 'Le bonnet de la liberté étoit blanc, le bonnet de Guillaume Tell est brun; pourquoi avons-nous choisi la couleur rouge? Est-ce pour annoncer aux nations qu'on ne peut conquérir la liberté qu'en arrosant ses autels de sang humain?' (*Gazette française*, 20 vent. an III (10 March 1795), cit. F.A. Aulard, *Paris pendant la*

réaction thermidorienne et sous le Directoire, 5 vols (Paris, 1899–1902), vol. 1, p. 539). A post-revolutionary view is provided by Louis-Sébastien Mercier: 'On vouloit bien du bonnet, signe de la liberté, mais non sa couleur rouge, emblème de sang' (*Le Nouveau Paris*, ed. Jean-Claude Bonnet (Mercure de France: Paris, 1994), p. 113). See also J. Grasset de Saint-Sauveur, for whom red 'annonce ambition bien-marquée, le non-repos, le trouble, l'esprit de révolution, les combats, les massacres et l'insensibilité' (*L'Esprit des Ana, ou de tout un peu*, 2 vols (Paris, 1801), vol. 2, p. 165, cit. Aileen Ribeiro, *Fashion in the French Revolution* (London, 1988), p. 165, note 8). This accusation is a leitmotif of nineteenth-century polemic against the *bonnet rouge*; see Maurice Agulhon, *Marianne au combat*, p. 73.

44. In the Ancien Régime, parricides had been dressed in a red shirt before execution. On the abolition of this practice, see *Thermomètre du jour*, 25 April 1792, no. 116, p. 198. Those sent for execution in prairial an II were to be dressed in red robes 'comme assassins des représentants du peuple' ('Instructions données par le Comité de Salut public à l'accusateur public du Tribunal révolutionnaire pour la marche à suivre dans la rédaction de son acte d'accusation', 28 prairial an II, cit. Tuetey, vol. 11, no. 2553, pp. 676–7). An anti-Jacobin pamphlet from 1798-99 relied on the earlier stigma attaching to the red shirt to incriminate the whole era: Antoine Jean Thomas Bonnemaison, *Les Chemises rouges, ou mémoire pour servir à l'histoire du règne des Anarchistes*, 2 vols ([Paris] an VII).

45. See M. Dommanget, *Histoire du drapeau rouge* (Paris, n.d.); Louis Combes, 'A propos du drapeau rouge', in *Épisodes et curiosités révolutionnaires*, pp. 305–8; and A. Mathiez, 'Le Drapeau rouge, symbole d'insurrection', *AHRF*, 1930, vol. 7, p. 274. Geffroy notes a reference in which the red flag and parricide converge: the flag was torn up to cries of: 'Tenez, le voici, c'est un parricide, qu'on le couvre d'un sac et qu'on le jette à la rivière' (Chaumette, *Mémoires sur la révolution de 10 août* (1794), p. 45, cit. 'Etude en rouge', p. 137).

46. *Courrier extraordinaire*, 20 September 1791, p. 6.

47. G. Lefebvre, *La Révolution française* (Paris, 1957), p. 240. See also Combes, *Épisodes*, p. 132. Likewise Hippolyte Taine, *Les Origines de la France contemporaine*, 5 vols (Paris, 1904), vol. 5, p. 181. For a synthesis of views on the category 'Girondin', see Mona Ozouf's entry in François Furet and Mona Ozouf (eds), *Dictionnaire critique de la Révolution française* (Flammarion: Paris, 1988), pp. 374–85.

48. 'Sur la reforme à faire dans le costume des François' (6 February 1792, no. 910, pp. 149–50). Pigott's speech was published as *Discours prononcé à l'Assemblée des Amis de la Constitution de Dijon, en faveur du bonnet de la liberté le 26 décembre 1791, par R. Pigott, Anglois, et Citoyen français* (BL, R.645 (22)).

49. See also Richard Cobb, 'The Revolutionary Mentality in France 1793–94', *History*, October 1957, vol. 42, no. 148, p. 191.

50. Cit. *Patriote françois*, 6 February, no. 910, p. 150.

51. In the vignette, the cap radiates light. On the iconographical roots of this feature see Gombrich, 'The Dream of Reason', p. 201. Other examples of liberty caps in this condition can be found in Boppe and Bonnet, *Vignettes emblématiques*, plate 130, p. 87, plate no. 9, p. 6. On the quasi-sacred qualities ascribed to the liberty cap, see below note 150.

52. On Pigott see also Louis Hugueney, *Les Clubs dijonnais sous la Révolution, leur rôle politique et économique* (Dijon, 1905), pp. 144-7.

53. *Patriote françois*, 13 February 1791, no. 917, pp. 176–7, 'Sur les piques'.

54. *Journal de la seconde législature*, 2 October 1791, no. 1, p. 3, 'Nouvelles'. Compare the following satire on new military uniform in the summer of 1791: 'Un haut-de-chasse et un hoqueton de peau de loup, un manteau de peau de tigre, une chaussure romaine, un bonnet de sapeur, une massue sur l'épaule, des pistolets à la ceinture. Plusieurs s'écrient que cet uniforme sentoit trop le sauvage, mais le président répondit qu'il seroit plus imposant, qu'un soldat ne devoit pas chercher des habits élégans, une coiffure de parade, des escarpins à cire luisante, ni un luxe qui pût le faire mépriser de son ennemi' (*La Révolution dans le royaume de Pluton opérée par l'arrivée de l'ombre de Mirabeau* [May–June 1791], no. 2, pp. 14–15).

55. *Chronique de Paris*, 10 July 1790, p. 762.

56. See for example '30 May 1790, Lyon, fête fédératif', ill. Robiquet and Sagnac, *Révolution de 1789*, vol. 1, p. 221; and a print showing the site of the Bastille on 19 July 1790, ibid., p. 236.

57. See letter from Jean-Claude Fougères, *Chronique de Paris*, 19 March 1792, no. 79, p. 313.

58. Madame de Genlis was noted to have visited the 1791 Salon wearing a 'bonnet de la liberté . . . qui sied même aux visages ennemis de nos libertés' (*Journal de Paris*, 29 September 1791, no. 270, p. 1101, cit. Philippe Bordes, *Le Serment du Jeu de Paume de Jacques-Louis David* (Éditions de la Réunion des Musées Nationaux: Paris, 1983), pp. 20, 95 note 34). Antoine Giroust's portrait of the Duc de Chartres showed him wearing buttons on which was written 'Liberté' (Bordes, ibid., pp. 19, 95 note 27). On revolutionary buttons, see *Modes et Révolutions 1780-1804* (Musée de la mode et du costume, Palais Galliéra: Paris, 1989), pp. 164–6. The Convention decreed on 4 October 1792 that French troops should wear buttons showing fasces surmounted by a liberty cap; see Maurice Bottet, *Le Bouton de l'Armée française* (Paris, 1908), p. 22.

59. In November 1791, a letter from Geneva to the *Patriote françois* reported a number of individuals as provocatively wearing 'des bonnets rouges, avec un G, signe de l'esclavage', who were then disciplined by the Genevan administration, 'qui veut . . . absolument que les Genevois *esclaves* croient être *libres*' (*Patriote françois*, 30 November, 1791, no. 842, p. 631). The 'G' might signify 'galérien', 'Geneva' or both.

60. *Courrier des LXXXIII Départements*, 13 July 1791, no. 12, p. 185; *Chronique de Paris*, 12 July 1791, no. 193, p. 781; Combes, *Épisodes*, p. 128. See the full description in D.L. Dowd, *Pageant Master of the Republic: Jacques-Louis David and trhe French Revolution* (University of Nebraska Press: Lincoln, NE, 1948), pp. 55–61. In the *Révolutions de Paris*, the distinctiveness of 'bonnets de laine' at this *fête* was pointed up by claiming that they had eclipsed the 'bonnets d'ours' of royal troops (no. 102, 18-25 June 1791, p. 533, cit. R. Monnier, *Un bourgeois sans-culotte, le général Santerre* (Paris, 1985), p. 35). The *bonnet rouge de laine* still carried this meaning in the spring of 1792 (*Le Réviseur universel et impartial*, 11 April 1792, no. 44, p. 2).

61. 'Le bonnet rouge est celui des forçats, que portaient les Suisses de Châteauvieux, lorsqu'ils furent ramenés' (F. Brunot, *Histoire de la langue française* (Paris, 1967), vol. 9, deuxième partie, p. 625); A. Soboul, *Les Sans-culottes parisiens en l'an II* (Clavreuil: Paris, 1958), p. 650); J. Quicherat, *Histoire du costume en France depuis les temps les plus reculés jusqu'à la fin du XVIIIme siècle* (Paris, 1875), p. 628; J.M. Thompson, *The French Revolution*, 5th edn (Oxford University Press: Oxford, 1955), pp. 263–4. Combes queried this assertion ('L'Archéologie du bonnet rouge', p. 135).

62. 6 April 1792, F.A. Aulard, *La Société des Jacobins*, 6 vols (Paris, 1889–97), vol. 3, p. 463.

63. *Idée générale de la fête civique proposée pour la réception des soldats de Châteauvieux* (n.d.n [1792]), p. 4; 'On ne distinguait nos quarante martyrs qu'à leurs épaulettes jaunes' (*Révolutions de Paris*, cited M. Ozouf, *La Fête révolutionnaire 1789–1799* (Gallimard: Paris, 1976), p. 83).

64. *Idée générale*, p. 3.

65. Preceded by 'les citoyens du faubourg St-Antoine dont l'un portoit au bout d'une pique le bonnet de laine rouge' (*Le Réviseur universel et impartial*, 11 April 1792, no. 44, p. 2). See the chapter on hats and their role as *the* standard sign of urban respectability and status in Michael Sonenscher, *The Hatters of Eighteenth-century France* (Cambridge University Press: Cambridge, 1987).

66. Ozouf, *La Fête révolutionnaire*, p. 85.

67. 'Le bonnet de la liberté s'est flétri et quoique pour relever son éclat nous lui avons donné la couleur de Châteauvieux, un présage funeste m'annonce que les tyrans le fouilleront aux pieds' (*L'Ordre de Marche et les cérémonies de l'entrée des soldats de Châteauvieux au club des Jacobins, du Manège* (n.d. [1792]), p. 6). This anonymous satirical pamphlet was presumably produced at a date close to the *fête*, as it resembles the descriptive programmes for the event, e.g., *Détail et ordre de la Marche et cérémonie de l'entrée de la fête en l'honneur des soldats de Châteauvieux* (Paris, 2 April 1792). Jean-Charles Benzaken notes a medal struck by Palloy to commemorate the *fête* which shows a *galérien* wearing a cap, standing in front of the Bastille, his broken chains at his feet, and crying: 'La liberté a rompu mes fers' (op. cit., p. 362, Fig. 16).

68. Dowd, *Pageant Master,* pp. 55–61. According to the *Ordre de marche de l'entrée triomphante des martyrs de la liberté, du régiment de Châteauvieux dans la ville de Paris* (pp. 4–5), in addition to the 'statue du despote', other royal statues on the procession's route, such as that to Louis XIV in the place des Victoires would also be veiled. See Andrew McClellan, 'The Life and Death of a Royal Monument: Bouchardon's *Louis XV*', *Oxford Art Journal*, 2000, vol. 23, no. 2, pp. 24–5.

69. *L'Ami des patriotes, ou la défenseur de la constitution*, 11 April 1792, no. 27, p. 261, quoting from the *Journal de Paris*.

70. A. Dayot, *La Révolution française. Constituante, Législative, Convention, Directoire, d'après les peintures, sculptures, gravures, médaillons, objets . . . du temps* (Paris, 1903), Fig. 468; also reproduced in M. Vovelle, *La Révolution française, images et récits*, 5 vols (Paris, 1986), vol. 2, p. 84. Jean-François Fourgeret referred to 'cette sale coiffure qui rappeloit les galériens' (letter to Nicolas Lecoy, 25 March 1792, cit. Pierre de Vaissière, *Lettres d' 'Aristocrates'. La Révolution racontée par des correspondances privées 1789–1794* (Paris, 1907), p. 419). See also *A deux liards, à deux liards, mon journal* [1792], no. 6, p. 4 and no. 10, p. 2; *Courrier républicain*, 20 vent. an III/10 May 1795, no. 491, pp. 77-8: 'un bonet [sic] . . . qui . . . étoit la principale toilette des forçats'.

71. *RAM*, vol. 17, 23 September 1793, p. 717, cit. Soboul, *Sans-culottes*, p. 651, note 12.

72. See *Journal historique de bagne par Regnaud (1825–6)*, vol. 2, plate 10, cit. *Quand voguaient les galères* (Musée de la Marine, Paris, 1991), p. 215. One source maintains that *bonnets verts* were worn in the galley ships by those convicts condemned to more than six years' hard labour (*La Grande Encyclopédie* (31 vols; Paris, n.d.), vol. 7, p. 325, 'bonnet

vert'). The fact that one of the liberty caps included on the standards of the *Garde nationale* in 1789 was red and green suggests that this was not an immediately recognizable connection.

73. *Encyclopédie, ou Dictionnaire raisonné des sciences, des arts et des métiers, par une société de gens de lettres*, D. Diderot and d'Alembert (eds), 17 vols (1751–65), 'Bonnet'. J.B. La Curne de Sainte-Palaye conjectured that the *bonnet vert* was borrowed from 'le bonnet que l'on donnoit aux fous' (*Dictionnaire historique de l'ancien langage françois*, 10 vols (Paris, 1875–82). These two meanings may help to make sense of the following comments of *Les Sabats jacobites* on Jacobins' use of the *bonnet rouge*: 'On croit que, sous beaucoup de rapports, le bonnet verd conviendrait mieux, mais la couleur rouge séduit davantage ces tigres affamés' (vol. 3 (1792), no. 62, p. 188).

74. Gibelin, *De l'origine*, p. 6. The following song accompanied the demolition of liberty trees: 'Arbre de misère / Bonnet de galère / Planté par des brigands / Abattu par des chouans', cit. J. Buisson, 'L'Arbre de la Liberté de Lingeard', *Revue du departement de la Manche*, vol. 4, no. 13, 1962, p. 40, cit. M. Ozouf, *Fête révolutionnaire*, p. 438. See also *Gazette française*, 19 vent. an III/5 March 1795, cit. Aulard, *Paris pendant la réaction thermidorienne*, vol. 1, p. 539: 'A voir la sotte adoration que l'on a montré pour les bonnets rouges, on serait tenté de croire que notre révolution a été faite par des galériens; car c'est dans les galères, et non point sur l'autel de la liberté qu'on arborat autrefois ce signe de révolte, qu'on apprécie aujourd'hui à sa juste valeur.'

75. On Jacobins' desire to make others wear *bonnets rouges* 'comme eux à la manière des forçats', see *Journal du Peuple, par M. Boyer de Nîmes*, 10 March 1792, no. 39, p. 148.

76. As in Lemaire's characterization of David as 'Un Jacobin, un sans-culotte, un enragé bonnet rouge, David enfin' (*Père Duchêne de Lemaire*, 348th letter, 17 March 1792, cit. Geffroy, 'Étude en rouge', p. 140).

77. 'The variety and sophistication of the Parisian trades meant that the capital's many artisanal enterprises were well able to develop their own political artefacts, or subcontract out work to enterprises in provincial cities' (Michael Sonenscher, *Work and Wages: Natural Law, Politics and the Eighteenth-century French Trades* (Cambridge University Press: Cambridge, 1989), p. 353).

78. *Patriote françois*, 28 February 1792, no. 932, p. 236, 'Paris'.

79. Aulard, *Société des Jacobins*, vol. 3, p. 471, 9 April 1792.

80. *Patriote françois*, 15 February 1792, no. 919, p. 184, 'Paris'.

81. 'M. Doppet, coiffé du bonnet rouge (et cette coiffure est saluée par des applaudisse-ments universels)' (Aulard, *Société des Jacobins*, vol. 3, p. 432). In the same meeting, the *fête* to greet the soldiers of Châteauvieux was discussed, but no suggestion that there was any particular connection between the two is evident.

82. Pétion's letter is given in full in A. Aulard, *Société des Jacobins*, vol. 3, p. 439. This letter was partially published in *Chronique de Paris*, 23 March 1792, no. 83, p. 331. This is probably echoed in *Révolutions de Paris*: 'déjà on parlait d'opposer aux bonnets rouges quantité de bonnets verts, avec le coupable espoir de faire dégénérer notre grande révolution en petites factions bien ridicules et bien meurtrières tout ensemble' (17–24 March 1792, no. 141, p. 536).

83. 19 March 1792, Aulard, *Société des Jacobins*, vol. 3, p. 142. This figure is repeated in *L'Ordre de marche et les cérémonies*: 'nous serons forcés nous mêmes de le cacher honteusement dans nos poches' (p. 6). On the symbolic and strategic role of pockets, see Chapter 6 of the present volume.

84. As Pétion feared, manifestations of the *bonnet rouge* often provoked violence. Fontenay claimed: 'l'anarchie prend toujours un nouveau degré d'extension et férocité', and cites the behaviour of 'une foule conduite par M. Santere [sic], et par M. S. Hurugue [sic], [qui] a traversé les rues de Paris, avec des étendards et des bonnets rouges au bout des piques, et s'est rendue aux Champs Elysées, où on a chanté, bu, mangé, dansé, et crié Vive M. Pétion' (*Journal général de France*, 27 March 1792, no. 87, pp. 350–1). Santerre is recorded as having been at the meeting of the Jacobins at which Pétion's letter arrived (Aulard, *Société des Jacobins*, p. 442). He did not, however, speak up in favour of the *bonnet rouge*.

85. This was not, however, a unanimous decision. In discussing the Assembly's abolition of religious congregations and their costume, M.A. Julien defended the cap, claiming that 'la robe monacale, la soutane, la culotte' were much more contentious signs of 'esprit de parti', likely to disturb 'l'esprit public' (Société des Jacobins, 18 April 1792, cit. Devocelle, 'Costume politique et politique du costume', vol. 1, p. 27).

86. no. 141, 17–24 March 1792, cit. Combes, 'L'Archéologie du bonnet rouge', p. 134.

87. See Patrice Higonnet, *Goodness beyond Virtue. Jacobins during the French Revolution* (Harvard University Press: Cambridge MA and London, 1998), pp. 186, 227.

88. *Patriote françois*, 21 March 1792, no. 954, p. 524, 'Paris du mardi 17 mars 1792'. Caps had been used as crowns as early as April 1790, when a *vainqueur de la Bastille*, the grenadier Joseph Arné was given a 'bonnet d'ouvrier' by way of a crown at a performance of *La Liberté conquise, ou le despotisme renversé* (Hans-Jürgen Lüsebrink and Rolf Reichardt, *The Bastille: A History of a Symbol of Despotism and Freedom* (Duke University Press: Durham and London, 1997), p. 92).

89. *Révolutions de Paris*, 17-24 March 1792, no. 141, p. 534. To this probable exaggeration should be compared André Chénier's qualitative, rather than quantitative, assessment of the climate of Paris at this time: 'les piques et bonnets n'avoient pu rien produire. Il a bien fallu envoyer une plus grande machine pour attrouper les oisifs, et réchauffer cette ville de Paris, qui quoiqu'on fasse, manifeste un étrange dégout pour l'anarchie' (*Journal de Paris*, supplément no. 38, 29 March 1792). Other commentators asserted that the combination of pikes, *bonnets rouges* and 'la dégoûtante et scandaleuse fête triomphale des soldats de Châteauvieux' alienated thousands of people from the Jacobins ('Idées sur le moment présent . . .' (24 April 1792), from *Troisième recueil [des] pièces [du procès de Louis XVI] déposées à la Commission extraordinaire du 12 (papiers trouvés dans l'armoire de fer)*, vol. 2, no. 204. cit. Tuetey, *Sources manuscrites*, vol. 4, pp. 24–5, no. 167).

90. *Journal général de France*, 15 March, no. 75, p. 303, 'Mélanges'; *Chronique de Paris*, 17 March, no. 77, p. 307, 'Variétés'.

91. *Courrier des LXXXIII Départements*, 19 March 1792, no. 19, p. 298.

92. *Journal général de France*, 25 March 1792, no. 85, pp. 343-4); ibid., 21 March 1792, no. 81, p. 327; *Feuille du jour*, 21 March 1792, no. 81, p. 640.

93. comte de Fersen, letter to King of Sweden in Brussels (24 March 1792), Gazlan de Vautibault and H. Vautibault, *Les d'Orléans au tribunal de l'histoire*, 7 vols (Paris, 1888–92), vol. 5, pp. 135–8, cit. Hubert La Marle, *Philippe Égalité. 'Grand Maître de la Révolution'* (Nouvelles Éditions Latines: Paris, 1989), p. 629.

94. Marquis de Romé to M. de Salaberry, March 1792, cit. Vaissière, *Lettres d' 'Aristocrates'*, pp. 487–8.

95. *Journal général de France*, 25 March 1792, no. 85, pp. 343–4.

96. *Journal général de France*, 21 March 1792, no. 81, p. 327.

97. Cf. A. Soboul, *Sans-culottes parisiens*, pp. 650ff. See also A. Geffroy, 'Sans-culotte (novembre 1790–juin 1792)', in *Dictionnaire des usages socio-politiques (1770–1815)* (Klincksieck: Saint-Claud, 1985), *passim*.

98. *Journal général de France*, 21 March 1792, no. 81, p. 327. Fontenay's opinion that the *bonnet rouge* was coming to be worn by criminals and vagrants is repeated on 25 March 1792, *Journal général de France*, no. 85, pp. 343–4: 'Les escrocs et les voleurs en avoient si avidement adopté ce costume que [même les gens] les moins délicats ont rougi de s'en affubler.'

99. The appearance of *bonnets rouges* was 'subite et momentanée' according to *Révolutions de Paris*, 17-24 March 1792, p. 534. This alliance of commerce and fashionable political accessories had been noted in 1777 when a *bonnetier* had proposed a 'bonnet aux insurgents', to appeal to supporters of the American war; in the event, the initiative was suppressed by official intervention (*Mémoires secrets*, 4 December 1777, cit. J. Sgard (ed.), *Histoire de France à travers les journaux du temps passé. Lumières et lueurs du XVIIIe siècle (1715–1789)* (A l'enseigne de l'arbre verdoyant: Paris, 1986), p. 234.

100. *Courrier des LXXXIII départements*, 20 March 1792, no. 20, p. 315.

101. 22 March 1792, no. 82, p. 650.

102. 19 March 1792, no. 110, pp. 75–6; see also 21 March 1792, no. 112, p. 84). See Michael Sonenscher's comment on this point, note 77.

103. Letter to Nicolas Lecoy, cit. Vaissière, *Lettres d' 'Aristocrates'*, p. 419. *L'Ami des patriotes, ou le défenseur de la constitution* noted the abrupt disappearance of *bonnets rouges* (11 April 1792, no. 27, p. 261).

104. *Courrier des LXXXVIII Départements*, 28 March 1792, no. 28, p. 440.

105. *Journal général de France*, no. 83, p. 335, 'Mélanges'.

106. On *fédérés* wearing *bonnets rouges* and their provocative behaviour in the Palais Royal (15 July 1792), see Tuetey, vol. 4, no. 1311, and *Arch Parl*, vol. 47, p. 598, for another incident on 9 August 1792; see also Thompson, *The French Revolution*, p. 278, on 14 July 1792.

107. See Laura B. Pfeiffer, 'The Uprising of June 20 1792', *University Studies of the University of Nebraska (Lincoln)*, July 1912, vol. 12, no. 3, pp. 199–343.

108. Georges Rudé, *The Crowd in the French Revolution* (Oxford, 1959), pp. 98–100.

109. A. Chuquet, *Lettres de 1792*, 1st series (Paris, 1911), p. 18. The parallel with the later censure of women who wore the *bonnet rouge* may be noted; see Soboul, *Sans-culottes parisiens*, p. 652.

110. *Déposition sur les tristes événemens de la journée du 20 juin 1792, comme témoin oculaire, et réflexions politiques* ([1792]) p. 5.

111. Vaissière, *Lettres d' 'Aristocrates'*, pp. 490, 502; Vaissière also publishes Rosoi's, *Récit exact et circonstancié de ce qui s'est dit et passé au Château des Tuileries, le mercredi 20 juin 1792*, pp. 511–24, reprinted from the *Gazette de France*.

112. Aulard, *Société des Jacobins*, vol. 4, p. 17, 19 June 1792. This event gave rise to numerous reprints of portraits of Louis XVI with a *bonnet rouge* added (e.g., Hennin Collection, no. 11176). But it is by no means certain that all representations of Louis wearing the cap are responses to this episode; see *L'Art de l'estampe et la Révolution française* (Musée Carnavalet, Paris, 1977), no. 343, p. 64.

113. *Journal de Paris*, 22 June 1792, no. 174, p. 7702. See also *Arch Parl*, vol. 45, pp. 421–4.

114. Aulard, *Société des Jacobins*, vol. 4, pp. 22–4, 20 June 1792. A variation on this riposte to Dumas's account is the claim reported in the words of an anonymous eyewitness that Louis had not been forced to don the cap; rather he had had a cap in his pocket ready to put on 'pour remercier le peuple de sa visite' (J.G. Peltier, *Correspondance politique des véritables amis du roi et de la patrie*, 26 June 1792, no. 65, p. 4).

115. Lefevre d'Arcy to Vanlarberghe, 20 June 1791, Vaissière, *Lettres d' 'Aristocrates'*, p. 463.

116. See Annie Duprat, 'Louis XVI condamné par les images', *L'Information historique*, 1992, vol. 5, no. 4, pp. 133-41, and her thesis, 'Repique est Capet: Louis XVI dans la caricature, naissance d'une langage politique', 3 vols, Université de Rouen, 1991.

117. See the Hennin collection for different versions: either hand-on-heart or with cap on (11174–11185), and the De Vinck collection, nos 4866–4880; J. Cuno (ed.), *French Caricature and the French Revolution, 1789–1799* (Los Angeles, 1989), nos 65, 66.

118. See *Arch Parl*, vol. 45, pp. 422–4.

119. Anon. (published by Villeneuve), 1792?, de Vinck Collection no. 4878, Cabinet des Estampes, BNF, Paris: 'LOUIS XVI avoit mis le Bonnet rouge, il avoit crié vive la nation, il avoit bu à la santé des sans-culottes, il avoit affecté le plus grand calme, il avoit dit hautement qu'il ne craindroit jamais, que jamais il n'auroit à craindre au milieu du peuple; enfin il avoit semblé prendre une part personelle à l'insurrection du 20 juin. Eh bien! ce même Louis XVI a bravement attendu que ses concitoyens fussent rentrés dans leurs foyers pour leur faire une guerre occulte et exercer sa vengeance.'

120. 'Un d'eux s'arrête ayant près de lui un petit arbre *pavoisé* comme celui qu'on alloit planter. Il prononce un discours dans lequel il invite l'Assemblée à assister à l'apothéose du bonnet qui va effacer les couronnes' (*Journal de Paris*, 21 June 1792, no. 172, p. 693); see also the print 'Congrès des rois coalisés, ou les Tyrans découronnés' (*c*.1793), which shows the liberty cap in a central position dazzling the surrounding kings with light; see Cuno (ed.), *French Caricature*, p. 215.

121. 'le monarque Jacobin mit son diadème rouge' (*L'Ordre de Marche . . . au Club des Jacobins, Du Manège*, p. 10); or, regarding 20 June 1792 and Legendre's supposed responsibility for placing the *bonnet rouge* on Louis's head: 'Il ose de son club poser le vil emblème / Sur ce front qui jadis reignoit le diadème' (Peltier, *Correspondance politique*, 30 June 1792, no. 67, p. 4, 'Sur l'attentat du 20 juin').

122. Charles de Villette, *Chronique de Paris*, 12 July 1791, cit. *Intermédiaire des chercheurs et des curieux*, 10 May 1888, cols. 277–81. These examples would tend to modify Agulhon's remarks concerning the pre-eminence of the 'femme-liberté': 'son bonnet ne courait pas le risque d'être confondu avec une couronne' (*Marianne au combat*, p. 26). Rather, the significance of the liberty cap is all the greater precisely because of its status as a substitute for the crown. The cap as both substitute for, and effacement of, the royal crown had a special relevance for the Dauphin during his confinement, for he had a *bonnet rouge* specially bought for him in the summer of 1793 (A. Tuetey, vol. 10, p. 7, no. 44). Quicherat notes a historical precedent, or echo of earlier French history: 'Le bonnet fût même mis sur la tête du roi, comme autrefois le chaperon révolutionnaire d'Etienne Marcel l'avait été sur la tête de Charles V dauphin' (*Histoire du costume*, p. 628).

123. P.L. Roederer, *Chronique de cinquante jours, du 20 juin au 10 août 1792, rédigés sur des pièces authentiques*, in *Mémoires sur les journées révolutionnaires et les coups d'état*, ed.

M. Lescure (Paris, 1875), vol. 1, p. 51. This act was approvingly accompanied by cries of 'Vive la nation!'

124. L.M. de Gouy, *Journal de Paris*, 14 July 1792, no. 196, supplement III, p. 3. Combes's claim that the cap worn by Louis was taken as a trophy, half carried in procession, half preserved as a 'relic' in the club electoral de l'Evêché, has the ring of hyperbole ('L'Archéologie', p. 135). On the repercussions of this incident, see 'Un habitant de l'Ile St-Louis. Le peintre Fr. Mouchet officier municipal, qui donna le 20 juin 1792, le bonnet à Louis XVI', *La Cité*, July 1918, pp. 169–87, October 1918, pp. 249–64, January 1919, pp. 32–55.

125. Rosoi, *Récit exact et circonstancié*, p. 12. The counter-discourse on the *bonnet rouge* extended to claiming that three 'Ministres Jacobites' had been the subject of a 'décret d'immortalité', which would one day be revealed as the brand on the shoulder of the *galérien* (p. 14). On comparisons of Christ to Louis XVI, 'saviour of the monarchy', see William Murray, *The Right-wing Press in the French Revolution 1789–92* (Boydell Press: Woodbridge, 1986), pp. 178–9. Extreme as this appropriation may seem, it is not unusual. In *Charlotte Corday* (n.d.), Adam Lux, 'député extraordinaire de Mayence', claimed the guillotine as an altar-like object of reverence after Charlotte Corday's execution. He also proposed that a monument be erected to her with the inscription 'Greater than Brutus' on the pedestal; see Helen Maria Williams, *Letters containing a Sketch of the Politics of France, from the thirty-first of May 1793, till the twenty-eighth of July 1794, and of the scenes which have passed in the prisons of Paris* (Dublin, 1795), p. 98.

126. Annie Duprat, 'Louis XVI condamné par les images', pp. 133–41.

127. See *Proclamation du roi, et Recueil de pièces relatives à l'arrêté du conseil du département, du 6 juin 1792, concernant le Maire et le Procureur de la Commune de Paris* (Paris, 1792).

128. Philip Mansel, 'Monarchy, Uniform and the Rise of the *Frac* 1760–1830', *Past and Present*, August 1982, no. 96, p. 130.

129. For example, in September 1792, the adoption of the *bonnet rouge* by the 'Assemblée électorale' in the department of L'Yonne led to them being compared to: 'un champ de coquelicots' (Aulard, *Société des Jacobins*, vol. 4, p. 266 (8 September 1792)). This floral association is evident in the decoration of a teapot (1793–94?) with a red Phrygian cap framed by a golden star on the side, and red poppies covering the rest of the white ground (Musée Carnavalet, Paris). Such hyperbole was amenable to caricature, as in Gillray's 'The Zenith of French Glory', showing the king's execution, surrounded by a uniform mass of cap-wearing spectators (D. Bindman, *The Shadow of the Guillotine: Britain and the French Revolution* (British Museum: London, 1989), no. 108, pp. 136–7). This naturalisation of the cap as symbol is expressed in a print, 'L'Abolition de l'esclavage' (decreed 4 February 1794), found on a fan in 1794, where caps appear as if they were fruit or blossom on a tree (illustrated *Modes et Révolution*, p. 201). The cap as fruit appears in a biblical idiom in Gillray's 'The Tree of LIBERTY, – with the devil tempting John Bull' (23 May 1798), which has Fox as the edenic serpent, hiding behind a tree which bears medlars labelled 'Plunder', 'Conspiracy', 'Revolution' etc., among which is a giant liberty cap. John Bull resists this offer, his pockets being full of apples from the tree labelled 'Justice, Religion, Laws', in which a crown echoes the cap (*The Satirical Prints of James Gillray*, ed. Draper Hill (Dover: New York, 1976), ill. 56). For a review of the cap's iconographical roots, see Harden, 'Liberty Caps and Liberty Trees'.

130. Maurice Dommanget, 'Le Symbolisme et le prosélytisme révolutionnaire à Beauvais et dans l'Oise: le bonnet rouge, le livre de la loi, l'arche et la bannière constit-utionnelle', *AHRF*, vol. 3, 1926, p. 49.

131. Caron, vol. 1, p. 178 (23 September 1793); Tuetey, vol. 9, no. 1397 (23 September 1793).

132. In 1792 the *Journal des décrets pour les habitants des campagnes* noted: 'Les bonnets antiques symboles de la liberté, sont fort en vogue à Paris. Il est peu de patriotes qui n'avaient dans sa poche un bonnet de laine rouge' (G. Isambert, *La Vie à Paris pendant une année de la Révolution, 1791–1792* (Paris, 1896), p. 33.

133. On the imitation of the Parisian Jacobin 'mother society' by provincial clubs see Michael L. Kennedy, *The Jacobin Club in the French Revolution. The First Years* (Princeton University Press: Princeton, New Jersey, 1982), pp. 31–5; *The Jacobin Club in the French Revolution. The Middle Years* (Princeton University Press: Princeton, NJ, 1988), pp. 220–2.

134. Chateaubriand recalled having seen *bonnets rouges* at the Cordeliers club on the president's table ready for speakers (*Mémoires d'outretombe* (3 vols; Paris, 1951), p. 310, cit. Aileen Ribeiro, *Fashion in the French Revolution*, p. 85); see also *Journal du Peuple, par M. Boyer de Nîmes*, 21 March 1792, no. 50, p. 201. In Bayeux the *bonnet rouge* was adopted by new councillors 'à l'exemple de la municipalité parisienne, et le rendirent obligatoire aux séances' (Alfred Dédouit, *Souvenirs inédits. Bayeux sous la Révolution, le Consulat et l'Empire* (Bellême, 1892), pp. 40–1). Nicolas Ruault claimed that the vogue for *bonnets rouges* in March 1792 spread from Strasbourg (*Gazette*, cit. Richard Cobb and Colin Jones (eds), *The French Revolution* (Simon & Schuster: London, 1988), p. 138). However, in Strasbourg on 8 March 1792, the appearance of a *bonnet rouge* on a pike in a theatre parterre, later paraded around the town to the strains of 'Ça ira!', was described as following 'l'exemple des Parisiens' (*Courrier des LXXXIII Départements*, 15 March 1792, no. 15, p. 225).

135. G. Walter, *Histoire des Jacobins* (Paris, 1946), p. 366.

136. Alisson de Chazet, *Mémoires, souvenirs, œuvres et portraits*, 3 vols (Paris, 1837), vol. 1, p. 387.

137. The *assemblées générales* of several sections adopted it: Droits de l'Homme (8 December 1792), Pont-Neuf (17 April 1793), Contrat Social (21 April 1793), Sans-culottes (4 May 1793) (Soboul, *Sans-culottes*, p. 651).

138. Soboul, *Sans-culottes*, p. 651. Interestingly, in his *mémoire justificatif* produced after his arrest in the autumn of 1793, he claimed that he had worn a cap, but a *bonnet tricolore*, and used this to argue for innocence: 'mais depuis quand les trois couleurs sont-elles un signe de contre-révolution?' (ibid.). As early as September 1791, some 'patriots' wanted to exclude citizens 'soupçonné d'incivisme' from wearing liberty caps (Hugueney, *Les Clubs dijonnais*, pp. 144-70.

139. *RAM*, 18 brum. an II, vol. 18, p. 358, cit. Devocelle, 'Costume politique et politique du costume', vol. 1, p. 49.

140. *Gazette nationale*, 4 frim. an II/25 November 1793, no. 64, p. 489.

141. Caron, vol. 3, pp. 114–15, 4 pluv. an II/23 January 1794.

142. Caron, vol. 3, pp. 393–40, 20 pluv. an II/8 February 1794.

143. *RACSP*, vol. 10, pp. 423–4. Unfortunately, the *arrêté* that Le Bon introduced to deal with this situation is not recorded.

144. Caron, vol. 6, pp. 240–1, 25 September 1793. Prévost, the police agent, who reported this incident, shared the women's suspicion that the *marchande* had been paid to display a non-standard cap.

145. Dommanget, 'Symbolisme: le bonnet rouge', p. 47. In Le Grand's print after the drawing, the caps were removed; see Sagnac and Robiquet, *Révolution de 1789*, vol. 2, p. 82.

146. Francis Lefeuvre, *Souvenirs de Nantes avant et pendant le Révolution* (Nantes, 1882), p. 34, cit. Robert Orceau, 'Le Bonnet phrygien', *Bulletin de la société archéologique et historique de Nantes et de la Loire-inférieure*, 1955, vol. 94, p. 25. 147. Michael L. Kennedy, *The Jacobin Club in the French Revolution. 1793–1795* (Berghahn: New York and Oxford, 2000), pp. 82–3.

148. *Courier républicain*, 20 brum. an II, pp. 65–6.

149. See Mona Ozouf, *La Fête révolutionnaire*, chapter 10 'La fête révolutionnaire: un transfert de sacralité', and Albert Soboul's classic study, '*Sentiment* religieux et cultes populaires: saintes patriotes et martyrs de la liberté', *AHRF*, 1957, no. 3, pp. 192–213, reprinted in *Paysans, sans-culottes et Jacobins* (Clavreuil: Paris, 1966), pp. 183-202.

150. Aulard, *Société des Jacobins*, vol. 4, p. 467. The *Chronique de Paris* described a meeting of the Société des patriotes habitués du café Raisson, rue de Bourbon, on March 2nd 1792: 'A l'aspect de ces signes vénérés [a tricolore and pike with liberty cap] l'on eut vu les nombreux patriotes, les mains et les chapeaux levés vers les symboles patriotiques, suspendus aux deux côtés de la salle, éprouver [sic] la délire de la joie et de la liberté' (supplement, 7 March). Pious veneration of the cap could also be a parodic device: 'Saint, saint, saint, trois fois saint bonnet, qui est le chapeau, la culotte et la coiffure des anchorettes marines, et que les enfans nouveaux nés de Jacob et de Saint Domingue ont adoptés' (*Le Club des Halles, du règne de la loi, sous le bon plaisir des piques et des bayonnettes, an IVe de la liberté*, vol. 1 (1792), pp. 19–21).

151. See Shilliam, op. cit., pp. 120–1, Figures 4 and 13. Philippe Bordes has noted that the image is derived from a print (De Vinck no. 5337) (Bonnet de la liberté dossier, Documentation, Musée de la Révolution française, Vizille).

152. *Patriote françois*, no. 957, 24 March 1792, p. 336. In Nantes, on 23 September 1793, a group of women offered a *bonnet rouge* to the Société des amis de la liberté et de l'égalité (Orceau, 'Le Bonnet phrygien', p. 30).

153. Froger, *Histoire de Saint-Calais*, cit. Marc de Villiers, *Histoire des clubs des femmes* (Paris, 1910), pp. 143–4 (7 September 1792). For a similar instance of a cap presented by women to the Jacobin club of Le Mans, see Kennedy, *The Jacobin Club . . . Middle Years*, p. 220.

154. To hoist a hat or cap on a pole or stick was itself understood as a sign of 'liberté' (Aulard, *Société des Jacobins*, vol. 3, p. 471 (9 April 1792).

155. The combination of *bonnet rouge* and pike was primarily emblematic but, as Geffroy has observed, might also be construed as carrying the violent subtext of the severed head ('Étude en rouge', pp. 122, 138). The significance of verticality is discussed by Elisabeth Liris, 'Autour des vignettes révolutionnaires: le symbolisme du bonnnet phrygien', in M. Vovelle (ed.), *Les Images de la Révolution française* (Paris, 1988), pp. 307–16.

156. *Histoire parlementaire de la Révolution*, vol. 16, p. 261, cit. Combes, 'Archéologie', pp. 130–1. The Conseil général of the Paris Commune granted the request from the band

of the Parisian *force armée* that they be allowed to wear *bonnets rouges* in view of their record of stalwart patriotism (*Procès-verbaux du Comité d'Instruction publique*, M.J. Guillaume (ed), 7 vols (Paris, 1891–1957), vol. 2, p. 804 (18 brum. an II).

157. *Annales de la république française*, 18 August 1793, no. 251, p. 1135. For an Austrian print which includes a 'Jacobin cap', see Ernst Wangerman, *The Austrian Achievement 1700-1800* (Thames & Hudson: London, 1973), Fig. 111, p. 181.

158. *RAM*, 9 March 1793, cit. Dommanget, 'Le Symbolisme et le prosélytisme révolutionnaire, le bonnet rouge', p. 48. See also P. Jouve, 'L'Image du sans-culotte dans la caricature politique anglaise', *Gazette des beaux-arts*, 1978, vol. 92, pp. 187–96. Examples of 'Jakobinmütze' are illustrated and discussed in *Kleider und Leute* (Bregenz, 1991), nos 12/1, 12/2, p. 283; see also *Freiheit, Gleichheit, Brüderlichheit* (Germanisches National Museum: Nürnberg, 1989), no. 202. Many thanks to Ann Curtis for her help with this weighty volume.

159. Mercier, in his *Le Nouveau Paris*, opened his chapter entitled 'Bonnet rouge', with the bitter cry: 'Étendard de perfection jacobinique!' (vol. 1, ch. 20, p. 134). The *bonnet rouge* became a touchstone for retrospective reviling and mocking of the Jacobins and *sans-culottes*, e.g. Alisson de Chazet's *Mémoires, souvenirs, œuvres et portraits*, vol. 1, pp. 387–90, 'De mon bonnet rouge'. Vera Schuster kindly pointed out this reference.

160. Soboul, *Sans-culottes parisiens*, pp. 650–3.

161. Caron, vol. 1, pp. 412–13, 5 niv. an II/25 December 1793. See also vol. 1, p. 337, 2 niv. an II/22 December 1793.

162. Aulard, *Société des Jacobins*, vol. 5, 19 December 1793/25 frim. an II, p. 56.

163. R.B. Rose, *The Making of the Sans-culottes* (Manchester University Press: Manchester, 1983), pp. 7–9. See also M. Sonenscher, 'Artisans, *sans-culottes* and the French Revolution', in Allan Forrest and Peter Jones (eds) *Reshaping France: Town, Country and Region during the French Revolution* (Manchester, 1991), pp. 106–7; and Annie Geffroy, 'Désignation, dénégation: la légende des sans-culottes (1780–1980)', in Christian Croisille, Jean Ehrard, Mari-Claude Chemin (eds), *La Légende de la Révolution*, Actes du colloque international de Clermont-Ferrand (June 1986) (Université Blaise Pascal: Clermont-Ferrand, 1988), pp. 581–93.

164. Michelet identifies the *bonnet rouge* as that 'universellement porté alors par les plus pauvres paysans' (*Histoire de la Révolution française*, vol. 1, p. 675).

165. I discuss Janot's transformation into a figure of revolutionary polemic in 'From Ancien Régime Fall-Guy to Revolutionary Hero: Changing Interpretations of Janot and Dorvigny's *Les Battus qui paient l'amende* in Later Eighteenth-century France', *British Journal of Eighteenth-Century Studies*, 1996, vol. 19, no. 2, 1996, pp. 124–54.

166. Soboul, *Sans-culottes*, p. 653.

167. Schmidt, vol. 2, p. 265, note 248, 'Tableau de frimaire et de nivôse an III, rapports journaliers'.

168. Ibid., 19 vent. an III/9 March 1795, p. 298. This transition is mirrored in the changing name of the Parisian 'Section de la Croix Rouge', which became 'Section du Bonnet Rouge' on 3 October 1793, then 'Section du Bonnet de la Liberté' from germinal an III/March–June 1795, and finally 'Section de l'Ouest' between prairial an III and an IV (Soboul, *Sans-culottes parisiens*, p. 248). In Beauvais, the *bonnet rouge* displayed on the Maison Commune was changed to a *bonnet tricolore* on 11 prairial an III/30 May 1795 (Dommanget, 'Symbolisme . . .: bonnet rouge', p.); the rue du Bonnet Rouge returned to its original name, rue du Sachat, on 17 fruct. an III/3 September 1795.

169. *L'Orateur du peuple*, 16 vent. an III/6 March 1795, cit. François Gendron, *La Jeunesse dorée* (Presses de l'Université de Québec: Montreal), p. 126.

170. *Messager du Soir*, 20 vent. an III/10 March 1795, 'Paris 19 ventôse', cited in A. Aulard, *Paris pendant la réaction thermidorienne*, vol. 1, p. 542. On 'La destruction de la symbolique révolutionnaire', see Gendron, *Jeunesse dorée*, pp. 120–7.

171. prairial an III/May–June 1795, *Intermédiaire des chercheurs et des curieux*, 10 March 1897, no. 755, col. 315. Two metal liberty caps taken from captured French vessels are to be found in England: one in the Royal Naval Museum, Portsmouth (see David Bindman, *Shadow of the Guillotine*, p. 185), another is in the possession of the Viscount Exmouth, whose ancestor, Captain Edward Pellew, took it from the French frigate *Cléopatre* on 19 June 1793 (although one should note that at some point repainting seems to have taken place). I would like to thank Viscount Exmouth for kindly bringing his heirloom to London for me to inspect and photograph.

172. *Gazette française*, 18 November 1796/28 brum. an V, no. 1778, p. 3. A *bonnet rouge* on the bell tower of the church of St Nicolas in Nantes was still visible on 16 August 1796, though removed shortly thereafter (Orceau, 'Le Bonnet phrygien', p. 31). A *bonnet* remained atop the Hôtel de Ville until a vote to have it removed as a 'bannière de crime et de malheurs' on 7 messidor an VII/25 June 1799 (Dommanget, 'Symbolisme', p. 51). In 1802, The removal of the liberty cap on top of the Invalides dome stirred up protests from 'exclusifs' (F.A. Aulard, *Paris sous le Consulat*, 4 vols (Cerf: Paris, 1903–1909), vol. 3, p. 504, 22 December 1802).

173. A *bonnet tricolore* (private collection, Paris) from the 42nd demi-brigade, 1st and 3rd batallions is illustrated in Pierre Charrié, *Drapeaux et étendards de la Révolution et de l'Empire* (Paris, 1982), pp. 16–17.

174. It has been claimed that Babeuf was the last to wear the 'bonnet rouge des Montagnards' (*Le Bonnet phrygien*, no. 1, 1907, p. 2), but I have not been able to confirm this.

175. 1 vend. an V/22 September 1796, no. 172, p. 1.

176. 30 pluv. an III, cit. Soboul, *Sans-culottes*, p. 653.

177. *Le Bonnet de la République, air de vaudeville des Visitandines* (Paris, n.d.), BNF Ye 56375 (56). See also the advertisement for Dolleman, 'culottier-gantier' from floréal an II, which evokes the scope for diversity of dress and fabrication of individual pieces: 'il fait et fournit . . . Bonnets à poil pour les voyageurs dans un nouveau goût, et beaucoup plus légers que ceux qui ont paru jusqu'actuellement, Bonnets en drap, et autres à la République' (*Affiches, annonces et avis divers*, 13 floréal an II/2 May 1794, no. 485, p. 7434).

178. Etienne-Jean Delécluze, a pupil of David at this time, recalled how Hilaire wore 'vêtements antiques', including a tunic, white mousseline trousers, and a purple cloak (*Journal de Delécluze 1824–1828*, ed. R. Baschet (Grasset: Paris, 1948), p. 60).

179. Valerie Mainz has discussed the presence of these caps in the *Sabines* in terms of their veiled evocation of the picture's political subtext; see 'David's *Les Sabines* and the Colouring of History Painting Post-Thermidor', *Interfaces: image, texte, langage*, February 1996, no. 10, pp. 45–59.

180. On David's *Sabines*, see *Jacques-Louis David 1748–1824* (Éditions de la Réunion des Musées Nationaux: Paris, 1989), pp. 323–53. On Regnault's *La Liberté ou la mort*, see *French Painting 1774–1830: The Age of Revolution* (Detroit Institute of Arts, Cleveland: Metropolitan Museum of Art, New York, 1974), pp. 580–1.

181. *L'Antidote moral, politique et littéraire*, 18 niv. an VIII, no. 108, pp. 2–3.

182. 26 brum. an II/16 November 1794, no. 3, p. 4.

183. J. Grasset de Saint-Sauveur, *Costumes des représentants du peuple, membres des deux conseils, du directoire exécutif, des ministres, des tribunaux, des messagers d'état, huissiers, et autres fonctionnaires publics etc.* (Paris, an IV, 1795), pp. 2–3. A caption to one of the Lesueur gouaches in the Musée Carnavalet, Paris plays up the perceived artificiality of political costume: 'Jeunes filles considérant un jeune homme en nouveau costume . . . le peuple les regardant comme des acteurs'. Claiming that behaviour or appearances was theatrical was a means of distancing and trivializing otherwise threatening events. Alisson de Chazet, for example, described the invasion of the Tuileries on 20 June 1792 as 'la répétition en costumes des scènes tragiques du 10 août' (*Mémoires, souvenirs, œuvres et portraits*, vol. 3, p. 11).

5

Sans-culottes: *the Formation, Currency, and Representation of a Vestimentary Stereotype*

THE CASE of the *sans-culotte* is one of the most well-known examples of the use of vestimentary vocabulary to identify a distinctive mode of collective political identity.[1] Within the historiography of the Revolution, there is an ongoing debate about the social constitution the *sans-culotte* movement, and how this affects our understanding of the nature and extent of their political engagement.[2] Albert Soboul argued that the *sans-culottes* were at heart a genuinely popular phenomenon, creators and beneficiaries of a new political culture of radical democracy. Subsequent commentators have disputed this, on the one hand pointing out the socially heterogeneous constitution of the *sociétés populaires* of the local *sections* of Paris, and on the other hand proposing that such activists made up a kind of incipient local political cadre. These scholarly arguments are in a sense merely an extension of the contestation that surrounded the arrival and the demise of *sans-culottes* from the revolutionary stage. Indeed, the image of the *sans-culotte* – a man of the people, wearing *bonnet rouge* (red woollen cap), *pantalon* (loose trousers), and *carmagnole* (short jacket) – is best known through retrospective satire and caricature.[3] The pungency of the visual and discursive rhetoric of such images has, however, been an obstacle to recognizing the various antecedents and tributaries that fed into the stereotype, and the complexities and uncertainties that surrounded the adoption and currency of versions of *sans-culotte* dress.

This chapter will explore aspects of the formation and currency of the *sans-culotte* type with the aim of understanding some of the ways in which this vestimentary ensemble functioned as a site for the assertion and challenging of political values. We will see that the stereotype was considerably less stable than usually presumed. Dress was a powerful and multifarious index of revolutionary ideas, but, here as elsewhere, one cannot separate questions of the currency of a type of dress from the interpretations, both intended and critical, which it elicited. Indeed, in seeking to focus on the image of the *sans-culotte,* and more specifically on its vestimentary dimension, a key consideration is that its constitution, and in due course dissolution, occurred without any legislation or official direction.[4] This was a phenomenon defined and negotiated in the turbulent public realm of revolutionary Paris.

Annie Geffroy has argued that the currency of *sans-culotte* costume as a form of political self-identification can only be understood in the light of a pre-existing discourse:

> If trousers became fashionable in 1792, I think this is because they provided a respectable explanation for a socio-political indicator already well-established in language, rather than the reverse. The 'costume of the sans-culottes' is based on popular dress, but transforms it into a symbol; it should therefore be detached from its social determinations.[5]

Trousers were, of course, identified with working men and their menial activities, distinguishing them from their masters and those artisans who aspired to the degree of relative respectability that breeches (*culotte*) signified.[6] Geffroy's argument is consistent with the fact that elements of what was to crystallize as the *sans-culotte* vestimentary stereotype are in evidence in prints and drawings showing contemporary revolutionary scenes well before the spring of 1792. In a 1791 drawing by the history painter Louis Lafitte (1770–1828), showing Louis XVI and the royal family in June 1791, being escorted back into Paris after their interception at Varennes (Figure 19), we find a group on the far left (Figure 20), made up of a member of the National Guard, a soldier, and *fort de la halle* (market porter), identifiable by his broad-brimmed hat, sloping back-wards over the shoulders, who also wears the striped trousers which were to become a standard part of the *sans-culotte* image. Here, these figures have been fused into a composite group by the exchange of dress and arms: the guard wears a liberty cap, the *fort* carries a sword, and the soldier carries a pike. The consolidation of the image of the *sans-culotte* was only possible because a set of conventions for representing men of the people already existed, which it was possible to harness to new political ends.[7]

Geffroy has meticulously and revealingly mapped out the changing meanings of 'sans culotte' (without breeches) and 'sans-culotte' (a person without breeches) during the later eighteenth century and the early years

Figure 19 Louis Lafitte: 'Le Retour de Louis XVI à Paris' (The Return of Louis XVI to Paris), 1791, drawing. Département des Arts Graphiques, Hennin Collection, vol. 125, no. 11002 (Qb 25th June 1791), Bibliothèque Nationale de France, Paris. Photograph: Bibliothèque Nationale de France.

Figure 20 Detail.

of the Revolution. Until February 1792, the term *sans culotte* was primarily used in a mocking sense carried over from the later Ancien Régime as a way of satirizing people's failed claims to respectability. To be deemed 'sans culotte' was equivalent to lacking an essential sign of proper dress, and therefore to be consigned to society's lower ranks. In the early years of the Revolution, the term was given a political dimension, being employed to distinguish *propriétaires* (property owners) and *honnêtes gens* (respectable people) – legitimate beneficiaries of the new political order – from their social inferiors. The establishment of meaning within a binary polarity was to remain a fundamental strategy in revolutionary rhetoric. For example, Robespierre contrasted 'sans-culottes' and 'culottes dorées' (gilded breeches).[8] It is only after February 1792 that the term begins to be given a positive, polemical meaning, in the form of a collective noun, to invoke a constituency which was claimed to be united by their espousal of a politics of radical populism.[9] After the invasion of the Tuileries palace on 10 August 1792, it came to be synonymous with the militant politics of the Parisian sections,[10] and occupied the foreground of political vocabulary until the spring of 1794, when the *sans-culottes*' presence on the political stage was forcibly eclipsed by the Convention. However, throughout this period, as will be noted later, old and new meanings continued to co-exist in fractious tension.[11]

Although historians continue to argue about the social constituency and political agenda of those gathered under the rubric *sans-culotte*, it is nonetheless the case that, as a vestimentary phenomenon, it has almost been taken for granted. That is, it has been presumed to have a fairly clearly defined inception and demise.[12] In what follows, however, I emphasize the extent to which pre-existing conventions for representing men of the people in the later Ancien Régime and the early Revolution not only feed into the *sans-culotte* stereotype, but remain essential to its meaning.[13] We find a set of representational elements which are at once more eclectic and less novel than has usually been presumed to be the case. To this extent, the new political function of the *sans-culotte* stereotype can be seen as having a significant degree of continuity with inherited protocols for dealing with the representation of men of the people.[14]

A hitherto unrecognized antecedent for the politicized notion of the *sans-culotte*, and one which also relies on an item of dress as its key referent, is the term *bonnets de laine* (woollen caps), and its currency between 1791 and the summer of 1792.[15] This looks back to the Ancien Régime and the association of the woollen cap with male artisans and labourers. It was also one of the semantic and vestimentary tributaries which were to feed into the later, much more widespread emblematic phenomenon of the *bonnet rouge* as liberty cap. In the early history of the Revolution, the term *bonnets de laine* acquired a specific meaning at once topographical and political, being used to refer collectively to men from the faubourg Saint-Antoine who had been active in the taking of the Bastille in the summer of 1789. Moreover, in usage of the term after 1789, the weight of reference was inherently retrospective, in so far as 14 July became consolidated as a foundational moment of popular activism.[16] The context and content of references to *bonnets de laine* exemplify the tension between innovation and redesignation in the formation of new vocabularies for defining the revolutionary landscape, its institutions and allegiances. The case of *bonnet(s) de laine* anticipates that of *sans-culotte(s)* in that the constitution of this political language predominantly relied on changing the meaning of already existing terms: antithesis and inversion are more in evidence than neologism.[17] The two terms also share an essentially distanced relation to their vestimentary referents – dress functioned as a form of stylized shorthand for signalling a socio-political allegiance.

In the spring of 1791, references to *bonnets de laine* articulate the increasingly polarized and fragmented language of politics – that is, with specific regard to what sort of people were, or should be, legitimately involved in political activity, both organized and spontaneous. On the one hand, we find satirical references to the faubourg Saint-Antoine as 'the glorious faubourg', which dispute the notion that 'with a free people, real glory consists in wearing a woollen cap, walking in clogs and without breeches'.[18] We can see here usage of the Ancien Régime form of mocking reference to vulgar clothing, a state of demeaning undress signalled by the comic and shameful absence of *culottes*. On the other hand, there are also positive references which, within a legitimizing but containing narrative framework, rely on the idea of a kind of cross-class collaboration at times of emergency or national crisis, as in the case of the construction of the arena for the Festival of Federation in July 1790,[19] in which people identified by their *bonnets de laine* lend their physical vigour to patriotic activities. In the context of the highly charged world of revolutionary politics, the ideological resonance of such a narrative could assume a momentous, potentially destabilizing import, in so far as the 'people' threaten to take on a more established and independent political role.[20]

Examples of the polarized language of contestation surrounding the visibility of *bonnets de laine* can be found in accounts of the translation of Voltaire's remains to the Panthéon on 11 July 1791. References to the presence of men from the faubourg Saint-Antoine in contemporary commentaries on this occasion are to some extent explained by the fact that the procession set out from the site of the Bastille, on the edge of the faubourg. Commentaries on the pantheonization of Voltaire illustrate a sense of the way in which figures from the 'peuple' could be represented as integral to the cohesively enthusiastic spectacle of such celebratory and commemorative occasions. For example, in his *Courrier des LXXXIII Départements*, Antoine Gorsas previewed the event by describing part of the procession as follows:

> The [model of the] Bastille will be carried successively by Bourgeois, former French guards with their uniforms, and valiant citizens of the faubourg St-Antoine, vulgarly known as woollen caps.[21]

Here, the qualification of *bonnets de laine* as vulgar is given patriotic legitimacy by highlighting their privileged role in sharing the responsibility for carrying the model of the Bastille, and by qualifying them as 'valiant', alluding to their heroic actions on 14 July 1789. Gorsas also pointed out that these men 'are honoured by this glorious title'.[22] In his euphoric report on the day's events, he played up the presence of *bonnets de laine* from the faubourg Saint-Antoine, but also claimed that *bonnets de la liberté* were worn by many of the other spectators. When it came to carrying the sarcophagus onto the site of the demolished Bastille, extra help was needed, and spontaneously provided:

> all of a sudden, a crowd of people threw themselves forward; a thousand arms strained to take hold of it, and a thousand heads wearing the liberty cap, threw themselves forward to carry it across an alley of poplars and oaks.[23]

The terminological slippage between *bonnets de laine* and the *bonnet de la liberté* is symptomatic of the coded way in which the popular was assimilated into political language. Given the problematic nature of the press as a documentary source for information on festivals, this tacit identification of *bonnets de laine* as liberty caps tells us more about revolutionary rhetoric than it does about the existence of any self-conscious policy on the part of the faubourg Saint-Antoine men themselves. Indeed, as one might have expected, these references to the unifying effects of patriotic enthusiasm are complemented by royalist commentaries which are at once sarcastic and baffled, where the occasion is dismissed as 'burlesque and magnificent'.[24] That the term *bonnets de laine* was still pivoting between a meaning associated with a backward-looking satire, and taking on a new political function, is illustrated by the fact that Charles de Villette, writing in the *Chronique de Paris* in July 1791, defended the people who were given this name by asserting that such caps were, in fact, proudly worn by men from the faubourg because they were a 'symbole de la liberté' (symbol of freedom).[25] However, he ensures that this symbol operates on a national level, rather than tieing it to the local identity of the faubourg Saint-Antoine: 'Since France recovered her sovereignty, this headgear is the civic crown of free men and regenerated Frenchmen.'[26]

Despite Gorsas's claim that the *bonnets de laine* embraced the idea that their headgear had taken on the role of liberty cap, it is surely more accurate to see this as a form of political rhetoric, in which the active role of the ordinary inhabitants of the faubourg Saint-Antoine was given a dignified cultural legitimacy by reference to a Roman emblem. On the one hand, the term *bonnets de laine* slides homophonically into *bonnet de la liberté*. On the other hand, the idea of the cap of liberty as an allegorical attribute is shifted to signify the enfranchisement of those that wore them. To this extent, such terminological elision marks a deeper political transition, corresponding to the invention of a language which could conceive of and recommend the role of popular activism, albeit in terms which restrict such activism within a vision of united patriotic endeavour.

Within the larger field of political language, the terminology of dress played an important role in articulating this transition. The way that the common *bonnets de laine* of artisans from the faubourg Saint-Antoine were given a collective emblematic role is paralleled in commentaries on the procession by references to the way in which items of ordinary clothing, and especially working clothes, were elevated to a ceremonial status. Thus, the journal *La Bouche de fer* described the presence of a contingent of printers 'in their working dress', between the chariot bearing Voltaire's sarcophagus and copies of his works as a mark of the 'goodness of the public spirit'. They had made themselves paper caps, on the front of which was the inscription 'freedom of the press', on the rear 'live free or die', and gathered around a tricolore banner with the words 'universal confederation of the friends of truth'.[27] A less sympathetic source, *L'Ami du roi*, also noted a hybrid form of dress sported by 'market porters in military outfits, but in jackets covered in flour, and in large hats similarly whitened'.[28] The context of the festival gave these clothes a new meaning, transforming them into a form of celebratory costume. Whether the wearing of such dress in the festival is to be seen as a sign of spontaneity, or, rather, as the result of a deliberate decision to display collective pride in the distinctive trappings of professional labourers, placed at the service of the celebration of one of the Revolution's great pioneers, these examples suggest that, within the ceremonial space of the festival, and also the discursive space of commentaries on such events, ordinary dress was acquiring an increasingly politically resonant visibility. It is significant that, in the case of the market porters, the promotion of such forms of costume is closely linked to the phenomenon of popular militarization, something that also applies to the proliferation of *sans-culotte* costume.[29]

Working dress had been used as a form of officially condoned cere-monial attire in the later eighteenth century, but the profoundly different context provided by the Revolution inevitably changed the meanings of such forms of public display.[30] The key issue in these texts from the summer of 1791 is, I would argue, the idea of popular self-representation.[31] This is exemplified in disputes over the obligation to acquire and pay for a uniform in order to serve in the National Guard.[32] Prudhomme raised this point in referring to, and speaking for, the masons and *forts de la halle* in the procession:

> They had no uniforms, and were not the less noticed. It is said that they are going to be given uniforms. So much the worse! this would only make them ordinary national guards; they would cease to be men, and they would certainly not become better patriots.[33]

Indeed, it was precisely the issue of the refusal of uniform which Prudhomme, in November 1793, cited as a defining moment when sketching a typological genealogy for 'patriots *par excellence*, born republicans'. He claimed that this could be traced back to 1790: 'at this time the men of this group were known as "woollen caps", and it referred to the true republican people who did their national guard service in working clothes', despite the disdain of the (royalist) 'habits bleus du roi' (king's blue uniforms) and (bourgeois) 'lafayettistes'.[34] These comments only make sense, of course, in the light of the later crystallization of the stereotype of the *sans-culotte* as exemplary popular militant. They nonetheless point back to a phase in the Revolution when the visibility of popular political activity was legitimized through a vocabulary in which the vestimentary became emblematic, in a way which was polemically construed as signalling a form of political authenticity.

This is also found in Gorsas's account of the invasion of the Tuileries on 20 June 1792, where he picks out a group of coalmen in order to assert the virtue of honest, and ingenuously unwashed, labouring men. The establishment of their symbolic status is defined within a binary opposition to the cosmetic dissimulation of *aristocrates*:[35]

> Your faces, blackened by a labour which provides for the rich who disdain you the means to transform coarse meat into succulent dishes; these symbolic figures of virtue, who do not seek to disguise their colours, command the respect of all these perfumed Achilles from the Palais Royal, whose complexions are as cold as their lemonade, and whose hearts are as soft as the fish soup which nourishes their feeble constitutions.[36]

For all Gorsas's enthusiasm, his adoption of an emblematic register inscribes a degree of necessary distancing, achieved by means of linking popular participation in revolutionary action to a pre-existing discourse of the virtue of labour. Indeed, one of the defining strands underpinning *sans-culotte* ideology was the idea of productive work, revalorized in aggressive political terms. As the *Journal des sans-culottes* asserted in 1792:

> The *sans-culottes*, ferocious and proud men, make up the majority of the nation, the *sans-culottes* sustain the state, the *sans-culottes* provide defenders of the motherland, dress you, nourish you, they can do without you and you only exist because of them, you consume, and it is they who produce.[37]

Such rhetoric pushes the idea that the morally desirable condition of transparency was most irreducibly evident in the form of men of the people engaged in political activity. Remarks such as Gorsas's on the events of 20 June 1792 highlight the way that working dress was taken to be a sign of such transparency by virtue of its grubby quotidian lack of artifice. Yet in April 1792, the idea that working dress had become a political symbol was resisted. A letter from Gorsas to Palloy regarding the preparations for the Festival of Liberty honouring the liberated soldiers of the Châteauvieux regiment ironically plays on the need for precisely this kind of palliative representational artifice. Gorsas notes the likely protests at Palloy's 'bizarre project' to have a stone model of the Bastille carried 'by authentic *sans-culottes*' (par des véritables sans-culottes). Although he mocks the unease at the spectacle of common men of the people participating in the procession, his recommendation of caution to Palloy – so as not to play into the hands of satirical commentators – registers a recognition of the need to translate the popular into a stylized, codified form.[38]

It is perhaps not surprising that accounts of revolutionary festivals and moments of political crisis promote the emblematization of ordinary dress.[39] For example, the events surrounding the invasion of the Tuileries on 20 June 1792 – a key moment in the radicalization of revolutionary politics – in fact see dress being represented in manifold emblematic ways. As Annie Geffroy has noted, although the vestimentary element most notoriously connected with this episode is the *bonnet rouge* as donned by Louis XVI, accounts of the massed deputations from the faubourgs Saint-Antoine and Saint-Marcel in the procession through the National Assembly on 19 June also contain another pungent but puzzling vestimentary ingredient.[40] This reportedly took the form of a pair of old and torn black *culottes* with *tricolore* ribbons attached being paraded on the end of a pike, creating a threateningly emblematic trophy. Significantly, on the same occasion, commentaries note that the slogan 'Long live the sans-culottes' appeared on banners.[41] The meaning of the term can be seen to be pivoting between its previous deprecatory sense and being a way of asserting the existence of a new constituency. As Richard Twiss observed, the people carrying this 'standard' wore breeches; 'sans-culottes' was 'the name that has been given to the mob'.[42] Indeed, for the *Révolutions de Paris*, 20 June became the 'Journée des sans-culottes'.[43] The notion of *sans-culottes* as a mobilized collectivity was thus named, at least in reported form (as emblems and *tableaux* in festivals often had labels or placards), at the same time as it was visually evoked in the form of a pair of black *culottes*, whose symbolic function was signalled both by their having been hoisted on a pike and by the attached ribbons. Moreover, the way that the meaning of the term *sans-culottes* was established within a strongly polarized binary vocabulary was doubly evident in that reports also refer to the pairing in the procession of the *culottes* with the attached inscription 'long live the *sans-culottes*' and a calf's heart skewered on a pike with the label 'aristocrat's heart'.[44] In this text, the *culottes* antithetically substantiate the slogan 'Long live the *sans-culottes*', in a way that is at once formalized and improvised, literal and allusive, as the calf's heart spells out a complementary kind of brutal triumphalism.[45] The pungency of such descriptions is, I would suggest, precisely a response to the disturbing spectacle of the quotidian being infused with emblematic significance. That this is so might be seen as being confirmed by the attempts to consign it to the realms of satire. The *Mercure universel* referred to the *culottes* as a 'caricature',[46] and even Gorsas, who loquaciously enthused over the events of 19–20 June, saw in the parading of 'a pennant analogous to their honourable poverty', 'an old pair of black breeches', evidence of 'French gaiety and the piquant originality which distinguishes the nation'.[47] The rest of his remarks treat the procession as having a pronounced carnivalesque flavour.[48]

The prevalence of this kind of contested semantic manipulation can also be found in evidence in the spring of 1792 in references to one of the *sans-culotte*'s 'popular' avatars. This is the soiled woollen cap worn by the theatrical character Janot in Dorvigny's *Les battus qui paient l'amende* (The Downtrodden who Pay the Fine), a tremendously popular Parisian vaudeville first performed at the boulevard theatre of the Variétés Amusantes during the winter of 1779–80, and still vividly remembered in the Revolution, especially during the early months of 1792 when, as we have seen, the *bonnet rouge* was coming to be associated with exponents of militant populist politics, notably the Jacobin club.[49] Janot's cap had been soiled by the contents of a chamber pot poured from a first-floor window by the disapproving father of his paramour, Suzanne; he spends the rest of the play trying ineptly and unsuccessfully to obtain retribution, ending up being fined for his pains, hence the title of the piece. Janot and his cap were recalled during the spring and summer of 1792 either to vaunt the progress made in the active participation of the 'downtrodden' in political life, or else to decry the appallingly vulgar nature of would-be patriots and their champions. Janot's soiled woollen cap points, so to speak, both back to its comic connotation of unhygienic commonness and, also, to the crystallization of the *bonnet rouge* as an item of challengingly novel political symbolism. But the descriptive energy of both types of commentary relies on a recognition of the transformation of a piece of humdrum clothing into a tremendously powerful symbol – whether inspiring or threatening – associated with the intervention of *le peuple* in political activities.

One indication of the process of terminological evolution in question is the way that, from 1791, the collective terms *bonnets de laine* and *sans-culottes* come to be treated as equivalent. In February 1791, Hébert's *Père Duchesne* cites *bonnets de laine* and *sans-culottes* together, but as separate entities: 'Honour, a thousand millions of thunder, to the great general Pike, great burner of moustaches, of capuchin's beards, the most worthy of confidence of the fifty thousand *bonnets de laine* and the fifty thousand *sans-culottes*').[50] The novel nature of this terminology is registered in the equivocal way it is invoked in a review of Jean-Jacques Barbier's *La Prise de la Bastille* published by Gorsas in his *Courrier des LXXXIII Départements* in August 1791. The mix of social classes in the audience was euphemistically evoked: 'For all were there, down to the citizens of the faubourgs, who have been baptized by Messieurs of the aristocracy woollen caps and something more or less'.[51] Here these terms are treated as polemical and deprecatory inventions, thus denying any positive identification with them. By December 1793, the convention of referring to *bonnets de laine* from the faubourg Saint-Antoine had been superseded by the phrase 'sans-culottes du faubourg Saint-Antoine'.[52]

In the aftermath of the second invasion of the Tuileries palace on 10 August 1792, and the effective removal of Louis XVI from political power, to be superseded by the declaration of a republic, the term *sans-culottes* shifted from the contested margins of the political landscape to a more central, prominent position. However, it remained a term which was employed and defined in a variety of ways.

A complement to the ways in which we have seen working dress being treated as emblematic in the summer of 1792 is found in the attempts to determine a legitimating historical pedigree for *sans-culotte* costume. Reflecting on the rise of popular political involvement in July 1792, Mercier invoked the historical precedents of the 'Gueux' (Poor) in Holland, who revolted against their Spanish oppressor, Philip II, as well as the Greeks and Romans, 'all people without breeches'.[53] In a paean of praise to the *sans-culottes* from the same period, references embraced Spartacus, the Romans, the Swiss, the Dutch, Christ, Mohammed, Rousseau, Homer, Shakespeare, and Franklin.[54] The scheme for republican costume proposed by the artist and *conventionnel* Sergent in 1793 invoked working dress – 'This outfit is nothing other than the daily dress of Men of the countryside and Workers of the towns' – implying that his design amounted to the elevation of the generic dress of the common working man to quasi-official status. Yet he also claimed it as equivalent to the honorific Roman toga.[55] In discussing the etymology for *sans-culottide* in a report on the introduction of the republican calendar on 24 October 1793, Fabre d'Eglantine pointed out that 'aristocrates' were mistaken in assuming that the term 'sans-culotte' was

inherently demeaning, for it had Gallic origins, part of France having
been known as 'la Gaule nonculottée' (breechless Gaul): 'Whatever may
be the case regarding the origin of this term, ancient or modern, having
been made illustrious by liberty, it should be dear to us; this is enough
to consecrate it solemnly'.[56] In his ambivalent description of the legit-
imation of disordered commonness in female dress, C.F.X. Mercier
nonetheless noted that it conformed to antique precedent:

> Never was a woman more beautiful than with her hair unkempt, without
> powder, falling freely on her shoulders: never was she more interesting, and
> more worthy of the sublime title of Republican, than when her pretty and
> delicate feet were encased in clogs. Antique customs of the Teutons, you are
> going to be reborn among us.[57]

Like Sergent, Mercier proposed a new system of regularized republican
costume, in part, surely, as a more dignified alternative to this kind of
dishevelment.

Although a degree of legitimacy and accepted currency was achieved
by the term in the wake of 10 August 1792,[58] there was still no formal
legislative or official codification of *sans-culotte* costume. This is consistent with its identification with the Parisian *sections*, whose political
culture was in the nature of an aggregate of local pressure groups.
The nearest equivalent would be an occasion such as the Section des
sans-culottes voting that its president should present an address to the
Convention wearing *bonnet rouge* and trousers ('pantalon').[59] Equally,
and perhaps surprisingly, it is rare to find *sans-culottes* included in the
descriptions of festival programmes and processions. When they are
present as part of the processions, they are auxiliary to monumental
allegorical elements. Thus, in the festival on 10 nivôse an II/30 December
1793, honouring military casualties in general, and in particular those
from the taking of Toulon, the 'Chariot of Victory, carrying the national
fasces, with the statue of Victory on it' was to be surrounded by '50
veterans and 100 valiant *sans-culottes* wearing *bonnets rouges*';[60] it is likely
that it was only the caps which were uniform. *Sans-culotte* costume also
appears in the carnivalesque festivals and processions associated with
dechristianization. In these, it was often worn under religious vestments
which were to be cast off, revealing the 'true' *sans-culotte* beneath.[61]

The idea that *sans-culotte* costume enjoyed a distinctly restrictive
currency is consistent with 'revisionist' accounts of the movement, which
argue that the *sans-culottes* were more of a political cadre or oligarchy

than a mass movement. According to this view, summarized by Patrice Higonnet: 'sans-culottism became, to adapt Soboul's expression, an ideologised revolutionary democracy, rather than a truly popular manifestation'.[62] This reinforces the idea that *sans-culotte* costume was a form of unofficial political uniform whose utilization was probably confined principally to club meetings, and participation in deputations.[63]

The extremely limited adoption of *sans-culotte* costume in the Convention corresponds to the fact that it was identified with the local, and increasingly rival, power base of the *sociétés populaires*. Those who wore the same dress in the Convention as they did in *sociétés populaires*, such as Omer Granet from Marseille, Chabot[64] and Thibaudeau, were noted as standing out (though we must acknowledge that references to this are retrospective and therefore of uncertain reliability).[65] Some sources claim that only Armonville wore the *bonnet rouge* in the Convention.[66] The implicit incongruity between the degree of respect for authority expected of those in the National Assembly and the odour of street politics attaching to the *bonnet rouge* is exemplified by Mercier's retrospective claim that, when Chabot appeared in the Convention *en sans-culotte*, he held his cap 'honteusement' (shamefully) in his hand.[67] When Chaumette encouraged the members of the Conseil Général of the Paris Commune to wear clogs, this was as part of the war effort, in response to the chronic shortage of clothing and equipment, notably shoes, for the struggling revolutionary army, rather than a recommendation that popular dress be adopted as such.[68] When prominent figures took to wearing *sans-culotte* costume, this was seized on as a sign of suspicious exaggeration, a conclusion that was repeatedly and vehemently rammed home as such figures fell victim to censure, arrest, or execution, most notoriously Philippe Égalité, the king's regicide cousin, the former duc d'Orléans,[69] and Hébert, the voice, through Père Duchesne, of intransigent, iconoclastic *sans-culottisme*.[70] In the course of a review of his own impeccable republican credentials, Saint-Just claimed credit for putting 'all France' on guard against false patriots who 'marched with the counter-revolution wearing *bonnets rouges*', a strategy he saw as tantamount to trying 'to make the Republic hideous'.[71] After Thermidor, the wholesale repudiation of 'maratisme' gathered force. What had been intended as a virtuous modesty and simplicity of dress was castigated as merely dishevelled dirtiness and repugnant filthiness, constituting a kind of hierarchical aesthetic rationale for the unworthiness of its associated populist politics.[72]

A measure of *sans-culotte* costume having achieved a normative function (though not of its being ubiquitously adopted) is, precisely, evidence of its subversion, which is recorded as occurring between late 1793 and the spring of 1794. Detailed police reports filed for the Minister of the Interior give us an unusual degree of detail on how *sans-culotte* costume was misused. We have, of course, to acknowledge that it was the business of the police agents who compiled these reports to be able to provide information on the vagaries of *l'esprit public*, above all when dissent was manifest – they were looking for troublemakers; reports are least detailed when they are able to report calm and solid consensus.[73] Nonetheless, these texts provide a considerable degree of precision regarding the currency of *sans-culotte* costume, and more specifically evidence of its misappropriation, since for all their bureaucratized sloganizing, in delineating the features of suspect individuals they are extremely precisely observed in matters of physical appearance and dress.[74]

During this period, the *sans-culotte* outfit – *carmagnole*, *pantalon*, and *bonnet rouge*, but sometimes only one or two of these elements[75] – was described as having been put to subversive use in order to provoke and insult people who had presumably become habituated to its status as a sign of republican rectitude. In some cases named individuals were noted as deliberately concealing their dubious political credentials by adopting *sans-culotte* costume. In December 1793, the *ci-devant* marquis d'Audelot 'walks about as a *sans-culotte*; he only lacks a *bonnet rouge* for people who don't know him as a royalist take him to be a patriot, which he will never be'.[76] The implication is that the more complete the costume, the more it was likely to be the result of contrived concealment. As we noted earlier, in 1792 the type of the *sans-culotte* was also linked to that of the *forts de la halle*. In September 1793, a police report warned that, among 'several very poorly dressed people', who were in fact suspected of being 'well-born people', there were some who had dressed up as 'forts de la halle' (market porters).[77]

By March 1794, *sans-culotte* costume was reckoned to have been comprehensively compromised by its subversive misuse:

Aristocrates have absolutely adopted republican costume. We are reliably informed that two thirds of the *bonnets rouges* and short jackets are the most avowed scoundrels who only seek to corrupt public morale and who, by their costume, intimidate true *sans-culottes*.[78]

Saint-Just put it more pithily: 'The Revolution is frozen; all principles are weakened; all that is left are *bonnets rouges* worn by intrigue.'[79] Opinion therefore turned against men in such costumes:

> We must scorn [military] busbies, police caps, trousers and short jackets. It is with these insignificant symbols that, since the affair of the second of September [prison massacres], they insinuated themselves into the sections, that they secured the most important positions, and that they seek to halt the chariot of the Revolution in its course by exaggerated measures.[80]

A few days later it was reported that: 'Citizens dressed in short jackets [*carmagnoles*] are brazenly insulted'.[81] However, beyond the shifting status accorded to the essentially stylized ingredients of *sans-culotte* costume, it is important to note that, with the establishment of a ubiquitous régime of surveillance, dress in general had become a site for apprehensive scrutiny, and moreover that this applied to the most ordinary items of dress. As Père Duchesne had earlier recommended: 'if an apron was a rallying sign, it would be necessary to prevent even cooks from wearing them'.[82]

This repudiation of *sans-culotte* costume in the spring of 1794 was complemented by observations that there had been a relaxation of republican dress codes: dressing down was no longer obligatory in order to conform – willingly or opportunistically – to the vestimentary status quo.[83] Nonetheless, we continue to find references to people adopting the outfit well into 1795. In an essay on dress in the *Décade philosophique*, Amaury Duval, a resolute republican, recorded observing an ostentatiously stylish *muscadin* (previously known as a 'fat' (fop)) teetering down the Champs-Elysées in discomfortingly tight *culottes*, followed by a group of five or six 'prétendus sans-culottes en pantalons et vestes' (would-be *sans-culottes* in trousers and jackets). It was the former sight which disturbed him, since it seemed to be a throwback to pre-revolutionary *moeurs*. He reflected bitterly: 'I thought I had dreamt the Revolution'.[84] The survival of '*sans-culotte* style' was little more than a bitter reminder of lost ground. Nonetheless, it seems to have been possible to continue wearing elements of *sans-culotte* dress, notably the *bonnet rouge*, throughout the later 1790s, if at the risk of insult. In 1795, the *conventionnel* Armonville was mockingly described as tenaciously refusing to abandon his *bonnet rouge*, to the extent of eating and sleeping in it.[85] At the end of the 1790s, such items of dress are disparagingly referred to as 'relics', implying that they are merely obsolete and impotent vestiges of a past age, hence no longer threatening.[86]

By way of conclusion, I would like to turn to a selection of images of *sans-culottes*, and explore them as a source in terms of what they reveal about the representation of this important but contentious form of politicized dress. This is necessarily a fragmentary sampling of the complex problems involved in analysing the visual representation of *sans-culottes*. The images have been chosen because they correspond to significant strands within the rather limited repertoire of *sans-culotte* imagery.[87] These are predominantly prints; there are, in fact, almost no surviving paintings of men dressed as *sans-culottes* (the nearest one might get to this are occasional portraits).[88]

Before addressing the *sans-culotte*, it is necessary to review certain aspects of inherited conventions for representing the 'peuple'. The first point to make, which remains the case with regard to *sans-culottes*, is that representations of 'le peuple' were always collective, never individualized. Figures from the lower strata of society only became visible when they could be identified with various forms of commercial collectivity, as exponents of trades, or in the form of the deserving or criminalized poor.[89] In terms of the narrow conventions of high art, primarily genre painting, the most appealing and ideologically decorous vehicle for such visualization was the family unit. Following 1789, this easily lent itself to being imagined in terms of the ideal Greuzian happy family, experiencing a newly expanded form of patriotic happiness. In an anonymous print of 1790, *Hommage à la Constitution* (Figure 21), among the figures gathered to salute the statue of the Constitution, 'le peuple' are represented in the foreground by a family group similar to those in later eighteenth-century French genre paintings. They are identified as pseudo-popular by their dress: the woman wears a broad skirt, mob cap and shawl; her dress is of the informal kind that became fashionable in later eighteenth-century France; the man a round hat, loose cravat and jacket, waistcoat, with a sash around his waist, striped trousers and shoes; his outfit resembles the kind of theatrical costume used for male characters in *drames*, theatrical renditions of 'modern' subjects. It is hardly surprising that such recourse to available models was to recur later in the Revolution. What is at stake in the current discussion is precisely the question of the extent to which such available models were perceived as having become inadequate to new ideological demands. In the early Revolution, recycling ready-made visual stereotypes of the popular had the advantage of providing a recognizable vocabulary, but one whose meaning was changed by being employed to illustrate a new political language. Thus, in Debucourt's *L'Almanach national* of January 1791, 'the people' are represented by a

Figure 21 Anonymous: 'Hommage à la Constitution', 1791, coloured etching. 'La Constitution paroit sur un pied destal d'une main elle tient la Charte Constitutionnelle, de l'autre elle tient une pique surmontée d'un Bonnet de la Liberté, l'Ange Tutelaire de la France la couvre de son Égide d'une main, et de l'autre foudroient les Monstres qui veulent approcher de la Constitution, autour de la Statue l'on voit le Peuple François et la Garde Nationale qui viennent jurer fidélité aux nouvelles Lois de la Constitution; sur le devant l'on voit le Commerce qui rend grace à la Divinité de l'avenement de la Constitution en France. Sur le pied destal l'on voit un Flambeau et un Faisseau d'arme, simbole des Lumières et de l'union' (The Constitution appears on a pedestal, with one hand she holds the Constitutional Charter, with the other she holds a pike surmounted by a Liberty cap, France's Tutelary Angel covers her with her shield with one hand, and with the other she strikes with thunderbolts the Monsters who want to approach the Constitution, around the Statue one sees the French People and the National Guard who come to swear fidelity to the new laws of the Constitution in France. On the pedestal one sees a torch and a fasces of armes, symbol of Englightenment and union). Musée de la Révolution Française, Vizille, MRF 1984–87. Photograph: Musée de la Révolution Française, Vizille.

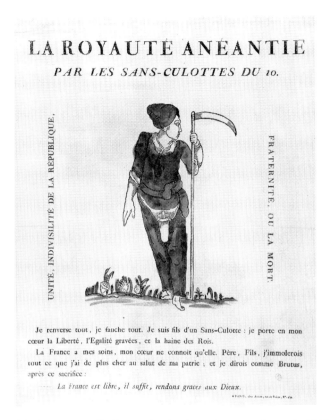

Figure 22 Anonymous: 'La Royauté anéantie par les sans-culottes du 10 [Août] (Royalty annihilated by the *sans-culottes* of the 10th August), 1792, woodcut. Musée Carnavalet, Paris, HIST GC 023. Photograph: Photothèque des Musées de la Ville de Paris (Chevallier).

diverse set of figures: national guards, children, fashionable figures wearing wigs and bonnets, and a Turk. Here the people correspond to a diverse but inclusive entity; the only figure who could be called popular is a woman selling pamphlets. These are essentially Ancien Régime spectators drafted in to witness the inspiring allegorical spectacle of the Constitution that floats above them.

The dramatic end to the monarchy on 10 August 1792 consolidated the political visibility of the *sans-culotte* and its representability. At first sight, the image of a *sans-culotte* in the print *La Royauté anéantie par les sans culottes du 10* [août] (Figure 22) might be said to achieve a brutally abbreviated graphic directness, enhanced by the coarseness of the woodcut.[90]

Figure 23 Pierre-Etienne Lesueur: 'L'Exécution de Philippe Égalité), 1794, pencil, 26 × 38.5 cm. Hennin Collection, vol. 133, no. 11675, Département des Arts Graphiques, Bibliothèque Nationale de France, Paris. Photograph: Bibliothèque Nationale de France.

As an image of a *sans-culotte*, it relies on a minimal set of ingredients: the trousers, jacket (with rolled-up sleeves), cap, and bare feet. Yet the dagger, as an instrument of merciless retribution, echoes the quotation from Voltaire's *Brutus* in the caption below. The scyth is decidedly polysemic. It connotes both the judicial blade of the guillotine and the grim reaper. But, in being substituted for the *sans-culotte*'s characteristic *pique*, it also locates the figure in a representational tradition, not only of Death, but also of the harvest – fallen royal heads mingle with stumps of foliage at the *sans-culotte*'s feet (an unavoidable subtext here is the fertilizing function of the blood of the Revolution's enemies: 'Qu'un sang impur abreuve nos sillons'). This is the son of a *sans-culotte*, who has come of age in decisively intervening in the annihilation of the monarchy. The figure stands upright, isolated, posed like a personification in a iconographical manual (something reinforced by his bare feet), but also inscribes a temporal dimension, as he looks back over his left shoulder to the human debris of the past. Significantly, in the caption, it is the *sans-culotte* who speaks, reinforcing his identity as an autonomous agent of the political freedom he has fought to achieve. Yet the figure is rudimentary; it is the slogans and quotations which hem him in that enrich the print with historical and cultural depth. Taken together, the ingredients do not cohere, except in the sense that they form a kind of fragmented collage.

A drawing by Pierre-Etienne Lesueur showing the execution of Philippe Égalité displaces its image of celebrating *sans-culottes* into a combination of grotesque and classicizing elements (Figure 23).[91] The figures are delineated in delicate outline which gives the image a strongly neoclassical flavour. Most of the poses resemble those employed in contemporaneous representations of subjects from classical history and literature. However, in the centre of the composition, a dancing figure cavorts in front of the scaffold in a way that is almost Callot-like in its energy, and also recalls figures of satyrs – a conventional form of animalistic antithesis to the perfect bodies of deities, heroes and heroines of classical mythology. In their different ways both figural idioms translate the violence of the subject into a quasi-carnivalesque scene of celebration and triumph which is stabilized by the employment of elements drawn from a well-established visual language.[92] For all the historical specificity and retributive energy of the episode depicted, the drawing owes more to a kind of stylized euphemism than it is an affirmation of a new republican social world. Alternatively, we could see the image as prescriptive, projecting the kind of authentically celebratory form of behaviour that should be adopted by *sans-culottes* on such occasions.

This kind of amalgam can be found in images whose representation of the politically active popular at first sight seems less obviously compromised by observance of the protocols of figurative decorum. *Le Peuple mangeur des rois*, published in the *Révolutions de Paris* (10–18 frimaire an II/30 November–8 December 1793) (Figure 24),[93] appears exceptional in the way that it articulates a naked, almost unbridled violence. But on closer examination, this turns out to be an exercise in the calculated subversion of established conventions regarding the representation of the male body; moreover, the accompanying text situates the image in relation to various strands of mythological and classical culture.

The immediate context for this project and commentary was David's proposal to the Convention for a giant figure of the French people to be sited on the Pont-Neuf, royal debris providing the material for the monument's pedestal.[94] For the *Révolutions de Paris*, such a monument should rival those known from the history of Antiquity; representing national vengeance, it would stand as a latter-day equivalent to the columns of Hercules, constituting a powerful deterrent to kings who

Figure 24 Anonymous: 'Le Peuple mangeur des rois' (The People Eater of Kings), etching, published in the *Révolutions de Paris* (10–18 frimaire an II/30 November–8 December 1793). Musée de la Révolution Francaise, Vizille. Photograph: Musée de la Révolution Française.

contemplated any incursion onto the territory of the Republic. Altern-atively, the frontier could be equipped with war machines which would themselves personify the French people: 'with the features of a colossal divinity, hurling down thunder, or else of the Carthaginian god, who opens his arms to smother the victims offered'. As Homer had described the kings of his time as 'eaters of peoples', so this figure of a French *sans-culotte* should have inscribed on its brow 'THE PEOPLE EATER OF KINGS'. The equivalence between the French people and the figure of a *sans-culotte* is insisted upon: among entries to the competition for this monument, preference should be given to those that most effectively translated the features of a *sans-culotte* into those of the French people.[95]

The physique of this figure is brawny, his chest and limbs hairy – in short, the complete antithesis to the idealized noble body of high art. Nonetheless, as the text explains, the figure's gigantic proportions cor-respond to its role as an animate anti-monarchical monument on France's embattled borders, and the unmistakable Herculean club firmly places him within literary and mythological traditions involving feats of superhuman strength. At the same time, as James Leith notes, the image is given extra bite because of associations of ritualistic cannibalism,[96] here legitimized by political rhetoric.

In vestimentary terms, his *bonnet de laine* is grubby and vulgar, lacking any visual cue to encourage recognition of it as a liberty cap, and his loose trousers – rolled up to reveal his powerful legs – remain an item of coarse dress, without any ennobling resemblance to classical drapery. The elaborately layered nature of this image is entirely consistent with the way that the representation of 'men of the people' was a problematic enterprise. Indeed, this also applies generally to the visual stereotype of the *sans-culotte*, which, far from being a consistent form of visual reference, is surprisingly diverse both in its visual ingredients and the way that such images were interpreted.

If we look ahead to David's projected theatre curtain for the Opéra, *Le Triomphe du Peuple français* (1794) (Figure 25), we find *sans-culottes* represented in the context of an elaborate assemblage of allegorical and historical figures. The image is dominated by the statuesque and superhuman allegorical figure of the 'French People' riding in the chariot; to the right march a procession of martyrs to liberty (Marat, William Tell, Brutus, Lepeletier, etc.). To the left, beneath a winged figure, two *sans-culottes* attack fallen 'fleeing tyrants', their swords signalling their militaristic function (Figure 26). One is nude, with a Roman coiffure, the other wears trousers and a long shirt, and has swept-back hair. This differentiation makes explicit what is in effect an oscillation between two registers – the antique and the contemporary. However, even in the latter case, the figure has a heroic, athletic stature: this remains an antique figure to which has been added a layer of politically symbolic modern dress.[97]

What is at stake in the representation of *sans-culottes* is the relation between the understanding of a polemical socio-political idea and how this could be translated into visual form. That is, rather than images of *sans-culottes* merely being a direct illustration of a normative socio-political category, they have a flexible and often problematic correspondance to their referent. On the one hand, the language of simplicity, authenticity and republican virtue which informed the idea of the *sans-culotte* could be translated into images of benign figures living out such ideals. For example, *Le Bon Sans-culotte* relies on an updated version of ideal Greuzian domesticity. Alternatively, the conventions of the fashion plate could be used to naturalize the type (as in the print from 1792, *Sans-culottes du 10 août, 1er an de la République française*).[98] On the other hand, when it was a question of representing the *sans-culotte* in militant,

Figure 25 Jacques-Louis David: 'Le Triomphe du Peuple français' (The Triumph of the French People), pencil and grey wash, 1794, 38.6 × 71 cm. Musée Carnavalet, Paris, Inv. I.E.D. 4856. Photograph: Photothèque des Musées de la Ville de Paris (Briant).

Figure 26 Detail.

aggressive mode there was a fundamental incompatibility or resistance between the political language used to identify *sans-culotte* social life and its translation into generic visual forms. Even when essentially celebratory, such images have a predominantly caricatural vocabulary, a register more easily employed when, as in the case of the coarsely pugnacious Père Duchesne, it takes the form of an imaginary portrait.[99]

Figure 27 Godefroy: 'Le Jongleur Pitt soutenant avec une loterie l'équilibre de l'Angleterre et les subsides de la coalition' (The Juggler Pitt maintaining England's balance and her subsidies for the coalition with a lottery), etching, first half of 1794, 36.5 × 45.5 cm. De Vinck Collection, vol. 26, no. 4387, Département des Arts Graphiques, Bibliothèque Nationale de France, Paris. Photograph: Bibliothèque Nationale de France.

Godefroy's etching *Le Jongleur Pitt soutenant avec une loterie l'équilibre de l'Angleterre et les subsides de la coalition* (The juggler Pitt maintaining England's balance and her subsidies for the coalition with a lottery) (1794) (Figure 27), is one of many anti-British images from this period. On the right, Pitt's left ankle is held by an athletic *sans-culotte*, who raises his right hand in a sign of warning and admonition. His idealized muscular legs and arms suggest that Godefroy had some awareness of the heroic conventions of history painting; the box-like space which contains the figures is also directly linked to current compositional conventions. Although the *sans-culotte* acts from a position in the corner, he is not an incidental character, but more a powerful personification of the French Republic, nonchalantly throwing his gawky adversary off balance, to the

LE CHARLATAN POLITIQUE OU LE LÉOPARD APPRIVOISÉ.

Figure 28 Antoine-Denis Chaudet: 'Le Charlatan politique, ou le léopard apprivoisé' (The Political Charlatan, or the leopard tamed), etching, first half of 1794, 46.1 × 60.3 cm. De Vinck Collection, vol. 26, no. 4388. Département des Arts Graphiques, Bibliothèque Nationale de France, Paris. Photograph: Bibliothèque Nationale de France.

dismay of king 'Georges Dandin'. This image is interesting because it shows the combination of two complementary representational modes: the extreme caricature applied to Pitt, and the more idealized treatment of the *sans-culotte*. The *sans-culotte* wears an apron, with a hammer tucked into his belt, thus evoking the continued presence of residually emblematic eighteenth-century iconographical conventions for representing male artisans. However, there is a further level of meaning here, in that aprons and hammers were also the attributes of *sapeurs* (sappers). Thus, the image inscribes a sign of national militarization, celebrating the heroic endeavour of this personification of the *peuple* as French People.

In another image from the same period, Antoine-Denis Chaudet's *Le Charlatan politique, ou le léopard apprivoisé* (The Political Charlatan, or the leopard tamed) (Figure 28), the delineation of two *sans-culottes* is strikingly different. They emphasize the caricatural more than the heroic, with the result that there is some ambiguity in how we might read them. In the middle distance, we see the head of the République also wearing a liberty cap, topped by the tricolore, placed on the prow of 'the vessel of the French Republic'. They are heavily muscled, but in a way that suggests plebeian 'Hercules forains' rather than the conventions of academic drawing. Yet beneath their short-sleeved jackets they wear loose-fitting long shirts which, in the manner of high art drapery, part to reveal the body beneath – not the elegant outlines of an academically idealized anatomy, but massive hips and thighs. Their faces are coarse, their joints thickened, and they wear sagging stockings and heavy clogs; they are placed in the left- and right-hand corners, in a way that seems like a paro-dic echo of the use of repoussoir figures in history painting. We might also read the figures as echoing the earlier satirical use of the term 'sans culotte', for they are not clothed in any kind of stylized popular dress; rather, they literally illustrate a state of comic undress. That this rendition of *sans-culottes* was not deemed subversive, but rather a legitimate element in caricature, is demonstrated by the fact that both prints were subsidized by the Comité de Salut public (Committee of Public Safety) as part of a campaign of anti-British propaganda.[100]

These two images exemplify the way that representations of the *sans-culotte* are predominantly either markedly idealized, or virulently caricatural – a polarization which parallels what Geffroy calls the 'black' and 'white legend' surrounding the historiography of the *sans-culotte*.[101] Forging an image of a *sans-culotte* or cognate types seems to rely on two main sets of conventions: those governing the representation of the heroic male body, as associated with history painting; and the varied kinds of exaggeration found in caricature, which are analogous to the theatrical modes of burlesque and vaudeville. They also employ quite different strategies for dealing with the symbolism of *sans-culotte* dress. In Chaudet's image, the *sans-culotte*'s costume is tailored to emphasize his athleticism. By contrast Godefroy's *sans-culottes* are much more stylized. The exag-gerated features of their ill-fitting clothes conform to the image's satirical idiom; even so they are capable of a comic mastery over the dehumanized English.

The print, 'Dansons la Carmagnole' (Figure 29), a frontispiece to a 1793 almanac, illustrates the residual presence of the earlier, pre-1792 deprecatory meaning of 'sans culotte'. On the one hand, for all that the figure wears a woollen cap (presumably red), and is armed with the popular pike and sword, this image of a daintily dancing *sans-culotte*

Dansons la Carmagnole.

Figure 29 Anonymous: 'Dansons la Carmagnole', etching, frontispiece, Anonymous [François Marchant], *La République en vaudevilles. Précédées d'une notice des principaux événemens de la révolution, pour servir de Calendrier à l'année 1793* (Paris, 1793). British Library, F.1881 (1). By permission of the British Library.

seems deliberately to refuse any more tangible evocation of the physical power of the 'peuple armé' (and it is set in a vaguely rural, rather than obviously urban, context). Rather, we notice the presence of exaggerated ragged tears in his clothes (which contrast with his neatly laced shoes). To this extent, the image could be said to represent an equivocal confluence of the new positive meaning of *sans-culotte* with its pre-revolutionary antecedent, the disparaging stereotype of the risibly underdressed 'sans culotte'.[102] This semantic discordance was remarked on at the time. In one of the police reports from November 1793 published by Caron, the term *sans-culotte* was used licentiously – playing on the sexual overtones of being 'sans culotte' – in a way that holds on to the eighteenth-century usage noted by Geffroy, rather than, or perhaps deliberately instead of, its new politicized meaning.[103]

The vestimentary ensemble of the *sans-culotte* had a short career, only being actively adopted between late 1792 and the spring of 1794. We have seen, however, that for all its intended polemical simplicity as a form of political statement, it drew on, and generated, a complex semantic baggage surrounding the representation of working men, specifically the men of the artisanal centre of the faubourg St-Antoine, and the emblem with which they became identified, the *bonnet de laine*. A sampling of the currency of *bonnets de laine* in 1791 underlines the latent ambiguities that fed into the *sans-culotte* stereotype, and which were exploited in the rhetorical contestation which accompanied its crystallization during the course of 1792. As Annie Geffroy has argued, the history of *sans-culotte* costume owes more to the dynamic, antithetical evolution of revolutionary language than it does to mere stylistic vestimentary innovation. It has only been possible to touch on the various ways in which the multi-layered richness of this discourse also found expression in visual imagery. Nonetheless, even within the limits of an exposition of a small number of prints and drawings, it is clear that the representation of the *sans-culotte* was anything but consensual, and drew on divergent referential ingredients, exemplifying the contestatory nature of such imagery, and the multi-layered symbolic power of dress.

After 1794, the phenomenon of the *sans-culottes* remained present in the language of politics, but predominantly in the form, on the one hand, of satire and caricature, and on the other, of the mythologization of the republican cause. In due course, nineteenth-century historical genre painting consolidated and recyled the ferocious and sanguinary *sans-culotte* stereotype.[104]

It has proved to be extremely difficult to recover the precise empirical history of the utilization of *sans-culotte* costume. This follows partly from the way in which it was employed. The *sans-culotte* ensemble – primarily *bonnet rouge*, trousers, and short jacket – could be achieved through the combination of all or only some of its overall set of elements, which were enough to signify identification with a position at once political and rhetorical. Precise details of dress themselves were subordinate to the assertion of a point of view; what passed for *sans-culotte* costume was to that extent always a stylized, instrumental approximation. In so far as *sans-culotte* costume was never the subject of legislation, it was all too easy for its adoption to pivot ambiguously between a calculated simulation and an authentic statement of identification; it depended, that is to say, on the enunciation and, so to speak, performance of an ideology, rather than being simply a matter of choosing to wear certain items of dress. Indeed, ironically, and perplexingly, full *sans-culotte* dress was evidently as often assumed by those who mimicked the stereotype as by those who sincerely identified with what it was meant to stand for; or, at least, this is how in 1793–94 police agents responded to encounters with exemplarily kitted-out *sans-culottes*. As we have seen, they came to believe that excessively fastidious concern with assembling and being seen in a full *sans-culotte* outfit was suspiciously redolent of a desire to mask other, contrary motives or identities – in this reiterating a deep-seated scepticism about the superfluous and morally questionable value of dress as a form of ephemeral, decorative, inherently unreliable self-presentation. Given this undercurrent of subversion, and the distrust of an outward, skin-deep show of orthodoxy, it is not surprising that this vestimentary stereotype came to be comprehensively devalued and discarded. In contrast to the quite protracted and eclectic process of its crystallization through 1791 and 1792, *sans-culotte* costume was to lose its ideological *raison d'être* with remarkable abruptness, a phenomenon which exposed its lack of any legislatively anchored norm, and the fact that it was compromisingly identified with a political formation which dramatically forfeited its temporary position of dominance on the stage of revolutionary politics.

Notes

1. This a revised and expanded version of my 'The Formation and Currency of a Vestimentary Stereotype: the *sans-culotte* in the French Revolution', in Wendy Parkins (ed.), *Fashioning the Body Politic* (Berg: Oxford, 2002), pp. 19–43.

2. See Albert Soboul, *Les Sans-culottes parisiens en l'an II. Mouvement populaire et gouvernement révolutionnaire 2 juin 1793–9 thermidor an II* (Clavreuil: Paris, 1958); Richard M. Andrews, 'Social Structures, Political Élites and Ideology in Revolutionary Paris, 1792–1794: A Critical Evaluation of Albert Soboul's *Les Sans-culottes parisiens en l'an II*', *Journal of Social History*, 1985, vol. 19, pp. 71–112; R.B. Rose, *The Making of the Sans-culottes. Democratic Ideas and Institutions in Paris, 1789–1792* (Manchester University Press: Manchester, 1983); Richard Cobb, *The Police and the People: French Popular Protest 1789–1820* (Oxford University Press: Oxford, 1970). For a recent summary of the historiographical dimension, and references to the main contributory studies, see Patrice Higonnet, 'Sans-culottes', in François Furet and Mona Ozouf (eds), *Dictionnaire critique de la Révolution française* (Flammarion: Paris, 1988), pp. 418–23.

3. Michel Jouve, 'L'Image du sans-culotte dans la caricature politique anglaise: création d'un stéréotype pictural', *Gazette des beaux-arts*, November 1978, vol. 91, pp. 187–96; David Bindman, *The Shadow of the Guillotine. Britain and the French Revolution* (British Museum: London, 1989); Claude Langlois, *La Caricature contre-révolutionnaire* (CNRS: Paris, 1988); James Leith, 'Images of *Sans-culottes*', in Claudette Hould and James Leith (eds), *Iconographie et image de la Révolution française*, Actes du colloque tenu dans le cadre du 59e congrès de l'Association canadienne française pour l'avancement des sciences (15–16 May 1989) (Montreal, 1990), pp. 130–59; Michel Naudin, 'La réaction culturelle en l'an III: la représentation du Jacobin et du sans-culotte dans l'imaginaire de leurs adversaires', in Michel Vovelle (ed.), *Le Tournant de l'an III. Réaction et Terreur blanche dans la France révolutionnaire* (Comité des travaux historiques et scientifiques: Paris, 1997), pp. 279–92.

4. Carol Eliel states that the *carmagnole* was banned when Bonaparte became First Consul (Alan Wintermute (ed.), *1789: French Art during the Revolution* (Colnaghi: New York, 1989), p. 93), referencing Jennifer Harris's article 'The Red Cap of Liberty: a study of dress worn by French revolutionary partisans 1789–94', *Eighteenth-century Studies*, Spring 1981, vol. 14, no. 3, p. 286. However, no supporting reference is given here.

5. Annie Geffroy, 'Désignation, dénégation: la légende des sans-culottes (1780–1980)', in Christian Croisille, Jean Ehrard and Marie-Claude Chemin (eds), *La Légende de la Révolution*, Actes du colloque international de Clermont-Ferrand (June 1986) (Université Blaise Pascal: Clermont-Ferrand, 1988), p. 586, and also her, 'Sans-culotte(s) (novembre 1790–juin 1792)', in A. Geffroy, J. Guilhaumou and S. Moreno, *Dictionnaire des usages socio-politiques (1770–1815)* (Klincksieck: Saint-Cloud, 1985), pp. 157–86, and Marcel Reinhard, *Nouvelle Histoire de Paris. La Révolution 1789–1799* (Hachette: Paris, 1971), pp. 214, 420.

6. On the cognate role played by hats and their absence, see Michael Sonenscher, *The Hatters of Eighteenth-century France* (Cambridge University Press: Cambridge, 1987).

7. On Lafitte, see Jean-François Heim, Claire Béraud, Philippe Heim, *Les Salons de peinture de la Révolution française (1789–1799)* (C.A.C. Edition: Paris, 1989), p. 249. A fan illustrated with an image of 5/6 October 1789 includes a man in cap and striped trousers (*Modes et révolutions 1789–1804* (Musée de la mode et du costume, Paris, 1989), no. 154, ill. p. 187, Musée de la Mode et du Costume, Inv. 86.22312). In the print 'époque du vendredi 19 Février 1791' (*Révolutions de Paris*, 1791, no. 32, p. 29), showing men from the faubourg Saint-Antoine, we find, in the bottom left-hand corner, a man wearing a cap, striped trousers and short jacket, and carrying a pike (Bibliothèque Nationale de France, Hennin Collection, no. 10650). See also the anonymous print, *L'Idole renversée*, c.1791, where a *fort de la halle* in striped trousers and broad-brimmed hat joins soldiers, a policeman, a grenadier of the national guard, holding up the crown vacated by the fallen bust of Louis XVI (James Cuno (ed.), *French Caricature and the French Revolution, 1789–1799* (Grunwald Center for the Graphic Arts, Wight Art Gallery, University of California, Los Angeles: 1989), cat. no. 85, pp. 191–2).

8. Soboul, *Sans-culottes*, p. 408.

9. Geffroy notes that 'sans-culotte' is not used in pamphlets from between February 1790 and July 1791, reprinted in F.A. Aulard, *La Société des Jacobins*, 6 vols (Paris, 1889–97) ('Sans-culotte', *Dictionnaire des usages socio-politiques*, p. 180, note 7). George Rudé dated the shift from old to new meanings of *sans-culotte* to June 1792, i.e. the invasion of

the Tuileries (*The Crowd in the French Revolution* (Oxford University Press: Oxford, 1959), p. 12).

10. See Soboul's *Sans-culottes parisiens*, and also Maurice Genty, *L'Apprentissage de la citoyenneté. Paris 1789–1795* (Messidor/Éditions sociales: Paris, 1987).

11. For example, a satirical response to the prominence of the term's new meaning: 'Mais aujourd'hui sans qu'on me hue / Je me promène dans la rue, / Que je sois ou non culotté, / Vive, vive la liberté!' (*Le Réviseur universel et impartial et bulletin de Madame de Beaumont*, no. 44, 11 April 1792, p. 2).

12. To this extent, the idea that the costume was instigated by the appearance of the actor Simon Chenard in a prototype *sans-culotte* outfit, at the festival celebrating the liberation of Savoy in October 1792, as commemorated in a painting by Louis-Léopold Boilly (Musée Carnavalet), is anachronistic, and erroneous. On Boilly's picture, see Susan Siegfried, *The Art of Louis-Léopold Boilly. Modern Life in Napoleonic France* (Yale University Press: New Haven and London, 1995), pp. 41–2, and Aileen Ribeiro, *The Art of Dress. Fashion in England and France 1750–1820* (Yale University Press: New Haven and London, 1995), pp. 146–7. The assumption that the painting is contemporaneous with the festival is, however, problematic. As Siegfried notes, Chenard wears a hat, not a *bonnet rouge*, which would have been *de rigueur* in late 1792. This opens up the idea that the picture was in fact made later, the cap being omitted as a way of excluding any explicit reference to the heyday of the Republic, with the result that the image is shifted into the domain of portraits of actors in character. Copia's print after the picture was announced in the *Journal de Paris* on 7 February 1795 (price 6 *livres*).

13. See Michael Sonenscher, *Work and Wages: Natural Law, Politics, and the Eighteenth-century French Trades* (Cambridge University Press: Cambridge, 1989), for a brilliantly illuminating rereading of the language of *sans-culotterie*, not in terms of historians' interpretations of the course of the Revolution, but rather its relation to the world of artisanal labour.

14. This chapter deliberately focuses on male *sans-culottes*, because it is they who dominate revolutionary texts and images. The topic of female *sans-culottes* seems not to have attracted a comparable degree of attention, except in so far as female participation in revolutionary political culture was seen as anomalous by their male counterparts. See Dominique Godineau, *Citoyennes tricoteuses. Les Femmes du peuple à Paris pendant la Révolution* (Alinéa: Paris, 1988), and Darlene Gay Levy and Harriet B. Applewhite, 'Women and Militant Citizenship in Revolutionary Paris', in Sara E. Melzer and Leslie W. Rabine (eds), *Rebel Daughters. Women and the French Revolution* (Oxford University Press: Oxford and New York, 1992), pp. 79–101.

15. As yet, I have not located any images which explicitly incorporate the *bonnets de laine*.

16. Indeed, as Raymonde Monnier has shown, in 1791 the faubourg was less actively at the forefront of organized public political action, rather than spontaneous protest, than in the early days of the Revolution. For example, in elections in June 1791, voting turn-out in the faubourg was relatively low compared to that in other areas of Paris, and the general tenor of the participation in the new revolutionary political culture was still predominantly bourgeois, and did not involve any organized popular militancy (*Le Faubourg Saint-Antoine (1789–1815)* (Société des Études robespierristes: Paris, 1981), pp. 120, 125).

17. For detailed explorations of the complexities of the revolutionary lexicon, see the exemplary studies that make up the *Dictionnaire des usages socio-politiques (1770–1815)*, 4 vols (Klincksieck: Saint-Cloud, 1985–89).

18. François Marchant, *Les Sabats jacobites*, no. 8 [*c*.17 March 1791], cit. Geffroy, 'Sans-culotte(s)', p. 165.

19. See *Essai sur la méthode à employer pour juger les ouvrages des beaux-arts du dessin, et principalement ceux qui sont exposés au Salon du Louvre, par une société d'artistes* (Paris, 1791), pp. 7–8), cit. Philippe Bordes, *Le 'Serment du Jeu de paume' de Jacques-Louis David* (éditions de la Réunion des Musées Nationaux: Paris, 1983), p. 73. Lynn Hunt notes a similar example of this in July 1793 applied by Fouché to times when 'liberty was in danger' (*Arch Parl*, vol. 68, p. 73, cit. *Politics, Culture, and Class in the French Revolution* (University of California Press: Berkeley and London, 1984), p. 101). This could be seen as a dramatic, newly politicized version of the idea of special cultural events as exceptional moments of class convergence. On the example of the Académie royale de peinture et de sculpture's Salon exhibitions as a pre-revolutionary site for evoking the symbolic reconciliation of social difference, see Richard Wrigley, *The Origins of French Art Criticism: from the Ancien Régime to the Restoration* (Oxford University Press: Oxford, 1993), pp. 88–90.

20. For later development of this discourse, see Christian Alain Muller, 'Du "peuple égaré" au "peuple enfant": le discours politique à l'épreuve de la révolte populaire en 1793', *Revue d'histoire moderne et contemporaine*, January–March 2000, vol. 47, no. 1, pp. 93–112.

21. 12 July 1791, no. 11, p. 170. The literature on this occasion is summarized in David Dowd, *Pageant Master of the Republic: Jacques-Louis David and the French Revolution* (University of Nebraska Press: Lincoln, 1948), pp. 48–54, and Tourneux, vol. 2.

22. 13 July 1791, no. 12, p. 185.

23. Ibid.. Brissot explained the cohesive role played by 'l'enthousiasme qu'a inspiré cette cérémonie aux amis de la liberté et au peuple' (*Patriote françois*, 13 July 1791, no. 703, p. 50).

24. *L'Ami du roi*, 13 July 1791, no. 194, pp. 775–6; in Fontenay's *Journal général de France*, the word 'burlesque' is also used to describe the occasion, suggesting that it would have provided Rabelais with ample matter for a new chapter to add to his account of the exploits of Gargantua and Pantagruel (16 July 1791, no. 166, p. 692).

25. 12 July 1791, no. 193, p. 781. Significantly, when reprinted in Villette's *Lettres choisies de C. V. sur les principaux événemens de la Révolution* (Paris, 1792), references to *bonnets rouges* were edited out (e.g., p. 182), presumably so as to minimize what might have retrospectively appeared as the progressive intervention of militant *sans-culottes* and Jacobins for whom the *bonnet rouge* had, by this date, become a rallying sign.

26. *Lettres choisies*, p. 186.

27. *La Bouche de fer*, 12 July 1791, no. 90, pp. 4–5. This was the paper of the Cercle social, of which the 'Amis de la Vérité' was the public manifestation (David Andress, *Massacre at the Champ de Mars. Popular Dissent and Political Culture in the French Revolution* (The Royal Historical Society and Boydell Press: Woodbridge, 2000), p. 121). Hence, this would seem to be a self-congratulatory reference to a group of the Cercle's adherents. On the Cercle social, see G. Kates, *The Cercle social, the Girondins, and the French Revolution* (Princeton University Press: Princeton, 1985). Printers had also appeared at the earlier Festival of Federation on 14 July 1790 with a banner proclaiming 'L'Imprimerie,

flambeau de la Liberté', and generally made a point of wearing their paper hats with the inscribed motto 'Liberté de la presse' in 'manifestations patriotiques' (Philippe Minard, 'Identité corporative et dignité ouvrière: le cas des typographes parisiens, 1789–1791', in Michel Vovelle (ed.), *Paris et la Révolution*, Actes du colloque de Paris I, 14–16 avril 1989 (Paris, 1989), p. 27).

28. *L'Ami du roi, des français, de l'ordre, et sur-tout de la vérité, par les continuateurs de Fréron, sous la direction de M. Montjoye*, 13 July 1791, no. 194, pp. 775–6. During the Revolution, inscribing headgear is a recurrent enunciatory device. On 22 prairial an III/ 10 June 1795, demonstrators from the faubourg Saint-Antoine wrote on their hats 'Du pain et la constitution démocratique de 1793' (Schmidt, vol. 2, p. 343).

29. On the *forts de la halle* as 'les aînés de la Révolution' (the elders of the Revolution), see *Arch. Parl.*, vol. 44 pp. 551–2. In an address to the Assembly on 4 June 1792 by a deputation of *forts*, it was proposed that, at the head of the army, 'l'arche sainte de la loi' be carried by the *forts*, in the manner of the Hebrews. The term 'les aînés de la liberté' was also used in a description of a banquet on the Champs Elysées, 25 March 1792, where *Vainqueurs de la Bastille* fraternised with *forts* (*Courrier des LXXXIII Départements*, no. 26, 26 March 1792, p. 409, no. 28, 28 March 1792, pp. 440–1, and no. 29, 29 March 1792, p. 458). Once again, we find the inversion of established power relations in the celebration of: 'cette classe si dénigrée de l'ancien régime, et traitée de bonnets de laine et de sans-culotte, sous le nouveau'. On the close-knit community of the *forts*, see David Garrioch, *Neighbourhood and Community in Paris 1740–1790* (Cambridge University Press: Cambridge, 1986), pp. 119, 124, 253.

30. Working clothes had been an element in Ancien Régime ceremonies such as the laying of the foundation of Ste Geneviève in 1764, which included masons wearing jackets, aprons, and white stockings, their hats decorated with ribbons and cockades; see Alain Gruber, *Les Grandes Fêtes et leurs décors à l'époque de Louis XVI* (Droz: Paris, Geneva, 1972), p. 28.

31. This remains the case later, as in the use of costume associated with defunct *corps de métiers* as part of a carnivalesque festival procession which also included religious dress, adopted so as to provide a parodic spectacle. See Pellegrin, *Vêtements*, pp. 125–6, on a festival at Poitiers on 20 frimaire an II/10 December 1793).

32. See Maurice Genty, *L'Apprentissage du citoyenneté*, pp. 28–9.

33. *Révolutions de Paris*, no. 105, 9–16 July 1791, p. 5. In his next issue he reported that they were to have their uniforms paid for, but that they resented this, preferring to pay for themselves (no. 106, 16–23 July 1791, p. 90).

34. *Révolutions de Paris*, 15 brum. an II/5 November 1793, no. 214, pp. 77–8, cit. Jean-Marc Devocelle, 'Costume politique et politique du costume: approches théoriques et idéologiques du costume pendant la Révolution française', mémoire de maîtrise, Université de Paris I, 1988, 2 vols, vol. 1, p. 77–8.

35. *Aristocrate* was an all-purpose pejorative term for counter-revolutionaries. See *Dictionnaire des usages socio-politiques* (Saint-Cloud, 1985), vol. 1, pp. 9–38.

36. 'Vos figures, noircies par un travail qui fournit aux riches qui vous dédaignent les moyens de faire convertir en mets succulens les viandes des plus grossières; *ces figures symboliques de la vertu*, qui ne cherchent pas à farder ses couleurs, en imposoient à tous ces Achilles parfumés du Palais Royal, dont le teint est aussi froid que leurs limonades, et le coeur aussi mou que les bisques qui repaissent leur frêle individu' (*Courrier des LXXXIII*

départements, no. 22, 22 June 1792, p. 334). Mercier also noted among the 'bataillons populaires' 'les charbonniers qui n'avaient pour armes que leurs bâtons, et pour drapeau qu'un sac à charbon attaché au bout d'un gourdin' (*Le Nouveau Paris*, ed. Jean-Claude Bonnet et al. (Mercure de France: Paris, 1994), p. 152).

37. *Journal des sans-culottes*, no. 1, p. 3 (1792). On the representation of work and workers, see Vincent Milliot, *Les Cris de Paris, ou le peuple travesti. Les représentations des petits métiers parisiens (XVIe–XVIIIe siècles)* (Publications de la Sorbonne: Paris, 1995); Jacques Proust, 'L'Image du peuple au travail dans les planches de l'*Encyclopédie*', in *Images du peuple au dix-huitième siècle*, Colloque d'Aix-en-Provence, 25 et 26 octobre 1969, Centre Aixois d'Études et de Recherches sur le dix-huitième siècle (Armand Colin: Paris, 1973), pp. 65–85; William H. Sewell Jr, 'Visions of Labour: illustrations of the mechanical arts before, in, and after Diderot's *Encyclopédie*', in Steven Kaplan and Cynthia J. Knoepp (eds), *Work in France: Representation, Meaning, Organization, and Practice* (Cornell University Press: Ithaca and London, 1986), pp. 258–86; Valerie Mainz, *L'Image du travail et la Révolution française* (Musée de la Révolution française, Vizille, 1999).

38. BNF, Paris, MS Nouv. Acq. Fr. 308 fol. 278.

39. Interestingly, one festival held in Poitiers on 20 frim. an II/10 December 1793 involved a parodic disposal of costumes used by the *corps de métiers* along with religious outfits, suggesting that these tradesmen were, so to speak, thereafter revealed in their own ordinary dress (Nicole Pellegrin, *Les Vêtements de la Liberté. Abécédaire des pratiques vestimentaires françaises de 1780 à 1800* (Alinéa: Paris, 1989), pp. 125–6).

40. See Geffroy, 'Sans-culote(s)', pp. 175–6; Laura B. Pfeiffer, 'The Uprising of June 20, 1792', *University Studies* [University of Nebraska, Lincoln], July 1912, vol. 12, no. 3, pp. 1–147/197–343 (the volume has double pagination).

41. Cf. the print 'Fameuse journée du 20 juin 1792', in *Révolutions de Paris*, no. 134, p. 348, with the caption 'Réunion des citoyens du faubourg St Antoine et St Marceau allant à l'assemblée nationale présenter une pétition et de suite une autre chez le Roi'.

42. Richard Twiss, *A Trip to Paris in July and August 1792* (Dublin, 1793), p. 137, cit. Aileen Ribeiro, *Fashion in the French Revolution* (Batsford: London, 1988), p. 86. Twiss's observation fits with the point made by Colin Jones (who kindly drew my attention to this) and Rebecca Spang, drawing on Daniel Roche's analysis of popular dress before the Revolution (*The People of Paris* (Berg: Leamington Spa, 1987), p. 189), that the artisans, shopkeepers, servants, and petty officials who made up the social core of revolutionary *sans-culottes*, in fact tended to wear breeches rather than *pantalon* (C. Jones and R. Spang, 'Sans-culottes, sans café, sans tabac: shifting realms of necessity and luxury in eighteenth-century France', in Maxine Berg and Helen Clifford (eds), *Consumers and Luxury. Consumer Culture in Europe 1650–1850* (Manchester University Press: Manchester, 1999), p. 47).

43. 'Les citoyens du faubourg St-Antoine et St-Marcel chez le Roi, lui font une pétition, Louis 16 prend un bonnet rouge et le met sur sa tête en criant vive la Nation et buvant à la santé des sans-culottes', *Révolutions de Paris*, no. 154, p. 554 (Hennin Collection, vol. 127, no. 11176, Qb20 juin 1792; 59.B.23615). Similarly, Fontenay encapsulated the significance of the day as one of a simple, lamentable conflict: 'On a vu les Sans-Culottes lutter contre leur Roi constitutionnel, et l'assiéger dans son château avec des piques et des canons'. He used the euphemistic term of 'une paire de hauts-de-chausses' to refer to the *culotte*, thus fastidiously refusing the link with *sans-culottes* (*Journal général de France*, 21 June 1792, pp. 698, 700).

44. Geffroy, 'Sans-culotte(s)', *Dictionnaire des usages socio-politiques*, p. 175, quoting *Moniteur*, 22 June 1792, *RAM*, vol 12, p. 718; *Journal des débats*, 22 June 1792, p. 218. Other versions give 'le peuple est las de souffrir' ([Stephen Weston], *Letters from Paris during the Summer of 1792* (Debrett: London, 1793), p. 33). An alternative way of reading the incident is that this brandishing of a pair of breeches was intended as a satire on the status quo, utilizing the association of breeches with respectability and therefore authority, that is to say recalling the pre-revolutionary meaning of *sans-culotte*. Indeed, perhaps one could see this latter reading as consistent with the cultural trope of the 'battle of the trousers', shifted from a matter of domestic conflict to the public political arena.

45. As noted by both Leith ('Images of *Sans-culottes*') and Geffroy, a fascinating example of iconographical euphemism is Villeneuve's print, *L'Amour sans culotte* (Cabinet des Estampes, Bibliothèque Nationale de France, Paris: Qb1 10 Novembre 1793, ill. Geffroy, 'Désignation, dénégation', p. 593). This shows a pair of culottes hoist on an arrow by a winged cupid who wears a liberty cap. The image has the motto: 'Quand l'amour en bonnet se trouve sans culotte, la liberté lui plaît, il en fait sa marmotte.'

46. 21 June 1792, cit. Pfeiffer, 'The Uprising of June 20, 1792', p. 84/280.

47. *Courrier des LXXXIII départements*, 22 June 1792, no. 22, p. 336.

48. On this phenomenon, see Antoine de Baecque, *Le Corps de l'histoire. Métaphores et politique (1770–1800)* (Calmann-Lévy: Paris, 1993), pp. 303–74. Georges Duval's memoir treats the inception of *sans-culotte* costume in the same vein. He recalls how two men who appeared at Meudon in *sans-culotte* outfits were greeted by local children with 'les cris usités dans la cérémonie du mardi gras' (*Souvenirs de la Terreur, de 1788 à 1793*, 4 vols (Paris, 1841), vol. 2, pp. 35–42.

49. See Richard Wrigley, 'From Ancien Régime Fall-guy to Revolutionary Hero: Changing Interpretations of Janot and Dorvigny's *Les battus qui paient l'amende* in Later Eighteenth-century France', *British Journal of Eighteenth-century Studies*, Autumn 1996, vol. 19, no. 2, pp. 124–54.

50. No. 38, 28 February 1791, cit. Geffroy, 'Sans-culotte(s)', *Dictionnaire des usages socio-politiques*, p. 163.

51. 28 August 1791, cit. *Actes Comm*, 2nd series, vol. 7, pp. 658–9.

52. Tuetey, vol. 4, p. 110.

53. *Chronique de Paris*, July 1792, p. 62, cit. Pellegrin, *Vêtements*, p. 162; see also Sonenscher, *Work and Wages*, p. 344.

54. *Journal des sans-culottes*, [1792] no. 1, p. 4.

55. 'Costume Républicain (de Sans-culotte), adopté, proposé & dessiné par Sergent, Député de Paris à la Convention Nationale. Ce costume n'est autre chose que l'habit journalier des Hommes de la campagne et des Ouvriers des villes, il n'y auroit de différence entre les Citoyens que dans la qualité des Etoffes. Toutes les articulations ne sont plus gênées par des attaches; il est de forme demi-circulaire, et se jette sur les bras ou les épaules. Il pourroit n'être porté qu'à 21 ans, âge où les Citoyens commencent à exercer leurs droits, et tiendroit lieu de la Robe Virile des Romains. Ce Dessin à l'aquarelle porte 12 po. de large, sur 14 de haut' (*Description des ouvrages de peinture, sculpture, architecture et gravure exposés au Sallon du Louvre, par les artistes composans la Commune générale des Arts, le 10 Août 1793, l'An 2e de la République Française, une et indivisible* (Paris, [n.d.]), *Supplément . . .*, no. 789, pp. 18–19). The drawing is lost.

56. P.F.N. Fabre d'Eglantine, *Rapport fait à la Convention nationale . . . au nom de la Commission chargée de la confection du calendrier* [24 October 1793], cit. James Guillaume (ed.), *Procès-verbaux du Comité d'Instruction publique de la Convention nationale*, vol. 2 (1894), p. 704, cit. Michael Sonenscher, 'Artisans, sans-culottes, and the French Revolution', in A. Forrest and P. Jones (eds), *Reshaping France: Town, Country, and Region during the French Revolution* (Manchester University Press: Manchester, 1991), p. 115.

57. C.F.X. Mercier, *Comment m'habillerai-je? Réflexions politiques et philosophiques sur l'habillement français, et sur la nécessité d'un costume national* (Paris, 1793), p. 3. The reference is to Tacitus.

58. The Section du Jardin-des-Plantes changed to its name to 'des Sans-culottes' on 13 August 1792; it reverted to its original name on 10 ventôse an III/8 February 1795. A decree of 7 fructidor an III/24 August 1795, replaced *sans-culottides* by *jours complémentaires*. In the royalist press, the term's currency was acknowledged through bitter parody; for example, after 10 August 1792, the *Gazette de Paris* created the euphemistic neologism 'invêtus salariés' (Laurence Condart, *La Gazette de Paris. Un journal royaliste pendant la Révolution française (1789–1792)* (L'Harmattan: Paris, 1995), p. 298).

59. Soboul, *Sans-culottes*, p. 651.

60. See *L'Ordre de la marche de la fête qui aura lieu décadi prochain 10 nivôse, l'an 2e de la République une et indivisible, en mémoire des armées françaises, et notamment à l'occasion de la prise de Toulon*, p. 1.

61. See Mona Ozouf, 'Le Simulacre et la fête', in J. Ehrard and P. Viallaneix (eds), *Les Fêtes de la Révolution. Colloque Clermont-Ferrand, juin 1974* (Société des Études Robespierristes: Paris, 1977), p. 345.

62. Higonnet, 'Sans-culottes', p. 424.

63. For example, when Chenard sang the Marseillaise in the Convention and also at place Louis XV in 1793, he is noted as having worn a *carmagnole* and clogs (Ch. Moisset in *Dictionnaire de Biographie française*, vol. 8, pp. 223–6).

64. Chabot is shown wearing a *bonnet rouge*, but not *pantalon* in 'La balance des abus' (described in *Journal de Paris* 23 April 1792), ill. C. Langlois, *La Caricature Contre-révolutionnaire* (CNRS: Paris, 1988), pp. 216–17, 247.

65. On Granet, see Pellegrin, *Vêtements*, p. 97. Granet was sufficiently notorious to have been drawn in one of Lesueur's gouaches (Musée Carnavalet, Paris). On Thibaudeau, see ibid., p. 175.

66. J. Quicherat, *Histoire du costume français depuis les temps les plus reculés jusqu'à la fin du XVIIIe siècle* (Paris, 1875), p. 630.

67. Mercier, *Le Nouveau Paris*, p. 113. By contrast, when Chabot was *en mission* in Amiens, he addressed the people from the cathedral pulpit 'coiffé d'un énorme bonnet rouge' (Vicomte de Bonald, *François Chabot, membre de la Convention (1756–1794)* (Émilc-Paul: Paris, 1908), pp. 202–3).

68. *RAM*, vol. 19, no. 96, 6 niv. an II/26 December 1793, p. 42.

69. No directly contemporary source has ever been cited to back up the claim that the duc d'Orléans wore *sans-culotte* costume. The only source for this seems to be Madame Tussaud's memoirs, which, if reliable, indicate that, at a date left imprecise, he adopted a more chic alternative to *sans-culotte* costume proper: 'a short jacket, pantaloons, and a round hat, with a handkerchief worn sailor fashion loose round the neck, with the ends long and hanging down . . . the hair cut short without powder *à la* Titus, and shoes tied

with string' (*Memoirs and Reminiscences of France*, ed. F. Hervé (London, 1838), p. 177, cit. Ribeiro, *Art of Dress*, p. 85). The representation of a similar kind of outfit in an anonymous print from 1790, *Hommage à la Constitution* (Musée de la Révolution française, Vizille, 1984–87) (Figure 21) suggests that Mme Tussaud's recollections relate to a period before that characterized by *sans-culotterie*. Other connections of the duc to revolutionary dress include his having sent his sons in National Guard uniform to meetings of the St Roch district (Quicherat, *Histoire du costume*, p. 626). In a letter (24 March 1792) from the comte de Fersen to the King of Sweden, the duc d'Orléans and his sons were described as having walked beneath the king's window in the Tuileries wearing *bonnets rouges* (G. de Vautibault and H. Daragon, *Les d'Orléans au tribunal de l'histoire*, 7 vols (1888–1892), vol. 5, pp. 135–8, cit. Hubert La Marle, *Philippe Égalité 'Grand Maître de la Révolution'. Le rôle politique du premier sérénissime frère du Grand Orient de France* (Nouvelles Editions Latines: Paris, 1989), pp. 628–9). See also Chapter 4 note 59 in the present volume.

70. At the moment of Hébert's execution, it was noted that there was popular disapproval of the way the executioner had mockingly waved a *bonnet rouge* in his face (Schmidt, vol. 2, p. 193, 26 March 1794). Although these examples would seem to go against Geffroy's assertion that 'aucun parlementaire ne s'est, sous la Révolution, présenté dans le "sanctuaire des lois" en pantalon', she is surely correct to make the point that when individuals are accused of wearing *sans-culotte* costume in the Convention, we should probably take this to mean that they were 'mal vêtu' (poorly dressed), rather than kitted out with *bonnet rouge*, *pantalon*, and *carmagnole* ('Sans-culotte(s)', p. 167).

71. *Le Vieux Cordelier*, Albert Mathiez and Henri Calvet (eds) (Colin: Paris, 1936), p. 285; the text is from an unpublished fragment dated to *c*.18 March 1794. Pellegrin notes the vestimentary ambivalence evident in the inventory of Saint-Just's effects, which included trousers in blue cloth and white silk, several *culottes*, a *bonnet de police*, and a number of hats (*Vêtements de la Liberté*, pp. 160–1).

72. Such views are evident before Thermidor, as in Saint-Just's self-justificatory note: 'qui a crié à toute la France de se tenir garde contre les faux patriotes? qu'ils marchaient à la contrerévolution couverts de bonnets rouges? qu'ils s'efforçaient de rendre la République hideuse?' (*Le Vieux Cordelier*, p. 285). For a post-Thermidor example, see Jean-François Barailon, *Projet sur le costume particulier à donner à chacun des deux conseils législatifs, et à tous les fonctionnaires publics de la République française, présenté à la Convention nationale* (13 fructidor an III [30 August 1795]), p. 3. On the alignment of a repugnant form of politics with a dirty, ugly body and dress, see Antoine de Baecque, 'La figure du jacobin dans l'imagerie politique (1795–1799): naissance d'une obsession', *Sources: travaux historiques*, 1988, no. 14, pp. 61–70.

73. The reports were published by Pierre Caron, *Paris pendant la Terreur. Rapports des agents secrets du Ministre de l'Intérieur*, 7 vols (Didier: Paris, 1910–1964). For a sceptical account of the mindset and bureaucratic procedures exemplified by these reports see Cobb, *Police and the People*, pp. 3–48. This is discussed further in the next chapter.

74. This mode of description can be found beyond such official realms, and well before the Terror; for example, the journal *Le Babillard, journal du Palais royal et des Thuileries* [sic] (June–October 1791), which employs almost exactly the same style of picking out both exemplary and dubious public speakers, though driven by a hard-edge constitutionalist outlook. Meticulous scrutiny of dress had become a widespread skill, driven by uncertainty

as much as suspicion, and the urgent need to know what socio-political identity lay behind visible outer layers. The journal's aim was 'répandre les principes de la constitution, inspirer le respect pour les lois, faire connoître l'opinion publique, démasquer les factieux de tous les partis' (*Prospectus*, pp. 1–2). See Chapter 6 of the present volume for further discussion of *Le Babillard*'s approach to the significance of dress.

75. As Devocelle has noted, during this period, the ensemble was rarely visible in its totality in the street and in assemblies. Jean-Marc Devocelle, 'Costume et Citoyenneté', *Révolution française*, Actes des 113e et 114e Congrès nationaux des sociétés savantes (Strasbourg 1988–Paris 1989) (Éditions du Comité des Travaux Historiques et Scientifiques: Paris, 1991), p. 314. Devocelle analyses this point more fully in his mémoire de maîtrise, 'Costume politique et politique du costume', vol. 1, pp. 76–81.

76. Caron, vol. 2, p. 36, 7 niv. an II/27 December 1793,

77. Caron, vol. 1, p. 157, 22 September 1793.

78. Caron, vol. 5, p. 213, 20 vent. an II/10 March 1794.

79. 'La Révolution est glacée; tous les principes sont affaiblis; il ne reste que des bonnets rouges portés par l'intrigue' (*Œuvres complètes*, Charles Vellay (ed.), 2 vols (Charpentier and Facquette: Paris, 1908), vol. 2, p. 508).

80. Caron, vol. 5, pp. 225–6, 21 vent. an II/11 March 1794.

81. Caron, vol. 5, pp. 441–2, 30 vent. an II/20 March 1794.

82. *Lettres bougrement patriotiques du véritable Père Duchêne*, no. 368, p. 5.

83. According to a text fom May 1794: 'on peut aujourd'hui s'habiller décemment même avec goût; plus de bonnets rouges, plus de tutoiement affecté; on peut aller aux spectacles, et chez les filles, sans y être insulté par les sans-culottes ou par les satellites de l'armée révolutionnaire' ('Extrait d'une lettre de la frontière, en date du 29 mai 1794', in *The Despatches of Earl Gower, English Ambassador at Paris from June 1790 to August 1792*, ed. Oscar Browning (Cambridge University Press: Cambridge, 1885), p. 364). See also a text from April 1794: 'Le luxe n'est point le goût, et en dépit des pantalons, des bonnets rouges, des cheveux coupés et des moustaches, il est permis à des républicains de porter d'élégants culottes, des chapeaux d'une forme heureuse, une chevelure où brille la main délicate et légère du perruquier' (cit. G. Walter, *La Révolution française vu par les journaux* (Paris, 1948), p. 410), quoted by Ribeiro, *Fashion*, p. 70). The belief that *sans-culotte* costume had been a repressively levelling but contrived vestimentary façade surfaces after Thermidor: 'distinguez donc l'homme de bien / Du paresseux et de vaurien / Et des faux patriotes! / Peuple honnête et laborieux, / Ne vous déguisez plus en gueux; / Remettez vos culottes' (A. Dauban, *Paris en 1794 et 1795* (Paris, 1869), pp. 539–40), cit. Pellegrin, *Vêtements*, p. 151). The second verse points out the economic drawbacks of the impoverishment of costume.

84. *Décade philosophique*, vol. 2, pp. 139–40, vol. 3, p. 527. Jean Starobinski noted that the muscadins' caricature of Ancien Régime clothes indicated that the Revolution had been brought to a halt (*The Invention of Liberty* (Skira/Rizzoli: Geneva, 1987), p. 102). On post-Thermidorian socio-political types and the role of vestimentary cues, see Susan L. Siegfried, *The Art of Louis Léopold Boilly*, pp. 70–84.

85. *Annales patriotiques*, 10/11 March 1795, p. 10, cit. L.S. Mercier, *Le Nouveau Paris*, p. 1395 note.

86. Beauvert, *Caricatures politiques* (an VI, 1798), cit. Ribeiro, *Fashion in the French Revolution*, p. 84. Jean-Marc Devocelle observes that, in the *Dictionnaire de l'Académie*

française, 5th edn (an VII), the *carmagnole* was 'rejetté dans un passé révolu' ('La Cocarde directorielle: dérives d'un symbole révolutionnaire', *AHRF*, 1992, vol. 69, no. 3, p. 356).

87. James Leith has discussed the image of the *sans-culotte*, but without paying attention to its early development: 'Images of *Sans-culottes*', in *Iconographie et image de la Révolution française*, pp. 130–59.

88. Portraits of men *en sans-culotte* are extremely rare. Moreover, certain instances are problematic. For example, the anonymous portrait (spuriously attributed to Greuze in an anecdote emanating from the family of Mme Tranchant, from whom the picture was bought in 1901), *Portrait du jeune Alloy en sans-culotte* (Musée des beaux-arts, Orléans), shows a man, traditionally identified as François Alloy, wearing a *bonnet de police*, with loose shirt and jacket with a double collar. The story that Alloy put on 'sans-culotte' costume in order to carry a message to Louis XVI at Versailles must be erroneous on the basis of chronology (the king had left Versailles in October 1789, long before the arrival of the *sans-culotte* phenomenon). For all that, there is a residual congruity with the proposed idea that the wearing of such outfit was connected to formal, official occasions. See Mary O'Neill, *Musée des beaux-arts d'Orléans. Catalogue critique: Les Peintures de l'Ecole française des XVIIe et XVIIIe siècles*, thèse de doctorat de troisième cycle (Paris-Sorbonne, 1980), 2 vols, vol. 1, p. 193. I would like to thank Annie Defarges for her assistance.

89. See the series of prints made by the comte de Caylus after Edme Bouchardon's *Études pris dans le bas peuple, ou cris de Paris*, and J. Duplessi-Bertaux, 'Suite de mendiants, gravés à l'eau-forte' (Musée des arts et traditions populaires, Paris), illustrated in Robert M. Schwartz, *Policing the Poor in Eighteenth-century France* (University of North Carolina Press: Chapel Hill and London, 1988), pp. 54, 134, 219–21, 242). See also Milliot, *Les Cris de Paris*; Proust, 'L'Image du peuple au travail', pp. 65–85; Sewell, 'Visions of Labour', pp. 258–86; Hans-Jürgen Lüsebrink, 'Images et représentations sociales de la criminalité en France au XVIIIe siècle: l'exemple de Mandrin', *Revue d'histoire moderne et contemporaine*, July–September 1979, vol. 26, pp. 345–64.

90. See Leith, 'Images of *Sans-culottes*', p. 136, where the framing text is not reproduced.

91. This was his submission to the *concours de l'an II*; illustrated in William Olander, 'French Painting and Politics in 1793: the Great Concours de l'an II', in Wintermute (ed.), *1789: French Art During the Revolution*, Fig. 9, p. 35 (Olander corrects the identification of the subject as the execution of Louis XVI); see also Daniel Arasse, *La Guillotine dans la Révolution française* (Musée de la Révolution française, Vizille, 1987), cat. no. 45, p. 50, and Daniel Arasse, *La Guillotine et l'imaginaire de la Terreur* (Flammarion: Paris, 1987), pp. 212–13.

92. Dorinda Outram cites a letter by the deputy Giraud to the Committee of Public Safety regarding the behaviour of crowds at executions, in which he recommends that such events 'soit une espèce de spectacle pour lui [the *peuple*]. Les chants, la danse, doivent preuver aux aristocrates que le peuple ne voit de bonheur que dans le supplice' (*Révolutions de Paris*, 1792, cit. G. Lenôtre, *La Guillotine et les exécuteurs des arrêtés criminels pendant la Révolution* (Paris, 1893), pp. 310–11, cit. *The Body in the French Revolution. Sex, Class and Political Culture* (Yale University Press: New Haven and London, 1989). p. 114). In its ritualized and formalized celebration of regicide, Lesueur's image seems consonant with this kind of thinking.

93. See Hunt, *Politics, Culture, and Class*, 'The Imagery of Radicalism', pp. 107–10.

94. On the ideological roots of this kind of emblematizing of the pedestal, see Etienne Jollet, 'Between Allegory and Topography: the Project for a Statue to Louis XVI in Brest (1785–86) and the Question of the Pedestal in Public Statuary in Eighteenth-century France', *Oxford Art Journal*, 2000, vol. 23, no. 2, pp. 49–78. 95. *Révolutions de Paris*, 10–18 frimaire an II/30 November–8 December 1793, pp. 289–90.

96. Leith, 'Images of *Sans-culottes*', pp. 144–6.

97. See Philippe Bordes's contextualization of the two versions of this drawing, and his observation that the representation of the *sans-culotte* on the left articulates the ambiguity of Jacobin attitudes to them ('"Brissotin enragé, ennemi de Robespierre": David, conventionnel et terroriste', in Régis Michel (ed.), *David contre David*, 2 vols (Éditions de la Réunion des Musées Nationaux: Paris, 1993), vol. 2, pp. 319–47). Bordes also notes that this element of David's composition derives from a drawing by his pupil, Jean-Germain Drouais, illustrated in *Jean-Germain Drouais 1763–1788* (Musée des Beaux-Arts, Rennes, 1985), p. 100, fig. 178.

98. Both are illustrated in Leith, 'Images of *Sans-culottes*', p. 138, Figs. 3 and 4 respectively.

99. On Père Duchesne, see F. Braesch, *Le Père Duchesne* (Paris, 1938), and Ouzi Itsikowitch-Elyada, 'Manipulation et théâtralité. Le Père Duchesne (1788–1791)', thèse de doctorat, Paris, École des Hautes Études en Sciences Sociales, 1985, 2 vols. On an anonymous print 'Père Duchesne, foutre', see Siegfried, *Art of Louis-Léopold Boilly*, pp. 120–1, Fig. 100.

100. Claudette Hould, 'La Propagande d'état par l'estampe devant la Terreur', in Michel Vovelle (ed.), *Les Images de la Révolution française* (Publications de la Sorbonne: Paris, 1988), pp. 29–37.

101. See Geffroy, 'Désignation, dénégation: la légende des sans-culottes'; Leith, 'Images of *Sans-culottes*'; Bindman, *The Shadow of the Guillotine*.

102. A similar instance of this is the anonymous drawing 'Sans culotte parisien' (Musée Carnavalet, Paris) (ill. Pellegrin, *Vêtements*, p. 164), which also has torn clothing, and a rather effete down-at-heel demeanour.

103. André Saintanac, a surgery pupil, interrogated by the Tribunal révolutionnaire on 5 prairial an II was cleared of any connection to aristocratic gatherings, 'mais a reconnu qu'en badinant avec une femme de la section des Lombards sur le mot sans-culotte, il avait été arrêté par le comité de cette section' (Tuetey, vol. 9, no. 2325).

104. Marie-Claude Chaudonneret, 'Le mythe de la Révolution', in Philippe Bordes and Régis Michel (eds), *Aux Armes et aux arts! Les arts de la Révolution 1789–1799* (Adam Biro: Paris, 1988), pp. 313–40.

6

Mistaken Identities: Disguise, Surveillance, and the Legibility of Appearances

THROUGHOUT the preceding chapters, we have seen how some of the key elements in revolutionary dress, costume, insignia, and badges were continually subject to interference, challenge, and abuse in their physical adoption and emblematic import. Although there was a shared desire across local, national and individual levels to give some form of vestimentary expression to new modes of political identity, putting this into practice proved to be chronically problematic. In this book, such problems have been emphasized as an antidote to habitual assumptions that this dimension of revolutionary emblematics – at once material and visual – constitutes a kind of ingenuously expressive and more or less ubiquitous layer of symbolism. As has been made plain through close analysis of the currency and interpretation of some of the most prominent instances of politicized dress, their creation and use was itself an important site for the negotiation of varieties of political and social identity.

In the case of the different forms given to official costume, the generic project was undermined by acute awareness of its potential for misappropriation, from the confusingly ad hoc nature of military uniform to the multiplicity of easily counterfeited badges. The very ubiquity of the cockade rendered it prone to manipulation and subversion. By contrast the liberty cap was much more restricted in its usage as a form of dress. In the form of the *bonnet rouge*, its association with radicalism, as when adopted by Jacobins in the spring of 1792, and in due course *sans-culottes*, made of it an instrument of partisan provocation, thereby rendering its subsequent claims to official status divisive – either perceived as an assertion of the dominance of militant radical politics, or a token of an oppressive but spurious authority (an authority, of course, also eventually repudiated and challenged by the Convention). The history of the stereotype of the *sans-culotte* has shown that, even in the case of this most pungent form of militant socio-political style, appearances could be deceptive. Not only in the sense that the ensemble was dependent on earlier conventions for representing working men, and also the inversion of an inherited vocabulary of satire, in a way which inevitably undermined the coherence of its partisan agenda, but also that even in its heyday, between late 1792 and early 1794, it engendered, and was to a significant degree disabled by, a kind of subversive simulation employed by prudent fellow-travellers and committed counter-revolutionaries alike.

In the light of this fragmented and unstable picture, we now need to look more widely across the politicized spectrum of appearances – at, indeed, its limits. More specifically, two complementary phenomena will run through the material discussed here. First, the modes of observation or recognition within which it was given meaning. Secondly, those features of dress which attracted special attention, picked up on because they were believed to be particularly revealing or alarmingly inscrutable indicators of meaning, and why and how they fulfilled these roles. The issue of how reliable such features might be, given their inherent manipulability and ephemeral nature, emerges as a key dimension in attitudes to the legibility of dress. Indeed, the central theme of this chapter is disguise, which became an almost institutionalized premise for the sceptical surveillance of appearances.[1]

Revolutionary attitudes to and expectations of dress predominantly rely on the Rousseauesque diagnosis of a damaging dissociation between external vestimentary presentation and inner moral self.[2] Rousseau had been convinced that beneath the sophisticated surface of the spectacle of modern society lay an awful inner corruption.[3] The pragmatic necessities of dress had been perversely transformed by the indulgent superfluities of fashion. For all its putative self-expressive register, fashion was at root a means to mask people's true nature; by virtue of its essentially dissimulatory function, it was inherently untrustworthy. Moreover, the example of high society provided a dangerously seductive model for the lower classes. He recommended utilitarian and more hygienic clothes, thereby facilitating the body's capacity to express truly natural feelings. Pre-revolutionary fashion could to some extent be said to have assimilated – and profited from – these criticisms, becoming simpler, and redefining modishness in terms of less opulent nuances of style.[4]

In the nascent revolutionary order, established beliefs in the reliability of a hierarchy of appearances were profoundly shaken. The sense of a cathartic regeneration having swept away the inherited forms of despotism and authority had as its corollary a willingness to disregard now obsolete signs of status. However, as we saw in relation to official costume, this euphoric sense of liberation was also accompanied by perplexity when having to address the practical consequences of revolution. The dissent which had been chronically manifest in the collapse of the Estates General was replayed, not only in the National Assembly, but across the nation, particularly in the proliferating political societies and clubs. The institutions and formations which made up revolutionary political culture were from the outset not only defined by partisan dispute, but also informed by a more specific discourse of denunciation.[5] Moreover, the price of political prominence was to be an object of sceptical, iconoclastic scrutiny in the press, which put into uninhibited practice the new freedom to test and challenge people's credentials, allegiances, and record of revolutionary participation. If the triumph of Enlightenment had opened up public space to unfettered examination, this left the problem of how to make sense of what Antoine de Baecque has called 'le grand spectacle de la transparence'.[6] De Baecque focuses on the body, and explores its legibility in terms of beliefs in its physiognomic coding. For all the richness of his analysis, however, he somewhat surprisingly ignores the further, closely related dimension of dress. As I will suggest in this chapter, although the body and dress are intimately related, they are far from being synonymous. Consideration of the specific roles dress played in the currency of such codes of legibility is therefore an essential component in understanding the complexities of the revolutionary culture of appearances.

As we have seen, projects for establishing a reformed system of official and vernacular costume were realized only slowly and in part; the latter, expressions of a utopian vision of a model citizenry, remained almost exclusively on paper. More typically, Rousseau's condemnation of fashion as deceitful was translated into revolutionary anxieties about disguise and subversion, which were to constitute a turbulent undercurrent running through the revolutionary discourse of transparent patriotic virtue.[7] The recognition that people's dress was – or should be – a revealing indication of who they were and what they stood for provided a plausible equivalent for the developing vocabulary of revolutionary politics. Matters of vestimentary vanity and self-conscious display took on an increasingly elaborate and urgent political resonance.

Dress was at once a key focus of observational attention and a metaphorical means by which the new socio-political landscape could be apprehended and delineated. It was believed to give access to a level of perceived identity that went deeper than fashion – habitually judged to be quintessentially superficial; in seeking to interrogate the semantic import of appearances, dress and the body were often regarded as a continuous or overlapping legible surface.

The language of politics and the language of dress were closely intertwined in ways that were not new as such (dress had long been read as a sign of identity and status), but certainly newly consequential in the sense that dress was presumed to express or correspond to changing formations within the nascent political culture. In the importance given to the currency of liberty caps – both as dress and as emblems – and the stylized outfit associated with *sans-culottes*, as with the primordial emblematic burden carried by the cockade, matters of dress were placed at the heart of revolutionary discourse.[8] As already noted, this was only possible because of the existence of what Daniel Roche has termed the Ancien Régime's elaborate 'culture of appearances'. This had provided an established set of assumptions about the legibility of identity and status through varieties of dress. Thus, in 1777, Pidansat de Mairobert had noted that, given her unique rank, the queen needed no external decoration; only social inferiors required external identifying features, placing them within the social order.[9] Catalogues of such a hierarchical spectrum of dress codes were as commonplace as they were uncontroversial.[10] Yet, at the same time, in terms of the lived experience of reading identity through dress and appearances, there was an established recognition of the way that such notional order had become undermined by what Roche calls the 'confusion of vestimentary signs'.[11] As was frequently commented upon in the later eighteenth century, status could be simulated through the mere acquisition and display of clothes which conferred undeserved respect and deference. In the light of the social tabula rasa initiated by the assertion of a spirit of universal equality, this confusion of vestimentary signs acquired a salutary political significance. In an episode recorded by the *Révolutions de Paris*, a young road sweeper failed to recognize Louis XVI, mistaking him for a 'chevalier', and asking him for a tip. That the king could be mistaken for a common-or-garden chevalier was recounted as being symptomatic of the desuetude of former codes of status, and the weakening of their hold over the popular political imagination.[12]

In the context of the destabilized social landscape and radically transformed framework of political institutions, questions of identity became urgently important. Politics as a publicly shared process and spectacle was a novelty. Thus, the correlation between groupings of opinion and types of more or less given social identity, as expressed through dress and manners, was perforce more likely to be the subject of uncertainty and speculation. Yet, at the same time, how far dress could be read as corresponding to probable political identification was a moot point. On the one hand, there were specific badges and emblems and styles of dress which located a person as a member of the proliferating numbers of clubs, *sociétés populaires*, 'factions', 'sectes' and 'castes'.[13] But these were, literally, superficial features. The propensity to assume a correspondance between style of dress and political attitudes took the form of a new, ever expanding vocabulary at once concrete and allusive.[14] On the other hand, dress was looked to as an already differentiated resource for the reading of identities, and therefore provided a tangible, readily apprehendable basis for making sense of the proliferating crystal-lization of different constituencies and collectivities. Dress was universally understood as enshrining a complex of invitingly explicit moral and social indicators. The assumption that dress was in large part the result of choice, of the fabrication of publicly recognizable individual identity, easily lent itself to being interpreted in terms of political allegiance, or, more fundamentally, degrees of patriotic enthusiasm.

The role of dress as a symptomatic indicator of the public expression of different political opinions is evident across a variety of texts. As a way into exploring the place of the vestimentary in revolutionary discourse, we may sample reports from the summer of 1791 in *Le Babillard du Palais Royal*. These rely on the assertion of a contrast between different, oppos-ing types of politically active men. On the one hand, certain individuals were recognizable because of their departure from established norms of appearance, or the adoption of new forms. These men manifested novel, worryingly extreme forms of political language and argument, associated with their propensity to 'declamation' and 'haranguing'. On the other hand, were bourgeois who became more distinctively visible precisely because their habitual forms of behaviour and dress remained unvaried. Problematic and provocative novelty was thus set against pre-revolutionary conventions of bourgeois respectability.[15] Hair styles were a particularly vivid index of reassuring normality or provocative deviance: 'An individual wearing his own unpowdered hair (filthy hallmark of a reviled sect) announced that M. de La Fayette was leaving for Lille to corrupt the garrison.'[16] In the café des Italiens, a man 'of average stature, pale and thin face, wild black eyes, wearing a brown coat, and with short hair', declaimed against the most notable members of the National Assembly: 'Robespierre alone, he cried, deserves the gratitude of the French people'.[17] Others fomenting unrest were less precisely evoked. A man described simply as 'badly dressed', further condemned as 'very similar to those who are paid to make the people riot', 'criticized the conduct of Messieurs Bailly and La Fayette in the affair of the Champ de Mars'.[18] By contrast, bourgeois orators are identified primarily in terms of commendably familiar forms of dress: 'a man of about 50 years old, wearing a coat of brown cloth, black jacket, breeches and stockings. His exterior and his speech identified him as a good bourgeois, a friend of his *patrie*, the constitution and calm'.[19] The *Babillard*, organ of the constitutionalist Cercle social, was extremely sensitive to any signs of misuse and manipulation of dress for ends that were directed at disturbing public order, and the authority of the Assembly and the National Guard.[20] Appearance and utterances are elided, forming a semantically continuous whole.

It is striking that these observations do not make fully explicit the justification for reading unpowdered hair as the sign of a 'sect', the Jacobins. This was possible in so far as they assume that dress played a central role in signalling conformity to established codes of propriety regarding men's public appearances. In the case of the sober outfit of the bourgeois, this is aligned with an updated set of political beliefs which yet draws on a well-established stereotype of bourgeois sobriety, at once vestimentary and moral. The detail provided is premised on the continued plausibility of such an identification between dress and opinions. Significantly, this form of journalistic judgement censured novelty, and the departure from constitutionalist consensus. The reliability of appearances and dress as a means to signal identity continued to provide a measure of the Revolution's political consolidation. Yet, as these examples from *Le Babillard* make explicit, such meanings were established within an expanding spectrum of difference – a spectrum that, in the summer of 1791, was clearly under stress.

Under the Republic, and especially the Terror, however, reliance on such a correspondance, which both underpinned and encouraged intensely apprehensive scrutiny of people's appearances, buckled under the increasing weight of suspicion. As we saw in the case of the *sans-culotte*, prescriptive visible norms of republican solidarity were renounced in so far as they were demonstrably being exploited, and thereby confusingly devalued, by prudent fellow travellers and subversive *agents provocateurs* alike. In the testing arena of street politics, dress had failed to live up to expectations of salutary transparency. Faced with the obligation to dispense with the coded language of external signs, the desire to be able somehow to distinguish true patriots from their enemies produced assertions of the irreducible nature of authentic patriotism, on a level deeper than that of the visible.[21] As Robespierre had asserted in the spring of 1792 regarding the symbolic properties of the cockade, true patriots had no need of supplementary external signs; they would unerringly recognize each other's pristine political virtue.[22] Colin Lucas has reminded us of the inherent circularity of such reasoning.[23] The vagaries of mere external appearances were no longer adequate to the more powerful ideology of republicanism. Claude Payan denounced the false priority of appearances that had hitherto been mistakenly indulged in, to the detriment of authentic patriotism: 'this system which wanted everywhere to substitute the exterior of patriotism for patriotism itself, and words for things'.[24] Thus, in March 1794, wearing mourning dress in public was censured by a police agent, not only because it was a morale-sapping admission of military losses, but also because it was incompatible with the new régime of appearances, where all exterior signs had been swept away: 'Mourning is in the heart; the severe spirit of the Republic has banished all that is merely exterior'.[25]

Rather than dress, with its troublingly manipulable nature, attention shifted to a deeper corporeal register, relying on the ubiquitous pseudo-science of physiognomy.[26] Significantly, this was applied not only to individuals, but also on a collective level. Reporting to the Minister of the Interior, Charmont claimed that the reassuringly calm and consensual condition of the body politic was registered on people's faces: 'One hardly encounters any people with cadaverous looks, faces are no longer distorted as they used to be'.[27] The Revolution, it was confidently asserted, had cathartically banished dissimulation; its citizens' features ingenuously expressed this new moral order. This was incontrovertible evidence of the achievement of a genuinely altered, comprehensively regenerated state of affairs.

But, however revealing of the observational *modus operandi* of police agents, these reassuring instances of official surveillance's confirmation of the populace's healthy moral condition are exceptional. The activities of the agents themselves were predicated on the need to monitor public manifestations of *l'esprit public* precisely in order to apprehend undercurrents of discontent, and the more dangerous phenomenon of deliberately concealed subversion. Moreover, it was a commonplace that appearances were inherently manipulable. What, under the Ancien Régime, had constituted morally dubious dissimulation, under the Revolution took on a much more consequential, and politically destabilizing significance. This discourse of surveillance, and the search to uncover plotting, was a hallmark of the republican years, especially under the Terror, exacerbated by the nation's condition of being on a war footing. François Furet has argued that the language of the conspiracy is central to Jacobin rhetoric.[28] It allowed an absolute political language, in which the Revolution and its enemies were locked together, the latter compromising or threatening the integrity of the former. Nonetheless, in Furet's account, the very absolutism of revolutionary rhetoric obscures, if not transcends material particularities of identity. This overlooks the frequency with which recourse to appearances in general and dress in particular were believed to provide evidence both of the threat of subversion and of its containment. Furthermore, for all the forthrightness of the vocabulary of denunciation, in practice as often as not we find attention to dress resulting in the articulation of uncertainty, apprehension, and admissions of the tangibly ambiguous nature of vestimentary legibility. In a sense, the willingness to engage in categorical denunciation can be partly understood as being a compensatory reaction to the manifestly equivocal nature of the evidence of appearances.

According to police agents writing about the state of Paris at the end of 1793, counter-revolutionary 'contagion' was spread by two complementary types of people. First, those paid by enemies of the Republic, who took great care to hide their evil intentions beneath 'the mask of humanity, of sensibility, indeed of patriotism, etc.'; secondly 'weak souls' who were easily susceptible to being led astray, especially by priests, habituated as they had become to treating their sermons as a source of guidance. Such people needed reliable advice on how to distinguish true from false patriots.[29] Indeed, for police agents surveying the public mood, a willingness to transform appearances was itself reckoned to be a characteristic of those who were working to undermine the nation: 'these adroit reptiles are never ashamed to take the form of the moment'; they seized every opportunity to attack patriots and 'seek every means to make them seem suspect'. The most insidious form of such subversion was to simulate the appearances of true patriots – 'evildoers' hiding beneath 'the cloak of patriotism'[30] – thereby sowing confusion, and mutual distrust.[31]

Yet, when Chaumette addressed the Paris Commune on 'the [eleven] characteristics which identify suspect people', although he included forms of behaviour and conduct – interrupting *assemblées du peuple*, drawing attention to the Republic's troubles and dwelling on bad news, having the words *liberté*, *république* and *patrie* on their lips, but frequenting former nobles, priests and *modérés* – the nearest he got to singling out visual features was to include a category of those who changed their conduct and language according to circumstances 'and affect a studied austerity and severity in order to appear to be republicans'; that is, their self-styled republican identity was essentially false. In eschewing precise details, whether deliberately or not, he left his characterizations open to inter-pretation, and hence more likely to be approved of.[32]

As James Johnson has noted, a *locus classicus* for the concern over the manipulation of appearances was the stage, a space dedicated to the temporary adoption of assumed identities. Actors, whose profession relied on chameleon-like switching of roles and identities – from heroes to villains and vice versa – were viewed highly sceptically as an anti-role model for virtuous republicans. Whatever the habitual pleasures of theatre attendance, these were outweighed by the dangerous moral behaviour on view.[33] In addition, concerns over actors wearing obsolete costumes from the past followed from the theatre's role as a particularly prominent aspect of public space. For all the artifice associated with the stage, the social and political signification of the actors and their costumes was assimilated to, and continuous with, the spectacle of dress-as-identity visible in the street, café, and club. Thus, in September 1793, as part of his surveillance of *l'esprit public*, embracing questions of food supply, markets, queues outside bakers, conversations in cafés, and gatherings on the boulevards, Latour-Lamontagne fulminated against a performance of Diderot's *Père de famille* at the Théâtre de la République. Plays such as this, he complained, which represented contemporary life in the Ancien Régime,

> depict the ancient abuses of the feudal régime in the most flattering form; privileged orders reappear once again on the stage; odious costumes afflict our sight; the language of tyranny echoes in our republican ears, and each day the counter-revolution takes place in our theatres.[34]

Moreover, the 'père de famille' reproached his son for wearing 'the honourable dress of the poor . . . which he dared to describe as a shameful disguise'.[35] This was tantamount to challenging the ideological rationale for the adoption of *sans-culotte* costume. The idea that dress could neither conceal nor alter ineffaceable social rank was politically repugnant, in that it challenged the abolition of hierarchy that had been achieved by the Revolution. In so far as dress codes were recognized as being inescapably ideological, he argued that they should conform to the new republican situation. This censure is consistent with the vigilant attention to evidence of disguise manifest in the reports by Latour-Lamontagne and his colleagues, who treated it as a direct expression of subversive deviance.[36]

Complementary to the essentially metaphorical evocation of the need for a régime of collective surveillance, we find a parallel language of empirical observation and report, which evolved its own analytical protocols. We have seen evidence of the elaborate nature of such reading of appearances in the complex careers of the cockade and liberty cap, and responses to new forms of official costume and badge. Attention focused not only on the significance of particular forms of dress, but also on specific details, singling them out as potentially incriminating evidence of 'rallying signs'. Such habits of surveillance are entirely consistent with police practices regularly employed in the Ancien Régime, in which it was incumbent on agents and observers to be able to identify the ringleaders behind public disturbances.[37] But a similar vocabulary is also found across a wide spectrum of revolutionary journalistic language, and also local monitoring in the Paris sections.[38] As with the inception of a discourse of denunciation mentioned above, this mode of observation is evident from the earliest days of the Revolution. In October 1789, for example, the *Révolutions de Paris* alerted its readers to a 'conspiracy' of 30,000 soldiers surreptitiously recruited to enable the king's escape; as their 'distinctive mark', they would be mutually identifiable by having removed the bottom button of their jackets.[39]

It was recognized as inherent in the use of such 'rallying signs' that they would be varied by the groups using them in order to confound adversaries. Hence we find a multiplicity of items singled out for warnings and denunciations. In these matters, vigilance was more important than practicalities.[40] Faced with such polymorphous forms of subversion, police vigilance inevitably became at times confused by its own conscientiousness. In May 1793 a police agent admitted his uncertainty about a group of young men observed on the Champs-Elysées who suspiciously all wore cockades on the right side of their hats, but nonetheless appeared to be engaged in nothing more sinister than the game they were playing:

'perhaps these were agents who had put their cockades on the right, in order to mingle with people with bad intentions, who wear cockades in this manner, and to be able to arrest them'.[41] Indeed, contrary to the sceptical judgement of historians such as Richard Cobb as to the form-ulaic predictability of this kind of document – agents seeing and reporting what they were conditioned to see and expected to report – they also bear witness to moments of self-critical caution. Recounting a long convers-ation with a man whom the agent had begun by suspecting of dubious motives, presuming that he was being bought drinks with the aim of a kind of subversive recruitment, he ends by admitting his uncertainty:

> it is possible that I here applied the eye of a policeman to a man who only wanted to do me a favour, and that I took for signs of a wicked or counter-revolutionary spirit [what were] the bad humour of poverty, outbursts produced by drink, and the effects of discontent that everyone shares on the subject of provisions.[42]

Wigs were an object of particular concern to observers and agents because of their suitability for disguise. The *conseil général* of the Paris Commune discussed wigs in tandem with *bonnets rouges* in November 1793, a time when the latter had become an object of derision on the part of 'muscadins' and 'aristocrates'. Whereas it was recommended that the use of *bonnets rouges* should be confined to meetings of sections' committees, a ban on wigs was called for because they facilitated the undesirable manipulation of people's identity. It was claimed that some people revelled in switching their identity from that of 'old republican' with a wig, to *muscadin*, displaying their abundant unrepublican locks, a strategy designed to confound the exigent surveillance of public appearances, and expectations of ingenuous self-presentation.[43]

In a sense, this reaction against the misuse of what had become standard forms of signalling patriotism and revolutionary committment was merely an extension of the general phenomenon whereby the currency of vestimentary norms, whether informally practiced or officially instit-uted, actually had the effect of encouraging deviance and infringement.[44] In the context of the Revolution, however, such practices were perceived as both symptomatic of, and a catalyst to, partisan conflict. Sensibilities habituated to recognize the changing forms of fashion were correspond-ingly skilled at noticing topically highlighted nuances and varieties of dress. Such skills, which had become in effect naturalized, were therefore easily able to adapt to the new dynamically unstable, régime of appear-ances, less because of commercial competition and innovations of style than as a consequence of the fragmented social and political landscape.

After the cathartic watershed of Thermidor, anti-republican dress codes emerged, providing ample material to occupy the highly developed scrutiny of dress and appearances by journalists, agents, and the inhabit-ants of public space generally. For example, in 1794 an anti-Jacobin pamphlet drew attention to the disputes arising over men wearing their hair in plaits ('nattes'). The author explained that the context for this was an earlier form of proscription pursued by the Jacobins: 'who, I believe, had wanted to punish those who wore their hair in plaits in public places'. Current agitation against plaits worn by genuine patriots was evidence that the Jacobin cause was still far from extinct, manifest in the ongoing and excessively zealous harassment of innocent citizens because of their appearance:

> Will we continually see Jacobinism raise its hideous head, to indoctrinate the French with impunity, and when they find themselves abandoned by their followers, to attack people of moderate opinions [honnêtes gens], taking them to task for their dress, criticizing their hairstyle in order to convert new ones, to presume to destroy long-established customs and to find in these pretexts for accusations.[45]

The author pointed out that plaits, having been popular for over six years, were no longer fashionable; also, ribbon for tying up hair was now expensive, so plaits had become a necessary alternative. For good measure, he condemned Jacobins because of their hairstyle and rebarbative behav-iour: 'These vile intriguers with their plain hair, who have already been executed by the gibbet of opinion, should flee far from my unfortunate country!'[46]

François Gendron has noted the pamphlet literature around the time of the demise of the *jeunesse dorée*, which picks up on 'black collars' and plaits as provocative catalysts to disputes between *jeunesse dorée* and 'Jacobins'.[47] In 1796, the *Gazette française* explained that a ban on plaits, justified by seeking to re-establish public order, risked being seriously counterproductive:

> It is arbitrary, it embitters [people's] minds, it give a kind of favour to Jacobins who were the first to ban plaits; *and the bureau central should be well enough informed of what is being hatched in Paris*, to know how dangerous it is to let

the Jacobins believe that they will find support among the authorities of this town.[48]

Behind this recommendation was a consciousness of the insidiously destabilizing effects of miscellaneous species of deviant badge and dress code, which had frustrated the consolidation of successive phases of revolutionary authority, continually serving to undermine consensus, through the provocation of dissent and violent disputes, which threatened to compromise public order.

The identification of political opponents was a highly fraught and contested issue. As we saw with the episode of the *bonnet rouge* in the spring of 1792, Jacobins had tried to appropriate it for their own ends. Their opponents imagined extreme forms of condemnatory identification. A satirical pamphlet from May 1791 went as far as recommending that they be branded with the letter F – for *filou* (thief) – on their faces. This would correspond to a kind of antithesis to the ribbons and medals that the nation had awarded to its faithful servants; however, it would share with these decorations the possibility of being awarded to all, regardless of birth or wealth. Its physically indelible nature would guarantee the impossibility of Jacobins' return after they had been banished. As the author noted, this recycled the Ancien Régime practice of branding galley convicts; unlike the convicts' branded shoulders, which were normally concealed by their dress, this mark would be constantly publicly visible.[49]

These ideas should be seen in the context of the review of penal legislation in the summer of 1791. Garat argued that the practice of branding should be discontinued, since marking criminals for life would prevent a 'return to virtue'.[50] Nonetheless, the advantages of branding – at once punitive and pragmatic – led to its recommendation in the case of dissident priests who had been found guilty of organizing resistance to the Revolution.[51] Other proposals for dealing with the significant problem of non-juring priests included a label on their chests proclaiming 'Priest suspected of sedition'.[52] More generally, marks on the body, such as tattoos, were seized on as evidence of royalist allegiance. Tattoos found on a man arrested after he had walked in Marie-Antoinette's blood after her execution included a cross, a necklace, a heart and a medallion, aligning him suggestively with Chouan iconography; but he was released once it had been established that these had been acquired before the Revolution.[53]

The desire for new forms of identity which would articulate the fully achieved characteristics of a republican order can be understood as a response to the disturbing vicissitudes that had dogged attempts to introduce official costume. (As noted in Chapter two, none was realized except in fragmentary form before the Directory).[54] One of the fullest, and characteristically most uncompromising, of such schemes was that drafted by Saint-Just. The primary social categories to be identified corresponded to age and public role. The forms of identification conceived by Saint-Just were accompanied by punitive regulations for their misuse. Thus, murderers were to wear black, but would be executed if they failed to do so. Priests of all persuasions were forbidden to wear their 'attributes' in public. Men who had lived blameless lives would be granted a white sash when they reached sixty years of age; this would be conferred on them in 'le Temple'. Soldiers who had been wounded would be awarded a gold star, worn on the part of their body where they had been wounded; if this was the face, or they had lost a limb, it would be worn over the heart.[55] Such essentially authoritarian schemes refashioned the world of social relations within a restrictive framework, from which all turbulence and indeed scope for individual self-expression were ruthlessly excluded.

Saint-Just's disciplinarian conception of a transparent régime of appearances was an extreme form of compensation, or discursive rectification, for the disordered and unmanageable nature of public life under the Republic. Indicative of the troublingly unstable state of affairs was the attention given to disguise, a wholesale – and indeed calculated – antithesis to the desire for visible authenticity. Adoption of disguise corresponded to a repudiation, at once pragmatic and symbolic, of the prevailing revolutionary order. As we will see in the special case of crossdressing, it therefore provoked extreme legislative condemnation.

Disguise was synonymous with the machinations of the Revolution's enemies. It was a means to escape, as well as to engage in subversive activity. In the language of surveillance and suspicion, disguise was an extension of the notion of masking. Masking operated on two complementary levels: dissimulation of physical expression and behaviour, and manipulation of forms of dress. However, in practice these are treated as continuous, especially when they were believed to correspond to threatening forms of evasion and subterfuge.

Concern over the practice of disguise found expression in warnings in which commonplace items of dress are invested with disturbing subversive potential. That this form of active disavowal of the Revolution required concealment of true identity aligned troublemaking with incorrigible dissembling. Indeed, disguise was habitually assumed to be inherently compromising. In July 1791, a spoof article in the *Journal de la cour et de la ville* warned that the wardrobes of *agents provocateurs* preparing themselves for emigration included: 'Woollen jackets and woollen caps, suitable to represent when the occasion arises workers from a suburb, and to insult rich or respectable people'.[56] When Manuel offered the duchesse de Tourzel the chance to escape fom the prison of La Force in September 1792, he provided a suitably fully concealing outfit – 'trousers, coat, jacket' – designed to allow her to merge with crowds in the street. She, however, could not bring herself to put the plan into action, not because of the idea of dressing as a man, but rather out of a desire to die in her own clothes: 'it was repugnant to me to perish in clothes that would not have been my own'.[57] Other émigrés were less fastidious. A Parisian boatwoman's dress surviving in the collections of Corsham Court was allegedly used by Mrs Henry Seymour to facilitate her escape to England.[58]

Accounts of émigrés and politicians in flight adopting a variety of disguises are legion.[59] Such episodes served to demean the fugitives, willing to abjure their true identities in the interests of self-preservation from revolutionary justice, and also played on the amusing incongruousness of nobles' desperate dressing down.[60] Disguise could take on a legitimizing rationale when employed to engage in what in retrospect came to be seen as justified plotting, as in the case of Fouché's preparation of the downfall of Robespierre. In order to avoid being compromised, he had stayed away from the Convention, and not slept at home, circulating among his confederates in various disguises to elude surveillance.[61] Equally for royalists, disguise could be a necessary means of manoeuvre in moments when the king was threatened. Two of the queen's women were only able to rejoin the royal family in the Tuileries on 20 June 1792 by dressing in 'outfits of women of the people'.[62] And of course, none other than Louis XVI and Marie-Antoinette had dressed down as valet and governess on their momentously unsuccessful escape bid which terminated prematurely and ingloriously when they were intercepted at Varennes.

Concern over the uses of dress for disguise treated it not just as a simple, unified legible surface, but as a series of opaque layers, between which alternative signs of identity could be concealed.[63] In 1790, a

satirical pamphlet played on the metaphor of the fit of clothes in order
to evoke the new diversity of political disposition, both honourable
and otherwise. Thus, figures such as the abbé Maury or Mirabeau would
need extremely loose-fitting clothes to accommodate their prodigious
propensity to vice; Lafayette, who had less to hide, would manage with
close-fitting garments.[64] Waistcoats were a convenient place to conceal
symbolic motifs as they were covered by jackets, which might in the right
company be opened to reveal royalist *fleurs de lys*. An article in *Le Feuille
du jour* on the discovery of such waistcoats in Bordeaux in September
1791 gave full details: 'the background is decorated with fleurs de lys, on
which are printed the arms of the empire with this double legend: Long
live the King! Long live the Queen! . . . these waistcoats could be the
rallying sign for the enemies of the constitution'. Large numbers of them
were to have been made, but searches had failed to reveal who had been
producing these elaborately subversive clothes. This revelation posed a
problem for patriots who wished to uphold freedom of dress as part of
the general legislative protection of freedom. On the one hand, individual
liberty was sacrosanct; on the other, potential causes of trouble and dissent
needed to be stamped out – especially now that the Revolution was
believed to be almost accomplished. But there are some circumstances
'where what at first sight seems innocent, can serve as a mask for the most
dangerous plots'. Such machinations were predictably contrasted with
the cockade which, for 'right-minded people', was the only 'sign of
union . . . because this cockade alone is the emblem of French liberty.
Indeed, it should be enough for well-intentioned citizens to learn that a
particular form of costume could be the cause of alarm, that they make
it a law not to adopt it.'[65] Yet, in late 1792 it was still possible for a royalist
such as Antoine-Vincent Arnault to declare his loyalty to the king by
having fleurs de lys embroidered on his waistcoat, cravat and gloves.[66]

The greater the degree of suspicion, the more likely it was that
attention would latch on to banal details offering a key to the revelation
of conspiratorial motives; in the summer of 1795, for example, alarm was
raised concerning the green cravats worn by new, counter-revolutionary
terrorists.[67] Thieves and other undesirables could, however, easily change
their 'rallying sign'; as the *Gazette française* pointed out, this could lead
to the absurd spectacle of the authorities overzealously and in all likeli-
hood erroneously pursuing fashionable novelties: 'Large hats, little boots,
square coat tails, bleu-barbeux jackets, can also be regarded as a rallying
sign.'[68] This kind of obsessive anxiety over potentially meaningful details

of dress is exemplified in the municipal *arrêté* issued in Montpellier on 6 April 1796 threatening arrest for those who 'wore their hair in plaits, a green or yellow cockade, and a hat with crêpe band whose ends are knotted on the left side'.[69]

Perhaps the most vivid example of the revelation of dress as a means of disguise is the recurrent claim that *agents provocateurs* had been discovered to be wearing linen beneath their assumed outfits of ragged *sans-culottes*. This is a resonant image for, on the one hand, it implies that such counter-revolutionaries gave themselves away because they were unable to dispense with the personal comforts to which they had been accustomed before the Revolution, and, on the other hand, it demonstrates that such people could not slough off their pernicious 'aristocratic' identity. The motif can be found applied retrospectively to what is claimed to be the first sighting of a *bonnet rouge* as worn by a 'leader' in 1788.[70] A later example of this reporting strategy concerns disturbances in the markets at Melun and Agen in 1792: 'Everywhere there are large gatherings, moving in an orderly fashion, perfectly under the control of leaders who, in *sans-culotte* costume, conceal fine white shirts and display a thorough education'.[71] *Les Sabats jacobites* parodied a Jacobin denunciation: 'beneath their rags, they hide white linen and even breeches'.[72] In October 1795, the *Journal des hommes libres* alerted patriots to watch out for fine linen under rough clothes; rebel casualties had been found to be wearing linen with *fleurs de lys* embroidered on it.[73]

A leitmotif within the discourse of disguise is the way that items of dress, among other things, were kept in pockets, conveniently ready for misuse. As we have seen in relation to the currency of the *bonnet rouge*, this quintessentially republican emblem was predominantly worn in specific quasi-official locations; otherwise, they were kept in readiness in pockets.[74] Indeed, one account of Louis XVI's encounter with the crowds who invaded the Tuileries on 20 June 1792 claimed that he, too, had had a *bonnet rouge* in his pocket 'to thank the people for their visit'.[75] However, this habitual practice, which corresponded to a form of respect for and conservation of the cap's emblematic power, was all too easily exploitable for contrary ends. In December 1793, false *sans-culottes* were reported as being at large, their *bonnets rouges* ready in their pockets, which they donned before entering cafés and other places of public gathering to provoke and insult citizens, put off their guard by the insignia of popular republicanism.[76] In so far as the cap was a separate item, it lent itself to strategies which aimed to undermine its authority.

Thus the pocket became an ambiguous space whose practicality could be abused. The pocket was also a place to protect evidence in the form of incriminating papers, ready to be produced as part of an explicit denunciation. At the Jacobin club, Saint-Just claimed that he had the proof of Hébert's accusation in his pocket.[77] Similarly, compromising documents were said to have been found in the lining of the king's breeches after his execution.[78]

A counterpoint to this mode of concealment is the attention given to hats as the site for signs that were at once strategically visible and coded. Following the invasion of the Tuileries on 20 June 1792, men who led the cheering in favour of Pétion on the occasion of the second festival of Federation were claimed to have chalk marks on their hats.[79] On the *journée* of 2 prairial an III/21 May 1795, men from the sections in the faubourg St-Antoine took to the street with a similar hat-borne motto: 'Bread and the democratic constitution of 1793'.[80] Again, in February 1796, men were reported to be plotting to protest at the price of bread, planning to take to the streets; the leaders would give the signal by displaying the exhortation: 'People rise up, it is time, bread!' on their hats.[81] The latter plan was all the more seditious in that any 'sign' other than the cockade, especially when written on hats, had been banned. Women's hats had always been subject to fashionably topical fabrications. In the aftermath of Marat's assassination by Charlotte Corday, fashion merged with partisan allusion. In the first place, it was noticed that she had worn a green hat on the day of her murderous act. Accordingly, such hats were banned by the Paris Commune, although this was not enough to prevent the practice being boldly and contentiously adopted.[82]

At its most extreme, the problematizing of the relation between exterior appearances and interior moral identity during the Revolution led to scepticism about the most fundamental of vestimentary codes, those which signalled gender.[83] The initiative for changing accepted conventions which determined the mutually exclusive divide between male and female dress was primarily taken by radical women, but with only brief success. Moreover, it is striking that cross-dressing stirred extremely strong negative reactions from radicals and royalists alike. The most prominent form of cross-dressing was in the form of subversive disguise, a subject where it is difficult to distinguish between accusation and observation. Yet it was also part of a more general repertoire of caricature. In an English print denouncing Philippe d'Orléans' role in the downfall and execution of the king, 'The near in blood, the nearer bloody . . .', Robespierre appears 'en poissarde'.[84]

In a pre-revolutionary context, censure of cross-dressing relied on Biblical authority, backed up by medical argument.[85] Only exceptionally, as part of the rituals of carnivalesque inversion, was women's adoption of items of male dress fleetingly permissible. But it took on a much more threatening aspect when it formed part of a challenge to authority. One of the earliest instances of this was the often repeated claim that the march to Versailles on 5 October 1789 was instigated by men dressed as *poissardes*.[86] Equally, when in the summer of 1791 *poissardes* were observed wearing elements of the uniform of the National Guard, this was found repugnant, in that such illicit 'freedom' exemplified the profound disorder that disturbed critics of revolutionary politics.[87] Outrage at this kind of vestimentary misappropriation articulated the anxiety that the Revolution was fundamentally aberrant. In a similar but politically contrasting manner, it was also possible to ridicule Jacobins' world-view as being so obsessed with political orthodoxy and deviation that they insisted on denouncing a case of crossdressing as an example of seditious subterfuge, ignoring the more fundamental principle of confusion of gender at stake. Thus, commenting in October 1796 on the arrest of a man who had aroused suspicion because he was dressed as a woman, the *Gazette française* quipped with weary sarcasm: 'The Jacobins will say that he is an émigré.'[88] Such anxieties were widespread – rumours, perhaps, but designed to confirm the worst fears of police agents on the lookout for deviance. As noted in May 1793: 'We are assured that there are in this great city many émigrés, above all women of good birth, disguised as men, while some former nobles are concealed in women's clothes.'[89] This episode corresponds to a period when concern over the malevolent intentions of émigrés, who were believed to be returning to add their weight to a politically regressive current of opinion, was intense.

The ritualized adoption of masks and festive, irreverent disguise in carnival was early on recognized as a potentially convenient cover for political troublemaking. In Paris, carnival and its associated masks were banned on 31 January 1790.[90] It was not until 1796 that people in Paris once again emerged at carnival time with masks.[91] In the provinces local traditions were more resistant to suppression. It was only in 1793 that carnival in Toulon was forbidden because of fears of its exploitation by 'ill-intentioned people'.[92] In January 1797, the departmental administration of the Gironde forebade the use of masks or disguises, fully aware of the seditious uses to which they might be put.[93] Yet, as Antoine de Baecque has reminded us, the carnivalesque mode of parody resurfaced in the eclectic, unmanageable language of pamphlet literature celebrating the cathartic effect of the old world turned upside down.[94] The metaphor of carnival could be turned both against and in favour of the Revolution. Sceptical responses to festivals decried their disorder; this was epitomized by citing the unseemly prominence of *poissardes*, and treating them as merely temporary expressions of carnivalesque aberration. Georges Duval gleefully recalled how two men essaying *sans-culotte* costume in Meudon were greeted by small boys who delightedly called to them using terms associated with carnival[95] – a response which enshrined what Duval regarded as a salutary misrecognition of the vestimentary paraphernalia of extreme politics. On the other hand, the carnivalesque could be construed as a form of anti-aristocratic denunciation. Thus, as James Johnson has noted, according to an anecdote in the *Journal des clubs ou sociétés patriotiques*, the proscribed carnival masks had, in fact, been displaced into the form of 'former tyrants and former slaves disguised as legislators fanning the flames of discord instead of making laws, and . . . humiliated aristocrats, who've donned a popular costume, affecting a popular language, acting in a popular fashion'.[96]

In 1792, a song had optimistically envisaged the universal wearing of the *bonnet rouge* by men, women and children.[97] However, rather in the manner of the problems encountered with the cockade, the reality of such equality was that it brought to the surface entrenched sentiments about the sexual division of political rights and responsibility. As discussed in Chapter three, disputes over the wearing of the cockade by women had, on the one hand, led to a decree (8 brumaire an II/29 October 1793) which formally stated that all men and women were free to wear what they wished, unconstrained by any attempt to impose a particular form of dress, and on the other hand had provoked concerted official repression of women's involvement in public political life. Significantly, cross-dressing was, with the wearing of religious costume and the requirement for all to wear the cockade, one of the exceptions to the decree's notional freedom. A decree of 7 August 1793 had already ordered that any man found dressed as a women in a 'rassemblement' was to be sentenced to death; this was a response to fears about the exploitation of crowds outside bakers as a means to foment discontent.[98] Antoine de Baecque has found an instance where this was carried out.[99] However, police reports continue to draw attention to this alleged practice without calling down the full force of the law.[100] Jean-Marc Devocelle notes the Directory's intolerance of the illegal practice of women wearing uniform or trousers:

'cross-dressing is only authorized to sick women, at home, with a doctor's certificate, approved by the municipality'.[101]

The discussions around the cockade spilled over onto other modes of the wearing of political dress by women. In a well-known episode from October 1793, a group of women from *les Halles* came to blows with an overzealous party of proselytizing women from the *Société des Femmes révolutionnaires* when refusing to emulate their adoption of the *bonnet rouge*.[102] In the *Conseil général* of the Paris Commune, Chaumette denounced the idea that women should wear the *bonnet rouge*. It was 'contrary to all the laws of nature that a women should want to make herself into a man . . . be simple in your dress, hardworking in your homes'.[103] Women should not, therefore, presume to adopt politicized dress. Apart from the fact that such dress had proved to be a cause of unwanted contestation, it should also, he asserted, remain the exclusive preserve of men. In fact, as Dominique Godineau has shown, considerable numbers of women did engage in cross-dressing in order to enter the ranks of the army; moreover, the needs of recruitment, and the exemplary courage of some of these women, meant that this practice could be publicly applauded.[104]

Chronic uncertainty regarding the status of appearances as an indicator of people's politicized identity followed from the recognition that it was not only unreliable but also subject to insidious manipulation. Such variability eluded any overarching legislation; rather, official attention was translated into localized exhortations to vigilance, recurrently reanimated by warnings of new forms of 'rallying sign'.

It would, however, surely be mistaken to attribute all such incidents to an over-anxious, pathologically suspicious régime of surveillance. Although difficult, if not impossible, to ascertain the degree of currency of disguise and deviant dress codes, these were not mere inventions of overzealous police agents or scaremongering journalists. Rather, we should see such attitudes as part of the general problem of making sense of the fluctuating and fragmented forms of publicly visible political culture as it was experienced in terms of the spectacle of social interaction. By definition, 'rallying signs' connected the individual, or small groups, with larger clandestine networks. Unlike the 'signs' looked for in the Ancien Régime, where the leaders and confederates were – riotously – out in the open, revolutionary cues were predominantly understood as uniting covert, concealed communities, who needed to be identified and dealt with precisely in order to pre-empt the realization of their schemes. Preventing disorder was, of course, the prime objective. It was also a more realistically achievable end through vigilant surveillance and prompt action. Yet disguise and its polymorphic manifestations remained as an insidiously elusive undercurrent – literally existing beneath the surface of appearances. In revolutionary perceptions of dress, it is figured as a complexly constituted register. In physical, material terms, this is expressed in the attention given to its disturbingly layered nature, thus potentially harbouring other counter-revolutionary motives and identities.

The accoutrements associated with the new political culture proved to be alarmingly vulnerable. This was not only a consequence of the inherited discourse on the unreliability of vestimentary appearances. In the Revolution, the manifold manipulations of outward appearances took on a political significance at once fundamental and circumstantial. The very items of dress which had been adopted to proclaim a new political order had, by virtue of the nature of their self-conscious display, facilitated their opportunistic appropriation and subversive simulation. Indeed, legislative attempts to restrict the wearing of the signs of official authority could be seen as having been counterproductive, in the sense that this left open a symbolic vacuum, which was filled both by ingenuous individualistic expressions of patriotic solidarity and their dissenting alternatives.

We need not share the predisposition of pragmatically suspicious police agents reporting to the Minister of the Interior and apprehensively interventionist national guards to read unfamiliar manifestations of dress and its accessories as provocative evidence of covert conspiracies. For all the fears articulated in police reports and alarmist journalistic *faits divers* about conspiratorial networks and counter-revolutionary cells, it is probable that such troubling manifestations of vestimentary diversity were as often the result of unco-ordinated but patriotically well-intentioned individual initiative as they might have been a coded front for *agents provocateurs*. The confusion generated by the contrary motives that might explain similar forms of variety in dress and its accessories points to what is perhaps the central feaure of the politics of revolutionary appearances, namely an uncertain and frequently unresolved process of (mis)recognition whereby the heterogeneous spectacle of people visible in the street, club, and café had continually to be tested against expectations of how dress should signify new modes of identity.

Notes

1. On the need for study of such 'politiques de surveillance', see Daniel Roche, *La Culture des apparences. Une histoire du vêtement (XVII–XVIIIe siècles)* (Fayard: Paris, 1989), p. 507 note 74.

2. On changing paradigms of the construction of appearances, see J.P. Cavailhé, 'De la construction des apparences au culte de la transparence. Simulation et dissimulation 16e–18e siècles', *Littératures classiques*, Autumn 1998, vol. 34, pp. 73–102; Caroline Jacot Grapa, *L'Homme dissonant au dix-huitième siècle* (Studies on Voltaire and the Eighteenth Century, 1997, vol. 354).

3. See Jean Starobinski, *J.J. Rousseau, la transparence et l'obstacle* (Plon: Paris, 1958), and Philippe Perrot, *Le Travail des apparences, ou les transformations du corps féminin XVIIIe–XIXe siècles* (Seuil: Paris, 1984), Chapter 4, 'Le chiffre des apparences'. The extent to which the established figuring of vestimentary vanity as essentially feminine was appropriated to castigate 'aristocrates' is discussed below in relation to *muscadins* and the *jeunesse dorée*.

4. Aileen Ribeiro, *Dress in Eighteenth-century Europe 1715–1789* (Batsford: London, 1984), pp. 140–62. The new 'simplicity' of fashion was, of course, merely a reconfigured form of urban sophistication.

5. See Lynn Hunt, *Politics, Culture and Class in the French Revolution* (University of California Press: Berkeley, Los Angeles and London, 1984), p. 39; Geoffrey Cubitt, 'Denouncing Conspiracy in the French Revolution', *Renaissance and Modern Studies*, 1989, vol. 33, pp. 143–58; Antoine de Baecque, *Le Corps de l'histoire. Métaphores et politique (1770–1800)* (Calmann-Lévy: Paris, 1993), pp. 257–302; Jacques Guilhaumou, 'Fragments of a Discourse of Denunciation (1789–1794)', *The French Revolution and the Creation of Modern Political Culture*, vol. 4, Keith Michael Baker (ed.), *The Terror* (Pergamon/Elsevier: Oxford, 1994), pp. 139–55; and Colin Lucas, 'The Theory and Practice of Denunciation in the French Revolution', *Journal of Modern History*, December 1996, vol. 68, no. 4, pp. 768–85.

6. de Baecque, *Corps de l'histoire*, pp. 257–302.

7. See Roche, *Culture des apparences*, p. 149.

8. Lynn Hunt, 'Freedom of Dress in Revolutionary France', in Sara E. Melzer and Kathryn Norberg (eds), *From the Royal to the Republican Body: Incorporating the Political in Seventeenth- and Eighteenth-century France* (University of California Press: Berkeley, Los Angeles, London, 1998), p. 248.

9. *Mémoires secrets pour servir à l'histoire de la république des lettres en France, depuis 1762 jusqu'à nos jours*, 36 vols (London, 1779–1789), vol. 10, 8 October 1777, p. 263.

10. For example, J.F. Sobry, *Le Mode françois* (Paris, 1786). See Robert Darnton, 'A Bourgeois Puts his World in Order: the City as a Text', *The Great Cat Massacre, and Other Episodes in French Cultural History* (Vintage: New York, 1985), pp. 107–43. A graphic equivalent is the anonymous *Les Costumes françois representans les différens états du royaume avec les habillemens propres à chaque état et accompagné de réflexions critiques et morales* (Paris, 1776). However, as John Shovlin observes regarding Augustin Rouillé's *L'Ami des françois* (Constantinople, 1771), tabulations of the social order could be a means to cast doubt on its justifiability ('The Cultural Politics of Luxury in Eighteenth-century France', *French Historical Studies*, fall 2000, vol. 23, no. 4, p. 593).

11. Roche, *Culture des apparences*, p. 92.

12. *Révolutions de Paris*, 1789–90, vol. 2, no. 16, pp. 20/21, 'Anecdote arrivée à Louis XVI quelques jours après sa résidence à Paris'. The incident reworks the topos of the incognito sovereign mingling among his subjects; see Richard Wrigley, 'Protokollierte Identität. Anmerkungen über das inkognito in der Reisepraxis und der Reiseliteratur des 18. Jahrhunderts', in Joachim Rees, Winifried Siebers, Hilmar Tilgner (eds), *Europareisen politisch-sozialer Eliten im 18. Jahrhundert. Theoretische Neuorientierung – kommunikative Praxis – Kultur – und Wissenstransfer*, Spitz: Berlin, 2002, pp. 209–18.

13. See Chapter 4 on Jacobins and *bonnets rouges*, Chapter 3 on the Société des amis de la constitution monarchique and *cocardes blanches*, and Chapter 2 on the badges of *sociétés populaires*.

14. See the indispensable *Dictionnaire des usages socio-politiques (1770–1815)*, 4 vols (Klincksieck: Saint-Cloud, 1985–89).

15. During the Ancien Régime, the image of the bourgeois had, of course, hardly been a consistently stable phenomenon; see Richard Wrigley, 'The Class of '89': cultural aspects of bourgeois identity in France in the aftermath of the French Revolution', in Andrew Hemingway and William Vaughan (eds), *Art in Bourgeois Society 1790–1850* (Cambridge University Press: Cambridge, 1998), pp. 130–53.

16. *Le Babillard*, 16 September 1791, no. 95, p. 441.

17. *Le Babillard*, 31 August 1791, no. 79, pp. 315–16.

18. *Le Babillard*, 7 August 1791, no. 55, p. 89. See David Andress, *Massacre at the Champ de Mars. Popular Dissent and Political Culture in the French Revolution* (Boydell for the Royal Historical Society: Woodbridge, 2000).

19. *Le Babillard*, 14 October 1791, no. 123, p. 735.

20. For example, on *gardes suisses* who wore the cockade in a distinctive way, 7 August 1791, no. 55, p. 72 ; on 'brigands' who appropriated the uniform of the National Guard, 19 August 1791, no. 67, pp. 213–14; on disguised priests, 24 August 1791, no. 72, p. 255; on the fabrication of royalist army uniforms, 22 August 1791, no. 70, p. 237.

21. See Lucien Jamme, 'St-Just: la lutte contre les masques', *Le Discours jacobin et la démocratie* (Fayard: Paris, 1989), pp. 210–12.

22. See Chapter 3.

23. Lucas, 'Theory and Practice of Denunciation', pp. 768–85.

24. *RAM*, vol. 21, 17 mess. an II/5 July 1794, p. 237, cit. Albert Soboul, *Les Sans-culottes parisiens en l'an II* (Clavreuil: Paris, 1958), p. 953 note 145. Such remarks can be found from the outset of the Revolution; for example, the *Révolutions de Paris* reproached bourgeois members of the National Guard who were more concerned for their *toilette* than their duty: 'il seroit à souhaiter qu'on s'enthousiasmât réellement pour la chose et non pas pour l'habit' (9–12 September 1789, p. 132). On bourgeois vanity see also *Le Fouet national*, no. 2, pp. 22–3. Such distinctions took on a quite different resonance under the Terror. On the pre-revolutionary sensationalist critique of the social order through censure of the apparatus of representation on which it relied, see Shovlin, 'Cultural Politics of Luxury', pp. 577–606.

25. Caron, vol. 6, p. 172, 8 germ. an II/28 March 1794.

26. See Antoine de Baecque, *Corps*, pp. 286–302, and for a general survey, Jean-Jacques Courtine and Claudine Haroche, *Histoire du visage. Exprimer et taire ses émotions (XVIe–XIXe siècles)* (Payot: Paris, 1988).

27. Caron, vol. 3, pp. 318–19, 16 pluv. an II/4 February 1794. Of a criminal 'qui a ordinairement une redingote de peluche mêlée, dont le pan droit se trouve déchiré', Letassey remarked: 'il porte sur sa figure ce qu'il est' (*ibid.*, vol. 4, p. 28, 22 pluv. an II/10 February 1794).

28. François Furet, *Penser la Révolution française* (Gallimard: Paris, 1978), pp. 90–102.

29. Caron, vol. 1, pp. 12–16, 'Fin d'août 1793'.

30. Caron, vol. 2, p. 60, 8 niv. an II/28 December 1793.

31. Caron, vol. 1, p. 95, 14 September 1793.

32. *RAM*, vol. 18, pp. 89–90, 21 vend. an II, 12 October 1793.

33. James H. Johnson, *Listening in Paris: a Cultural History* (University of California Press: Berkeley, Los Angeles, London, 1995), p. 123, and 'Revolutionary Audiences and the Impossible Imperatives of Fraternity', in Bryant T. Ragan Jr and Elizabeth A. Williams (eds), *Re-creating Authority in Revolutionary France* (Rutgers University Press: New Brunswick, New Jersey, 1992), pp. 57–78.

34. Caron, vol. 1, p. 129, 18 September 1793.

35. Ibid.

36. Jean-Marc Devocelle publishes a 'Lettre des administrateurs du Bureau des moeurs, du bureau central du Canton de Paris aux entrepreneurs de l'opéra comique' (3 frimaire an VII/23 November 1798, BHVP MSS 773, f° 120), which insists on the exclusion of 'les livrées de noblesse' and foreign uniforms from the stage unless absolutely essential to the play, to avoid offering 'les amis de la royauté' the opportunity to treat such features as cues to assert noisily their allegiance ('Costume politique et politique du costume: approches théoriques et idéologiques du costume pendant la Révolution française', Université de Paris I, mémoire de maîtrise, 1988, 2 vols, vol. 2, pp. 34–5).

37. For pre-revolutionary cases where changed identity, including cross-dressing, had been observed, see Arlette Farge, *Vivre dans la rue à Paris au XVIIIe siècle* (Gallimard: Paris, 1979), pp. 94–100.

38. See Richard Cobb, *The Police and the People. French Popular Protest 1789–1820* (Oxford University Press: Oxford, 1970), pp. 17–36. Accounts of disguise as a criminal device are legion; the *Mémoires de Vidocq, forçat et chef de la Police de sûreté écrits par lui-même*, 2 vols (Gründ: Paris, n.d.), give an authoritative survey. See also *Les Ruses des escrocs et des filous dévoilées*, 2 vols (Paris, 1811). On the Paris police's intimidating reputation for streetwise omniscience, see *A Sketch of Modern France, in a series of letters to a lady of fashion, written in the years 1796 and 1797, during a tour through France*, ed. C. L. Moody (London, 1798), pp. 216–17. The Paris Commune set up a *comité de recherches* in October 1789; the Legislative Assembly created its own in November 1791 (Lucas, 'Theory and Practice of Denunciation', p. 770); on *comités de surveillance* set up in sections in the immediate aftermath of 10 August 1792, see Maurice Genty, *L'Apprentissage de la citoyenneté. Paris 1789–1795* (Messidor/Éditions sociales: Paris, 1987), pp. 203–4. See also Timothy Tackett, 'Conspiracy Obsession in a Time of Revolution: French Élites and the Origins of the Terror 1789–1792', *American Historical Review*, June 2000, pp. 691–713.

39. *Révolutions de Paris*, 1789, vol. 1, no. 13, 3–10 October 1789, p. 33.

40. Patrice Higonnet has noted a similar form of renunciation of passwords and codes used by Jacobins to allow mutual recognition, since they might facilitate 'aristocrates' in the forging of false identities (*Goodness Beyond Virtue. Jacobins during the French Revolution* (Harvard University Press: Cambridge, MA, and London, 1998), p. 169). An example of

overdetermined proscription from 1799 is the arrest of a pharmacy student, who had hung up a white sheet to dry, on suspicion of having displayed the Bourbon white flag (*L'Aristarque français*, 18 frim. an VIII/9 December 1799, no. 18, pp. 3–4).

41.   Tuetey, vol. 9, no. 598, 16 May 1793.

42.   Caron, vol. 6, 3 germ. an II/23 March 1794. For an instance of over-zealous police intervention, when a 'bon patriote jacobin et bon républicain' had been mistreated by agents 'à cause de sa mise', who presumably took him for a suspiciously well-kitted out pseudo-*sans-culotte*, see Caron, vol. 1, p. 234 (29 September 1793).

43.   Black wigs *à la jacobine* had earlier been banned (*RAM*, vol. 18, 5 frim. an II/25 November 1793, no. 65, p. 497).

44.   See Daniel Roche, *Histoire des choses banales. Naissance de la consommation XVIIe– XIXe siècles* (Fayard: Paris, 1997), p. 220.

45.   *Pensées sur les coupeurs de Tresses. Par un homme libre, qui ne l'est pas* (n.d. [1794]).

46.   Ibid.

47.   F. Gendron, *La Jeunesse dorée* (Presses de l'Université du Québec: Montréal, 1979), pp. 320–1.

48.   no. 1777, 27 brum. an V/17 November 1796, pp. 3–4.

49.   *Départ de Filous et des brigands, contrôlé sur le visage de la lettre F. Prononcé le dimanche 29 Mai 1791, à la société des amis de la constitution, séante à Paris, par N. Citoyen actif*, pp. 2–6. In the print *Le Jacobin royaliste*, a Jacobin is shown as a convict, also relying on the parallel of the *bonnet rouge* form of liberty cap with the cap worn by convicts (Hennin collection, vol. 142, 12469 (68 C 35246). See also the print *Ce que j'étois, ce que je suis, ce que je vais être* (De Vinck collection, vol. 51, 1797 Qb, 52 C 8050), in which a transition from *sans-culotte* to *parvenu* to branded convict is represented.

50.   *Arch Parl*, vol. 26, p. 689, 1 June 1791. See Antoinette Wills, *Crime and Punishment in Revolutionary Paris* (Greenwood: Westport, CT, London, 1981), pp. 192, 201–2.

51.   Higonnet, *Goodness*, p. 228.

52.   This was suggested in the Legislative Assembly by Duval according to Aimée de Coigny in October 1791 (*Journal* (1981), p. 75, cit. Nicole Pellegrin, *Les Vêtements de la Liberté* (Alinéa: Paris, 1989), p. 124).

53.   E. Campardon (ed.), *Marie-Antoinette à la Conciergerie* (Paris, 1863), p. 161.

54.   For a full discussion of projects for new official costumes, see Jean-Marc Devocelle, 'Costume et citoyenneté', *Révolution française 1988–1989. Actes des 113e et 114e congrès nationaux des sociétés savantes* (Strasbourg, 1988–Paris, 1989). Section d'histoire moderne et contemporaine (Comité des Travaux Historiques et Scientifiques: Paris, 1991), pp. 313–32. Such schemes had been a feature of pre-revolutionary utopian texts; see Roche, *Culture des apparences*, pp. 398, 400–11. They were also part of post-revolutionary conceptions of a new order. Bonald's compartmentalized image of a durably stable society relied on age, sex, and profession – akin, he believed, to a truly natural order. See Gérard Gengembre, 'Bonald, 1796–1801: contre-Révolution et politique du possible', in François Furet and Mona Ozouf (eds), *The French Revolution and the Creation of Modern Political Culture*, vol. 3, *The Transformation of Political Culture 1789–1848* (Pergamon: Oxford, 1989), pp. 309–21. I am grateful to Tony Halliday for encouraging me to look at Bonald as a fruitful source for such opinions.

55.   Saint-Just, 'Fragments d'institutions républicaines', *Œuvres complètes*, 2 vols, ed. Charles Vellay (Charpentier: Paris, 1908), vol. 2, pp. 524–30. That Saint-Just's scheme was

not merely an extreme manifestation of authoritarian wishful thinking is evident in the call for legislation on dress from a deputation from the Section des Quinze-Vingts: 'Législateurs, décrétez l'uniformité dans les costumes, vous décrétez l'uniformité des coeurs' (*Arch Parl*, vol. 59, p. 712, 8 March 1793).

56. Supplément du no. 8, pp. 2–3.

57. *Mémoires de Madame la duchesse de Tourzel, gouvernante des enfans de France de 1789 à 1795*, ed. Jean Chalon (Mercure de France: Paris, 1969), p. 411.

58. Many thanks to Daru Rooke, who alerted me to the existence of this dress; to Adam White and Chris Ridgway for advice on tracking it down; and James Methuen Campbell for kindly sending me a copy of Patricia Raine's, *A Dress of the Revolution worn for Escape 1793* (Northern Society of Costume and Textiles, 1989).

59. The Baron de Batz was reported to be in hiding dressed as a coachman (Tuetey, vol. 10, nos 2667–70). For other examples, see Dorinda Outram, *The Body and the French Revolution. Sex, Class, and Political Culture* (Yale University Press: New Haven and London, 1989), p. 81.

60. 'Fragments inédits des mémoires de Dulaure', cit. Georges Lenôtre, *La Guillotine et les exécuteurs des arrêts criminels pendant la Révolution* (Paris, 1893), pp. 184–5.

61. Barras, 'Fragments des Mémoires de Barras', in *Bibliothèque des mémoires relatifs à l'histoire de France pendant le dix-huitième siècle*, nouvelle série, vol. 29, ed. M. de Lescure (Paris, 1875), vol. 29, p. 291. Moulin, imprisoned in the Luxembourg because of his doubts on 18 brumaire, escaped disguised as a woman (H. Viel-Castel, *Collection de costumes* (1834), p. 42).

62. Barnabé Farmain de Rosoi, *Récit exact et circonstancié de ce qui s'est dit et passé au Château des Tuileries, le mercredi 20 juin 1792*, p. 6. Disguise was a subtext of the whole event in that Rosoi claimed that the crowd's entry to the palace was allegedly facilitated by 'brigands . . . travestis en gardes nationaux'.

63. Richard Cobb has noted how the dress of the poor, who habitually wore their meagre wardrobes on their backs, was habitually made up of several layers of dress (*Death in Paris* (Oxford University Press: Oxford, 1978), p. 25).

64. *Le Tailleur patriote, ou les Habits de Jean-Foutre* (Paris, 1790), no. 1, pp. 2–4. Attr. to J. Duffay.

65. *Le Feuille du jour*, 21 September 1791, no. 270, pp. 708–9, 'Bordeaux'. The *Journal des hommes libres* also published a warning about royalist waistcoats (20 vend. an IV/12 October 1795, no. 131, p. 509).

66. A.-V. Arnault, *Souvenirs d'un sexagénaire*, 4 vols (Paris, 1833), vol. 1, pp. 267–8.

67. *La Sentinelle*, 29 mess. an III/17 July 1795, p. 95.

68. *Gazette française*, 27 brum. an V/17 November 1796, pp. 3–4.

69. 17 germ. an IV/6 April 1796, cit. J. Duval-Jouve, *Montpellier pendant la Révolution*, 2 vols (Montpellier, 1881), vol. 2, pp. 293–4.

70. Quenard, in the 'Tableau historique', prefacing François Bonneville's *Portraits des personnages célèbres de la Révolution*, 2 vols (Paris, 1796), vol. 1, pp. 32–3, noted C.L. Chassin (ed.), *Les Elections et les cahiers de Paris en 1789* (Paris, 1888), p. 7, note 2.

71. *Le Spectateur et modérateur*, 13 March 1792, no. 104, pp. 50–1. See also Caron, vol. 4, p. 156 (28 pluv. an II), on 'un reste de noblesse' visible beneath *carmagnole* and *bonnet de rouge*.

72. vol. 3 (1792), no. 62, p. 178.

73. *Journal des hommes libres*, 20 vend. an IV/12 October 1795, no. 131, pp. 509–10.

74. In 1792, a journal aimed at provincial readers reported:'il est peu de patriotes qui n'avaient dans sa poche un bonnet de laine rouge' (*Journal des décrets pour les habitants des campagnes*, cit. G. Isambert, *La Vie à Paris pendant une année de la Révolution, 1791–1792* (Paris, 1896), p. 33). Members of the Commune des arts kept their identification cards in their pockets; indeed, this practice was preferred to that of wearing them on lapels (H. Lapauze, *Procès-Verbaux de la Commune des arts* (Paris, 1903) p. 173, 29 vend. an II).

75. J.G. Peltier, *Correspondance politique des véritables amis du roi et de la patrie*, 26 June 1792, no. 65, p. 4.

76. Caron, vol. 2, p. 33, 7 niv. an II/27 December 1793.

77. Caron, vol. 2, p. 191, 16 niv. an II/5 January 1794.

78. *Appendix. Les dix articles des juremens, des faux sermens, prononcés par Louis Capet, en présence des chevaliers à Poignards, trouvés dans la doublure de sa culotte le jour de sa mort* (Paris [1793]). Other examples of this location for compromising documents include the *Lettre à la comtesse Henriette, sur les assignats . . . trouvées dans le gousset d'une culotte etc.* (Paris, 1790), and *Les Grandes Prédictions du grand Nostradamus, trouvées dans la grande culotte de peau de messire Honoré Barnave* (1790).

79. *Journal de Paris*, no. 197, 15 July 1792, pp. 794–5.

80. Schmidt, vol. 2, p. 343, 2 prairial an III/21 May 1795.

81. Schmidt, vol. 3, p. 97, 22 pluv. an IV/11 February 1796.

82. *Annales de la République française*, cit. Jacques Guilhaumou, 'La Mort de Marat à Paris (13 juillet–16 juillet 1793)', in Jean-Claude Bonnet (ed.), *La Mort de Marat* (Flammarion: Paris, 1986), p. 71.

83. On the long and complex pre-revolutionary history of cross-dressing, see Sylvie Steinberg, *La Confusion des sexes. Le travestissement de la Renaissance à la Révolution* (Fayard: Paris, 2001).

84. London 26 January 1793, ed. Fores, De Vinck collection no. 5795, Cabinet des Estampes, BNF.

85. Abbé Gauthier, *Traité contre l'amour des parures, et le luxe des habits*, 2nd edn (Paris, 1780), pp. 194–5.

86. Tourzel, *Mémoires de la duchesse de Tourzel, gouvernante des enfants de France pendant les années 1789, 1790, 1791, 1792, 1793, 1795*, 2 vols (Paris, 1883), vol. 1, p. 18. M. Monnier, *Appel au Tribunal de l'opinion publique, du rapport de M. Chabroud, et du Décret rendu par l'Assemblée Nationale le 2 octobre 1790. Examen du Mémoire du duc d'Orléans, et du plaidoyer du comte de Mirabeau, et nouveaux Eclaircissemens sur les crimes du 5 et du 6 octobre 1789* (Geneva, 1790), p. 57. The duc d'Aiguillon was accused in the royalist press of having been at Versailles *en poissarde*; see *Lettre de M. le duc d'Aiguillon à Madame la princesse de Chimay, dame d'honneur de la Reine* (n.d.). See also Baron Marc de Villiers, *Histoire des clubs des femmes* (Paris, 1910), p. 248.

87. Ferdinand Dutailly to Joseph Faine, 10 July 1791, in Pierre de Vaissière, *Lettres d' 'aristocrates'* (Paris, 1907), p. 297.

88. 15 vend. an V/6 October 1796, no. 1735, p. 2.

89. Tuetey, vol. 9, no. 597 (15/16 May 1793).

90. *RAM*, vol. 3, 5 February 1790, p. 287, cit. Jean-Marc Devocelle, 'Costume politique et politique du costume, vol. 2, p. 40. See also *Actes Comm*, 1st series, vol. 3, pp. 663–4. However, Jacques Guilhaumou notes that, before its suppression, carnival was

also an opportunity to assert patriotic enthusiasm; Père Duchesne was a popular role, useful for provoking monarchists (*La Langue politique et la Révolution française. De l'événement à la raison linguistique* (Paris, 1989), p. 59). See also Antoine de Baecque and Jacques Guilhaumou, 'Le Dernier Carnaval', in *Le Monde de la Révolution française,* February 1989, no. 2, p. 12.

91. Schmidt, vol. 3, p. 95, 21 pluv. an IV/10 Febrruary 1796. In 1793, when Georges Duval and his friends dressed in carnival garb, they were almost arrested (*Souvenirs de la Terreur, de 1788 à 1793*, 4 vols (Paris, 1841), vol. 3, pp. 162–3).

92. Pellegrin, *Vêtements*, p. 64.

93. Lynn Hunt, *Politics, Culture, and Class*, pp. 66–7. A degree of control was ensured under the Consulate, in that masks were forbidden to be worn in the street and public places (Louis-Sébastien Mercier, *Le Nouveau Paris*, ed. Jean-Claude Bonnet (Mercure de France: Paris, 1994), p. 1730).

94. Antoine de Baecque, 'Les corps du carnaval politique', in *Le Corps de l'histoire,* pp. 303–42. See also Ouzi Elyada, 'La presse populaire parisienne et le temps de carnaval: 1788–1791', in Michel Vovelle (ed.), *Les Images de la Révolution française*, 4 vols (Pergamon: Oxford, 1990), vol. 1, pp. 108–17.

95. Duval, *Souvenirs de la Terreur*, vol. 3, pp. 162–3.

96. *Journal des clubs ou sociétés patriotiques*, no. 17, 2–10 March 1791, p. 166, cit. James H. Johnson, 'Versailles, Meet Les Halles: Masks, Carnival and the French Revolution', *Representations*, winter 2001, no. 73, p. 99.

97. *Paris, an Ier de la République française 1792*, cit. *Intermédiaire des chercheurs et des curieux*, 10 July 1878, no. 244.

98. *Arch Parl*, vol. 70, p. 451.

99. *Moniteur*, 11 germ. an II, cit. De Baecque, *Le Corps de l'histoire*, pp. 330, 419 note 50.

100. For example, Caron, vol. 6, p. 41, 2 germ. an II/22 March 1794.

101. 'La Cocarde directorielle: dérives d'un symbole révolutionnaire', *AHRF*, vol. 64, 1992, no. 41, p. 362, note 41. The prohibition on women wearing men's trousers was reiterated on 16 brumaire an IX (Philippe Perrot, *Les Dessus et les dessous de la bourgeoisie* (Fayard: Paris, 1981), p. 38). Perrot notes that this legislation is still in force.

102. Soboul, *Sans-culottes parisiens*, pp. 272–4.

103. Reported and applauded in the *Journal de Ville-Affranchie et des départements de Rhône et Loire*, 6 frim. an II, p. 32. Marie-Claude Chaudonneret kindly pointed out this reference. See also Darlene Gay Levy, Harriet Branson Applewhite, Mary Durham Johnson (eds), *Women in the French Revolution 1789–1795* (University of Illinois Press: Urbana, 1979), pp. 195–200, 205–17.

104. See Dominique Godineau, *Citoyennes tricoteuses. Les femmes du peuple à Paris pendant la Révolution française* (Alinéa: Paris, 1988), p. 264, cit. Higonnet, *Goodness Beyond Virtue*, pp. 93, 133–4, and Sylvie Steinberg, *La Confusion des sexes*, pp. 247–58.

Coda

All the distinction between conditions, nuance so essential to happiness today, almost resides in the way clothes are worn. (Stendhal, 1817)[1]

BY THE END of the 1790s, the ubiquitous and inescapable politicization of dress beyond the institutionalized forms of political life gave way to a renewed emphasis on its prime function as a signifier of social identity. Defining social identity by means of dress had, of course, always been a complex matter, but now the choices it involved also had to take account of a predominantly retrospective dimension, ranging from disavowal to selective fidelity to conventions forged during the revolutionary years. From the Thermidorean Reaction to the Directory, when individuals dressed to prepare themselves for public visibility, they could not but be acutely conscious of recent history, and the connotations of certain forms of dress. Under the Directory, the nature of revolutionary political culture shifted to a much more restricted, centralized concentration of power, leaving French citizens in a position of more self-conscious independence, increasingly removed from active participation in the flux of partisan participatory politics. This superseded the chronic proliferation of competing factions and 'partis' which had been synonymous with the internecine violence for which the Revolution was bitterly reproached and painfully remembered.

A leitmotif of the way in which this defunct political culture was represented, and simultaneously repudiated, was the compilation of lists of successively obsolete labels, symptomatic of the confusing, conflictual and what now seemed essentially artificial divisions which had riven society. In the autumn of 1796, with weary but knowing precision, Félix-Marie Faulcon, a former deputy in the National and Constituent Assembly, who had gone into hiding in Poitiers during the Terror,[2] enumerated a litany of such terms, which he claimed had disappeared as quickly as they had emerged. In 1792 and 1793, for example, the following inherently untranslatable series of terms had come and gone:

les ministériels, les amis de la liste civile, les chevaliers du poignard, les girondins, les hommes du 10 août, les septembristes, les modérés, les hommes d'état, les brissotins, les hommes du 31 mai, les fédéralistes, les montagnards, les membres de la plaine, les crapauds du marais . . .[3]

These were uncomfortable reminders of the progressively fractured nature of political culture, but which Faulcon devalued by asserting that they had mostly been identified with no more than a few noisy individuals. In the post-Thermidorian era, it was possible to enumerate catalogues of these superseded political identities as a way of effecting a kind of retrospective antidote. Such generalizations spawned an illustrated genre of catalogue in which forms of dress were delineated as corresponding to both a set of beliefs and also a trajectory through the Revolution's disjointed progress. Thus, Beauvert's *Caricatures politiques* (an VI, 1797–8) were caricatures not only in their censorious humour, but also in the sense that they delineated sets of distinctive outward physical features and dress.[4]

Beauvert distinguishes five classes of men within the generic term 'republican', each identifiable by their principles and opinions, their daily dress, and also their 'banner' – an ingredient which gives them the status of vernacular personifications. First come 'independents', otherwise known as 'democrats' or 'friends of the people', intimidatingly alluding to Marat's sobriquet (Figure 30). These men were proud and simple, close to nature, aware of the price of liberty, attached to laws, in so far as these were to the advantage of the majority, friends of the government, but independent from the 'governors', never divorcing their consciences and their patriotism. 'Their gaze is proud and noble, their bearing steady.' Their hair is clean, their linen white; their ordinary dress is close-fitting trousers of 'broadcloth' or 'knitted' fabric. On their feet, they wear small laced-up boots. They wear a short frac, and round hats of simple form. Their 'banner' is in the national colours, with the motto 'Liberty, Equality, Fraternity'.[5]

The second class are the 'exclusifs', 'vigorous patriots who only have faith in their relics', and whose heads are full of nothing but egoism, pride, and ignorance; they are only able to find fault with the present, and particularly with the government. Their hair is habitually neglected, their dress sometimes dirty. They wear short jackets and loose woollen trousers; their shoes are buckled with leather; their hats are 'extraordinary'. They almost always have pipes in their mouths, which renders them foul-smelling. A large knobbly stick in hand, they have an air of worry, illness,

Figure 30 Anonymous: 'L'Indépendant' (The Independent), etching, Beauvert, *Caricatures politiques* (Paris, an VI [1797–8]). Bibliothèque Nationale de France, Paris. Photograph: Bibliothèque Nationale de France.

and bad humour. Their banner echoes the intransigent motto of 1793–4: 'Vivre libre ou mourir' (Figure 31).

Thirdly, the 'achetés', or mercenaries, often only self-declared patriots once they have become employees of the government. They retain their old style of dress, whether that be casual or smart. Irascible, false, self-interested, self-important, they have a banner of the three national colours, but pale or faded, with the motto 'Vive la République' (Figure 32). The fourth class are the 'enrichis', whose patriotism is dubious. They fear denunciation by the 'independents', and shun the 'achetés'. Although not uniform, their dress is brilliant and luxurious. They normally wear large hats with almost imperceptible cockades. They are only seen in public on fine horses or in superb coaches. Their banner is blue and white; their motto is 'abondance de bien ne nuit pas' (wealth does no harm) (Figure 33). Finally, the fifth class, the 'systematics', who remain faithful

Figure 31 Anonymous: 'L'Exclusif' (The Exclusive), etching, Beauvert, *Caricatures politiques* (Paris, an VI [1797–8]). Bibliothèque Nationale de France, Paris. Photograph: Bibliothèque Nationale de France.

to their old prejudices, and dislike the republic, whose end they await, 'like Jews the coming of the Messiah'. Their appearance is continually changing. They have no sense of solidarity among their peers. 'Fanatics without religion, royalists out of stubbornness and pride'. Their banner is white, with small red crosses and gold fleur-de-lys, with green bows on top, with the motto: 'This won't last for ever' (Figure 34).

Such reassuringly parodic images were situated in an ambiguous temporal dimension. On the one hand, they present such types as constituting salient features of the current socio-political landscape. On the other hand, the assumptions and attitudes associated with each type articulate a strategic self-positioning in relation to values inherited from the founding era of republicanism in 1793–4, ranging from dogmatic fidelity to opportunistic self-interest. What these caricatures emphasize

Figure 32 Anonymous: 'L'Acheté' (The Mercenary), etching, Beauvert, *Caricatures politiques* (Paris, an VI [1797–8]). Bibliothèque Nationale de France, Paris. Photograph: Bibliothèque Nationale de France.

is the importance of dress as a means to slip in and out of politicized personae, with varying degrees of ingenuousness. They draw on different levels of iconographical register, reworking the format of the more mundane *cris de Paris* and moralizing 'types', articulating a level of characterization at once more particular and more complex, in so far as these 'political caricatures' are precisely located in the dynamic, shifting landscape of the present.

More schematically, but with a rhetorical force undiluted by its graphic abbreviation, the frontispiece to Fabien Pillet's *Etrennes dramatiques* for 1798 (Figure 35) spanned the Revolution in four images, illustrating the reconfigured features of the French citizen: the joker of 1788 – harbinger of the imminent inception of a carnivalesque restructuring of Ancien Régime society; the national guard of 1789, superseded by the *sans-culotte*

Figure 33 Anonymous: 'L'Enrichi' (The Enriched), etching, Beauvert, *Caricatures politiques* (Paris, an VI [1797–8]). Bibliothèque Nationale de France, Paris. Photograph: Bibliothèque Nationale de France.

of 1793 – agents of the newly, and necessarily, militarized identity of constitutional and republican régimes; closing with a shift to the allegorical register in 1798, consecrating the constitution of an III. One might also see this classically draped female figure as connoting the contemporary phenomenon of the *merveilleuses*, whose simple pseudo-antique dresses signified a new freedom, indeed licence, at once political and vestimentary, when set against the memory of the oppressive rigours of the Jacobin republic.

In place of the spectrum of finely tuned, and chronologically specific, politicized identities articulated by Faulcon and Beauvert, the revival of fashion both celebrated and obscured the renewed importance invested in the public visibility of social difference, in which, as Ewa Lajer-Burcharth has recently argued, the interplay of gendered identities was

Figure 34 Anonymous: 'Le Systématique' (The Systematic), etching, Beauvert, *Caricatures politiques* (Paris, an VI [1797–8]). Bibliothèque Nationale de France, Paris. Photograph: Bibliothèque Nationale de France.

also importantly at issue.[6] This rapidly became a distinctive way of translating the transformation of the political order into visible quotidian cultural form. Driven by the resources and pleasures of a renewed consumerism, fashions facilitated the expression of individually constructed identities, or at least an illusion thereof. The phenomenon of the *incroyables* inherited the stereotype of the *muscadin*, which, in the observational vocabulary of 1793–94, had been cast as the adversarial antithesis of the *sans-culotte*. Now, actively dressing up rather than down signalled an uninhibited liberation from and non-compliance with the residual post-Thermidorian republican ethos. After Thermidor, the *jeunesse dorée*, a militant and aggressive form of updated *muscadin*, publicized their repudiation of the republican state through their assaults on ex-Jacobins, and also by their evasion of conscription. Mercier defined

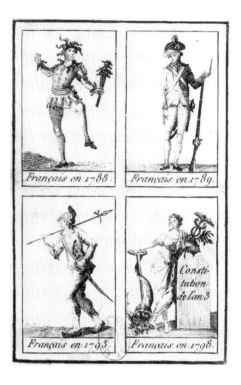

Figure 35 Canu: frontispiece, Fabien Pillet, *Etrennes dramatiques* (Paris, 1798), stipple engraving. Bibliothèque Nationale de France, Paris. Photograph: Bibliothèque Nationale de France.

these latter-day *muscadins* as 'rich and effeminate, wanting to distinguish themselves from those they called the bluecoats' – soldiers – which they did by feigning physical incapacity, and thus avoiding conscription.[7]

In this, however, they were acting against the grain, in that society was becoming increasingly visibly militarized.[8] The officially sanctioned and elaborately codified diversity of uniforms consequent upon the expansion of the army competed with, if not overshadowed, civilian fashion. Indeed, from the growth of the initially ill-equipped and eclectically dressed revolutionary army to the massed regiments of the Empire, uniform was to take over the role incompletely played by official dress as a signifier of social order. The ubiquitous social presence of military uniform inscribed a renewed recognition of hierarchy, shifted into a form of notionally apolitical appearances (notwithstanding the events of 18 brumaire).

The spectacle of militarism was a timely, and for many welcome, antidote to an endemic sense of social displacement. As an essay reviewing the state of France in 1797 concluded: 'We are all *ci-devant*[s] . . . we are all displaced'.[9] The structures and social forms of the Ancien Régime had been not so much lost, nor of course forgotten, as scrambled, their foundations irreversibly dissolved. In such diagnoses of the contemporary scene, there was evidently a deep-seated desire to deny the reality of the Revolution. As we have seen, for those such as Amaury Duval, who still held on to an updated form of republicanism, the spectacle of revived forms of showy dress, espoused by what he termed 'fats' (fops), seemed to have been deliberately adopted precisely in order to efface the reality of recent history.[10]

Social displacement was most scandalously manifest in the visibility of *parvenus* or *nouveaux riches*. *Parvenus* treated dress as a readily assumed means to assert new forms of status founded on recently acquired wealth; they rehearsed the established topos of adopting styles of dress to which they were not entitled, in the interests of their own newly acquired status, founded on money, not on birth or virtue. The *locus classicus* for this phenomenon in the later 1790s was the vaudeville character Madame Angot, first launched on the Parisian stage in 1796 in A.F. Eve's *Madame Angot, ou la poissarde parvenue*, and the subject of numerous sequels. This character has tended to be taken rather literally as an index, albeit censorious, of the *parvenu* phenomenon, but in fact can be shown to inscribe a rather more complexly layered statement about the vitiated veracity of outward forms of appearance. Madame Angot was a newly widowed wealthy fishwife, ostentatiously dressed up to suit her pretentions to superior status. The plausibility of her ambition is undercut by the stink of fish that clings to her, her frequent swigs from a flask of brandy, and above all her outbursts in Parisian slang. She aimed to marry her daughter into the aristocracy, in the person of a chevalier Giraud, but he turns out to be a fraud, thus reinforcing the narrative's message about the perils of mendacious, illegitimate dissimulation. The play's parodic effect was further enhanced by the fact that Madame Angot was played (up) by a man, the actor Jean-Baptiste Labenette, usually known by his stage name of Corsse.

As Pierre Frantz has noted, Eve's adaptation of the theatrical *poissarde* genre transformed disguise – at once social and vestimentary – which had hitherto been a subsidiary theme within the genre, into a central ideological narrative.[11] In the post-revolutionary context, theatrical cross-dressing would have had a further associational dimension, in that it figured at the comic end of a discourse on the unreliability of appearances which, as has been seen, included the more serious matters of conspiracy, disguise and unmasking, a discourse which accorded particular attention to the alleged incidence of men cloaking their subversive intentions by disguising themselves as women. This figure of a ludicrously pretentious fishwife had a further essentially political undercurrent in that it was a reassuringly farcical antidote to the memory of aggressive and intrusive women who had been visible from the march to Versailles on 5–6 October 1789 to the stereotype of the bloodthirsty *tricoteuses*. Responses to the play read it as both culturally and socially significant. On the one hand, such coarse slapstick was symptomatic of the degradation of taste wrought by the Revolution, a consequence of the deadening of sensibilities.[12] On the other hand, and more importantly, Madame Angot was celebrated as a form of deserved censure of the phenomenon of the *parvenu(e)*. Mercier specifically attributed the play's success to the rueful enthusiasm of those landowners who had lost property – and therefore the basis of their wealth – in the Revolution, a period during which all 'estates' had been confused, revelling in a theatrically enacted revenge on the *nouveaux riches*.[13]

In a slightly later play on the still troublesome theme of post-revolutionary *parvenus*, Jean-Baptiste Pujoulx's *Les Modernes enrichis* (1798), the mismatch between dress and corporeal identity is the prime cue to exposing unjustified pretentions. The protagonist is presented as thoroughly disreputable, having been bankrupt before 1789; a reviewer described his wife as still smacking of the village, and who continued to speak 'a patois which betrays at every moment his lack of education', and their son as 'a great ninny in gaiters and clogs'.[14]

The way that the dress and comportment of such figures gives away their essentially false identities is the central theme of prints accompanying the publication of the plays on this social phenomenon. In a print showing Corsse as Madame Angot in one of the later sequels (Figure 36), the figure's stiff, awkward pose is a parody of the gestures that were used in eighteenth-century theatrical portraits of actors declaiming their roles. The parodic nature of the image is heightened by the knowledge – spelt out in the caption – that this is a man dressed as a woman, and the woman in question is a fishwife got up as a *grande dame*. In the case of a frontispiece to another of Pujoulx's parodic polemics, *Le parvenu* (1801), the protagonist's self-compromising physical identity is played off against the antithetically elegant form and gesture of his interlocutor (Figure 37).

Figure 36 Anonymous: 'Physionomie théâtrale de Corsse, au Théâtre Montausier', from Le Mésangère, *Journal des dames et des modes*, no. 155, 25 messidor an VII/ 13 July 1799, plate 13, etching. British Library, London. Photograph: British Library.

The *parvenu* displays a grotesque mismatch between his fashionable *frac* and mid-calf-length *culottes*, and a thickened, bony body obtruding beneath. The figure's fundamental, irreducible vulgarity is shown in the way his body refuses to be disguised by modish tailoring; its coarse identity is indissimulable. In the same way that it was claimed that the adoption of new forms of signalling political authority had failed to disguise the inherent commonness and base morals of the Revolution's demagogues, the expensive artifice of new forms of fashions failed to mask the parvenu's true identity. The recognition of revolutionary appearances as at once mendacious and transitory is also the subject of a print from 1797, *Ce que j'étais, ce que je suis, ce que je vais être*, in which a *sans-culotte* metamorphoses into a *parvenu*, before arriving at his true destiny as a convict.[15]

Figure 37 Mariage after Fracasse: frontispiece to Jean-Baptiste Pujoulx, *Le Parvenu* (1801), 'Bravo! Encore . . . c'est cela . . . au parfait! Admirable! Vous ressemblez à Zéphir prêt à rejoindre l'Amour' (Bravo! Encore! . . . That's it . . . Perfect! Admirable! You resemble Zephir ready to rejoin Cupid), engraving. Bibliothèque Nationale de France, Paris. Photograph: Bibliothèque Nationale de France.

A complementary social phenomenon to this censure of the failed assumption of new identity and status by *parvenus* was the vestimentary reticence practiced by returned *émigrés*. Writing of his sojourn in Paris during the Consulate, J.F. Reichardt noted that *émigrés* eschewed participation in the newly formed official and social élite, either because they couldn't afford, or refused to purchase, the formal dress ('costumes d'apparat') necessary for attendance at official gatherings. Those who were sufficiently wealthy did not adopt such costume out of an 'esprit de caste', thereby expressing solidarity with their less well-off peers. Instead, they wore the commonplace *frac*, round hat, and shoes tied with ribbons (not silver buckles), a means to signal a self-elected social marginality.[16]

In the early days of the Revolution, the adoption of such a simple style of dress had been a means to express patriotic allegiance; now it served to convey a more complex form of socio-political positioning. At the same time, and clearly contrary to Reichardt's expectations, and those of many of their Parisian contemporaries: 'They seem to repudiate systematically anything which might recall former fashions.' As a result, he observed, they were alienated from the governmental sphere, where their experience and *savoir faire* might have been useful.[17] These *émigrés*' refusal to resuscitate Ancien Régime dress codes constitutes a kind of negative politics of dress, signifying by virtue of an absence of the available, predictable signs of status, including those from the Ancien Régime which their detractors expected them to wish to revive. Through such non-conformity, they contrived an understated but nonetheless explicit assertion of independence from the reconfigured social order.

It would be a truism to observe that the politics of revolutionary dress did not end with the disappearance of the badges, emblems, and costumes by means of which the Revolution, and its evolving political culture, had been given an explicit, programmatic vestimentary form – some items, of course, such as the mayoral sashes and the tricolore cockade, were remarkably durable. As successive chapters have made clear, key items of politicized dress – official costume and its variants, the liberty cap, and *sans-culotte* outfit – were the subject of a much more limited degree of adoption than has usually been assumed to have been the case. Rather, its legacy was most significantly manifest in the recognition that what mattered most was not what people chose to wear, but how such self-consciously enacted choices were to be recognized and interpreted.[18] Paradoxically, nothing exemplifies this more than the phenomenon of retaining the same forms of dress throughout the revolutionary years.[19] In memoirs and recollections, this recurs as an anomalous leitmotif, signalling either blasé inflexibility or courageous integrity. Such insouciance or intransigence reminds us of the unevenness and inconsistency of the vestimentary spectrum within which revolutionary dress became part of the lived experience of public political culture, not only on the level of collective, institutionalized practice, but also in terms of individuals' self-fashioning. These instances were presented as reassuring evidence of the ephemeral nature of politicized dress, and also the fact that it had been possible to survive the Revolution without sacrificing personal integrity. To this extent, the politics of dress in revolutionary France outlived and extended beyond the new forms of institutionalised political culture, coming to be assimilated into the micro-politics of individual identity. At the same time, for better or for worse, as Horace de Viel-Castel recognized, the politics of dress was an ineffaceable hallmark of the Revolution's legacy.[20]

Notes

1. 'Toute la distinction des conditions, nuance si essentielle au bonheur aujourd'hui, est presque dans la manière de porter les vêtements (Stendhal, *Histoire de la peinture en Italie* (Gallimard: Paris, 1996 [1817]), pp. 340–1). In a note to this statement, Stendhal added the supplementary observation: 'voyez à l'école de natation: on ne peut distinguer les conditions. On sait qu'une duchesse n'a jamais que trente ans pour un bourgeois . . .'

2. See Edna Hindie Lemay, *Dictionnaire des Constituants 1789–1791*, 2 vols (Universitas: Paris, 1991), vol. 1, pp. 350–1.

3. Félix Faulcon, *Fruits de la solitude et du malheur* (Paris, fructidor an IV [1796]), p. 9 note 1. See Chapter 3 for his contribution to the discussion of the cockade in an VII/ 1798.

4. For a more general reading of these images and their context, see Susan L. Siegfried, *The Art of Louis-Léopold Boilly. Modern Life in Napoleonic France* (Yale University Press: New Haven and London, 1995), pp. 78–9; and Aileen Ribeiro, *Fashion in the French Revolution* (Batsford: London, 1988), pp. 113–14.

5. Beauvert, *Caricatures politiques* (an VI, 1798), p. 4.

6. Ewa Lajer-Burcharth, *Necklines. The Art of Jacques-Louis David after the Terror* (Yale University Press: New Haven and Yale,), pp. 181–204. On the revival of illustrated fashion literature, see Raymond Gaudriault, *Répertoire de la gravure de mode française des origines à 1815* (Promodis: Paris, 1988).

7. L.-S. Mercier, *Le Nouveau Paris*, ed. dir. Jean-Claude Bonnet (Mercure de France: Paris, 1994), p. 505. To this extent, their feminization was a matter of cynical simulation, rather than being symptomatic of a deeper 'confusion des sexes'.

8. William Serman and Jean-Paul Bertaud, *Nouvelle Histoire de la France 1789–1815* (Fayard: Paris, 1998), p. 143.

9. *Ci-devant* embraced those who had under the Aucien Régime held titles and official positions. [Anon.] *De la situation intérieure de la république* (Paris, an V), quoted in a review in *Journal de Paris*, 4 March 1797, pp. 657–8, cit. Nicolas Wagner, 'Fête et dissolution sociale. A propos de quelques notices du *Journal de Paris* (1797)', in J. Ehrard and P. Viallaneix (eds), *Les Fêtes de la Révolution.* Colloque de Clermont-Ferrand (juin 1974) (Société des Études robespierristes: Paris, 1977), p. 528.

10. *Décade philosophique*, vol. 2, 1795, pp. 139–40. On the elision of perceptions of the end of the Terror and the end of the Revolution, see Bronislaw Baczko, *Comment sortir de la Terreur. Thermidor et Révolution* (Gallimard: Paris, 1989), p. 306.

11.   Pierre Frantz, 'Travestis poissards', *Revue des sciences humaines*, April–June 1983, vol. 61, no. 190, p. 17. On Madame Angot see Georges D'Outrepont, *Les Types populaires de la littérature française*, 2 vols (Brussels, 1926), vol. 2, pp. 462–77.

12.   Grimod de la Reynière, *Le Censeur dramatique*, 1797, vol. 1, pp. 4–7.

13.   L.-S. Mercier, *Néologie ou vocabulaire des mots nouveaux, à renouveller ou pris dans des acceptions nouvelles*, 2 vols (Paris, 1801), vol. 1, p. 36.

14.   *Mercure de France*, 19 January 1798, pp. 354–5. See also *Décade philosophique*, niv. an VI, p. 37.

15.   De Vinck Collection, vol. 51 Qb (1797), 52 C. 8050; ill. Michel Vovelle, *La Révolution française*: *images et récits*, 5 vols (Livre Club Diderot, Messidor: Paris, 19) vol. 5, p. 94.

16.   J.F. Reichardt, *Un Hiver à Paris sous le Consulat, 1802–1803*, trans. A. Laquiante (Plon: Paris, 1896), pp. 156–7. I am grateful to Tony Halliday for drawing this remark to my attention. In a report on official costumes dated 15 floréal an VII (4 May 1799), it was noted that, as a sign of the ubiquitous assimiliation of a republican style of dress: 'une grande partie des citoyens a déjà adopté la coiffure sans poudre, l'habit croisé avec des ganses sur la poitrine, le gilet court, le pantalon, les bottines et le chapeau rond' (Arch Nat F17 1232, pièce 5, fo 38 [30–40]).

17.   Reichardt, *Un Hiver à Paris*, pp. 156–7.

18.   Philip Mansel makes the point that, in the complex social and political circumstances of the early nineteenth century, a given type of costume, be it the *frac*, or *habit habillé*, did not carry a consistent signification – if it ever had. He cites the case of Cambacérès, former revolutionary and regicide, who continued to wear the *habit habillé* under the Empire – an 'antiquated' outfit which was not only not an indication of 'antiquated political beliefs', but the very antithesis of those that Cambacérès had held ('Monarchy, Uniform, and the Rise of the *frac* 1760–1830', *Past and Present*, August 1982, no. 96, p. 125).

19.   See Alisson de Chazet, *Mémoires, souvenirs, œuvres et portraits*, 3 vols (Paris, 1837), vol. 1, p. 389; and, on Martin Michel Charles Gaudin, duc de Gaëte (1756–1841) who was noted as continuing to wear old-fashioned dress during the Consulate, Philippe Séguy, *Histoire des modes sous l'Empire* (Tallandier: Paris, 1988), p. 72, and J. Lucas-Dubreton, *Le Culte de Napoléon 1815–1848* (Albin Michel: Paris, 1960), pp. 56–7. The postrevolutionary lexicon had a word for this 'type', 'les immobiles'; see Rabbé, Vieille de Boisjolin, Sainte-Preuve (eds), *Biographie universelle et portative des contemporains*, 5 vols (Paris, 1835), vol. 1, 'Vocabulaire complet de nouvelles dignités, des termes introduits dans la langue française depuis la Révolution française, et de ceux dont la véritable acception a été dénaturée', pp. 1–14; and, more recently, Alan B. Spitzer, 'Malicious Memories: Restoration politics and a prosopography of turncoats', *French Historical Studies*, Winter 2001, vol. 24, no. 1, pp. 37–61.

20.   See for example F.C. de Damery, *Projet de loi supprimant les habits, chapeaux et redingotes et décrétant la blouse, la veste et la casquette comme costume national* (Paris, n.d. [1848–9]).

Bibliography

Manuscript and Archival Sources

Archives des Musées Nationaux, Louvre, Paris
Musée des Souverains. MS 1–23.

Archives Nationales, Paris
Report on official costume, 15th floréal an VII [4 May 1799]
F^{17} 1232, pièce 5 f° 30–40.

Bibliothèque Historique de la Ville de Paris
Alfred de Liesville papers. MS 2118–22.
Palloy Papers and Documents 104142.

Bibliothèque Nationale de France
Letter from Antoine Gorsas (April 1792) to Palloy, MS Nouv. Acq. Fr.
308 f° 278.

Published Works

Anonymous works are listed under their title.

89 Le Livre du bicentenaire, Mission du Bicentenaire de la Révolution française et de la déclaration des droits de l'homme et du citoyen, Le Chêne-Hachette: Paris, 1990.

A messieurs de la garde nationale parisienne, sur le prix qu'ils doivent attacher à leur uniforme, n.d.

Actes du Ier congrès international d'histoire du costume.Centro Internazionale delle Arti et del Costume, Palazzo Grassi, Venice 31 August–7 September 1952, Stampa Strada: Milan, 1955.

Adresse à l'Assemblée nationale, par les soldats du cent-deuxième régiment, accusés sans fondement d'avoir voulu arborer la cocarde blanche, ce signe de proscription qu'ils ont tous en horreur, présentée le 10 juin 1792, l'an quatrième de la liberté.

Adresse de la section du Marais à la Convention Nationale, n.d. [1792].

Adresse présentée par les clercs de notaires de Paris, n.d. [1789?].

Affiches de la Commune de Paris 1793–1794, Éditions d'Histoire Sociale: Paris, 1975.

➤ *The Age of Napoleon: Costume from Revolution to Empire: 1789–1815*, Metropolitan Museum of Art: New York, 1989.

Agulhon, Maurice, *Marianne au combat: l'imagerie et la symbolique républicaine de 1789 à 1880*, Flammarion: Paris, 1979.

—— *Marianne au pouvoir: l'imagerie et la symbolique républicaine de 1880 à 1914*, Flammarion: Paris, 1989.

Anatole Demidoff, Prince of San Donato (1812–70), Wallace Collection: London, 1994.

Andress, David, *Massacre at the Champ de Mars. Popular Dissent and Political Culture in the French Revolution*, Royal Historical Society and Boydell Press: Woodbridge, 2000.

Andrews, Richard M., 'Social Structures, Political Élites and Ideology in Revolutionary Paris, 1792–1794: a Critical Evaluation of Albert Soboul's *Les Sans-culottes parisiens en l'an II*', *Journal of Social History*, 1985, vol. 19, pp. 71–112.

Andrey, Georges, 'Guillaume Tell, héros républicain ou les métamorphoses d'un mythe (XVIe–XVIIIe siècles)', in Michel Vovelle (ed.), *Révolution et République, l'exception française*, Kiné: Paris, 1994.

Andrieux, François Guillaume Jean Stanislas, *Opinion d'Andrieux (de la Seine), sur le projet de loi relatif à la cocarde nationale. Séance du 14 floréal an 7.*

Anecdotes intéressantes et peu connues sur la Révolution, Paris, 1790.

Anninger, Anne. 'Costumes of the Convention: art as agent of social change in revolutionary France', *Harvard Library Bulletin*, vol. 30, 1952, pp. 179–203.

Appendice. Les dix articles des juremens, des faux sermens, prononcés par Louis Capet, en présence des chevaliers à Poignards, trouvés dans la doublure de sa culotte le jour de sa mort, Paris [1793].

Arasse, Daniel, *La Guillotine et l'imaginaire de la Terreur*, Flammarion: Paris, 1987.

—— *La Guillotine dans la Révolution française*, Musée de la Révolution française, Vizille, 1987.

Arnault, Antoine-Vincent, *Souvenirs d'un sexagénaire*, 4 vols, Paris, 1833.

L'Art de l'estampe et la Révolution française, Musée Carnavalet, Paris, 1977.

Asfour, Amal, 'Champfleury and the Popular Arts', Oxford University, D.Phil., 1990.

Aulard, François Alphonse, *Paris pendant la réaction thermidorienne et sous le Directoire. Recueil de documents pour l'histoire de l'esprit public à Paris*, 5 vols, Paris, 1899–1902.

—— *Paris sous le Consulat. Recueil de documents pour l'histoire de l'esprit ˙ public à Paris*, 4 vols, Cerf: Paris, 1903–1909.

—— *La Société des Jacobins. Recueil de documents pour l'histoire du club des Jacobins de Paris*, 6 vols, Paris, 1889–97.

Babeau, Albert, *Le Louvre et son histoire*, Paris, 1895.

Baczko, Bronislaw, *Comment sortir de la Terreur. Thermidor et Révolution*, Gallimard: Paris, 1989.

Baecque, Antoine de, 'La figure du jacobin dans l'imagerie politique (1795–1799): naissance d'une obsession', *Sources: travaux historiques*, 1988, no. 14, pp. 61–70.

—— 'Le discours anti-noble (1787–1792): aux origines d'un slogan "Le Peuple contre les gros"', *Revue d'histoire moderne et contemporaine*, 1989, vol. 36, pp. 3–28.

—— *Le Corps de l'histoire: métaphores et politique (1770–1800)*, Calmann-Lévy: Paris, 1993.

—— *La Gloire et l'effroi. Sept morts sous la Terreur*, Grasset: Paris, 1997.

—— and Jacques Guilhaumou, 'Le Dernier Carnaval', in *Le Monde de la Révolution française*, February 1989, no. 2, p. 12.

Baldet, Marcel, *La Vie quotidienne dans les armées de Napoléon*, Hachette: Paris, 1964.

Bann, Stephen, *The Clothing of Clio: a study of the representation of history in nineteenth-century Britain and France*, Cambridge University Press: Cambridge, 1984.

—— *Romanticism and the Rise of History*, Twayne: New York, 1995.

Barailon, Jean-François, *Projet sur le costume particulier à donner à chacun des deux conseils législatifs, et à tous les fonctionnaires publics de la République française, présenté à la Convention nationale, 13 fructidor an III*.

Barbet de Jouy, Henri, *Notice des antiquités, objets du Moyen Âge, de la Renaissance, et des temps modernes composant le Musée des Souverains*, Paris, 1866.

Barbier, Louis, *Notice sur l'exhumation du corps du roi Louis XVI*, Paris, 1815.

Barras, Jean-Nicolas-Paul-François, vicomte de, 'Fragments des Mémoires de Barras', in *Bibliothèque des mémoires relatifs à l'histoire de France pendant le dix-huitième siècle*, nouvelle série, vol. 29, ed. M. De Lescure, Paris, 1875.

Barthes, Roland, *Le bleu est à la mode cette année et autres articles*, Éditions de l'Institut Français de la Mode: Paris, 2001.

Baticle, Jeannine, 'La Seconde Mort de Lepeletier de Saint-Fargeau. Recherches sur le sort du tableau de David', *BSHAF*, 1988, pp. 131–45.

Bault, *Récit exact des derniers momens de captivité de la reine, depuis le 11 septembre 1793, jusqu'au 16 octobre suivante, par la dame Bault, veuve de son dernier concierge*, Paris, 1817.

Beaucourt, marquis de, *Captivité et derniers moments de Louis XVI, récits originaux et documents officiels, recueillis et publiés pour la société de l'histoire contemporaine par le marquis de Beaucourt*, 2 vols, Paris, 1892.

Beauvert, *Caricatures politiques*, an VI, 1798.

Bellet, Roger, 'Mythe jacobin et mythe révolutionnaire chez Jules Vallès de '93 à la Commune de Paris', in Yves Charles (ed.), *Mythe et Révolutions*, Presses Universitaires de Grenoble: Grenoble, 1990, pp. 227–44.

Benzaken, Jean-Charles, 'L'Allégorie de la Liberté et son bonnet dans l'iconologie des monnaies et médailles de la Révolution française', *Gazette des archives*, 1989, nos 146–7, pp. 338–77.

Bertrand, Jean-Paul, *La Révolution armée. Les soldats-citoyens et la Révolution française*, Laffont: Paris, 1979.

Bianchi, Serge, *La Révolution culturelle de l'an II. Élites et peuple 1789–1799*, Aubier: Paris, 1982.

Les Bienfaits de la Révolution, 1791.

Bindman, David, *The Shadow of the Guillotine: Britain and the French Revolution*, British Museum, London, 1989.

Bisaccioni, Majolino, *Historia delle guerre civili di questi ultimi tempi*, Venice, 1653.

Biver, Marie-Louise, *Le Panthéon à l'époque révolutionnaire*, PUF: Paris, 1982.

Blanc, Louis, *Histoire de la Révolution française*, 15 vols, Paris, 1878.

Blanc, Olivier, *La Dernière Lettre. Prisons et condamnés de la Révolution 1793–1794*, Robert Laffont: Paris, 1984.

Boedels, Jacques, 'Le costume des gens de justice pendant la Révolution de 1789 à 1793', in Robert Badinter (ed.), *Une Autre Justice, 1789–*

1799. Contributions à l'histoire de la justice sous la Révolution française, Fayard: Paris, 1989, pp. 325–44.

—— *Les habits du pouvoir. La Justice*, Antébi: Paris, 1992.

Boilleau d'Ausson, Jacques, *Instruction sur l'arbre et le bonnet et de la liberté* [1792].

Bonald, vicomte de, *François Chabot, membre de la Convention (1756–1794)*, Emile-Paul: Paris, 1908.

Bonnaffé, Edmond, *Les Collectionneurs de l'ancienne France*, Paris, 1873.

[Bonnemaison, Antoine Jean Thomas] *Les Chemises rouges, ou mémoir pour servir à l'histoire du règne des anarchistes*, 2 vols, Paris, an VIII.

Le Bonnet de la République, air de vaudeville des Visitandines, Paris, n.d.

Bonnet, Jean-Claude, 'La Mort de Simonneau', in *Mouvements populaires et conscience sociale XVe–XIXe siècles*, Maloire: Paris, 1985, pp. 671–6.

—— (ed.), *La Mort de Marat*, Flammarion: Paris, 1986.

—— and Philippe Roger (eds), *La Légende de la Révolution au XXe siècle. De Gance à Renoir, de Romain Rolland à Claude Simon*, Flammarion: Paris, 1988.

Bonneville, François, *Portraits des personnages célèbres de la Révolution*, 2 vols, Paris, 1796.

Boppe, A. and R. Bonnet, *Les Vignettes emblématiques sous la Révolution*, Berger-Levrault: Paris, 1911.

Bordes, Philippe, *Le Serment du jeu de paume de Jacques-Louis David*, Editions de la Réunion des Musées Nationaux: Paris, 1983.

—— '"Brissotin enragé, ennemi de Robespierre": David, conventionnel et terroriste', in Régis Michel (ed.), *David contre David*, 2 vols, Editions de la Réunion des Musées nationaux: Paris, 1993, vol. 2, pp. 319–47.

—— and Régis Michel (eds), *Aux Armes et aux arts! Les arts de la Révolution 1789–1799*, Adam Biro: Paris, 1988.

—— and Alain Chevalier, *Catalogue des Peintures, Sculptures et Dessins*, Musée de la Révolution francaise, Vizille, 1996.

Bosseno, Christian-Marc, 'Acteurs et spectateurs des fêtes officielles parisiennes', in Valérie Noëlle Jouffre (dir.), *Fêtes et Révolution*, Délégation à l'Action Artistique de la Ville de Paris: Paris, 1989, pp. 112–33.

Bottet, Maurice, *Le Bouton de l'Armée française*, Paris, 1908.

Bouineau, Jacques, *Les Toges du pouvoir (1789–1799), ou la Révolution de droit antique*, Université de Toulouse-le Mirail: Toulouse, 1986.

Bourdin, Isabelle, *Les Sociétés populaires à Paris pendant la Révolution française*, Sirey: Paris, 1937.

Bourdon, Léonard, *Recueil des actions héroïques et civiques des républicains français*, Paris, an II.

Boutier, Jean and Philippe Boutry, *Les Sociétés populaires*, Éditions de l'École des Hautes Etudes en Sciences Sociales: Paris, 1992, part 6 of *Atlas de la Révolution française*, eds Serge Bonin and Claude Langlois.

Boyer, Ferdinand, 'Deux documents sur les Tuileries: l'état des appartements en septembre 1792 et l'inventaire des peintures en décembre', *BSHAF*, 1964, pp. 193–9.

Braesch, Frédéric, *La Commune du dix août 1792. Etude sur l'histoire de Paris du 20 juin au 2 décembre 1792*, Hachette: Paris, 1911.

—— *Le Père Duchesne*, Paris, 1938.

Bretons ou Chouans . . . Les paysans bretons dans la peinture d'histoire d'inspiration révolutionnaire au XIXe siècle, Musée des beaux-arts, Quimper; Musée d'histoire, Saint-Brieuc, 1989.

Brodhurst, Audrey C., 'The French Revolution Collections in the British Library', *British Library Journal*, vol. 2, no. 2, Autumn 1976, pp. 138–58.

Brown, Howard G., *War, Revolution, and the Bureaucratic State. Politics and Army Administration in France 1791–1795*, Clarendon Press: Oxford, 1995.

Brunel, Françoise and Sylvain Goujon, *Les Martyrs de prairial: textes et documents inédits*, Georg: Geneva, 1992.

Brunon, Raoul, 'Uniforms of the Napoleonic Era', in *The Age of Napoleon: Costume from Revolution to Empire 1789–1815*, Metropolitan Museum of Art, New York, 1989, pp. 179–201.

Brunot, F. with C.G.E.M. Bruneau and A. François, *Histoire de la langue française*, 13 vols, Paris, 1906–79.

Bulletin de la société de l'histoire du costume, Paris, 1907–1911.

Burke, Bobby, 'The Liberty Cap in America and France 1765–1789', Masters thesis, University of Pennsylvania, 1971.

Burtin, H., *Le Faubourg Saint-Marcel à l'époque révolutionnaire*, Paris, 1983.

Cahuet, Albéric, 'Les souvenirs révolutionnaires de la collection Lavedan', *L'Illustration*, 15 April 1933, no. 4702, pp. 450–2.

Campardon, Emile. (ed.), *Marie-Antoinette à la Conciergerie du Ier août au 16 octobre 1793. Pièces originales conservés aux Archives de l'Empire, suivies de notes historiques et du procès imprimé de la reine*, Paris, 1863.

Carrot, Georges, 'La Garde nationale 1789–1871', 3e cycle doctoral thesis, Université de Nice, 1979.

Catalogue des objets d'art, de curiosité et d'ameublement . . . appartenant à M. Henri Lavedan, Hôtel Drouot, Paris, 26/27 April 1933.

Catalogue des objets formant l'exposition historique de la Révolution française, Société de la Révolution française: Paris, 1889.

Catalogue d'une très belle collection de recueils des costumes XVIIIe et début du XIXe siècle, aquarelles originales appartenant à M. le vicomte J. de Jonghe, Giraud-Badin: Paris, 1930.

Cavailhé, Jean-Pierre, 'De la construction des apparences au culte de la transparence. Simulation et dissimulation 16e–18e siècles', *Littératures classiques*, Autumn 1998, vol. 34, pp. 73–102.

Cave, Christophe, Denis Reynaud, Danièle Willemart, Henri Duranton (eds), *1793. L'Esprit des journaux*, Université de Saint-Etienne: Saint-Etienne, 1993.

Cérémonial de la confédération française, fixé par la ville de Paris pour le 14 juillet 1790.

Cérémonie funèbre en mémoire des ministres français assassinés près de Rastadt par les troupes autrichiens. Programme, 3 prairial an VII.

Champfleury [pseud. Jules François Félix Husson], *Histoire des faïences patriotiques sous la Révolution*, Paris, 1867.

Chang, Ting, 'Alfred Bruyas: the mythology and practice of art collecting and patronage in nineteenth-century France', University of Sussex, D.Phil., 1996.

Charavay, Etienne, *Le Centenaire de 1789 et le musée de la Révolution*, Paris, 1886.

Charles, Robert-Jean, 'Armes de récompense et armes d'honneur', *Revue de la société des amis du Musée de l'armée*, no. 60, 1957–1958, pp. 16–18.

Charrié, Pierre, *Drapeaux et étendards de la Révolution et de l'Empire*, Copernic: Paris, 1982.

Chassin, Charles Louis (ed.), *Les Élections et les cahiers de Paris en 1789*, Paris, 1888.

Chassin, C.L. and Hennet Léon, *Les Volontaires nationaux pendant la Révolution*, 3 vols, Paris, 1899–1906.

Chateaubriand, François René, vicomte de, *Mémoires d'outre-tombe*, 3 vols, Gallimard: Paris, 1951.

Chaudonneret, Marie-Claude, *La Figure de la République: le concours de 1848*, Éditions de la Réunion des Musées Nationaux: Paris, 1987.

—— 'Le Mythe de la Révolution', in Philippe Bordes and Régis Michel (eds), *Aux Armes et aux arts! Les arts de la Révolution 1789–1799*, Adam Biro: Paris, 1988, pp. 313–40.

Chaulsit, Hector, 'Couplet sur le bonnet rouge, par le citoyen Hector Chaulsit', *Portefeuille politique et littéraire par le citoyen L****, 16 April 1795/27 germ. an III, no. 25, p. 99.

Chazet, Alisson de, *Mémoires, souvenirs, œuvres et portraits*, 3 vols, Paris, 1837.

Le Chevalier Wicar, peintre, dessinateur et collectionneur lillois, Musée des beaux-arts, Lille, 1984.

Chuquet, *Lettres de 1792*, 1st series Paris, 1911.

Clay, Richard, 'Saint-Sulpice de Paris: art, politics, and sacred space in revolutionary Paris 1789–1795', *Object*, no. 1, October 1998, pp. 5–22.

—— 'Signs of Power: Iconoclasm in Paris 1789–1795', Ph.D., University College London, 1999.

Cléry, Jean-Baptiste, *Journal de ce qui s'est passé à la tour du Temple pendant la captivité du roi Louis XVI roi de France*, London 1798; and Jacques Brosses (ed.), Mercure de France: Paris, 1987.

Cobb, Richard, 'The Revolutionary Mentality in France 1793–94', *History*, October 1957, vol. 42, no. 146, pp. 181–96.

—— *Les Armées révolutionnaires, instrument de la Terreur dans les départements, avril 1793–floréal an II*, 2 vols, Paris, La Haye, 1961; trans. Marianne Elliott, *The People's Army: the armées révolutionnaires, instrument of the Terror in the departments April 1793 to Floréal Year II*, Yale University Press: New Haven and London, 1987.

——— *The Police and the People. French Popular Protest 1789–1820*, Oxford University Press: Oxford, 1970.

—— *Paris and its Provinces 1792–1802*, Oxford University Press: Oxford, 1975.

—— *Death in Paris. The Records of the Basse-Geôle de la Seine October 1795–September 1801 Vendémiaire Year IV–Fructidor Year IX*, Oxford University Press: Oxford, 1978.

—— and Colin Jones (eds), *The French Revolution*, Simon and Schuster: London, 1988.

Cochin, Auguste and Charles Charpentier, *Les Actes du gouvernement révolutionnaire 23 août–27 juillet 1794*, 3 vols, Picard: Paris, 1920.

Code pénal, 2 vols, Paris, 1810.

Collection d'un amateur. Révolution française. Dessins, estampes, médailles, livres, documents, Hôtel Drouot, 12 Oct. 1973.

Collection révolutionnaire de Monsieur X, Hôtel Drouot (Ader, Picard, Tajan), Paris, 16 May 1990.

Combes, Louis, *Épisodes et curiosités révolutionnaires*, Dreyfous: Paris, n.d.

Comité militaire de l'hôtel de ville de Paris, séant au palais Cardinal. Règlement concernant les abus introduits dan l'usage des habits d'uniforme, et dans la faculté de se faire remplacer, 14 April 1790.

Condart, Laurence, *La Gazette de Paris. Un journal royaliste pendant la Révolution française (1789–1792)*, L'Harmattan: Paris, 1995.

Considérations sur les avantages de changer le costume français par la société populaire et républicaine des arts, n.d.; reprinted in *Décade philosophique*, 10 floréal an II, pp. 60–2.

Corps législatif. Conseil des Cinq-Cents et des Anciens. Les commissions des inspecteurs des conseils des Cinq-Cents et des Anciens, réunies. Extrait du procès-verbal du 6 vendémiaire, l'an sixième de la République française, une et indivisible.

Correspondance de Napoléon Ier, 32 vols, Paris, 1858–1870.

Costumes et uniformes, revue historique, documentaire, 19 February 1914–

Les Costumes françois représentans les différens états du royaume, avec les habillemens propres à chaque état et accompagnés de réflexions critiques et morales, Paris, 1776.

Courtine, Jean-Jacques and Claudine Haroche, *Histoire du visage. Exprimer et taire ses émotions (XVIe–XIXe siècles)*, Payot: Paris, 1988.

Cubitt, Geoffrey, 'Denouncing conspiracy in the French Revolution', *Renaissance and Modern Studies*, 1989, vol. 33, pp. 143–58.

Cuno, James (ed.), *French Caricature and the French Revolution 1789–1799*, Grunwald Center for the Graphic Arts, Wight Art Gallery, University of California, Los Angeles, 1989.

Dallet, Sylvie, *La Révolution française et le cinéma. De Lumière à la Télévision*, L'Herminier: Paris, 1988.

—— and François Gendron, *Filmographie mondiale de la Révolution*, L'Herminier: Paris, 1989.

Damery, F.C. de, *Projet de loi supprimant les habits, chapeaux et redingotes, et décretant la blouse, la veste et la casquette comme costume national*, Paris, n.d. [1848]

Darnton, Robert, *The Great Cat Massacre, and other episodes in French Cultural History*, Vintage: New York, 1985.

Dauban, A., *Paris en 1794 et 1795*, Paris, 1869.

Jacques-Louis David 1748–1824, Editions de la Réunion des Musées Nationaux: Paris, 1989.

Dayot, A., *La Révolution française. Constituante, Législative, Convention, Directoire, d'après les peintures, sculptures, gravures, médaillons, objets du temps*, Paris, 1903.

Dédouit, Alfred, *Souvenirs inédits. Bayeux sous la Révolution, le Consulat et l'Empire*, Bellême, 1892.

Delécluze, Etienne-Jean, *Journal de Delécluze 1824–1828*, ed. R. Baschet, Grasset: Paris, 1948.

Delpierre, Madeleine, 'La collection de costumes du Musée Carnavalet', *Bulletin du Musée Carnavalet*, vol. 4, May 1951, pp. 9–11.

—— 'A propos d'un manteau de représentant du peuple de 1798 récemment offert au Musée du costume', *Bulletin du Musée Carnavalet*, no. 1, 1972, pp. 13–23.

—— 'Le Musée de la mode et du costume de la Ville de Paris au Palais Galliera', in *I Duchi di Galliera. Alta finanza, arte e filantropia tra Genova e l'Europa nell'Ottocento*, 2 vols, Marietti: Genoa, 1991, vol. 2, pp. 923–33.

De Neuville/Detaille: deux peintres témoins de l'histoire, Editions IOP: Musée du château de Vançay, 1981.

Départ de Filous et des brigands, contrôlé sur le visage de la lettre F. Prononcé le dimanche 29 mai 1791, à la société des amis de la constitution, séante à Paris, par N. Citoyen actif.

Déposition sur les tristes événemens de la journée du 20 juin 1792, comme témoin oculaire, et réflexions politiques [1792].

Description de la fête du pacte fédératif, du 14 juillet, fixé par la ville, avec règlement de la police. Grande Illumination [1790].

Description fidèle de tout ce qui a précédé, accompagné et suivi la cérémonie de la confédération nationale du 14 juillet 1790.

Desmoulins, Camille, *Œuvres de Camille Desmoulins*, 2 vols, Paris, 1838.

—— *Le Vieux Cordelier*, Albert Mathiez and Henri Calvet (eds), Colin: Paris, 1936.

Dessaux-Lebrethon, Louis, *Mes Angoisses de 30 heures, dans les journées des 5 et 6 avril 1814, pour avoir, le premier, arboré le signe chéri des français: la cocarde blanche*, Ghent, May 1815.

D'Estrée, Paul, *Le Théâtre sous la Terreur 1793–1794*, Émile-Paul: Paris, 1913.

Détail du combat qui a eu lieu à Metz, entre la Garde nationale, les troupes de la ligne, et des soldats de l'empereur, qui ont voulu forcer la garnison à prendre la cocarde blanche, 1790.

Détail et ordre de la Marche et cérémonie de l'entrée de la fête en l'honneur des soldats de Châteauvieux, Paris, 1792.

Devocelle, Jean-Marc, 'Costume politique et politique du costume: approches théoriques et idéologiques du costume pendant la Révolution française', mémoire de maîtrise, Université de Paris I, 1988, 2 vols.

—— 'D'un costume politique à une politique du costume', in *Modes et Révolution 1780–1804*, Editions Paris-Musées: Musée de la mode et du costume: Paris, 1989, pp. 83–103.

—— 'Costume et citoyenneté', *Révolution française*, Actes des 113e et 114e congrès nationaux des sociétés savantes (Strasbourg, 1988–Paris, 1989), section d'histoire moderne et contemporaine, Editions du Comité des Travaux Historiques et Scientifiques: Paris, 1991, pp. 313–32.

—— 'La Cocarde directorielle: dérives d'un symbole révolutionnaire', *AHRF*, 1992, vol. 69, no. 3, pp. 355–66.

Dialogue entre le ruban rouge et le ruban aux trois couleurs. Fable, Paris [1790?].

Dictionnaire des usages socio-politiques (1770–1815), 4 vols, Klincksieck: Saint-Cloud, 1985–89.

Dictionnaire national et anecdotique, pour servir à l'intelligence des mots dont notre langue s'est enrichie depuis la Révolution, etc., 1790.

Les Différens Effets de la cocarde nationale, dédiée à la nation, ou lettre écrite par Dominique-Antonio-François-Jean-Népomucène-Pancrace Meresos y Poralipipos, à sa soeur, le 4 septembre 1789, 1790.

Diogène à Paris, 1790.

Dix ans de médailles, insignes et récompenses révolutionnaires. Souvenirs historiques 1789–1799, Musée de Charleville-Mézières, 1989.

Dominique-Vivant Denon. L'œil de Napoléon, Éditions de la Réunion des Musées Nationaux: Paris, 1999.

Dommanget, Maurice, 'Le Symbolisme et le prosélytisme à Beauvais et dans l'Oise: la cocarde et l'autel de la patrie', *AHRF*, 1925, vol. 2, pp. 131–50.

—— 'Le Symbolisme et le prosélytisme révolutionnaire à Beauvais et dans l'Oise: le bonnet rouge, le livre de la loi, l'arche et la bannière constitutionnelle', *AHRF*, 1926, vol. 3, pp. 47–58.

—— 'Le Symbolisme et le prosélytisme à Beauvais et dans l'Oise: les arbres de la liberté', *AHRF*, 1926, vol. 3, pp. 345–62.

—— *Histoire du drapeau rouge*, Paris, n.d.

Donzelli, Giuseppe, *Partenope Liberata overo Racconto dell'Heroica risoluzione fatta dal Popolo di Napoli per sottarsi con tutto il Regno dall'Insopportabil; Giogo delli Spagnuoli*, Naples, 1647; re-ed. Antonio Altamura, Naples, 1974.

Dörner, Eleonore, *Études mithraïques*, Leiden, 1978.

Douene, Colonel Bernard, 'Hommage à Jean Brunon', *Revue de la société des amis du Musée de l'Armée*, 1984, no. 89, pp. 5–18.

D'Outrepont, Georges, *Les Types populaires de la littérature française*, 2 vols, Brussels, 1926.

Dowd, David. L., *Pageant Master of the Republic: Jacques-Louis David and the French Revolution*, University of Nebraska Press: Lincoln, NE, 1948.

Jean-Germain Drouais 1763–1788, Musée des beaux-arts, Rennes, 1988.

Drouot 1989. Art and Auction in France, Compagnie des Commissaires-priseurs de Paris: Paris,1989.

Dubois, Madeleine, 'Les Origines du Musée Carnavalet. La Formation des collections et leur accroissement 1870–1897', 3 vols, 1947, École du Louvre.

Duffay, J., [attr.] *Le Tailleur patriote, ou les Habits de Jean-Foutre*, Paris, 1790.

Duplantier, Jacques Paul Frontin, *Corps législatif. Conseil des Cinq-Cents. Opinion de J.P.F. Duplantier, député du département de la Gironde, sur le projet relatif à la cocarde nationale. Séance du 3 floréal an VII*.

Duprat, Annie, 'Repique est Capet: Louis XVI dans la caricature, naissance d'une langage politique', 3 vols, Université de Rouen, 1991.

—— 'Louis XVI condamné par les images', *L'Information historique*, 1992, vol. 5, no. 4, pp. 133–41.

Dupuy, Roger, *La Garde nationale et les débuts de la Révolution en Ille-et-Vilaine (1789–mars 1793)*, Klincksieck: Paris, 1972.

—— and Jean Meyer, 'Bonnets rouges et blancs bonnets', *Annales de Bretagne et des pays de l'Ouest*, 1975, vol. 72, pp. 405–26.

Durieux, Joseph, *Les Vainqueurs de la Bastille*, Paris, 1911.

Duval, Georges, *Souvenirs de la Terreur de 1788 à 1793*, 4 vols, Paris, 1841.

Duval-Jouve, J., *Montpellier pendant la Révolution*, 2 vols, Montpellier, 1881.

Ehrard, Jean and Paul Viallaneix (eds), *Les Fêtes de la Révolution*. Colloque Clermont-Ferrand (juin 1974), Société des Etudes robespierristes: Paris, 1977.

Elliott, Grace Dalrymple, *Journal of my Life during the French Revolution*, London, 1859.

Elyada, Ouzi, 'La Presse populaire parisienne et le temps de carnaval: 1788–1791', in Michel Vovelle (ed.), *Les Images de la Révolution française*, 4 vols, Pergamon: Oxford, 1990, vol. 1, pp. 108–17.

Emblèmes de la Liberté: L'image de la république dans l'art du XVe au XXe siècle, co-ord. Dario Gamboni and Georg Germann with François de Capitani, Bernisches Historisches Museum; Stampfli: Berne, 1991.

Encyclopédie, ou Dictionnaire raisonné des sciences, des arts, et des métiers, par une société de gens de lettres, D. Diderot and D'Alembert (eds), 17 vols, 1751–65.

Epstein, James A., 'Understanding the Cap of Liberty: Symbolic Practice and Social Conflict in Early 19th-century England', *Past and Present*, February 1989, no. 122, pp. 74–118.

—— *Radical Expression. Political Language, Ritual, and Symbol in England 1790–1850*, Oxford University Press: New York and Oxford, 1994.

E.S.B., A. de La Borderie, and Boris Porchev, *Les Bonnets rouges*, 10:18: Paris, 1975.

Eschasseriaux jeune, René, *Corps législatif. Conseil des Cinq-Cents. Opinion de Eschasseriaux sur le projet de résolution relatif à la cocarde nationale. 3 floréal an VII.*

Essai sur la méthode à employer pour juger les ouvrages des beaux-arts du dessin, et principalement ceux qui sont exposés au Salon du Louvre, par une société d'artistes, Paris, 1791.

La Famille royale à Paris. De l'histoire à la légende, Musée Carnavalet: Paris, 1993.

Farge, Arlette, *Vivre dans la rue à Paris au XVIIIe siècle*, Gallimard: Paris, 1979.

Farge, René, 'Camille Desmoulins au jardin du Palais-Royal', *Annales révolutionnaires*, 1914, vol. 7, pp. 646–74.

—— 'Le local du club des Cordeliers et le coeur de Marat', *AHRF*, 1927, no. 4, pp. 320–47.

Faulcon, Félix, *Opinion de Félix Faulcon, député de la Vienne, sur le projet de résolution relatif à la cocarde nationale. Prairial an VII.*

—— *Fruits de la solitude et du malheur*, Paris, fructidor an IV.

Faust, Bernard Christoph, *Sur le vêtement libre, unique et national à l'usage des enfants*, Paris, 1792.

Fénelon, François de Salignac de La Mothe, *Les Aventures de Télémaque, fils d'Ulysse (1699); Telemachus, son of Ulysses*, ed. and trans. Patrick Riley, Cambridge University Press: Cambridge, 1994.

Ferat, P.S., *Cocarde royale et de la liberté aux couleurs distinctives de l'Hôtel-de-Ville de Paris*, 1789.

Fleurs de lys et bonnet phrygien. Raymond Jeanvrot et Jacques Calvet. Deux collectionneurs bordelais regardent la Révolution française, Association des conservateurs des Musées d'Aquitaine: Périgueux, 1989.

Frantz, Pierre, 'Travestis poissards', *Revue des sciences humaines*, April–June 1983, vol. 61, no. 190, pp. 7–20.

Freiheit, Gleichheit, Brüderlichkeit, Germanisches Nationalmuseum: Nürnberg, 1989.

French Painting 1774–1830: The Age of Revolution, Detroit Institute of Arts; Cleveland; Metropolitan Museum of Art, New York, 1974.

Furet, François, *Penser la Révolution française*, Gallimard: Paris, 1978.

—— and Mona Ozouf, (eds), *Dictionnaire critique de la Révolution française*, Flammarion: Paris, 1988.

Gamboni, Dario, '"Instrument de la tyrannie, signe de la liberté": la fin de l'Ancien Régime en Suisse et la conservation des emblèmes politiques', in *L'Art et les révolutions. Actes du XXVIIe congrès international d'histoire de l'art. Strasbourg 1–7 Sept. 1989. section IV, Les Iconoclasmes*, Société alsacienne pour le développement de l'histoire de l'art: Strasbourg, 1992, pp. 213–28.

—— *The Destruction of Art: Iconoclasm and Vandalism since the French Revolution*, Reaktion: London, 1997.

Garrioch, David, *Neighbourhood and Community in Paris 1740–1790*, Cambridge University Press: Cambridge, 1986.

—— *The Formation of the Parisian Bourgeoisie, 1690–1830*, Harvard University Press: Cambridge MA and London, 1996.

—— 'Parisian Women and the October Days of 1789', *Social History*, vol. 24, no. 3, Oct. 1999, pp. 231–49.

Gastin, Louis-Alexandre, *Opinion de Gastin, sur le projet de résolution relatif à la cocarde nationale. Séance du 29 floréal an VII*.

Gaudriault, Raymond, *Répertoire de la gravure de mode française des origines à 1815*, Promodis: Paris, 1988.

Gauthier, abbé F.L., *Traité contre l'amour des parures, et le luxe des habits*, Paris, 1779; 2nd edn 1780.

Gautier de Syonnet, Jacques-Louis, see: Sionnet

Geffroy, Annie, 'Sans-culotte(s) (novembre 1790–juin 1792)', in A. Geffroy, J. Guilhaumou and S. Moreno, *Dictionnaire des usages sociopolitiques (1770–1815)*, Klincksieck: Saint-Cloud, 1985, pp. 157–86.

—— 'Étude en rouge 1789–98', *Cahiers de léxicologie*, 1987, no. 51, pp. 119–48.

—— 'Désignation, dénégation: la légende des sans-culottes (1780–1980)', in Christian Croisille, Jean Ehrard, and Marie-Claude Chemin (eds), *La Légende de la Révolution. Actes du colloque international de Clermont-Ferrand (juin 1986)*, Université de Blaise Pascal (Clermont II), Centre de Recherches Révolutionnaires et Romantiques; Clermont-Ferrand, 1988, pp. 581–93.

—— 'Les dictionnaires socio-politiques 1770–1815: une bibliographie', *Dictionnaire des usages socio-politiques (1770–1815)*, fasc. 3, Saint-Cloud, 1988, pp. 7–46.

—— '"A bas le bonnet rouge des femmes!": (octobre–novembre 1793)', in Marie France Brive (ed.), *Les Femmes et la Révolution française*. Actes du colloque international 12–13–14 avril 1989, Université de Toulouse-Mirail, 3 vols, Presse Universitaire du Mirail: Toulouse, 1989–90, vol. 3, pp. 345–52.

Gembloux, Pierquin de, *Le Bonnet de la liberté et le coq Gaulois fruits de l'ignorance. Lettre à M. Viennet, membre de l'Académie française, pair de France etc., etc.*, Bourges, n.d.

—— *Notices historiques, archéologiques et philologiques sur Bourges et le département de Cher*, Bourges, 1840.

Gendron, François, *La Jeunesse dorée: épisodes de la Révolution française*, Presses de l'Université du Québec: Sillery, Québec, 1979.

—— *La Jeunesse sous Thermidor*, PUF: Paris, 1983.

—— *The Gilded Youth of Thermidor*, trans. James Cookson, McGill–Queen's University Press: Montreal and Kingston, London, Buffalo, 1993.

Gengembre, Gérard, 'Bonald, 1796–1801: contre-Révolution et politique du possible', in François Furet and Mona Ozouf (eds), *The French Revolution and the Creation of Modern Political Culture*, vol. 3, *The Transformation of Political Culture 1789–1848*, Pergamon: Oxford, 1989, pp. 309–21.

Genty, Maurice, 'Le Mouvement démocratique dans les sections parisiennes du printemps 1790 au printemps 1792', thèse de doctorat d'état, Université de Paris I, 1981–82, 4 vols.

—— *L'Apprentissage de la citoyenneté. Paris 1789–1795*, Messidor/Éditions sociales: Paris, 1987.

—— 'Controverses autour de la garde nationale parisienne', *AHRF*, January–March 1993, pp. 61–88.

Gérard, Alice, 'Bonnet phrygien et Marseillaise', *L'Histoire*, July–August 1988, no. 113, pp. 44–50.

Gibelin, Alexandre Esprit, *De l'Origine et de la forme du bonnet de la liberté*, an IV.

Gildea, Robert, *The Past in French History*, Yale University Press: New Haven and London, 1994.

Giraffi, Alessandro, *Le rivoluzioni di Napoli*, Venice, 1648; trans. J. Howell, *An exact Historie of the late Revolution in Naples, and of their monstrous successes not to be paralleled by any Ancient or Modern History*, 2 parts, London, 1650–52.

Girardet, Raoul, 'Les Trois Couleurs', in Pierre Nora (ed.), *Les Lieux de mémoire*, vol. 1, *La République*, Gallimard: Paris, 1984, pp. 5–35.

Girault de Coursac, P. and P., *Louis XVI, un visage retrouvé*, Éditions de l'Œil: Paris, 1990.

Godechot, Jacques, *14 juillet 1789. La Prise de la Bastille*, Gallimard: Paris, 1965.

—— *Les Institutions de la France sous la Révolution et l'Empire*, PUF: Paris, 1968.

Godineau, Dominique, *Citoyennes tricoteuses. Les femmes du peuple à Paris pendant la Révolution française*, Alinéa: Paris, 1988.

Gombrich, E.H., 'The Dream of Reason: Symbolism in the French Revolution', *Journal of the British Society for Eighteenth-century Studies*, Autumn 1979, vol. 2, no. 3, pp. 187–217.

Goret, Charles, *Mon témoignage sur la détention de Louis XVI et de sa famille dans la tour du Temple*, Paris, 1825.

Gower, Earl, *The Despatches of Earl Gower, English Ambassador at Paris from June 1790 to August 1792*, ed. Oscar Browning, Cambridge, 1885.

La Grande Encyclopédie, 31 vols, Paris, n.d.

Les Grandes Prédictions du grand Nostradamus, trouvées dans la grande culotte de peau de messire Honoré Barnave, 1790.

Grapa, Caroline Jacot, *L'Homme dissonant au dix-huitième siècle*, Studies on Voltaire and the Eighteenth Century, 1997, vol. 154.

Grasset de Saint-Sauveur, Jacques, *Costumes des représentants du peuple, membres des deux conseils, du directoire exécutif, des ministres, des tribunaux, des messagers d'état, huissiers, et autres fonctionnaires publics etc.*, Paris, an IV, 1795.

—— *L'Esprit des Ana, ou de tout un peu*, 2 vols, Paris, 1801.

Grégoire, abbé, *Rapport et projet de décret présentés au nom du comité d'instruction publique sur les costumes des législateurs et des autres fonctionnaires publics, séance du vingt-huit fructidor, l'an trois*, in Bernard Deloche and Jean-Michel Leniaud (eds), *La Culture des sans-culottes. Le premier dossier du patrimoine 1789–1798*, Editions de Paris, Presses du Languedoc: Paris and Montpellier, 1989, pp. 295–303.

Grimod de la Reynière, *Le Censeur dramatique, ou Journal des principaux théâtres de Paris et des départements, par une société des lettres*, 1797–98.

Gruber, Alain, *Les Grandes Fêtes et leurs décors à l'époque de Louis XVI*, Droz: Paris, Geneva, 1972.

Guiffrey, J.J. and Anatole de, Montaiglon, *Correspondance des directeurs de l'Académie de Rome avec les surintendants des bâtiments 1666–1797*, 18 vols, Schemit: Paris, 1887–1912.

Guilhaumou, Jacques, 'La Mort de Marat à Paris (13 juillet–16 juillet 1793)', in Jean-Claude Bonnet (ed.), *La Mort de Marat*, Flammarion: Paris, 1986, pp. 39–80.

—— *La Langue politique et la Révolution française. De l'événement à la raison linguistique*, Klincksieck: Paris, 1989.

—— 'Fragments of a Discourse of Denunciation (1789–1794)', *The French Revolution and the Creation of Modern Political Culture*, vol. 4, Keith Michael Baker (ed.), *The Terror*, Pergamon/Elsevier: Oxford, 1994, pp. 139–55.

Guillaume, M. (ed.), *Procès-verbaux du Comité d'Instruction publique de la Convention nationale*, 7 vols, Paris, 1891–1957.

Guilletaux, V., *Monnaies françaises. Colonies 1670–1942. Métropole 1714–1942*, Chaix: Versailles, 1937–42.

Halliday, Tony, *Facing the Public: Portraiture in the aftermath of the French Revolution*, Manchester University Press: Manchester, 2000.

Hanet, Jean-Pierre-Louis, dit Cléry, *Mémoires de P.L. Hanet Cléry, ancien valet de chambre de Madame Royale, aujourd'hui Dauphine, et frère de Cléry, dernier valet de chambre de Louis XVI, 1776–1823*, 2 vols, Paris, 1825.

Harden, J. David, 'Liberty Caps and Liberty Trees', *Past and Present*, February 1995, no. 146, pp. 66–102.

Harris, Jennifer, 'The Red Cap of Liberty: a Study of Dress worn by French revolutionary Partisans 1789–1794', *Eighteenth-century Studies*, Spring 1981, vol. 14, no. 3, pp. 83–312.

Harvey, John, *Men in Black*, Reaktion: London, 1995.

Heim, Jean-François, Claire Béraud, and Philippe Heim, *Les Salons de peinture de la Révolution française (1789–1799)*, C.A.C. Édition: Paris, 1989.

Hellegouarc'h, J.M., 'Quelques termes relatifs à la mode sous la Révolution de 1789', *Cahiers de lexicologie*, 1978, vol. 33, no. 2, pp. 105–32.

Hennin, Michel, *Trésor de numismatique et glyptique: médailles de la Révolution*, Paris, 1826.

—— *Histoire numismatique de la Révolution française*, 2 vols, Paris, 1826.

Herz, Neil, 'Medusa's Head: male hysteria under political pressure', *Representations*, Fall 1983, no. 4, pp. 27–54.

Hesse, Carla, 'The Law of the Terror', *MLN*, vol. 114, no. 4, Sept. 1999, pp. 702–18.

Hier pour demain. Arts, traditions et patrimoine, Éditions de la Réunion des Musées Nationaux: Paris, 1986.

Higonnet, Patrice, 'Sans-culottes', in François Furet and Mona Ozouf (eds), *Dictionnaire critique de la Révolution française*, Flammarion: Paris, 1988, pp. 418–23.

—— *Goodness beyond Virtue. Jacobins during the French Revolution*, Harvard University Press: Cambridge MA and London, 1998.

Hill, Draper, *The Satirical Prints of James Gillray*, Dover: New York, 1976.

Hould, Claudette, 'La Propagande d'état par l'estampe devant la Terreur', in Michel Vovelle (ed.), *Les Images de la Révolution française*, Publications de la Sorbonne: Paris, 1988, pp. 29–37.

Hugueney, Louis, *Les Clubs dijonnais sous la Révolution, leur rôle politique et économique*, Dijon, 1905.

Hunt, Lynn, *Politics, Culture, and Class in the French Revolution*, University of California Press: Berkeley, Los Angeles, London, 1984.

—— 'Freedom of Dress in Revolutionary France', in Sara E. Melzer and Kathryn Norberg (eds), *From the Royal to the Republican Body. Incorporating the Political in Seventeenth- and Eighteenth-century France*, University of California Press: Berkeley, Los Angeles, London, 1998, pp. 224–49.

Icart, Roger, *La Révolution française et l'écran*, Éditions Milan: Toulouse, 1988.

Idée générale de la fête civique proposée pour la réception des soldats de Châteauvieux, n.d. [1792].

Isambert, Gustave, *La vie à Paris pendant une année de la Révolution, 1791–1792*, Alcan: Paris, 1896.

Itsikowitch-Elyada, Ouzi, 'Manipulation et théâtralité. Le Père Duchesne (1788–1791)', thèse de doctorat, Paris, École des Hautes Études en Sciences Sociales, 1985, 2 vols.

Jamme, Lucien, *Le Discours jacobin et la démocratie*, Fayard: Paris, 1989.

Jean-Richard, Pierrette and Gilbert Mondin, *Un Collectionneur pendant la Révolution: Jean-Louis Soulavie (1752–1813)*, Éditions de la Réunion des Musées Nationaux: Musée du Louvre, Paris, 1989.

Johnson, James H., 'Revolutionary Audiences and the Impossible Imperatives of Fraternity', in Bryant T. Ragan Jr and Elizabeth A. Williams (eds), *Re-creating Authority in Revolutionary France*, Rutgers University Press: New Brunswick, New Jersey, 1992, pp. 57–78.

—— *Listening in Paris: a Cultural History*, University of California Press: Berkeley, Los Angeles, London, 1995.

—— 'Versailles, Meet Les Halles: Masks, Carnival, and the French Revolution', *Representations*, winter 2001, no. 73, pp. 89–116.

Jollet, Etienne, 'Between Allegory and Topography: the Project for a Statue to Louis XVI in Brest (1785–86), and the Question of the Pedestal in Public Statuary in Eighteenth-century France', *Oxford Art Journal*, 2000, vol. 23, no. 2, pp. 49–78.

Jones, Colin, and and Rebecca Spang, 'Sans-culottes, sans café, sans tabac: shifting realms of necessity and luxury in eighteenth-century France', in Maxine Berg and Helen Clifford (eds), *Consumers and Luxury. Consumer Culture in Europe 1650–1850*, Manchester University Press: Manchester, 1999, pp. 37–62.

Jordan, David. P., *The King's Trial. The French Revolution vs. Louis XVI*, University of California Press: Berkeley, Los Angeles, London, 1979.

Jourand, Chanoine, 'De la suppression (1790) au rétablissement (1805) du costume ecclésiastique', *La Semaine religieuse du diocèse de Lyon*, 1963, no. 70, pp. 230–7.

Jourdain, Yves-Claude, *Table alphabétique des matières contenus dans les décrets rendus par les assemblées nationales de France, depuis 1789, jusqu'au 18 brumaire an VIII*. Paris, an X.

Jourdan, Annie, *Les Monuments de la Révolution 1770–1804. Une histoire de représentation*, Honoré Champion: Paris, 1997.

Jouve, P., 'L'Image du sans-culotte dans la caricature politique anglaise: création d'un stéréotype pictural', *Gazette des beaux-arts*, November 1978, vol. 91, pp. 187–96.

Kaplan, Steven Laurence, *Farewell Revolution. Disputed Legacies, France 1789/1989*, Cornell University Press: Ithaca and London, 1995,

Kates, G., *The Cercle social, the Girondins, and the French Revolution*, Princeton University Press: Princeton, 1995.

Kelly, George Armstrong, *Victims, Authority, and Terror. The parallel deaths of d'Orléans, Custine, Bailly, and Malesherbes*, University of North Carolina Press: Chapel Hill, 1982.

—— *Mortal Politics in Eighteenth-century France*, University of Waterloo Press: Waterloo, Ontario, 1986.

Kennedy, Michael L., *The Jacobin Club in the French Revolution. The First Years*, Princeton University Press: Princeton, 1982.

—— *The Jacobin Club in the French Revolution. The Middle Years*, Princeton University Press: Princeton, 1988.

—— *The Jacobin Club in the French Revolution. 1793–1795*, Berghahn: New York and Oxford, 2000.

Korshak, Yvonne, '*Paris and Helen* by Jacques-Louis David: Choice and Judgment on the Eve of the French Revolution', *Art Bulletin*, March 1987, vol. 69, no. 1, pp. 102–16.

—— 'The Liberty Cap as a Revolutionary Symbol in America and France', *Smithsonian Studies in American Art*, Fall 1987, pp. 53–69.

La Curne de Sainte-Palaye, Jean-Baptiste, *Dictionnaire historique de l'ancien langage françois*, L. Favre *et al.* (eds), 10 vols, Paris, 1875–82.

Lafont d'Aussonne, *Mémoires secrets et universels des malheurs et de la mort de la Reine de France*, Paris, 1825.

Lajer-Burcharth, Ewa, *Necklines. The Art of Jacques-Louis David after the Terror*, Yale University Press: New Haven and London, 1999.

La Marle, Hubert, *Philippe Égalité. "Grand Maître de la Révolution". Le rôle politique du premier sérénissime frère du Grand Orient de France*, Nouvelles Éditions Latines: Paris, 1989.

Langlois, Claude, *La Caricature contre-révolutionnaire*, CNRS: Paris, 1988.

Lapauze, Henry (ed.), *Procès-verbaux de la Commune générale des arts de peinture, sculpture et architecture et de la société populaire et républicaine des arts*, Bulloz: Paris, 1903.

Launay, Edmond, *Costumes, insignes, cartes, médailles des députés 1789–1898* (1899), revised André Souyris-Rolland 1981.

Lefebvre, Georges, *La Révolution française*, Paris, 1957.

Lefeuvre, Francis, *Souvenirs de Nantes avant et pendant la Révolution*, Nantes, 1882.

Leith, James, 'Images of Sans-culottes', in Claudette Hould and James Leith (eds), *Iconographie et image de la Révolution française*, Actes du colloque tenu dans le cadre du 59e congrès de l'Association canadienne française pour l'avancement des sciences (15–16 May 1989), Montreal, 1990.

Leloir, Maurice, *Histoire du costume de l'antiquité à 1914*, Paris, 1934–49.

Lemaire, Jean, *Le Testament de Napoléon. Un étonnant destin 1821–1857*, Plon: Paris, 1975.

Lemay, Edna Hindie, *Dictionnaire des constituants 1789–1791*, 2 vols, Universitas: Paris, 1991.

Lenk, Torsten, 'La Garde-robe royale historique du cabinet royal des armes de Stockholm', in *Actes du Ier congrès international d'histoire du costume*. Centro Internazionale delle Arti et del Costume, Palazzo Grassi, Venice, 31 August–7 September 1952, Stampa Strada: Milan, pp. 187–96.

Lenoir, Alexandre, *Description historique et chronologique des monumens de sculpture, réunis au Musée des monumens français*, 6th edn, Paris, an X/1802.

Lenôtre, Georges [pseud. Louis Léon Théodore Gosselin], *La Guillotine et les exécuteurs des arrêtés criminels pendant la Révolution*, Paris, 1893.

—— *Vieilles maisons, vieux papiers*, 3rd series, Paris, 1906.

—— *Notes et souvenirs*, Calmann-Lévy: Paris, 1940.

Lequime, Jean, *La Société de l'histoire du costume et le Musée du costume*, Proba: Paris, 1946.

Leroux, J.J., *Déclaration de M. J.J. Leroux, sur les événemens du 20 juin 1792*, 1792.

Lettre à la comtesse Henriette, sur les assignats . . . trouvées dans le gousset d'une culotte etc., Paris, 1790.

Lettre de M. le duc d'Aiguillon à Madame la princesse de Chimay, dame d'honneur de la Reine, n.d.

Le Verdier, Pierre, 'Les reliques de la famille royale et les descendants de Cléry', *Revue des questions historiques*, 1896, vol. 60, pp. 264–80.

Lever, Evelyne, *Philippe Égalité*, Arthème Fayard: Paris, 1996.

Levy, Darlene Gay, and Harriet Branson Applewhite, 'Women and Militant Citizenship in Revolutionary Paris', in Sara E. Melzer and Leslie W. Rabine (eds), *Rebel Daughters. Women and the French Revolution*, Oxford University Press: Oxford, 1992, pp. 79–101.

——, and Mary Durham Johnson (eds), *Women in Revolutionary France: Selected Documents*, University of Illinois Press: Urbana, 1979.

Liesville, Alfred de, *Histoire numismatique de la Révolution de 1848, ou Description raisonnée des médailles, monnaies, jetons, repoussés, etc., relatif aux affaires de la France*, Paris, 1877.

Lindsay, Suzanne Glover, 'Mummies and Tombs: Turenne, Napoleon, and Death Ritual', *Art Bulletin*, September 2000, vol. 82, no. 3, pp. 476–502.

Liris, Elizabeth, 'Autour des vignettes révolutionnaires: le symbolisme du bonnet phrygien', in Michel Vovelle (ed.), *Les Images de la Révolution française*, Paris, 1988, pp. 307–16.

—— 'De la liberté à l'union dans l'iconographie des drapeaux des districts parisiens', *AHRF*, 1992, vol. 64, no. 3, pp. 341–530.

Lucas, Colin (ed.), *The French Revolution and the Creation of Modern Political Culture*, vol. 2, *The Political Culture of the French Revolution*, Pergamon: Oxford, 1988.

—— 'The Theory and Practice of Denunciation in the French Revolution', *Journal of Modern History*, December 1996, vol. 68, no. 4, pp. 768–85.

Lucas-Dubreton, J., *Le Culte de Napoléon 1815–1848*, Albin Michel: Paris, 1960.

Lüsebrink, Hans-Jürgen, 'Images et représentations sociales de la criminalité en France au XVIIIe siècle: l'exemple de Mandrin', *Revue d'histoire moderne et contemporaine*, July–Septemebr 1979, vol. 26, pp. 345–64.

—— and Rolf Reichardt, *The Bastille. A History of a Symbol of Despotism and Freedom*, Duke University Press: Durham and London, 1997.

Lux, Adam, *Charlotte Corday*, n.d.

Luzzatto, Sergio, *Mémoires de la Terreur. Vieux montagnards et jeunes républicains au XIXe siècle*, Presses Universitaires de Lyon: Lyon, 1991.

Lynn, John A., *The Bayonets of the Republic. Motivation and Tactics in the Army of Revolutionary France, 1791–1794*, University of Illinois Press: Urbana and Chicago, 1984.

Macalister, Mrs Donald A., 'Lord Ernle's *faïence patriotique*', *Apollo*, 1927, vol. 6, pp. 175–80.

Macé de Lépinay, François, and Jacques Charles, *Marie-Antoinette du Temple à la Conciergerie*, Caisse Nationale des Monuments Historiques and Tallandier: Paris, 1989.

Mac'Vernoll, 'Visite au Musée des souverains par la Reine de Hollande', *Le Monde illustré*, 2 May 1858, no. 58, p. 324.

Mainz, Valerie, 'David's *Les Sabines* and the Colouring of History Painting Post-Thermidor', *Interfaces: image, texte, langage*, February 1996, no. 10, pp. 45–59.

—— *L'Image du travail et la Révolution française*, Musée de la Révolution française, Vizille, 1999.

Malmesbury, Earl of, *Diaries and Correspondence of the Earl of Malmesbury*, 3 vols, London, 1844.

Mansel, Philip, 'Monarchy, Uniform and the Rise of the *frac,* 1760–1830', *Past and Present*, August 1982, no. 96, pp. 103–32.

Marchand, *Mémoires de Marchand, premier valet de chambre et exécuteur testamentaire de l'Empereur*, Jean Bourguignon and Henry Lachouque (eds), 2 vols, Plon: Paris, 1955.

Marie-Antoinette et son temps, Galerie Sedelmeyer: Paris, 1894.

Markoff, John, *The Aboliton of Feudalism. Peasants, Lords, and Legislation in the French Revolution*, Pennsylvania State University Press: Philadelphia, 1996.

Markov, Walter and Soboul, Albert, *Die Sansculotten von Paris. Dokumente zur Geschichte des Volksbewegung, 1793–94*, Akademie Verlag: Berlin, 1957.

Mathiez, Alfred, *Les Origines des cultes révolutionnaires*, Paris, 1904.

—— 'L'Exposition de la Révolution française', *AHRF*, 1928, vol. 5, p. 169.

—— 'Une Exposition de souvenirs révolutionnaires à la Chambre des Députés', *AHRF*, 1930, vol. 7, pp. 206–7.

—— 'Le drapeau rouge, symbole d'insurrection', *AHRF*, 1930, vol. 7, p. 274.

Maurice Leloir: de Guy de Maupassant à Douglas Fairbanks, Maison Fournaise, Chatou, 1995.

McClellan, Andrew, 'The Life and Death of a Royal Monument: Bouchardon's *Louis XV*', *Oxford Art Journal*, 2000, vol. 23, no. 2, pp. 1–27.

Mémoires de mode, Palais Galliera, Musée de la mode et du costume: Paris, 1994.

Mémoires secrets pour servir à l'histoire de la république des lettres en France, depuis 1762 jusqu'à nos jours, 36 vols, London, 1779–1789.

Mercier, C.F.X., *Comment m'habillerai-je? Réflexions politiques et philosophiques sur l'habillement français, et sur la nécessité d'un costume national*, Paris, 1793.

Mercier, Louis-Sébastien, *Néologie, ou Vocabulaire des mots nouveaux, à renouveller ou pris dans des acceptions nouvelles*, 2 vols, Paris, 1801.

—— *Le Nouveau Paris*, ed. Jean-Claude Bonnet et al., Mercure de France: Paris, 1994.

Merrick, Jeffrey, *The Desacralisation of the French Monarchy in the Eighteenth Century*, Louisiana State University Press: Baton Rouge, 1998.

Michel, Régis (ed.), *David contre David*, 2 vols, Editions de la Réunion des Musées Nationaux: Paris, 1993.

Michelet, Jules, *Histoire de la Révolution française*, 2 vols, Bouquins: Paris, 1979.

Michon, Georges, 'La Maison de Robespierre, rue de Saintonge, à Paris', *AHRF*, 1924, vol. 1, pp. 64–6.

Milliot, Vincent, *Les Cris de Paris, ou le peuple travesti. Les représentations des petits métiers parisiens (XVIe–XVIIIe siècles)*, Publications de la Sorbonne: Paris, 1995.

Minard, Philippe, 'Identité corporative et dignité ouvrière: le cas des typographes parisiens, 1789–1791', in Michel Vovelle (ed.), *Paris et la Révolution*. Actes du colloque de Paris I, 14–16 avril 1989, Paris, 1989, pp. 23–33.

Modes et révolution, 1780–1804, Musée de la mode et du costume, Palais Galliera: Paris, 1989.

Moëlle, Claude-Antoine, *Six journées passées au Temple et autres détails sur la famille royale qui y a été détenue*, Paris, 1820.

Monin, H. 'L'Histoire de la Révolution aux Salons de peinture de 1896', *Révolution Française*, January–June 1896, pp. 554–6, *Ibid.*, 1885, pp. 1019–1031.

Monnier, M., *Appel au tribunal de l'opinion publique, du rapport de M. Chabroud, et du décret rendu par l'Assemblée Nationale le 2 octobre 1790. Examen du Mémoire du duc d'Orléans, et du plaidoyer du comte de Mirabeau, et nouveaux Éclaircissemens sur les crimes du 5 et du 6 octobre 1789*, Geneva, 1790.

Monnier, Raymonde, 'Le Culte de Bara en l'an II', *AHRF*, 1980, vol. 52, pp. 321–37.

—— *Le Faubourg Saint-Antoine (1789–1815)*, Société des Études robespierristes: Paris, 1981.

—— *Un bourgeois sans-culotte, le général Santerre*, Paris, 1985.

Montalot, P. and L. Pingaud (eds), *Le Congrès de Rastatt (11 juin 1798– 28 avril 1799). Correspondance et documents*, 3 vols, Picard: Paris, 1913.

Moore, John, *A Journal during a Residence in France, from the Beginning of August to the Middle of December, 1792*, 2 vols, London, 1794.

Moreau, *Corps législatif. Conseil des Anciens. Motion d'ordre de Moreau (de l'Yonne), séance du 21 prairial an VII.*

La Mort de Bara. De l'événement au mythe. Autour du tableau de Jacques-Louis David, Fondation du Musée Calvet: Avignon, 1989.

Mosse, Claude, *L'Antiquité dans la Révolution française*, Albin Michel: Paris, 1989.

Muller, Christian Alain, 'Du "peuple égaré" au "peuple enfant": le discours politique à l'épreuve de la révolte populaire en 1793', *Revue d'histoire moderne et contemporaine*, January–March 2000, vol. 47, no. 1, pp. 93–112.

Municipalité de Paris. Commissaires des 48 sections réunis à la Maison Commune. Extrait des délibérations du conseil général des commissaaires de la majorité des sections, du dimanche 12 août 1792, l'an 4me de la Liberté.

Murray, William, *The Right-wing Press in the French Revolution 1789–92*, Boydell Press: Woodbridge, 1986.

Musée rétrospectif des classes 85 et 86. Le costume et ses accessoires à l'Exposition universelle internationale de 1900 à Paris, Paris, 1900.

Myerly, Scott Hughes, *British Military Spectacle: From the Napoleonic Wars Through the Crimea*, Harvard University Press: Cambridge MA, London, 1996.

Naudin, Marcel, 'Les Souvenirs Napoléoniens du Musée de Châteauroux', *Revue de la société des amis du Musée de l'Armée*, 1958, no. 61, pp. 35–7.

Naudin, Michel, 'La réaction culturelle en l'an III: la représentation du Jacobin et du sans-culotte dans l'imaginaire de leurs adversaires', in Michel Vovelle (ed.), *Le Tournant de l'an III. Réaction et Terreur blanche dans la France révolutionnaire*, Comité des travaux historiques et scientifiques: Paris, 1997, pp. 279–92.

Nelms, Brenda, *The Third Republic and the Centennial of 1789*, Garland: New York and London, 1987.

Nineteenth-century French Drawings and Some Sculpture (15 June–14 July 2000), Hazlitt, Gooden and Fox, London.

Noël, F., 'Lettre au Rédacteur du Magazin encyclopédique, sur l'antiquité du BONNET ROUGE, considéré comme signe de la Liberté', *Magazin encyclopédique*, 1793, no. 41, pp. 327–8.

Notice sommaire des monuments et objets divers relatifs à l'histoire de Paris et de la Révolution française exposés au Musée Carnavalet suivant l'ordre des salles parcourues par les visiteurs, Paris: June, 1881.

Nouveau Dictionnaire françois, à l'usage de toutes les Municipalités, les milices nationales et de tous les Patriotes, composé par un Aristocrate, dédié à l'Assemblée Nationale, pour servir à l'histoire de la Révolution de France, et c'est la vérité comme on dit toute nue, Paris, 1790.

Oechslin, Werner, 'L'Architecture révolutionnaire: idéal et mythe', in *Les Architectes de la Liberté 1789–1799*, École des Beaux-Arts, Paris, 1989, pp. 351–61.

Olander, William, 'French Painting and Politics in 1793: the Great Concours de l'an II', in Alan Wintermute (ed.), *1789: French Art during the Revolution*, Colnaghi: New York, 1989, pp. 29–45.

O'Neill, Mary, *Musée des beaux-arts d'Orléans. Catalogue critique: Les peintures de l'Ecole française des XVIIe et XVIIIe siècles*, thèse de doctorat de troisième cycle, Paris-Sorbonne, 1980, 2 vols.

Orceau, Robert, 'Le Bonnet phrygien', *Bulletin de la société archéologique et historique de Nantes et de la Loire-inférieure*, 1955, vol. 94, pp. 23–33.

L'Ordre de la marche de la fête qui aura lieu décadi prochain 10 nivôse, l'an 2 de la République une et indivisible, en mémoire des armées françaises, et notamment à l'occasion de la prise de Toulon.

Ordre de marche de l'entrée triomphante des martyrs de la liberté, du régiment de Châteauvieux dans la ville de Paris [1792].

L'Ordre de Marche et les cérémonies de l'entrée des soldats de Châteauvieux au club des jacobins, du Manège, n.d. [1792].

Ory, Pascal, 'Le Cent-cinquantenaire', in Jean-Claude Bonnet and Philippe Roger (eds), *La Légende de la Révolution au XXe siècle. De Gance à Renoir, de Romain Rolland à Claude Simon,* Flammarion: Paris, 1988, pp. 139–56.

—— *La Belle Illusion. Culture et politique sous le signe du Front populaire 1935–1938,* Plon: Paris, 1994.

Outram, Dorinda, *The Body and the French Revolution. Sex, Class, and Political Culture,* Yale University Press: New Haven and London, 1989.

Ozouf, Mona, *La Fête révolutionnaire 1789–1799,* Gallimard: Paris, 1976.

—— 'Le Simulacre et la fête', in Jean Ehrard and Paul Viallaneix (eds), *Les Fêtes de la Révolution.* Colloque Clermont-Ferrand, (June 1974), Société des Etudes robespierristes: Paris, 1977, pp. 323–53.

Pageot, J., 'Le costume dans l'armée catholique et royale de Vendée', *Revue du souvenir vendéen,* March 1960, no. 50, pp. 4–7.

Palloy, Pierre-François, *Discours prononcé à la société de Sceaux-l'Unité, le 10 frimaire, jour de la Fête de la Raison, en présence de toutes les autorités constituées,* 1793.

Pardailhé-Galabrun, Annick, *La Naissance de l'intime. 3000 foyers parisiens, XVII–XVIIIe siècles,* PUF: Paris, 1988.

Parker, H.T., *The Cult of Antiquity and the French Revolutionaries,* University of Chicago Press: Chicago, 1937.

Pellegrin, Nicole, 'Les Chemises patriotiques. Essai sur les dons civiques en Haut-Poitou pendant la Révolution', in *Le Centre-Ouest dans la Révolution,* Poitiers, 1988, pp. 77–85.

—— *Les Vêtements de la Liberté. Abécédaire des pratiques vestimentaires françaises de 1780 à 1800,* Alinéa: Paris, 1989.

Peltier, J.G., *Correspondance politique des véritables amis du roi et de la patrie.*

Pensées sur les coupeurs des tresses. Par un homme libre, qui ne l'est pas, n.d. [1794].

Perrot, Philippe, *Les Dessus et les dessous de la bourgeoisie. Une histoire du vêtement au XIXe siècle*, Fayard: Paris, 1981.

—— *Le Travail des apparences, ou les transformations du corps féminin XVIIIe–XIXe siècles*, Seuil: Paris, 1984.

Pfeiffer, Laura B., 'The Uprising of June 20, 1792', *University Studies [University of Nebraska, Lincoln]*, July 1912, vol. 12, no. 3, pp. 197–343.

Pigott, Robert, *Discours prononcé à l'Assemblée des amis de la constitution de Dijon, en faveur du bonnet de la liberté, le 26 décembre 1791*.

Pointon, Marcia, 'Materialising Mourning: Hair, Jewellery, and the Body', in Marius Kwint, Christopher Breward and Jeremy Ainsley (eds), *Material Memories: Design and Evocation*, Berg: Oxford, 1999.

Pollart, Philippe Joseph, *Opinion de Pollart (de la Seine), sur le port de la cocarde nationale. Séance du 13 floréal an VII*.

Poulot, Dominique, 'Alexandre Lenoir et les musées des monuments français', in Piere Nora dir., *Les Lieux de mémoire*, II, *La Nation*, vol. 2, Gallimard: Paris, pp. 497–532.

—— 'Surveiller et s'instruire': la Révolution française et l'intelligence de l'héritage historique*, Studies on Voltaire and the Eighteenth Century, vol. 344, 1996.

—— *Musée, Nation, patrimoine 1789–1815*, Gallimard: Paris, 1997.

Pouy, F., *Histoire de la cocarde tricolore*, Paris, 1872.

Premières Collections. Musée de la Révolution française, Vizille, Conseil Général de l'Isère: 1985.

Procédure criminelle, instruite au Châtelet de Paris, sur la dénonciation des faits arrivés à Versailles dans la journée du 6 octobre 1789. Imprimé par ordre de l'Assemblée nationale, 1790.

Procès-verbal de la Confédération à Paris, le quatorze juillet mil sept-cent-quatre-vingt-dix, Paris, 1790.

Procès-verbal dressé sur les événemens du 20 juin 1792, par M. Sergent, Administrateur du département de la police, 1792.

Proclamation de Louis XVI lue à l'Assemblée nationale le 28 mai 1790, couleurs de la conciliation, Paris, 1790.

Proclamation du Roi, et Recueil de pièces relatives à l'arrêté du conseil de département, du 6 juin 1792, concernant le Maire de département et le Procureur de la Commune de Paris, Paris, 1792.

Programme de la fête de la victoire de 10 prairial l'an IV.

Projet sur le costume particulier à donner chacun des deux conseils législatifs, et à tous les fonctionnaires publics de la République française, présenté à la Convention nationale, 13 fructidor an III.

Proust, Jacques, 'L'Image du peuple au travail dans les planches de l'*Encyclopédie*', in *Images du peuple au dix-huitième siècle*, Colloque d'Aix-en-Provence, 25 et 26 octobre 1969, Centre Aixois d'Études et de Recherches sur le dix-huitième siècle, Armand Colin: Paris, 1973, pp. 65–85.

——, 'Sans-culotte malgré lui: contribution à la mythologie de Guillaume Tell', in *Essays on Diderot and the Enlightenment in Honor of Otis Fellows*, ed. John Pappas, Geneva, 1974, pp. 268–81.

Punition terrible et exemplaire de trois brigands aristocrates, arrêtés et mis à mort hier au soir par nos bons citoyens du fauxbourg Saint-Antoine. Cocarde nationale insultée aux Thuileries [1790].

Quand voguaient les galères, Musée de la Marine, Paris, 1991.

Quicherat, J., *Histoire du costume en France depuis les temps les plus reculés jusqu'à la fin du XVIIIe siècle*, Paris, 1875.

Rabbé, Vieille de Boisjolin, Sainte-Preuve (eds), *Biographie universelle et portative des contemporains*, 5 vols, Paris, 1835.

Raine, Patricia, *A Dress of the Revolution worn for Escape 1793*, Northern Society of Costume and Textiles, 1989.

Rapport et décret sur la fête de la réunion républicaine du 10 août.

Rathier, L., and F. Beaunier, *Recueil des costumes français, ou Collection des plus belles statues et figures françaises, des armes, armures, des instruments, des meubles, etc. dessinés d'après les monuments, manuscrits, peintures et vitraux, avec un texte explicatif suivi d'une notice historique et cronologique* [sic]; *devant servir à l'histoire de l'art du dessin en France depuis Clovis jusqu'à Louis XIV inclusivement*, Paris, 1810.

Ray, Monique and Jacques Payen, *Souvenirs iconographiques de la Révolution française à Lyon*, Éditions lyonnaises d'art et d'histoire: Lyon, 1989.

Reichardt, J.F., *Un Hiver à Paris sous le Consulat, 1802–1803*, trans. A. Laquiante, Paris, 1896.

Reinhard, Marcel, *La Chute de la royauté: 10 août 1792*, Gallimard: Paris, 1969.

—— *Nouvelle Histoire de Paris. La Révolution 1789–1799*, Hachette: Paris, 1971.

Reiset, comte de (ed.), *Livre-journal de Madame Eloffe*, 2 vols, Paris, 1885.

Représentations de la livrée de Paris à Monseigneur le Maire de ladite ville, n.d. [1789?].

La Révolution française et l'Europe 1789–1799, 3 vols, Council of Europe: Grand Palais, Paris, 1989.

Révolution française et 'Vandalisme'. Actes du colloque international de Clermont-Ferrand 15–17 décembre 1988, Simone Bernard-Griffiths, Marie-Claude Chemin, Jean Ehrard (eds), Universitas: Paris, 1992.

La Révolution française, le Premier Empire. Dessins du Musée Carnavalet, Paris, 1982.

Rheims, Maurice, *La Vie étrange des objets. Histoire de la curiosité*, Plon: Paris, 1959.

Ribeiro, Aileen, *Dress in Eighteenth-century Europe 1715–1789*, Batsford: London, 1984.

—— *Fashion in the French Revolution*, Batsford: London, 1988.

—— *The Art of Dress. Fashion in England and France 1750–1820*, Yale University Press: New Haven and London, 1995.

Richard, Bernard, 'Le Bonnet phrygien, couvre-chef de la République en France et ailleurs', in *Marianne: image féminine de la République*, Centre Culturel Français de Turin, n.d.

Rigney, Anne, *The Rhetoric of Historical Representation. Three Narrative Histories of the French Revolution*, Cambridge University Press: Cambridge, 1990.

Roche, Daniel, *Le Peuple de Paris* (Aubier Montaigne: Paris, 1981); *The People of Paris: an essay in popular culture in the eighteenth century*, trans. Marie Evans with Gwynne Lewis, Berg: Leamington Spa, 1987.

—— 'Apparences révolutionnaires ou révolution des apparences?', in Nicole Pellegrin, *Les Vêtements de la liberté. Abécédaire des pratiques vestimentaires françaises de 1780 à 1800*, Alinea: Paris, 1989, pp. 193–202.

—— 'Apparences révolutionnaires ou révolution des apparences?', in *Modes et Révolutions 1789–1804*, Musée de la mode et du costume: Paris, 1989, pp. 105–28.

—— *La Culture des apparences: une histoire du vêtement (XVIIe–XVIIIe siècles)*, Fayard: Paris, 1989.

—— *Histoire des choses banales. Naissance de la consommation XVIIe–XIXe siècles*, Fayard: Paris, 1997.

Roederer, Pierre Louis, *Chronique de cinquante jours, du 20 juin au 10 août 1792, rédigés sur des Pièces authentiques*, in *Mémoires sur les journées révolutionnaires et les coups d'état*, ed. M. Lescure, vol. 1, Paris, 1875.

Roëmers, *Corps législatif. Conseil des Cinq-Cents. Projet de résolution présenté par Roëmers au nom d'une commission spéciale, sur le port de la cocarde nationale. Séance du 8 frimaire an VII*.

Rose, R.B., *The Making of the Sans-culottes. Democratic Ideas and Institutions in Paris, 1789–1792*, Manchester University Press: Manchester, 1983.

[Rosoi, Barnabé Farmain de], *Récit exact et circonstancié de ce qui est passé au Château des Tuileries le mercredi 20 juin 1792*.

Rudé, Georges, *The Crowd in the French Revolution*, Oxford University Press: Oxford, 1959.

Les Ruses des escrocs et des filous dévoilées, 2 vols, Paris, 1811.

Sagnac, Philippe and Paul Robiquet, *La Révolution de 1789*, 2 vols, Paris, 1934.

Saint-Just, Louis Antoine Léon de, *Œuvres complètes*, ed. Charles Vellay, 2 vols, Charpentier and Facquette: Paris, 1908.

—— *Le Vieux Cordelier*, Albert Mathiez and Henri Calvet (eds), Colin: Paris, 1936.

Saint Mleux, Georges, *Souvenirs d'un fédéraliste Malouin*, Saint-Servan, 1911.

Samoyault-Verlet, Colombe, and Jean-Pierre Samoyault, *Château de Fontainebleau. Musée Napoléon Ier. Napoléon et la famille impériale*, Éditions de la Réunion des Musées Nationaux: Paris, 1986.

—— 'The Emperor's Wardrobe', *The Age of Napoleon: Costume from Revolution to Empire 1789–1815*, Metropolitan Museum of Art, New York, 1989, pp. 203–15.

Sandalo-Philos, *Le Costume des représentants conforme à la religion de nos pères*, n.d.

Schama, Simon, *Patriots and Liberators: Revolution in the Netherlands, 1780–1813*, Collins: London, 1977.

Schechter, Ronald, 'Gothic Thermidor: the *bals des victimes*, the fantastic, and the production of historical knowledge in post-Terror France', *Representations*, no. 61, winter 1998, pp. 78–94.

Schwartz, Robert M., *Policing the Poor in Eighteenth-century France*, University of North Carolina Press: Chapel Hill and London, 1988.

Séguy, Philippe, *Histoire des modes sous l'Empire*, Tallandier: Paris, 1988.

Seiterle, G., 'Die Urforme der Phrygischen Mütze', *Antike Welt*, 1985, vol. 3, pp. 2–13.

Seligman, Edmond, *La Justice en France pendant la Révolution 1791–1793*, 2 vols, 1901–1913.

Serman, William and Jean-Paul Bertaud, *Nouvelle Histoire de la France 1789–1919*, Fayard: Paris, 1998.

Sewell Jnr, William H., *Work and Revolution in France. The Language of Labour from the French Revolution to 1848*, Cambridge University Press: Cambridge, 1980.

—— 'Visions of Labour: illustrations of the mechanical arts before, in, and after Diderot's *Encyclopédie*', in Steven Kaplan and Cynthia J. Knoepp (eds), *Work in France: Representation, Meaning, Organization, and Practice*, Cornell University Press: Ithaca and London, 1986, pp. 258–86.

Sgard, Jean (ed.), *Histoire de France à travers les journaux du temps passé. Lumières et lueurs du XVIIIe siècle (1715–1789)*, A l'enseigne de l'arbre verdoyant: Paris, 1986.

Shilliam, Nicola J., '*Cocardes nationales* and *bonnets rouges*: Symbolic Headdresses of the French Revolution', *Journal of the Museum of Fine Arts, Boston*, 1993, vol. 5, pp. 105–31.

Shovlin, John, 'The Cultural Politics of Luxury in Eighteenth-century France', *French Historical Studies*, fall 2000, vol. 23, no. 4, pp. 577–606.

Siegfried, Susan L., *The Art of Louis-Léopold Boilly. Modern Life in Napoleonic France*, Yale University Press: New Haven and London, 1995.

Sionnet [Jacques Louis Gautier de Syonnet], *La Cocarde du Tiers Etat* [1789].

Siviniant, *Motion pour engager les Français et les Françaises à ne jamais cesser de porter la Cocarde nationale*, Brest, 1791.

A Sketch of Modern France, in a series of letters to a lady of fashion, written in the years 1796 and 1797, during a tour through France, ed. C.L. Moody, London, 1798.

Soboul, Albert, 'Sentiment religieux et cultes populaires: saintes patriotes et martyrs de la liberté', *AHRF*, 1957, no. 3, pp. 192–213.

—— *Les Sans-culottes parisiens en l'an II. Mouvement populaire et gouvernement révolutionnaire, 2 juin 1793–9 thermidor an II*, Clavreuil: Paris, 1958.

—— *Les soldats de l'an II*, Club français du livre: Paris, 1959

—— 'Un Episode des luttes populaires en septembre 1793', *AHRF*, 1961, vol. 33, pp. 52–5.

—— *Paysans, sans-culottes et Jacobins*, Clavreuil: Paris, 1966.

Sobry, J.F., *Le Mode françois, ou Discours sur les principaux usages de la nation françoise*, Paris, 1786.

Sonenscher, Michael, 'The *sans-culottes* of Year II: rethinking the language of labour in pre-revolutionary France', *Social History*, October 1984, vol. 9, no. 3, pp. 301–28.

—— *The Hatters of Eighteenth-century France*, Cambridge University Press: Cambridge, 1987.

—— *Work and Wages: Natural Law, Politics, and the Eighteenth-century French Trades*, Cambridge University Press: Cambridge, 1989.

—— 'Artisans, *sans-culottes* and the French Revolution', in Allan Forrest and Peter Jones (eds), *Reshaping France: Town, Country and Region during the French Revolution*, Manchester University Press: Manchester, 1991, pp. 105–21.

Le Soulier de Marie-Antoinette: essai muséographique, Musée des beaux-arts, Caen, 1989.

Souyris-Rolland, André, *Guide des ordres civiles français et étrangers, des médailles d'honneur et des médailles de sociétés*, Préal-Suplam: Paris, 1979.

—— 'Les Vainqueurs de la Bastille et leurs décorations', *Revue de la société des amis du Musée de l'Armée*, vol. 88, 1983, pp. 59–80.

—— *Histoire des distinctions et des récompenses nationales*, 2 vols, Préal: Paris, 1986–87.

Spitzer, Alan B., 'Malicious Memories: Restoration politics and a prosopography of turncoats', *French Historical Studies*, Winter 2001, vol. 24, no. 1, pp. 37–61.

Starobinski, Jean, *J.J. Rousseau, la transparence et l'obstacle*, Plon: Paris, 1958.

—— *The Invention of Liberty*, Skira/Rizzoli: Geneva, 1987.

Steinberg, Sylvie, *La Confusion des sexes. Le travestissement de la Renaissance à la Révolution*, Fayard: Paris, 2001.

Stendhal, *Histoire de la peinture en Italie*, Gallimard: Paris, 1996 [1817].

Sutherland, Donald, 'Chouannerie and Popular Royalism: the survival of the counter-revolutionary tradition in Upper Brittany', *Social History*, October 1984, vol. 9, no. 3, pp. 351–60.

Tackett, Timothy, *Becoming a Revolutionary. The Deputies of the French National Assembly and the Emergence of a Revolutionary culture (1789–1790)*, Princeton University Press: New Haven and London, 1996.

—— 'Conspiracy Obsession in a Time of Revolution: French Élites and the Origins of the Terror 1789–1792', *American Historical Review*, June 2000, pp. 691–713.

Taine, Hippolyte, *Les Origines de la France contemporaine*, 5 vols, Paris, 1904.

Taylor, Lou, 'Doing the Laundry?: an assessment of object-based dress history', *Fashion Theory*, December 1998, vol. 2, no. 4, pp. 339–44.

Thompson, J. M., *The French Revolution*, 5th edn, Oxford University Press: Oxford, 1955.

Thoumas, General Charles-Antoine, *Exposition rétrospective, militaire du Ministre de la Guerre en 1889*, 2 vols, Paris, 1890.

Torné, Pierre Anastase, *Discours de Pierre Anastase Torné, évêque de la métropole du centre (Bourges), sur la suppression des congrégations séculières et du costume écclestiatiques, 6 avril 1792*.

Toudouze, Georges Gustave, 'Maurice Leloir, la Société de l'Histoire du Costume, et le Musée du costume à Paris', *Revue du vêtement*, no. 15, August 1943.

—— *Le Costume français*, Larousse: Paris, 1945.

Tourneux, Maurice, 'L'Exposition historique de la Révolution française', *Gazette des beaux-arts*, 1889, vol. 30, pp. 405–6.

Tourzel, duchesse de, *Mémoires de la duchesse de Tourzel, gouvernante des enfants de France pendant les années 1789, 1790, 1791, 1792, 1793, 1795*, 2 vols, Paris: 1883.

—— *Mémoires de la duchesse de Tourzel, gouvernante des enfants de France, pendant les années 1789 à 1795*, ed. Jean Chalon, Mercure de France: Paris, 1969.

Trichet, Louis, *Le Costume du clergé, ses origines et son évolution en France d'après les règlements de l'église*, Cerf: Paris, 1986.

Trogan, Rosine, and Sorel Philippe, *Augustin Dupré (1748–1833), Graveur général des Monnaies de France. Collections du Musée Carnavalet*, Paris-Musées: Paris, 2000.

Truesdell, Matthew, *Spectacular Politics. Louis-Napoléon Bonaparte and the fête impériale 1849–1870*, Oxford University Press: Oxford, 1997.

Turckheim-Pey, Sophie, 'Les Insignes révolutionnaires de la collection Côte', in *Autour des mentalités et des pratiques politiques sous la Révolution française*, 112e congrès national des sociétés savantes, Lyon, Histoire moderne et contemporaine. Comité des travaux historiques et scientifiques: Paris, 1987, vol. 3, pp. 137–49.

Tussaud, Madame, *Memoirs and Reminiscences of France, forming an abridged history of the French Revolution*, ed. Francis Hervé, London, 1838.

Twiss, Richard, *A Trip to Paris in July and August 1792*, Dublin, 1793.

Vaissière, Pierre de, *Lettres d'Aristocrates'. La Révolution racontée par des correspondances privées 1789–1794*, Paris, 1907.

—— *La Mort du Roi (21 janvier 1793)*, Perrin: Paris, 1910.

Vatel, C., *Recherches historiques sur les Girondins: Vergniaud. Manuscrits, lettres et papiers, pièces pour la plupart inédites, classées et annotées*, 2 vols, Paris, 1873.

Vaughan, Megan, 'I am my own foundation', *London Review of Books*, 18 Octber 2000, pp. 15–17.

Vautibault, G. de, and Daragon, H. *Les d'Orléans au tribunal de l'histoire*, 7 vols, Paris, 1888–1892.

Venturino, Diego, 'La naissance de l' "Ancien Régime"', in *The French Revolution and the Creation of Modern Political Culture*, vol. 2, Colin Lucas (ed.), *The Political Culture of the French Revolution*, Pergamon: Oxford, 1988, pp. 11–40.

Vidocq, *Mémoires de Vidocq, forçat et chef de la Police de sûreté écrits par lui-même*, 2 vols, Paris, n.d.

Viel-Castel, Comte Horace de, *Collection de costumes, armes et meubles. pour servir à l'histoire de France*, 5 vols, Paris, 1827–45.

—— *Mémoires du comte Horace de Viel-Castel sur le règne de Napoléon III 1851–1864*, ed. Pierre Josserand, 2 vols, Le Prat: Paris, 1979.

Villari, Rosario, 'Masaniello: Contemporary and Recent Interpretations', *Past and Present*, 1985, no. 108, pp. 117–32.

—— *The Revolt of Naples*, Polity/Blackwell: Oxford, 1993.

Villette, Charles de, 'Sur les décorations', *Chronique de Paris*, 25 October 1791, no. 298, pp. 1199–200.

—— *Lettres choisies de C.V. sur les principaux événemens de la Révolution*, Paris, 1792.

Villiers, Baron Marc de, *Histoire des clubs des femmes et des légions d'amazones 1793–1848–1871*, Paris, 1910.

Vittu, Françoise, 'Maurice Leloir, peintre et historien du costume', in *Maurice Leloir: de Guy de Maupassant à Douglas Fairbanks*, Maison Fournaise, Chatou, 1995, pp. 2–7.

Vovelle, Michel, *La Chute de la royauté 1787–1792*, Paris, 1972.

—— (ed.), *Les Images de la Révolution française*, 4 vols, Pergamon: Oxford,1990.

—— *La Révolution française: images et récits*, 5 vols, Livre Club Diderot, Messidor: Paris, 1986.

—— (ed.), *Le Tournant de l'an III. Réaction et Terreur blanche dans la France révolutionnaire*, Comité des travaux historiques et scientifiques: Paris, 1997.

Wagner, Nicolas, 'Fête et dissolution sociale. A propos de quelques notices du *Journal de Paris* (1797)', in Jean Ehrard and P. Viallaneix (eds), *Les Fêtes de la Révolution*. Colloque de Clermont-Ferrand (juin 1974), Société des Études robespierristes: Paris, 1977, pp. 525–36.

Wallon, H., *Histoire du Tribunal révolutionnaire de Paris*, 5 vols, Hachette, Paris, 1880.

Walter, Gérard, *Robespierre*, Gallimard: Paris, 1936.

—— *La Révolution française vu par les journaux*, Tardy: Paris, 1948.

Wangerman, Ernst, *The Austrian Achievement 1700–1800*, Thames and Hudson: London, 1973.

Warner, Marina, *Monuments and Maidens: The Allegory of the Female Form*, Weidenfeld & Nicolson: London, 1985.

Wassyng Roworth, Wendy, 'The Evolution of History Painting: Masaniello's Revolt and Other Disasters in Seventeenth-century Naples', *Art Bulletin*, June 1993, vol. 75, no. 2, pp. 219–34.

Weiss, Louise, *Souvenirs d'une enfance républicaine*, Denoël: Paris, 1937.

Weston, Stephen, *Letters from Paris, during the Summer of 1792, with Reflections*, London, 1793.

Willemin, Nicole-Xavier, *Des Costumes civils et militaires. Armes et armures, instruments de masque, meubles de toute espèce, et décorations intérieurs et extérieurs des maisons, dessinés, coloriés, et gravés d'après les originaux pour servir à l'histoire des arts depuis le VIe siècle jusqu'au commencement du XVIIe siècle*, Paris, 1825.

Williams, Gwyn A., *Artisans and sans-culottes: popular movements in France and Britain during the French Revolution*, Edward Arnold: London, 1968.

Williams, Helen Maria, *Letters containing a Sketch of the Politics of France, from the thirty-first of May 1793, till the twenty-eighth of July 1794, and of the scenes which have passed in the prisons of Paris*, Dublin, 1795.

Wills, Antoinette, *Crime and Punishment in Revolutionary Paris*, Greenwood: Westport, CT, London, 1981.

Wintermute, Alan (ed.), *1789: French Art during the Revolution*, Colnaghi, New York, 1989.

Wright, Beth. S., *Painting and History during the French Restoration. Abandoned by the Past*, Cambridge University Press: Cambridge, 1997.

Wrigley, Richard, 'Breaking the Code: interpreting French revolutionary iconoclasm', in Alison Yarrington and Kelvin Everest (eds), *Reflections of Revolution, Images of Romanticism*, Routledge: London, 1993, pp. 182–95.

—— *The Origins of French Art Criticism: from the Ancien Régime to the Restoration*, Oxford University Press: Oxford, 1993.

—— 'From Ancien Régime Fall-guy to Revolutionary Hero: Changing Interpretations of Janot and Dorvigny's *Les Battus qui paient l'amende* in Later Eighteenth-century France', *British Journal of Eighteenth-century Studies*, 1996, vol. 19, no. 2, pp. 124–54.

—— 'Transformations of a Revolutionary Symbol: the Liberty Cap in the French Revolution', *French History*, 1997, vol. 11, no. 2, pp. 131–69.

—— 'The Class of '89?: cultural aspects of bourgeois identity in France in the aftermath of the French Revolution', in Andrew Hemingway and William Vaughan (eds), *Art in Bourgeois Society 1790–1850*, Cambridge University Press: Cambridge, 1998, pp. 130–53.

—— 'Revolutionary Relics: Survival and Consecration', *Fashion Theory*, 2002, vol. 6, no. 2, pp. 145–90.

—— 'The Formation and Currency of a Vestimentary Streotype: the *sans-culotte* in the French Revolution', in Wendy Parkins (ed.), *Fashioning the Body Politic*, Berg: Oxford, 2002.

—— 'Protokollierte Identität. Anmerkungen über das inkognito in der Reisepraxis und der Reiseliteratur des 18. Jahrhunderts', in Joachim Rees, Winifried Siebers, Hilmar Tilgner (eds), *Europareisen politisch-sozialer Eliten im 18. Jahrhundert. Theoretische Neuorientierung – kommunikative Praxis – Kultur – und Wissenstransfer*, Spitz: Berlin, 2002, pp. 209–18.

Index